'Henry Lawson 1896' by illustrator Walter Syer
(Dixson Library, State Library of New South Wales, DG P1/21; 22.3 x 17.0 cm)

'A tall, slight man, delicate in appearance, and with an air of refinement and sensitiveness, Lawson would give a first impression of femininity. This is deepened by his quiet, though decisive, style of speech. It is in the virility of his thoughts and the directness of his manner that his masculinity is manifested' (*Champion*, 17 October 1896, p. 452): from an interview with Henry Lawson as he passed through Melbourne en route to Sydney from Western Australia in 1896, shortly after the publication of *While the Billy Boils*.

BIOGRAPHY OF A BOOK

HENRY LAWSON'S *WHILE THE BILLY BOILS*

PAUL EGGERT

SYDNEY UNIVERSITY PRESS
THE PENNSYLVANIA STATE UNIVERSITY PRESS
2013

Published 2013 by SYDNEY UNIVERSITY PRESS
in association with The Pennsylvania State University Press
Penn State Studies in the History of the Book
Edited by James LW West III

© Paul Eggert 2013
© Sydney University Press 2013

Reproduction and Communication for other purposes
Except as permitted under the Act, no part of this edition may be reproduced, stored in a retrieval system, or communicated in any form or by any means without prior written permission. All requests for reproduction or communication should be made to Sydney University Press at the address below:

Sydney University Press
Fisher Library F03
University of Sydney NSW 2006 AUSTRALIA
Email: sup.info@sydney.edu.au
Web: sydney.edu.au/sup

National Library of Australia Cataloguing-in-Publication entry

Author: Eggert, Paul, 1951-
Title: Biography of a book : Henry Lawson's While the billy boils / Paul Eggert.
ISBN: 9781743320143 (hbk)
9781743320129 (pbk)
Series: Penn State Studies in the History of the Book.
Notes: Biography of a Book is co-published with The Pennsylvania State University Press in its History of the Book series, edited by James L. W. West III.
Includes bibliographical references and index.
Subjects: Lawson, Henry, 1867–1922 While the billy boils.
Lawson, Henry, 1867–1922 – Criticism and interpretation.
Australian prose literature – 19th century – History and criticism.
Australian prose literature – 20th century – History and criticism.
Other Authors/Contributors:
West, James L. W.
Dewey Number: A823.2

Cover images: Walter Syer's (uncaptioned) illustration for the inside front boards of the Angus & Robertson trial issue (1896) of *While the Billy Boils*, Mitchell Library, State Library of New South Wales; (*back cover*) detail of the marked-up printer's copy for *While the Billy Boils* of "'An Old Mate of your Father's'", Mitchell Library, State Library of New South Wales.

Cover design by Dushan Mrva-Montoya
Layout by Ampersand Duck in Minion Pro

CONTENTS

List of illustrations	*page*	vii
Preface		ix
Abbreviations		xiii
Note on currency		xv
Chronology		xvi
	Introduction: Lives of works	1
1	A writing career in the making: Lawson's early life	33
2	Lawson in the literary marketplace: The *Worker*, the *Bulletin* and *Short Stories in Prose and Verse*	45
3	Author and publisher: Lawson and Angus & Robertson	73
4	The revision and copy-editing of *While the Billy Boils*: Lawson and Arthur W. Jose	88
5	The making of a book: Texts and illustrations	107
6	Respecting the marketplace: The publishers' natural wish to make a fat 5s. volume	128
7	Lawson's no longer: Publication of *While the Billy Boils*	147
8	Early reception of *While the Billy Boils*: The first five years	162
9	Who made the money, and how much?; or, why Lawson went to England	199
10	'Pursuing Literature': Lawson's stories in Britain 1900–1902	222
11	The afterlife of *While the Billy Boils*	248

| 12 | Lawson's reputation in the postwar period | 272 |
| 13 | Australian literary criticism and scholarly editing from the 1980s: *While the Billy Boils* as cross-section | 311 |

Appendixes

1	A production history of Edward Dyson's *Rhymes from the Mines*	355
2	The curious history of the Frank Mahony illustrations in *While the Billy Boils*	358
3	Postwar printings of *While the Billy Boils* and prose selections	364
4	Angus & Robertson's record-keeping	371

Index — 375

ILLUSTRATIONS

'Henry Lawson 1896' by Walter Syer *frontispiece*

Title-page of first impression of *While the Billy Boils* with Frank Mahony's vignette dated '96' [1896] *page 32*

between pages 116 and 117

1 Printer's copy for 'That There Dog o' Mine'
2 Printer's copy for 'Going Blind'

Original illustrations reproduced in While the Billy Boils

3 Frank Mahony's illustration for '"An Old Mate of your Father's"': 'They would talk of some old lead.'
4 Frank Mahony's illustration used in the first impression for 'On the Edge of a Plain': 'Poured some water into the hollow.'
5 Frank Mahony's illustration used in the second impression for 'On the Edge of a Plain': 'Poured some water into the hollow.'
6 Frank Mahony's illustration for 'The Drover's Wife': 'Mother, I won't never go drovin'; blast me if I do!'
7 Frank Mahony's re-drawn illustration for 'The Drover's Wife' for 1900 cheap edition
8 Frank Mahony's illustration for '"Dossing Out" and "Camping"': 'Tenderly examining the seat of the trousers.'
9 Frank Mahony's illustration for 'A Visit of Condolence': 'I'm sorry mum. I didn't know.'

10   Frank Mahony's illustration for 'Two Dogs and a Fence': 'The inside dog generally starts it.'

11   Frank Mahony's illustration for 'Macquarie's Mate': 'His mate's alive.'

12   Walter Syer's (uncaptioned) illustration for the inside front boards of the trial issue (1896) of *While the Billy Boils*

All illustrations are courtesy of the State Library of New South Wales.[1]

---

[1]   The Walter Syer drawing of Lawson is held by the Dixson Library, State Library of New South Wales, filed at DG P1/21. Syer's (uncaptioned) illustration used for the trial issue of *While the Billy Boils* is at PX *D195. The printer's copy for *While the Billy Boils* and the Frank Mahony original drawings are held in the Mitchell Library, State Library of New South Wales, filed at A1867–A1868 and PX *D195 respectively.

PREFACE

THIS IS A book about the life of an Australian literary classic, Henry Lawson's *While the Billy Boils*. The idea that literary works can have 'lives' able to be studied over time was first introduced in the 1930s by the aesthetic philosopher Roman Ingarden. But the metaphor was slow to filter into anglophone literary-critical thinking. The postwar New Critical movement did not accommodate the insight, and even less so the quarter-century of high literary theory that succeeded it. Yet study of the production, distribution and reception of books – a still comparatively neglected source of evidence – potentially offers a way of testing longstanding generalisations and assumptions about literary works and periods such as the highly contested Australian 1890s.

Ultimately book history provides a model for studying the life of literary works across time and through the hands of many individuals, interested groups and institutions. Studying its material basis, both in documents and in the marketplace, makes one look at the literature differently. A book about the life of a literary work cannot be about the author's work alone. Yet the author does not retreat from view – as was typical of so much academic work in the last couple of decades of the twentieth century. Rather, in the kind of book-historical study pursued here, textual agency and material intervention of all kinds become relevant, along with the contexts for those interventions and decisions. The writer's actions are literally the *sine qua non*.

The publishing of newspapers, books and magazines is a business, like any other. Yet it is also *un*like others, in that it affords the rite of passage for virtually all literary works. This is the crux of its importance for students of literature, especially of works that have an enduring currency over time. And it is why it needs to be brought more centrally into the ongoing debate.

This book is aimed at two kinds of readers. I envisage the first as those whose interest in Henry Lawson or the Australian 1890s is mainly literary or cultural and who want to see how their view of Lawson or of that decade is changed by an intensive look at the material underpinnings both of his career as a writer and of the continuing currency of his works after his death in 1922. This reader will only occasionally be tempted to dip into the footnotes.

They contain a wealth of supporting and supplementary detail intended for the other category of reader: researchers with their different projects who may be looking for hard evidence, either for purposes of comparison or for what new thinking it might spark. Such archival and bibliographic evidence was something that the remarkable pioneer of Lawson scholarship, Colin Roderick, often failed to provide in his editorial commentary and in his biography of Lawson, thus leaving too many of his interpretations and conclusions at the level of assertion. At the present, early stage of the application of book-historical methodologies to Australian literary study, the need to document the material basis of interpretation is still a real one. As an enduring classic of Australian literature, *While the Billy Boils* happens to be a particularly demanding case – but quite fascinatingly so.

A new scholarly edition of *While the Billy Boils* is being published by Sydney University Press to accompany this book. Textually, the edition strips away the accretions, intentions and sequencing of the 1896 book, rather than treating them as the inevitable climax of a literary evolution. The new edition returns to the texts of the original newspaper versions, placing them in chronological order and allowing the textual changes that were made for later publication to be studied and understood.

Documentary sources are quoted without correcting errors of handwriting or typography. In the main text, 'sic' is only very sparingly used to set-off such errors, for they are far too common.

A monograph of the present kind inevitably leaves its author beholden to many institutions and individuals. Accordingly, there are many whom I would like to acknowledge. First and foremost I thank my long-time collaborator Elizabeth Webby who has given me helpful and detailed advice about the drafts of this book and who has prepared the explanatory notes to our accompanying edition of *While the Billy Boils*. I also wish to thank: the late Jennifer Alison for advice on the Angus & Robertson archive in the Mitchell Library, State Library of New South Wales; Paul Brunton and his colleagues at the Mitchell, especially Tracy Bradford and Wendy Holz in the Original Materials Branch and the staff at the Special Collections desk, including the late Arthur Easton, for many services; Dennis Bryans for his expert advice about 1890s technology for printing illustrations; Robert Dixon and Craig Munro for invaluable advice; Caren Florance of Ampersand Duck for her typesetting; Rod Kirkpatrick for information on the *Patriot*; Brian McMullin for confirming some details of a trial page design referred to elliptically in the Ledgers of Angus & Robertson; Annette Renshaw, Subsidiary Rights Manager at HarperCollins; Michael Sharkey for information on David McKee Wright; Meredith Sherlock for her highly skilled assistance with the accompanying edition, work which has also fed into this book; Cheryl Taylor for information on the *Patriot*; Chris Tiffin for preparing the index and for two readings of the completed MS that led to many improvements; Robert Trogdon and Michael Austin for information on Ernest Hemingway and Lawson; Jürgen Wegner for information on some aspects of printing history in Sydney; Tessa Wooldridge for tracking down many essential publications and documents; the many indexers and researchers who, together, have made the AUSTLIT database such a useful resource; the editors of *Textual Cultures*, *Variants* and *The Library* in whose pages some of the material in this book has appeared in a different form;[1] and, finally, the Australian Research Council for an Australian Professorial Fellowship and the University of New South Wales, which generously supported in other ways the research on which this book is based.

Paul Eggert   *May 2012*

---

[1] Respectively, 'A Convergence of Book History and Literary Criticism. Case-study: Henry Lawson in 1890s Sydney', *Textual Cultures*, 6 (2011), 76–96; 'Writing in a Language Not your Own: Editions as Arguments about the Work – D. H. Lawrence, Joseph Conrad and Henry Lawson', *Variants*, 9 (2012), 163–84; and 'Brought to Book: Bibliography, Book History and the Study of Literature', *The Library*, 7th series, 13.1 (2012), 3–32.

ABBREVIATIONS

ADB	*Australian Dictionary of Biography*, ed. Douglas Pike and others, 17 vols. (Carlton, Vic.: Melbourne University Press, 1966–2007).
Alison	*Doing Something for Australia: George Robertson and the Early Years of Angus & Robertson, Publishers 1888–1900* (Melbourne: Bibliographical Society of Australia and New Zealand, 2009).
Autobiographical	Henry Lawson, *Autobiographical and Other Writings 1887–1922*, ed. Colin Roderick (Sydney: Angus & Robertson, 1972).
Collected Verse	Henry Lawson, *Collected Verse, Volume One: 1885–1900, Volume Two: 1901–1909* and *Volume Three: 1910–1922*, ed. Colin Roderick (Sydney: Angus & Robertson, 1967, 1968, 1969).
Commentaries	Colin Roderick, *Henry Lawson: Commentaries on his Prose Writings* (Sydney: Angus & Robertson, 1985).
Criticism	Henry Lawson, *Criticism 1894–1971*, ed. Colin Roderick (Sydney: Angus & Robertson, 1972).
Eggert and Webby	Henry Lawson, *While the Billy Boils: The Original Newspaper Versions*, ed. Paul Eggert, with Explanatory Notes by Elizabeth Webby (Sydney: Sydney University Press, 2013).

In the Days	Henry Lawson, *In the Days When the World Was Wide and Other Verses* (Sydney: Angus & Robertson, 1896).
Lee	Christopher Lee, *City Bushman: Henry Lawson and the Australian Imagination* (Fremantle, WA: Fremantle Arts Centre Press, 2004).
Letters	Henry Lawson, *Letters 1890–1922*, ed. Colin Roderick (Sydney: Angus & Robertson, 1970).
Mackaness	*An Annotated Bibliography of Henry Lawson* (Sydney: Angus & Robertson, 1951).
Life	Colin Roderick, *Henry Lawson: A Life* (Angus & Robertson, 1991).
Prose Writings	*Henry Lawson the Master Story-teller: Prose Writings*, ed. Colin Roderick (Sydney: Angus & Robertson, 1984). A revision of Henry Lawson, *Short Stories and Sketches 1888–1922*, ed. Colin Roderick (Sydney: Angus & Robertson, 1972).

OTHER ABBREVIATIONS

A1867–8	Printer's copy for *While the Billy Boils* in two bound volumes, Mitchell Library, State Library of New South Wales (MSS 314/156–157, filed at A1867–A1868)
A&R	Angus & Robertson
GR	George Robertson of Angus & Robertson
HL	Henry Lawson
ML	Mitchell Library, State Library of New South Wales
NLA	National Library of Australia
SLNSW	State Library of New South Wales

THE TITLES OF LAWSON'S STORIES AND SKETCHES collected in *While the Billy Boils* (1896) are given in the wording and presentation of their original newspaper versions (as edited in Eggert and Webby). Where sufficiently different as to cause uncertainty, their 1896 titles are given instead in square brackets if that version is intended. The Contents page in Eggert and Webby allows a rapid identification of the original title.

NOTE ON CURRENCY

The unit of currency in use in the Australian colonies in the second half of the nineteenth century, and then in Australia after Federation, was the pound (£), divided into twenty shillings (s.), each of twelve pennies (d.). A sixpence and a threepence were small silver coins, and a half-crown (equivalent to 2s.6d.) a large one. The penny, halfpenny and farthing (one-quarter of a penny) were copper. A guinea was a notional unit equivalent to 21s., often used to price luxury goods in preference to the pound. Upon decimalisation in 1966 one Australian dollar equalled 10s. in the old system. Henry Lawson's portrait appeared on the ten-dollar note until 1993.

CHRONOLOGY

THIS IS A list of events in the life of Henry Lawson (HL) and in the production and reception of the stories and sketches collected for *While the Billy Boils* (1896), its impressions and later editions. The original titles of stories and sketches are preferred; if changed in 1896, the new title follows in square brackets. The appearance of some poems is also mentioned, and they are identified as such. Personal entries refer to HL unless otherwise specified. '*Worker*' refers to the Sydney weekly; if the Brisbane counterpart is intended, this is stated. Printer's charges, payments to HL and sales figures[1] are from Angus & Robertson's publishing ledgers housed at the Mitchell Library (exact locations are given in footnotes to the relevant chapters). Unsourced quotations are from *Letters*.

17 June 1867	Born, Grenfell, a goldfields town in New South Wales (NSW), to Niels Hertzberg ('Peter') Larsen (1832–88; arrived Melbourne from Norway 1855) and Louisa Albury (1848–1920; born NSW).
From December 1867	Childhood mainly at New Pipeclay (Eurunderee), between Mudgee and Gulgong (goldrush town from April 1870).
Late 1871–73	Family lives in a booming Gulgong; temporary prosperity, then they return to Eurunderee where HL's father 'selects' (leases) 40 acres to farm.
1875–79	At local bush schools, then Catholic school at Mudgee and with access to the School of Arts library.

[1] Charges were sometimes retrospective because of the (presumably monthly) billing cycle, and entries for 30 June usually represent a taking-in of data for end-of-financial-year reconciliation. Payments to HL and sales figures are in respect of *While the Billy Boils* only, for its first seven years (29 August 1896 – 30 June 1903).

1876	HL's partial deafness first noticed.
1880–83	Working with father on building contracts, at first locally and then in the Blue Mountains.
1882	GR to Sydney from Scotland, via New Zealand.
May 1883	HL's mother Louisa Lawson moves to Marrickville in Sydney; joined by HL.
1884	They move to 138 Phillip Street (central Sydney). HL works as coach-maker's apprentice; studies for but fails matriculation exam.
1885	Home becomes a meeting place for free thinkers and republican socialists; HL begins writing verse.
From 1886	Emergence of a radical labour movement in Queensland.
10 June 1887	Republican riot at Sydney Town Hall.
By 23 July 1887	First poem accepted by *Bulletin* (Sydney): 'A Song of the Republic' (published 1 October).
1888	Contributes to the *Republican* (Sydney). 'While the Billy Boils', poem by Keighley Goodchild in *Australian Ballads and Other Poems* (London: Walter Scott Company), ed. Douglas Sladen. First Labor member in Queensland parliament.
15 May 1888	Louisa Lawson establishes the feminist monthly the *Dawn*.
22 December 1888	'His Father's Mate', HL's first short story in *Bulletin*.
31 December 1888	Death of HL's father.
From 1888	Writing mainly bush ballads and political verse, but also some prose, for *Town and Country Journal* (Sydney) from 1888, *Truth* (Sydney) from 1890, Brisbane socialist *Boomerang* in 1891, *Worker* (Brisbane) from 1891, *Worker* (Sydney) from 1893.
22 June 1889	'The Story of Malachi' in *Bulletin*.
1890	Prolonged Maritime Strike in Melbourne and Sydney; broadens into a near-general strike. First *Bulletin* book, organised by J. F. Archibald, *A Golden Shanty: Australian Stories and Sketches in Prose and Verse* (Sydney) reprints revised 'His Father's Mate'.
c. January 1890	Meets Mary Cameron [later, Gilmore] in Sydney.
1 March 1890	First issue of the Brisbane *Worker*, ed. William Lane: monthly; fortnightly from October 1890; weekly from April 1892.

26 April 1890	Sails for Albany, Western Australia, with his brother Peter.
May–September 1890	In Albany; writes for *Albany Observer*.
October 1890	Returns to Sydney: works as builder's labourer, living 'in a third-rate hash-house'; then 'Up-country again . . . house-painting' ['Pursuing Literature'].
Early 1890s	Economic conditions gradually deteriorate. A labour provincial press spreads, dedicated to organised trades unionism, education of the workers and parliamentary representation, but with radical elements sympathetic to republican separation from Britain and violent revolution if necessary.
6 January 1891	Shearers' strike begins, western Queensland; spreads later in 1891 to NSW and Victoria.
By 4 April – 18 September 1891	On staff of *Boomerang* (Brisbane).
16 May 1891	'Freedom on the Wallaby' in Brisbane *Worker*, p. 8, by-line: 'Brisbane, May, 1891' and 'WRITTEN FOR THE "WORKER."': [freedom's] 'goin' to light another fire/ And boil another billy'.
23 May 1891	'Bogg of Geebung' in *Boomerang*.
17 June 1891	Election of 35 Labour Electoral League representatives to NSW parliament; 'The Triumph of the People' (poem) in *Boomerang* on 27 June.
10 October 1891	'The Shame of Going Back' (poem) in *Bulletin*.
By 2 December 1891	Living at 16 Thomas Street, Ashfield, Sydney.
1892	Living mainly in doss houses and with aunts at McMahon's Point, North Sydney and Dawes Point, near The Rocks, Sydney; working as a painter 'for nigger-driving bosses at 5s. a day' ['Pursuing Literature'].
April 1892	Secures letters of introduction to editors in Western Australia from various Sydney editors but does not go.
23 April 1892	'A Visit of Condolence: A Study from Life of a Sydney "Larrikin"' in *Bulletin*.
28 May 1892	'A Day on a Selection. A Sketch from Observation' in *Bulletin*.
11 June 1892	'Arvie Aspinall's Alarm Clock' in *Bulletin*.
9 July 1892	Begins manufactured controversy in *Bulletin* with A. B. Paterson on the merits of the city vs the bush.

CHRONOLOGY

23 July 1892	'The Drover's Wife' in *Bulletin*. Launch of the Maryborough *Patriot* by the Political Reform Association, owned and mostly edited by Irvine ('Jack') Perel.
September 1892	Sent by J. F. Archibald, editor of *Bulletin*, to Bourke.
21 September 1892	Arrives Great Western Hotel, Bourke (till 24 November): 'took notes all the way up'; thereafter, house-painting in Bourke.
November 1892	'A Christmas in the Far West; or, The Bush Undertaker' in the (intended) annual *Antipodean*, ed. George Essex Evans (London: Chatto & Windus).
5 November 1892	'In a Dry Season' in *Bulletin*.
6 November 1892	Defeat of miners strike in Broken Hill; many strikers destitute.
23 November 1892	Joins General Laborers Union of Australasia.
24 November – c. 26 December 1892	Working in shearing sheds on the Darling R.
27 December 1892	Walks, probably with James W. (Jim) Gordon, from Bourke to Hungerford on NSW–Queensland border; 'bushed on a lignum plain' on 8 January.
1893	Financial depression in the eastern colonies deepens; collapse of some banks.
17 January 1893	Hungerford to Bourke (a 'nine days' walk): '300 miles [return] ... That's all I ever intend to do with a swag'.
By 6 February 1893	In Bourke, working as a painter.
Mid March? 1893	Returns to Sydney.
15 April 1893	'Mitchell: A Character Sketch' in *Bulletin*.
16 April 1893	'The Union Buries its Dead. A Bushman's Funeral. A Sketch from Life' in Sydney *Truth*.
May 1893	16 Labor representatives elected to the Queensland parliament.
6 May 1893	'On the Edge of a Plain' in *Bulletin*.
13 May 1893	'Mitchell Doesn't Believe in the Sack' in *Bulletin*.
27 May 1893	'"Stragglers": A Sketch Out Back' in *Bulletin*.
June–?November 1893	Living with aunt (Emma Brooks) at North Sydney.
3 June 1893	'"Rats"' in *Bulletin*.
10 June 1893	HL's first known contribution to *Worker*, 'The Waving of the Red' (poem).

17 June 1893?	'The Shearing of the Cook's Dog', HL's first story in *Worker* (date unconfirmed).
24 June 1893	'"An Old Mate of your Father's"' in *Worker*.
1 July 1893	'Another of Mitchell's Plans for the Future' in *Bulletin*.
15 July 1893?	'"Some Day." A Swagman's Love Story' in *Worker* (date unconfirmed).
16 July 1893	William Lane leaves to set up New Australia colony in Paraguay.
5 August 1893?	'A Camp-fire Yarn' in *Worker* (date unconfirmed; stylistically develops '"Some Day"').
5 August 1893	'His Colonial Oath' in *Bulletin*.
6 August 1893	'The Man Who Forgot' in *Truth*.
19 August 1893	'When the Sun Went Down' in *Worker*.
9 September 1893	'"Tom's Selection." (A Sketch of Settling on the Land)' in *Bulletin*.
30 September 1893	'Selection Farms' in *Worker*.
21 October 1893?	'Macquarie's Mate' probably in Sydney *Worker* (unconfirmed).
28 October 1893	'Macquarie's Mate' in Brisbane *Worker*.
11 November 1893?	'"Brummy Usen"' in *Worker* (date unconfirmed).
18 November 1893	Sails for New Zealand (Auckland then Wellington), after failing to secure editorship of Sydney *Worker* in succession to Walter W. Head.
25 November 1893	'"Dossing Out" and "Camping"' in *Worker*.
27 November 1893	Arrives at Wellington, destitute. Taken in by journalist Tom Mills. Some verse and sketches appear in *Fair Play* and *New Zealand Times* and its weekly *New Zealand Mail* December–January.
2 December 1893	'"In a Wet Season." Along the Line' in *Bulletin*.
8 December 1893	'That There Dog o' Mine: An Australian Sketch' in *New Zealand Mail*, which announces HL's presence in Wellington and promises 'a short series of sketches' by him.
11 December 1893	'That There Dog o' Mine' reprinted in *New Zealand Times*.
15 and 29 December 1893	'Coming Across.—A Study in the Steerage' in *New Zealand Mail*; reprinted in *New Zealand Times* 30 December.
16 December 1893	'Hungerford' in *Bulletin*.
By 26 February 1894	In Pahiatua, then timber-getting in the Hutt Valley.

9 March 1894	'Stiffner and Jim (Thirdly Bill)' in *Pahiatua Herald*.
6 April 1894	Leaves Pahiatua for Wellington.
c. May 1894	Sails Wellington–Picton to work laying telegraph line on the Picton–Dunedin line near Kekerengu, South Island.
May 1894	Formation of Australian Workers Union from shearers, labourers and workers unions.
20 July 1894	Having sailed, probably from Picton or Lyttleton (the port of Christchurch), sails from Wellington to Sydney, after offer of a position on new *Daily Worker* (issued from 2 July 1894 in lead-up to NSW elections).
29 July 1894	Arrives in Sydney; lives mainly with aunt at North Sydney till February 1896.
1 August 1894	Last issue of *Daily Worker*; HL becomes provincial editor on the weekly issue.
11 August 1894	'Drifted Back' in *Worker*.
Soon after 16 August 1894	Meets John Le Gay Brereton; friendship quickly develops.
25 August 1894	'Remailed' in *Worker*.
1 September 1894	'Stiffner and Jim (Thirdly Bill)' reprinted in *Worker*.
15 September 1894	Loses staff position on *Worker*; becomes exclusive contributor.
22 September 1894	'Shooting the Moon' in *Worker*.
29 September 1894	'"Board and Residence."' in *Worker*.
13 October 1894	'Baldy Thompson. A Sketch of a Squatter' in *Worker*.
By 19 November 1894	Has fallen out with 'my feller wirkers' at the *Worker*.
20 November 1894	Brereton, 'Poetry in Australia', in *Hermes*: the first article on HL.
15 December 1894	'He'd Come Back' and 'That Swag' ['Enter Mitchell'] in *Bulletin*; 'She Wouldn't Speak' in *Worker*.
22 December 1894	'His Country—After All' in *Patriot* (Maryborough, Queensland). First HL volume: *Short Stories in Prose and Verse* (Sydney: L. Lawson) at 1s., collecting 'The Drover's Wife', '"Rats"', 'The Union Buries its Dead', '[The Bush Undertaker]' and 'Macquarie's Mate'. Has discussed publication of 'my first volume of verse' for 'some time next year' (Preface) – perhaps with Brereton.
5 January 1895	'The Old Bark School: An Echo' in *Bulletin*. A. G. Stephens's review in *Bulletin* of *Short Stories in Prose and Verse*.

12 January 1895	'Some Reflections on a Voyage across Cook's Straits (N.Z.)' ['Across the Straits'] in *Worker*.
19 January 1895	'Steelman' in *Bulletin*.
April 1895	A. B. Paterson and GR discuss publication of *The Man from Snowy River*.
Between April and July 1895	HL approaches GR, having heard of his agreement with Paterson; HL gathers his published poems.
11 May 1895	'Our Pipes' in *Bulletin*.
1, 8 and 15 June 1895	'Jones' Alley' serialised in *Worker*.
29 June 1895	'Going Blind' in *Worker*.
26 July 1895	Agreement between A&R and HL to publish a volume or volumes of verse and prose. HL receives advance of £14 on anticipated half-share of royalties; moves from cheap lodging house to John McGrath's Edinburgh Hotel.
From 26 July 1895	Likely start of process of gathering, clipping, mounting and then revising poems for *In the Days When the World Was Wide and Other Verses*.
October–mid-December 1895	Likely period of HL and Jose's work on first half of printer's copy for *Billy Boils*.
10 October 1895	Copyright buyout of contents of *In the Days*: HL receives £40 and struggles to revise 'The Star of Australasia' for it.
17 October 1895	A. B. Paterson, *The Man from Snowy River and Other Verses* (Sydney: A&R).
23 October 1895	'My book [*In the Days*] will be out in about two weeks'. Available to work fulltime on revising stories for *Billy Boils*.
c. November 1895	Meets Bertha Bredt (b. 1877 at Bairnsdale, Victoria; stepdaughter of socialist Sydney bookseller).
6 November 1895	Brereton's notice in *Hermes* of (the still untitled) *In the Days*.
15 November 1895	Mary Cameron [later, Gilmore] leaves Sydney for Paraguay.
30 November 1895	A&R purchases copy of Gaunt's *Moving Finger* (Methuen Colonial Library) as 'sample of type' for volume of HL stories [Ledger, ML].
14 December 1895	'Steelman's Pupil' in *Bulletin*.
21 December 1895	'Two Dogs and a Fence' in *Worker*. 'Setting up 3pp. in pica (Drover's Wife)' for page design [Ledger, ML].
28 December 1895	'Two Dogs and a Fence' reprinted in *Clipper* (Hobart).
January 1896	'Prose Sketches' by HL advertised by A&R as appearing

CHRONOLOGY

	'Shortly' [dated advertisement section in copies of *In the Days*]; writes dedicatory verses ('To an Old Mate') for *In the Days* 'in the early part of 1896' [*Collected Verse*, I. 457].
4 February 1896	Sample page-design for *Billy Boils* charged in Ledger.
14 February 1896	HL names Bertha Bredt as beneficiary in his estate.
14–15 February 1896	*In the Days When the World Was Wide and Other Verses* (Sydney: A&R).
19 February 1896	To Dunedin.
6 March 1896	Websdale, Shoosmith prepare quotation for printing *Billy Boils*.
10 March 1896	Arrives back in Sydney from New Zealand.
21 March 1896	'An Unfinished Love Story' in *Worker*. Last published story to be included in *Billy Boils*. First possible date for finalisation of second half of printer's copy of *Billy Boils*.
April–May 1896	Living at Forbes Street, Darlinghurst.
7 April 1896	A&R estimates cost of printing and paper for *Billy Boils*.
9 April 1896	GR sends Henry Hyde Champion, editor of *Champion*, 'a few page proofs' of part of *Billy Boils*.
15 April 1896	Marries Bertha Bredt at a matrimonial agency (Weldon's) in Sydney.
25 April 1896	Payment of £1.10s. for 'For Auld Lang Syne': first published in *Billy Boils*.
2 May 1896	Payment for 'The Geological Speiler' (£2.10s.): first published in *Billy Boils*.
5 May 1896	Charge against *Billy Boils* to A. W. Jose for 'Reading' (£2.2s.).
6, 7 May 1896	Mowbray Morris, Macmillan's reader, advises rejection for London re-publication of *In the Days*.
9 May 1896	Henry E. Boote: *In the Days* shows HL as 'the Poet of the Common Herd' (Brisbane *Worker*).
18 May 1896	Payment for 'title-page 'Vignette' for *Billy Boils* by Frank Mahony.
23 June 1896	'Agreement' for *Billy Boils* between A&R and HL; Schedule lists stories whose rights were being purchased, as well as verse.
24 June 1896	Copyright payment of £42 to HL for *Billy Boils*.
By 25 June 1896	James MacLehose, Edinburgh, has received several rejections from British publishers for *In the Days*.
30 June 1896	With Bertha to Western Australia; in Perth by 15 July.
July 1896	Blocks for 9 Mahony illustrations charged.

By 23 July 1896	Champion tells GR he has written to 'half a dozen English litterateurs about Lawson', including George Bernard Shaw [ML MSS 314].
August–September 1896	Living with Bertha at Government Camp, East Perth.
14 August 1896	Date of THE PUBLISHERS' preface. Cost of first of many advertisements for *Billy Boils* (in *Review of Reviews*, Melbourne) charged.
29 August 1896	*While the Billy Boils* (Sydney: A&R) published, in cloth, at 5s. retail; first reviews.
3 September 1896	Writes to GR from East Perth: 'Have seen the book and it looks alright. Expect to get my copies today'.
9 September 1896	'Am well pleased with book'.
19 September 1896	*Worker* announces direct sale of copies of *Billy Boils* at 5s.6d. 'posted to you direct', with profits to the Worker Improvement Fund. *In the Days* and Paterson's *The Man from Snowy River* also sold by Australian Workers Union offices around NSW.
23 September 1896	Charges for printing and binding first 3,000 copies.
By 30 September 1896	The 4th–6th Thousands ordered; bound copies received regularly in small batches from 24 October 1896.
Before 2 October 1896	HL writes to GR from Perth: 'Kindly advise me what you mean to do about the English edition. Better get a reliable reader to go through a copy'.
2 October 1896	Returns with Bertha to Sydney, via Melbourne.
13 October 1896	Arrives in Sydney.
By 23 October 1896 – 31 March 1897	Living at 91 Redfern Street, Redfern.
30 October 1896	Charge against *Billy Boils* for 'Mr Jose – Reading' (6s.6d.).
6 November 1896	A. P. Watt begins effort to place *Billy Boils* and *In the Days* with British publishers.
?8 December 1896	MacLehose, hearing from Watt of initial lack of success, advises GR to place *Billy Boils* and *In the Days* with book wholesaler Simpkin, Marshall.
By 26 December 1896	Edward Dyson, *Rhymes from the Mines* (Sydney: A&R).
30 December 1896	'Alteration to Stereos' charged in Ledger (10s.6d.) against *Billy Boils*.
By 22 January 1897	Methuen has agreed to issue *Billy Boils* but offering only 1s.8d. per unbound copy.

CHRONOLOGY

2 March 1897	A. P. Watt advises A&R to accept Methuen offer; unable to place *In the Days*.
10 March 1897	'50 [copies] in quires', the first from the 5th Thousand, received by A&R; final copies of the 5th thousand delivered 30 June 1897 [Progress Register, ML].
31 March 1897	To Wellington with Bertha; arrive 9 April.
By 3 May 1897	William Blackwood has written to A&R 'offering to bring out a home edition' of *Billy Boils*.
5 May 1897	Reaches Mangamaunu, South Island, and opens Native School the next day.
6 May 1897	MacLehose informs A&R that Methuen has withdrawn offer because paper used (by McCarron, Stewart) not of same standard as sample (from the first printing by Websdale, Shoosmith).
6 May – late October 1897	Teaching at Native School, Mangamaunu.
June 1897	Charges in Ledger for printing '2000 Spectator Reviews 1500 8vo Circulars', a further 8,000 on 3 July; and of 'Academy reviews' in August.
3 July 1897	Simpkin, Marshall issue of *Billy Boils* in London noted as among 'THIS WEEK'S BOOKS' (*Saturday Review*).
17 July 1897	E. V. Lucas's review of *Billy Boils* in *Academy*.
August and 28–30 September 1897	Charges for 'Pentland Binding' of the English (Simpkin, Marshall) issue and new title-pages [Ledger, ML].
11 September 1897	Copies of the 6th Thousand begin to come into stock; final delivery 10 March 1898.
From 7 November 1897	In Wellington.
29 November 1897	The 7th–9th Thousands: paperbound copies from Websdale, Shoosmith begin to come into stock; final copies received by 31 May 1898. Paper copies retail at 2s.6d.; cloth reduced to 3s.6d.
1898	Victor Daley, *Dawn and Dusk* (Sydney: A&R).
10 February 1898	Son, Joseph Henry Lawson born.
12 March 1898	Leaves Wellington for Sydney with family; live at 1 Regent Street, Newtown until July; then with brother-in-law J. T. Lang, August–September.
1 April – 30 June 1898	Works as a clerk in Government Statistician's Office, Sydney.

8 May 1898	GR explains to HL that the Blackwood offer for *Billy Boils* arrived after deal struck with Simpkin, Marshall.
30 June 1898	Ledger records credit balance for first 6,000 copies of *Billy Boils* (cloth, at 5s. retail) of £160.
4 July 1898	Charges for printing of 10th–12th Thousand [Ledger, ML]; 10th Thousand) into stock 9 July – 20 September 1898.
3 August 1898	£5 A&R cheque to HL.
27 August 1898	Date of Assignment to A&R of published and unpublished prose, which became *On the Track* and *Over the Sliprails*.
November – early December 1898	At Courtenay Smith's Rest Haven (for alcoholics), North Willoughby; then various North Sydney addresses till April 1900.
1899	Revising *In the Days* for revised edition.
12 January 1899	£15 A&R cheque to HL.
21 January 1899	'"Pursuing Literature" in Australia', *Bulletin*.
6, 10, 13 May 1899	Ledger charges for redrawing five of the illustrations in *Billy Boils*.
2 September 1899	£25 A&R cheque to HL.
By 30 June 1899	Sales of clothbound 3s.6d. issue for financial year: 675; paperbound 1,317. Only 38 cloth copies sold in London (at 5s.), July–December 1898.
18 July 1899	Agreement signed with A&R for volume of verse.
31 October 1899	Printing ordered for 11,000 copies of *Billy Boils* First Series (paperbound, at 1s. retail).
30 November 1899	Special issue of forthcoming First Series for E. W. Cole (Melbourne).
January 1900	*In the Days When the World Was Young and Other Verses* (revised edition).
11 February 1900	Daughter, Bertha, born.
28 February 1900	Printing ordered for 11,000 copies of *Billy Boils* Second Series.
7 April 1900	*On the Track* (Sydney, A&R).
20 April 1900	Leaves for England with family.
c. late May 1900	Arrival in London; July – c. 15 October in Harpenden, Herts.
9 June 1900	*Over the Sliprails* (Sydney: A&R).
By 30 June 1900	4,000 copies of *Billy Boils* First Series received (sales of 2,596) and 4,800 copies of Second Series (sales, 2,259); loss of £38 recorded.

July 1900	*On the Track and Over the Sliprails* as a combined volume.
by 13 July 1900	T. Fisher Unwin considers but does not accept a Lawson volume for his Over-Seas Library.
13 July 1900	Engages James Brand Pinker as agent.
August 1900	*Popular Verses* (Sydney: A&R).
September 1900	*Humorous Verses* (Sydney: A&R).
3 October 1900	Wife Bertha admitted to Bethnall House, a private asylum at Bethnall Green, London.
c. 16 October 1900	Moves to London, sharing flat in Gray's Inn Road with Arthur Maquarie; children boarded at Shepperton, 50 kms up the Thames.
7 December 1900	*Verses, Popular and Humorous* as a combined volume (Sydney: A&R).
31 December 1900	A&R (as copyright owner) receives royalty of £5.7s.9d. from Blackwood for the *Billy Boils* stories used in *The Country I Come From*.
31 March 1901	British Census records HL living in a three-room flat at Gray's Inn Road, London with his daughter and a servant, Lizzie Humphrey.
15 May 1901	Bertha's derangement worsens; committed to Bethlem Royal Hospital (mental asylum) until 14 August 1901; HL moves to Charlton, a village near Shepperton, till early winter where Bertha, upon release, joins him.
June 1901	*The Country I Come From* (Blackwood); first review, 4 July.
30 June 1901	Financial-year sales of *Billy Boils*: clothbound 3s.6d., 440; paperbound 2s.6d.: First Series, a further 3,479 received (sales 2,328); Second Series, 495 received (sales 2,337). Credit balance £90.
November 1901	*Joe Wilson and his Mates* (Blackwood), then Colonial issue for 'India and British colonies only'; A&R's issue for Australasia in 1902.
c. early winter 1901 – May 1902	Living in tiny flat in Paradise Lane, off Princess Street, London.
December 1901	'The Drover's Wife' reprinted in *The Bulletin Story Book*.
8 March 1902	Edward Garnett's 'Appreciation' in *Academy*.
end of April 1902	Bertha Lawson leaves for Sydney with Mary and Will Gilmore.
21 May 1902	HL leaves Antwerp for Colombo then Australia.

30 June 1902	Financial-year sales for First and Second Series (1,911 and 1,339); no details for 3s.6d. format; credit balance £96.
July 1902	*Children of the Bush* (London: Methuen); colonial issue advertisements dated September 1902.
12 July 1902	Arrives Adelaide; then Sydney: two successive Manly addresses.
December 1902	Period in Sydney Hospital.
1 April 1903	Admitted to Royal Prince Alfred Hospital, Sydney, for alcoholism; discharged 24 April.
4 June 1903	Judicial separation from Bertha. Living on the streets of Sydney; then at frequent intervals boarding with Mrs Isabel Byers, North Sydney.
30 June 1903	Financial year sales: 3s.6d., 337 after receipt of 499 copies; First and Second Series, 1,716 and 1,707. Credit balance of £103.
By 31 December 1903	Only 5 copies in 3s.6d. format sold since 1 January 1902 in London by A&R's agent, the Australian Book Company.
30 June 1904	Sales for financial year: 3s.6d., 325 after 200 returned from London; First and Second Series, 1,193 and 1,247. Credit balance not recorded.
4 April 1905	First of many short stays till January 1910 in Darlinghurst Prison for 'wife desertion', 'child desertion' and, later, failure to pay for maintenance of children.
November 1905	*When I Was King and Other Verses* (Sydney: A&R); also issued in two volumes by A&R as *When I Was King* and *The Elder Son*.
November 1906	First of various periods as a voluntary patient in Darlinghurst Mental Hospital, till 1911.
1907	*Children of the Bush* (Sydney: A&R), using English sheets; in two series as *Send Round the Hat* and *The Romance of the Swag*.
April 1907	At Victoria Coffee Palace, Melbourne; sells rights of a volume of prose and one of verse to Thomas Lothian.
1909	*Children of the Bush* (Sydney: A&R), new typesetting and without verse included in the 1902 and 1907 issues.
25 February – May 1910	Sails to Eden; thence to E. J. Brady's camp at Mallacoota, Victoria.
August 1910	*The Rising of the Court and Other Stories* (Sydney: A&R).
October 1910	*The Skyline Riders and Other Verses* (Sydney: Fergusson).

October 1913	*Triangles of Life and Other Stories* and *For Australia and Other Poems* (Melbourne: Standard Publishing [T. C. Lothian]).
April and June–July 1914	Trips to Eurunderee, NSW.
August 1915	*My Army, O, My Army!* (Sydney: Tyrrell's).
1916	*Song of the Dardanelles and Other Verses* (London: Harrap).
January 1916 – August 1917	At Leeton, NSW; with short periods in Sydney and one in Melbourne. Then lives in North Sydney till June 1921, with repeated hospitalisations.
November 1918	*Selected Poems of Henry Lawson* (Sydney: A&R), copy-edited by David McKee Wright.
From October 1921	Boarding in Ashfield, Sydney; then Katoomba, NSW; and finally Abbotsford, Sydney.
2 September 1922	Dies at Mrs Byers's home. Hailed as 'poet of the people'; state funeral on 4th.
1923	Cheap issue of *Billy Boils* in three slim volumes (Sydney: A&R).
1924	Second edition (new typesetting) of *Billy Boils* in two volumes in A&R's Platypus series.
1925	*Poetical Works of Henry Lawson* (Sydney: A&R), 3 vols.
2 September 1927	Brereton at fifth anniversary of HL's death: although 'the national poet' and his 'the voice of a great democracy', HL's prose is 'more highly prized by good judges of literature than his verse'.
1927	Third edition of *Billy Boils*: First and Second series in separate volumes (London: Jonathan Cape).
28 July 1931	Memorial statue of HL by G. W. Lambert unveiled in Sydney.
1933	Five stories from *Billy Boils* collected in *Capajon*, ed. Edward Garnett.
1933–35	Sale of A&R's literary archive to the Mitchell Library (MSS 314).
1935	*The Prose Works of Henry Lawson*, 2 vols., reprinted 1937; then in new (one-volume) typesettings 1940 and 1948.
October 1938	Article approving HL in *Communist Review* by Katharine Susannah Prichard. Other appropriations of his legacy

	followed by socialist and communist writers valorising the verse.
From 1947	Many selections of HL's stories published in Australia, usually with introductions by university-based literary critics; formalist and contemporary concerns influence selections.
1964	*The Stories of Henry Lawson*, ed. Cecil Mann, 3 vols (Sydney: A&R).
1967–84	Colin Roderick's scholarly editions (Sydney: A&R) of HL's collected verse, prose, letters and criticism.
1977	Sale of A&R's business archive to the Mitchell Library (MSS 3269).

INTRODUCTION

LIVES OF WORKS

At the end of my third year of high school I chose as my prize for doing well in, of all subjects, mathematics a hardback copy of *Henry Lawson's Best Stories*, edited by Cecil Mann and first published in that same year, 1966. I cannot remember now why my eye lingered on its black shiny dust jacket. I would have noticed the large sad eyes and scraggy moustache of a man at three-quarters turn, formally photographed, peering out of the darkness and looking piercingly at me. Perhaps the image struck a chord. In February of that same year Australia had changed its currency from pounds, shillings and pence to dollars and cents. Henry Lawson's image appeared on the ten-dollar note – of which, being a schoolboy, I had had precious few in my hands and of which I had therefore some reason to be respectful. If I vaguely knew Lawson was someone important I was not entirely sure why. Perhaps I had read some fragments of his prose in primary-school readers or heard some of his verse read out loud, or recited. In any case, it would be the first book by Lawson in my family home.

No doubt I felt the stories looked promising. I was interested in the Australian bush towns for I had spent the school holidays of my first fourteen years in Tenterfield, a country town on the Great Dividing Range, in northern New South Wales. It was my father's home town. Though I came from Sydney and though I was aware of being, in the eyes of my childhood friends there, something of a city-slicker from 500 miles away, I felt safely, if not fully, at home in Tenterfield. One much-admired uncle, though he lived in town, still had a very old 'two-roomed house … built of round timber, slabs, and stringybark', much the same as the one described in the opening sentence of the first story in that same volume, Lawson's most famous one, 'The Drover's Wife'. Rough slab floor and no electricity notwithstanding, my uncle slept there on weekends when he went to tend the cattle. He liked it there. It may have been a tall story, but he would recount his climbing into bed one night only to find an unexpected bedfellow – a snake, comfortably in occupation. Anyone who has read 'The Drover's Wife' will know why I mention the snake. So I had a half-understood and only half-earned link to my prize volume: the bush.

It was of course a 'Lawson volume' in other ways, of which I had no conception then. I could not ask the question, as I now do: what series of steps stood in between my choosing the book and the death of Lawson in 1922? By then he was known mainly around the streets of inner Sydney as a sad wreck of a man, an impoverished and sometimes cadging alcoholic, but also remembered for some stirring ballads and stories written long before. Why, then, had my prize volume been available at all in 1966? Why, in that year, was a smart-looking volume of Lawson prose felt to be appropriate for city schoolchildren as something worth prizing? And why these contents: the stories and sketches that Cecil Mann had chosen? What part of Lawson's life had they come from? And what, more broadly, was their source in the print culture in which Lawson had lived and moved?

Then the next logical question: how, after their initial publications, had these stories cut across the cultural history of Australia in the twentieth century so as to reach my hands? Even from the facts, or factoids, already adduced by my anecdote, they must have done so, since clearly they had not been forgotten. Learning how to answer this series of questions and to elicit the literary and cultural significance of the answers is the subject matter of this book. It is the biography of a book. It tells the life of a collection of Lawson's prose from 1896, *While the Billy Boils* – from which my 'Drover's Wife', and many others in Mann's selection, were stated in its Contents page to have come.

This biography of a book not only traces the cultural cross-section performed by Lawson's prose but also, by virtue of its book-historical approach, cuts across recent trends in literary studies in general and approaches to Australian literature in particular. Like many a scholarly book it comes out of a tradition while being critical of it, while trying at the same time to renovate it. In this book, narratives are generated about both makers and readers of Lawson's prose. Book productions are analysed with sometimes forensic attention. Reception histories are traced from archives and collections. Some surprising reversals of accepted wisdom occur, but it is the way of proceeding and the way of conceptualising the method that give the book its broader relevance. At its most general, it offers or implies a model for literary studies. In contrast to trends in recent decades, the model is deeply respectful of empirical evidence, including that of authorship. It finds ways of giving voice to the evidence, and of connecting it to insights generated from other areas and by other scholars. If there is a manifesto, however, it is only a modest one. There is no note of triumph on offer, only a certain satisfaction in understanding the thing one may have thought one knew well for the first time – or at least differently.

Biographical–textual–material

The pacing of that first sentence from 'The Drover's Wife' in Mann's selection is not, in fact, presented as Lawson originally wrote it. The sentence was rewritten by a publisher's editor for *While the Billy Boils* in 1896. There turned out to be, as I discovered, hundreds of such changes. If the story of Lawson's stories were to be told, I realised, the first obligation was to start at the beginning, or as close to it as could be achieved. So it is that the original newspaper texts of the short stories and sketches that appeared in *While the Billy Boils* in 1896 in revised form make their appearance, for the first time since the 1890s, in the edition that accompanies the present volume.[1] The 1896 collection, in

---

[1] Henry Lawson, *While the Billy Boils: The Original Newspaper Versions*, ed. Paul Eggert, with Explanatory Notes by Elizabeth Webby (Sydney: Sydney University Press, 2012). In

its complete form and as divided into smaller formats, has, in contrast, rarely been out of print. Its texts have also been collected in weighty tomes of Complete Works since the 1930s and widely anthologised. The stories and sketches have achieved classic status. Right from the start, Lawson's form of bush realism guaranteed the collection's popularity and meant that, to future generations, it would be seen as a defining document of the Australian cultural flowering of the 1890s, the decade before the Federation of the colonies into the Commonwealth of Australia in 1901.

Lawson's innovative narrative techniques were less visible but no less important. He had been developing them from the late 1880s as the stories and sketches appeared in various newspapers and periodicals, mainly in Sydney but also in Brisbane and Maryborough in Queensland, Wellington and Pahiatua in New Zealand, and in London. This development has been, until now, obscured by the circumstances of the original productions. More surprisingly, the only previous scholarly edition of the stories – in a Collected Prose whose publication spanned 1972–84 – did less than it might have done to clarify and give readers access to the phases of Lawson's literary coming-of-age.[2]

The motives behind his revisions and the copy-editing for *While the Billy Boils* were mixed. The collection would be advantageously positioned in the available marketplaces by its ambitious new Sydney publisher, Angus & Robertson. This affected its preparation, of which the author was by no means in complete control. The implications of this fact, explored in later chapters, are many. Archival research in the Angus & Robertson papers in the Mitchell Library in Sydney, together with a systematic collation of the stories' versions, has shown that *While the Billy Boils* cannot be adequately understood whether approached in a traditional way as a self-contained literary classic or, alternatively, as the discursive expression of a nationalist mindset of the 1890s.

---

the following footnotes, *While the Billy Boils* is abbreviated to *Billy Boils*. See also the List of Abbreviations. Where pagination has been added to manuscript and other folios by the holding library, it is cited; otherwise foliation is given.

[2]   This criticism of Colin Roderick's scholarly editions of HL's prose fiction is pursued in Chapter 13. The editions are cited in full in the List of Abbreviations.

These two approaches, the first typical of the period up to the mid-1970s and the second of the following couple of decades, do not account sufficiently for the new evidence. The argument of the present volume is that a broader book-historical perspective must come into play. Here, the scholarly edition is crucial. It presents the stories in the order of their first publication, thus reinserting the relevance of biographical fact and bibliographical chronology into the debate. By tabulating and attributing responsibility for the many hundreds of changes made to the original texts as they moved forward to the versions that appeared in *While the Billy Boils*, the edition respects the principle of individual human agency. The author, however, is by no means the only agent in which the edition or this book is interested – although, without him, there would be no story to be told.

Study of the evidence, textual and archival, importantly assists in a reconstruction of the literary and publishing environment of Sydney, in which, before 1896, this new talent from the bush was obliged to operate if he were to achieve an income, secure a readership and hone his literary skills. Lawson went on to revise sixteen of the fifty-two stories and sketches in *While the Billy Boils* for *The Country I Come From*, a Lawson collection published by Blackwood in Edinburgh in 1901.[3] These later versions are also documented in the edition, thus facilitating a focused study of the various Lawsons encountered by his early readerships.[4] A reception history is therefore pursued in Chapters 8 and 11–13, drawing in part upon the work of previous scholars but mainly upon the extraordinary gathering of reviews that George Robertson put together for each of the early titles in his firm's brave publishing venture from the mid-1890s.

Promotion and production go hand in hand in this account, which, in its sweep from 1896 to the 1980s and after, becomes more broadly cultural

---

[3] The Blackwood collection is discussed in Chapter 10: its n. 27 lists the sixteen inclusions.
[4] Explanatory notes in the accompanying edition also help to locate the stories in their biographical, literary and other contexts, including in their overlaps with HL's verse and other writings. Other notes gloss the Australianisms, idiomatic and slang usages, in the sinuous use of which HL became a master.

and cultural-political in its purview. Nevertheless, the solid foundation of bibliographical fact and archival resource prevents Lawson and his prose from being reduced to the passive role of exemplum of broader discursive formations. Respecting the claims of chronology and agency is the key here. It opens the door to a broadened understanding of the literary *work*, one that circumvents the narrower emphasis on the verbal icon – the self-sufficient text of the New Critical movement from the 1930s and subsequent decades.

When in 1931 the German aesthetic philosopher Roman Ingarden published *Das literarische Kunstwerk*, and especially after its appearance in English in 1967, the idea of literary works as having a 'life', as 'com[ing] into being and exist[ing] only by our grace' as readers, rather than being seen as autonomous aesthetic objects, began slowly to gain ground.[5] E. D. Hirsch's *Validity in Interpretation* (1967) was significant here, but even he tended to close down the existential gap that Ingarden's careful descriptions of the phenomena associated with the work had opened up. If we were to validly interpret literary works, Hirsch argued, then there must be something held in common that was the object of interpretation. Since, as the philosophers of the New Critical movement René Wellek and Austin Warren had shown in the 1940s, that could not be the author's private intention it must be what Hirsch called the communicated intention.[6] This move papered over the philosophical cracks, leaving the idea of the aesthetic work-as-object gingerly in place. In due course it would lend support to a scholarly editorial methodology based on final authorial intention, as complete-works editorial projects began to be organised for nineteenth- and twentieth-century writers. Thus editors tended to reinforce the objective status of the work that their textual apparatuses – showing the existence of competing versions,

---

[5] Roman Ingarden, *The Literary Work of Art: An Investigation on the Borderlines of Ontology, Logic and Theory of Literature*, tr. George G. Grabowicz (1931; Evanston, IL: Northwestern University Press, 1973), p. 373. The 'life of the literary work' is the name of one of the chapters.
[6] E. D. Hirsch, *Validity in Interpretation* (New Haven: Yale University Press, 1967); René Wellek and Austin Warren, 'The Mode of Existence of a Literary Work of Art': first published in 1942 in *Southern Review* and in Wellek and Warren, *Theory of Literature* (1948) as 'The Analysis of the Literary Work of Art'; then with revised title (London: Cape, 1966), pp. 142–57.

some authorial, some not – were potentially dismantling. Alert readers of scholarly editions found they could read the editions to some effect, both with the grain and against. Rejected versions were lurking in those apparatuses, but they were hard to get at.

The rug was more effectively, indeed powerfully, pulled from under the existing commitment to the close study of aesthetic objects by the burgeoning poststructuralist theory movement. Its success, in its evolving forms and especially from the early 1980s in anglophone countries, meant that interest in studying the life of individual literary works, in their detailed interaction with the agents of their production and reception, became the pursuit of only a tiny minority.

Scholarly editors and some textual critics necessarily engaged the theme. They were emboldened in part by the new editorial-theory movement of the 1980s and 1990s, with its defence of the editorial documentation of textual 'process' rather than finalised 'product', its redefinition of rejected versions recorded in the apparatuses as alternative ones, and a newfound interest in the signifying qualities of the material carriers of text. This last interest gradually legitimated study of the readerships that engaged with those text-carriers, typically magazines and books. So now works were not only textual (and in multiple versions); they were material as well.

The advent from the early 1990s of the new book-history movement gave a broadening impetus to the debate. It opened up some long-closed corridors. The Australian case was no exception. The book trade lurched unbidden into the purview of the literary scholar and suddenly declared its relevance. The gradual consolidation from the 1860s of properly established book importing and retailing businesses in Melbourne (Mullens, George Robertson of Melbourne) and then Sydney (Dymocks, Angus & Robertson), and the role of colonial editions in driving down the local price of fiction thus extending potential readerships, began to be better understood.[7] Recent work

---

[7] See Paul Eggert, '*Robbery Under Arms:* The Colonial Market, Imperial Publishers and the Demise of the Three-Decker Novel', *Book History*, 6 (2003), 127–46; and 'Australian Classics and

has shown that opportunities for Australian authors to achieve first or simultaneous publication in the USA would emerge strongly in the twentieth century, despite continuing domination of the local scene by British publishing houses.[8] But the pattern had already been set in the nineteenth century, and especially during the 1890s after the US Chace Act (1891) finally regulated international copyright arrangements. To maximise income in one another's marketplaces from the intellectual property purchased from authors, American and British publishers had to come to terms. Typically, the ensuing sale of rights (or sheets) by their London publishers allowed some fortunate colonial Australian writers to gain a hearing, via New York publishers, in the USA.[9]

In Australia, where it was usually associated with editorial projects, textual criticism revealed previously overlooked versions, sometimes authorised for different readerships or superseded when the author, under production pressures, lost control of the text's evolution. These

---

the Price of Books: The Puzzle of the 1890s', *Journal of the Association for the Study of Australian Literature* (special issue *The Colonial Present*, ed. Gillian Whitlock), 8 (2008), 130–57.

[8] See David Carter, 'Transpacific or Transatlantic Traffic? Australian Books and American Publishers', *Reading Across the Pacific: Australia–United States Intellectual Histories*, ed. Robert Dixon and Nicholas Birns (Sydney: Sydney University Press, 2010), pp. 339–59; and Roger Osborne, 'New York City Limits: Australian Novels and American Print Culture', *ibid.*, pp. 299–308.

[9] The AUSTLIT database records nearly 100 cases of publication of Australian novels and short-story collections in the USA before 1901: 13 cases of first publication in USA and another 84 of simultaneous publication there (www.austlit.edu.au, accessed December 2011). These numbers exclude works by short-term visitors to Australia but include works not specifically identified in AUSTLIT as simultaneous. 27 cases precede the Chace Act, the great majority during 1880–90. The earliest was in 1846 (Charles Rowcroft, *The Bushranger of Van Diemen's Land*); works by Henry Kingsley, B. L. Farjeon and Tasma are the most notable. Of the 70 cases during 1891–1900, works by Rolf Boldrewood, Guy Boothby, Rosa Praed, E. W. Hornung and Ada Cambridge are the most frequent.

In some cases the US publications are or appear to be different versions of a work. Their significance is yet to be studied systematically, but four cases have been illuminated by scholarly editions. See the Introductions to the Academy Editions (St Lucia: University of Queensland Press): Henry Kingsley, *The Recollections of Geoffry Hamlyn*, ed. Stanton Mellick, Patrick Morgan and Paul Eggert (1996), pp. l–li; and Marcus Clarke, *His Natural Life*, ed. Lurline Stuart (2001), pp. xlviii–li. See also the Introductions to the Colonial Texts Series editions: Catherine Martin, *The Silent Sea*, ed. Rosemary Foxton (Sydney: University of New South Wales Press, 1995), p. xxvi; and Ada Cambridge, *A Black Sheep: Some Episodes in his Life* (the serial version of *A Marked Man*), ed. Elizabeth Morrison (Canberra: Australian Scholarly Editions Centre, 2004) pp. xxxvi–xxxvii.

latter explanations themselves raised wider book-historical questions about the relationship of author to publisher, editor and literary agent, and each of these in turn raised questions of the literary marketplace and authors' accommodations to it.

A return to the literary

At the most general level in this book I am trying to show by example that it can be productive, as a form of literary study, to follow the lives of works over time, both at the hands of the author and his or her collaborators in production, and in the reception of readers.

The aesthetic experience engendered by the act of reading is very real to us. Indeed, it can be profoundly real. Reflective people have been trying for centuries to describe and analyse that experience – to replay it, as it were, in different voices. When readers name the thing that they are describing or analysing they give it the name of the particular work, almost as if it were timeless. The reader's situation is somewhat like that of the concert pianist on the public stage, for whom it would be paralysing to believe other than that the interpretation he or she is in fact rendering, right now, *is* the work.

Yet, stepping back a little, we can agree that the reading itself (like the interpretation itself) is in history, that readings in the past of the same work have been different and that readings in the future will doubtless be differently inflected again, as they respond to changed cultural climates. So if reading is inevitably part of the functioning of works, and if works therefore inevitably inhabit history, it would be strange to exclude reading from the definition of the work, as if we were discussing something that is objective, timeless, self-sufficient.[10]

If the logic of *in*clusion is granted, if the 'work' necessarily exists in relation to the operations of time and human agency, then it follows that there can be no such thing as 'the work itself' – even if, as a regulative idea

---

[10] Cf. Paul Armstrong: 'Reading is coming back as a legitimate topic of enquiry after a long period of neglect': 'In Defense of Reading: Or, Why Reading Still Matters in a Contextualist Age', *New Literary History*, 42 (2011), 87–113.

for discussion of the reading experience, the term remains pragmatically indispensable. There is little point trying to escape from the clutches of this paradox, uncomfortable though it may be at first, because it throws light on some ticklish problems of definition.

For the text of a work to be read it must be in material form of some kind, usually on screen or on paper. Time and human agency leave their marks on the production of materialised texts, and readers are affected by these material productions. Their reading of a text of a work – their aesthetic experience – is a realisation of meanings that lie dormant in the materialised form of the lexical text and in its presentation: in its design, dust jacket, blurb, illustrations and so on. Each presentation keys us into the history of its own moment of production, just as each version of the lexical text keys into the life of the author and into the intentions and motivations of the author's collaborators.

The capacity of a work to index cultural change over time is a dimension of its existence that can in principle be read off the production features and inferred from the reception that each new edition receives. The indexing can form part of literary study. It can stand in for or access discursive criticism. At the same time, because of its emphasis on the act of reading, this model of the work underwrites the practice of close reading upon which literary-critical training has traditionally centred. A philosophical underwriting for close reading – and by extension for literary appreciation, to the extent that it is intrinsic to reading – has been sadly lacking for some time now, ever since the literary as a category found itself in ill odour.[11]

---

[11] Cf. Jane Gallop: 'If practiced here and there, [close reading] is seldom theorized, much less defended. It has been, I think, tarred with the elitist brush applied in our rejection of the New Critics' canon, and I fear it is being thrown out with the dirty bathwater of timeless universals': 'The Historicization of Literary Studies and the Fate of Close Reading', *Profession* (2007), 181–6 [p. 182]; and James F. English, *The Global Future of English Studies* (Chichester, West Sussex: Wiley-Blackwell, 2012), p. 13.

Cf. also David Carter: 'literary "appreciation" is something we will still want to teach in one form or another'. Yet, he asks: 'Is the object of our research still literature or is it books, publishing, or print culture? Is what we're doing still *literary* history or is it book history, the history of reading, or something else again – the history of cultures or subjectivities? Are we still talking about "literary studies" or is the literary simply dispersed into all other studies?'

The reason why is well known. Michel Foucault's *The Archaeology of Knowledge* first appeared in French in 1969 and then in 1972 in English. Reprinted another thirteen times in English by 2000, it tended to remove the existing grounds of work-definition, and it had a diversionary effect on the study of the book as material object.

Given what Foucault calls 'the density of discursive practices' at any one time, he argues:

> if there are things said – and those only – one should seek the immediate reason for them in the things that were said not in them, nor in the men that said them, but in the system of discursivity, in the enunciative possibilities and impossibilities that it lays down. The archive is first the law of what can be said, the system that governs the appearance of statements as unique events.[12]

In his typically sinuous prose, accumulating as it proceeds through elegant turns until it reaches the generalising and decisive statement, Foucault was wanting, extraordinarily, to define and centralise the archive of *discourses*, not of documents. He was, as it were, rolling the material-documentary stone out of the way to provide entrance to the philosopher's cave where would be found the immaterial-discursive system. Foucault's 'archive' is what he calls at first the *historical a priori*. By this he does not mean any actual archive of documents organised according to certain principles nor, more generally, the idea of a possible archive of all documents.[13] Rather, he was wanting to validate the study of the set of relationships exterior to any and all enunciations of meaning at any one time when, as he puts is, 'there are things said – and those only'. Analysis of texts and documents would necessarily henceforth

---

Furthermore, he notes, the current study of book history is methodologically 'agnostic towards literature': 'Structures, Networks, Institutions: The New Empiricism, Book History and Literary History', in *Resourceful Reading: The New Empiricism, eResearch and Australian Literary Culture*, ed. Katherine Bode and Robert Dixon (Sydney: Sydney University Press, 2009), pp. 31–52 [pp. 35, 34]. For a reply to Carter, see Paul Eggert, 'Brought to Book: Bibliography, Book History and the Study of Literature', *The Library*, 7th series, 13.1 (2012), 3–32. This is the source of some of the argument here.
[12] Michel Foucault, *The Archaeology of Knowledge* (London: Routledge, 2000), pp. 128, 129.
[13] What an empiricist might think of as the categorical difference between the archive and the library (as holders predominantly of documents as against books) turns out not to be of any moment if viewed in terms of Foucault's history of discursive formations.

occur in the passive voice, since agency was implicitly now transferred to the discursive system.

Texts are, under this generalising purview, reduced to instances of some discursive event or thing. In practical terms, the material records of moments of writing and of reading get swallowed up into a far larger-scale form of cultural explanation. In the 1970s and 1980s this was intoxicating stuff. Foucault helped open up the way for what proved to be an avalanche of postcolonial thinking about the archive. Knowledge turned out to be, as Foucault had predicted, an exercise of power over, not a neutral understanding of, an objective real world. There was complicity in the act of knowing. Enunciating and thereby decloaking the discursive system, tracing the ramifications of its power, was the point of the enterprise. After Foucault, the trajectory of understanding has been, then, away from the document to the text, to the discourse, to the conditions of possibility of the underlying discursive system.

Under this dispensation there would be casualties. As Foucault had put it, with some courtesy, in 'The Statement and the Archive':

> to posit the existence of . . . discursive formations . . . we have put to one side, not in a definitive way, but for a time and out of methodological rigour, the traditional unities of the book and the *oeuvre*.[14]

A series of agreements, Foucault quite reasonably points out, goes along with this. It means that, in doing so,

> we have ceased to accept as a principle of unity the laws of constructing discourse (with the formal organization that results), or the situation of the speaking subject (with the context and the psychological nucleus that characterize it); that we no longer relate discourse to the primary ground of experience, nor to the *a priori* authority of knowledge; but that we seek the rules of its formation in discourse itself.[15]

That was a lot to put to one side, even for the purposes of an intellectual experiment and despite the new flexibilities for cultural analysis that it ushered in.

---

[14] Foucault, *Archaeology of Knowledge*, p. 79.
[15] *Ibid.*

No wonder then that, in the 1980s, we began to refer rather lazily to 'the literary text' (or, as in the present case, 'Lawson's text'), and then just 'the text', almost as if the literary dimension could not be defended any longer, or had become illegible as such. In a situation where authorship was first disentangled from the biographical author and then deemed to be a constricting regime of interpretation, where was the ground to defend 'the literary' as other than a floating discourse; or, after Pierre Bourdieu, as a field in which cultural capital could be accrued and contested; or as an institutionalisation of a politically conservative kind? The 'literary work' as a term seemed, suddenly, very old-fashioned.

The past had bequeathed other answers to the question of grounding the literary; but they too now felt unsatisfactory in various ways. The literary work consorted with hierarchies and canons: it had been behaving badly all along, only we had not noticed. Better then to ignore it: others might take care of the question of its grounding anyway and, for now, there were more interesting things to explore. Various forms of discursive critique began to flourish. They promised much more than traditional literary study by ranging more widely. Cultural studies had already set off down this road and, through its flexibilities, offered attractive models. Whether cultural study would ultimately absorb literary study as a sub-section of itself became a real question.

Yet there was a cost to all of this, which we hardly noticed at the time: the cost of leaving the essential thing that had brought us to literary study in the first place unattended, almost uninspected. How to name the thing (that, in the strongly creative sense of the term, we *realise* in reading) remains the question, and then how to understand its confluence with the many contextual flows that writing and reading inevitably recall and initiate. Discursive and other forms of critique had asked the latter question in a way that old-fashioned study of 'historical contexts' – which left the literary text in a self-sustaining category of its own – could not.

To want to recruit these discursive insights while yet addressing the abiding but unanswered question is not the same as wishing to reify the literary work into an aesthetic object. That would amount to a return to the philosophic premises of 1940s New Criticism, which is the opposite of my intention in this book. Its title uses the word 'biography'. The term lays stress on the unfolding of the literary work over time. Reading is always central to its operations, a process that starts from the moment the writer's first stuttering thoughts are got down on paper or on screen, and then as they develop into a more or less finished version that itself may be discarded or further developed. There is, in other words, a textual genesis in which writers are their own first readers. And editors, agents and typesetters become readers well before the public reception starts.

There is a feedback loop. Anticipation of the reception will have affected the developing text or texts of the work right from the very start, a process that will proceed through production. Records of the subsequent reception – marginalia in printed or digital copies, personal diary entries, reviews – will likely be made and some will survive.

This model so far assumes only the one publication event. A work that becomes a favourite and ultimately perhaps a classic for a reading community will enjoy many such events. The author, publisher, typesetter or the designer may intervene in any one of them, creating new versions or a new organisation of contents, or adding new introductions or notes or illustrations, while almost certainly providing new packaging or blurbs intended to influence potential purchasers. None of these considerations will leave the new reading experiences unaffected.

Yet all readers of the work, in later discussing their experience of reading (which is really their memory of the experience), profess to be discussing 'the work' or 'the text'. Rightly so, since the experience is theirs, and it needs a name. When they find they disagree they each return to the bibliographic object, which was the site of the reading experience. If they had the experience but fear they missed the meaning, at least they know where to return to refresh that experience, or to draw authority for their first interpretation, or to check or correct it. The stable thing in all of this is not so much the realised textual meaning (which is inherently shifting) as the bibliographic site of it: the material document, which scarcely changes at all. The two are always in a dialectic: they need each other, as it were, to secure their different but linked identities. Thus it is not a matter of 'the work' somehow transcending the process: the work (broadly considered) *is* the process. It is also how we name it.

Text and its material carrier have always been, from a bibliographical perspective, two different things. But the eclipse of bibliography from participation in the broader debate, especially acute in and after the 1980s, meant that the routine distinction was lost to us. If bibliography was, as argued at the time, merely a positivist hangover from a discredited New Critical idealism then its passing would not be mourned. There is, indeed, a grain of truth in this objection, a point I develop in Chapter 13 and again in the Introduction to the scholarly edition. I observe here only that the forcible submersion of bibliography to an even deeper undercurrent than before meant that we lost the interpretative leverage that flowed from the distinction between text and document. Yet to 'read' production in the indexical way suggested above sometimes requires close attention to that distinction. Analytical bibliography necessarily comes into play (as seen in Chapters 4 and 5), because it is a technology for recovering the production history of printed matter.

Its discrediting was a hard pill to swallow for scholarly editors in the 1980s. They were dealing on a daily basis with text-versions whose variant inscriptions, witnessed by their material carriers, required, for their explanation, the ascription of individual agency – even if not the solitary, inspired author of Romantic figuring. The materiality of manuscripts, proofs and successive editions was the irrepressible source of the editorial dissent. There was evidence here, the editors believed, that needed to be brought to the table of literary debate.

So, gradually, the bibliographical undercurrent, chastened but refreshed, bubbled up in the renewed editorial theory of the 1980s, and then in the new book-history movement some few years later. The mantra of the latter movement, 'the material book', signalled distance from its belles-lettristic past where publishers had memorialised themselves in histories of their firms as handmaidens in the publication of what became classic literary works. Now, suddenly, in the 'democratized spaces' of the printshop all works, literary or otherwise, were equal since all were books, material objects.[16] That way clarity lay – or at least that was the hope. Studies of the history of reading, shading off into reception studies of individual works, were fine too, for there were to be many rooms in the mansion of book history when the professional society SHARP was established in the early 1990s, its first conference being held in 1993. But that still left the literary work – that 'manifestly relegated term', as Kathryn Sutherland referred to it in 1996 – unattended and its study undefended.[17]

My larger argument, in response, is that to retrieve the distinction between text and document is to pay heed to the empirical questions that it implicitly raises. Further, it is to be able to conceptualise, as a literary methodology, the tracing of the 'life' of a work. A demonstration of this process for Henry Lawson's *While the Billy Boils* is the central subject matter of this book. It is offered, primarily, as a contribution to Australian literary studies and to studies of Lawson in particular. Yet it will be clear that its methodological implications go considerably further.

The national, postcolonial and transnational paradigms

The nationalist paradigm in Australia – and its recruitment of Lawson as a founding figure – is one of the themes that study of the life of *While the Billy Boils* allows one to pursue in a peculiarly focused way. One result of the study is a revisionary reading of the 1890s as a literary decade. What I call the Long 1890s carried on until the 1950s and after, when the cultural nationalists gave it a definition that expressed their own contemporary ideals. This re-creation of the 1890s was tacitly accepted

---

[16] David Finkelstein, *The House of Blackwood: Author-Publisher Relations in the Victorian Era* (University Park: Pennsylvania State University Press, 2002), p. 19. See further, Chapter 13 below.

[17] Kathryn Sutherland, 'Looking and Knowing: Textual Encounters of a Postponed Kind', in *Beyond the Book: Theory, Culture and the Politics of Cyberspace*, ed. Warren Chernaik, Marilyn Deegan and Andrew Gibson (Oxford: Office for Humanities Communication, 1996), pp. 11–22 [p. 16]. 'SHARP' is the Society for the History of Authorship, Reading and Publishing (www.sharpweb.org).

by 1980s feminist commentators despite their reversals of its ideological significance. In Chapter 12 I argue that the nationalist frame for both 1950s celebrations of the 1890s, and 1980s critique of its ideological formation, has seriously distorted understanding of that literary decade. This argument emerges from the successive receptions of *While the Billy Boils* recounted in Chapters 8, 11 and 13.

The common account of the formation of 1890s radical nationalism tended to draw attention away from more significant influences on the literary scene that were simultaneously global and colonial. The book-historical perspective of this book brings this truth out in empirically precise ways, lifting it from the fragile level of an ambitious claim. In this way the book cuts across, and speaks to, the recent transnational turn in literary studies. Although this movement now claims its founding figures from the late 1990s and early 2000s – Pascale Casanova, David Damrosch and Wai-chee Dimock, amongst others – a prehistory, of relevance here, can usefully be traced back to the new Imperial history movement of the 1990s, itself an outgrowth, in important ways, of postcolonialism in literary studies, which in its turn flourished from the late 1980s.

Inspired originally by poststructuralist thinking of the kind described above, early postcolonialist commentators aimed to reveal the hidden tensions and exploitations that centre–periphery power relations built into the everyday culture of the colonies, not just at governmental level but as interpolated into the social and racial fabric of the societies as well. Critics traced the various forms, psychic complicities and hybridising reactions that the discourse of Orientalism, to choose one important example, took or fostered.[18] Travel writings, novels, official documentation, cartography, the expansion or establishment of museums, first in Europe and then in the colonies: all these proved

---

[18] The initiator was *Orientalism* (New York: Pantheon, 1978) by Edward Said. He described an Imperial system of knowledge that incorporated the scientific classification of plants and animals, and the archive of official documents that notated, classified and regulated trade, government, social and especially indigenous affairs in the European colonies. See also, e.g., Mary Louise Pratt, *Imperial Eyes: Travel Writing and Transculturation* (London: Routledge, 1992); and Thomas Richards, *The Imperial Archive: Knowledge and the Fantasy of Empire* (London: Verso, 1993).

grist to the mill. The deployment of English literature in educational settings in the Empire was found to have been part of a normalising of Englishness and of the power disparities that went with it. In these ways and in others, isolated national or colonial-national models of historical explanation were effectively bypassed. This is the key point here.

A sharpened oppositional politics grew out of this theorising amongst the (literary-cultural) postcolonialists and the new Imperial historians. If Empire was now to be understood as 'a cultural artifact as a well as a geopolitical entity', if 'it belongs to a geography of the mind as well as a geography of power' as Eric Hinderaker described it, then it would be mandatory to find ways of giving voice to the 'subaltern' – indigenous peoples especially – via explorations of culturally hybrid colonial environments, especially the non-settler cultures in Africa and Asia and the Caribbean.[19] With this shift in attention to questions of cultural identity, often analysed through its discourses, the new Imperial historians seemed to deny the primacy of the economic and political evidence, upon which earlier Imperial historians had traditionally focussed. Yet, as new Imperial thinking has had to acknowledge what Kathleen Wilson calls the 'unevenness of metropolitan power … the disjunctures between metropolitan and colonial intentions', the two sides in the dispute have tended to grow closer in their need to account for empirical evidence, even if their frames for analysing it remain at odds. One test of this colonial discourse theory (as the historians call it), indeed, is its capacity to explain existing and new archival evidence, not just to rehearse its own positions, subtle though they may be. Where explanation has failed, the theory has been recognised to need revision.[20]

[19] Eric Hinderaker, 'The "Four Indian Kings" and the Imaginative Construction of the First British Empire', *William and Mary Quarterly*, 3rd series, 53 (1996), 487–526 [p. 487].
[20] E.g., see Kathleen Wilson, 'Introduction: Histories, Empires, Modernities', in *A New Imperial History: Culture, Identity and Modernity in Britain and the Empire, 1660-1840*, ed. Wilson (Cambridge: Cambridge University Press, 2004), [quotations, p. 17]. For the opposite point of view, see Robin W. Winks, 'The Future of Imperial History', in *Historiography*, ed. Winks, vol. 5 of the *Oxford History of the British Empire* (Oxford: Oxford University Press, 1999), pp. 653–68.

Nevertheless, the criticisms have been polemical and severe. The new Imperial history has been accused of 'cultural reductionism', the counterpart of a Marxist economic reductionism, and for tending only to invert the centre–periphery essentialism it sought to dispel (with the Empire now seen as defining the British character and cultural system rather than vice versa). Whatever the force of these and other criticisms, the new movement certainly licensed renewed attention to the Imperial system, whether seen as monolithic and epistemic or as a series of underplanned and opportunistic arrangements and of informal networks.[21]

The latter approach looks to have potential for the present study if only because it touches hands with the empirical. Discussing the historical phenomenon of globalisation the geographer Miles Ogborn has observed:

> For many, understanding global changes in the past – for example, tracing histories of migrations, the development of trade, the building of empires or the uses of technologies – is also a matter of the many geographies of globalisation. Thinking about this can usefully develop ideas of networks or webs of global connection that are built in various ways to link people, places, ideas and objects together in dynamic configurations. The advantage of thinking in this way is that it allows for multiple webs or networks to come into view, all with different shapes and different sorts of connections, rather than trying to construct a single big picture into which all must fit ... This produces much more nuanced historical geographies than ones that speak simply of core and periphery.[22]

To apply this perspective to the imperial booktrade, with which the colonial trade in Australia was simultaneously both in commercial partnership and competition, we need to pay attention to how publishers in London and Edinburgh operated in a practical workaday manner to secure their territories, to promote their titles, and to organise their sales and distribution to and within the colonies. The workings of that

---

[21] Stephen Howe, 'Introduction: New Imperial Histories', in *The New Imperial Histories Reader*, ed. Howe (London: Routledge, 2010), pp. 1–20 [p. 7].
[22] Miles Ogborn, *Global Lives: Britain and the World, 1550–1800* (Cambridge: Cambridge University Press, 2008), p. 5.

booktrade, being in a continuous state of competitive evolution, cannot have been fully comprehended by any of the players as each one strove for commercial advantage and forged and reforged the many links in their networks.

Colonial writers, being further from the action than their Home counterparts, were at a distinct disadvantage. Lawson's decision to go to London at the end of 1899, as we shall see in Chapters 9 and 10, was an attempt to overcome it. Some colonially authored works that were written and set in the colonies made their way back to Britain to be republished, typically after having been serialised in colonial newspapers. The texts of these works were usually altered, or abridged, or at least copy-edited, creating versions different from those already available in the colonies. Through the channels of the Imperial book trade, those altered versions made their way back to the colonies, generally displacing or superseding whatever local forms there had been.

In striking out in a brave new direction in the mid-1890s and in face of the competition from London, Lawson's publisher George Robertson (of Angus & Robertson in Sydney) had to find a way both of matching the standards of production of the British books that he was simultaneously selling from the firm's bookshop and of devising a sales campaign that would capture the public's attention. Playing the nationalist card – or, more precisely in his case, that of pride in local colonial achievement – was an obvious stratagem. Robertson was far more intent on the latter aspect than on the ideological relevance of Lawson's stories to the Bushman experience outback. This was a barrow that some reviewers and cultural entrepreneurs – discussed in Chapter 8 – nevertheless seized on and proceeded to push. As we shall see in Chapters 11 and 12, later interpreters of the 1890s mistook this sales pitch for a decisive swing in cultural temperament.

Transnational perspectives

It was perhaps inevitable that the trade and cultural phenomenon of globalisation, much remarked from the early 1990s, would call forth a corresponding literary response. The nation as an organising category in literary history, book history and in educational curricula was already overdue for such a response when Pascale Casanova argued in 1999 for a new model of a world literary system. The imagined community of the nation, as Benedict Anderson described it in 1983, partly grew out of its representations in newspapers and literary forms such as the novel. Similarly, at more local levels the socially formative effects of literary reading have been demonstrated by various histories of reading groups and circulating libraries. Understandably, then, a recent collection of essays declares the shared intention of its contributors to focus 'on literary *sociability* ... to shift attention from individual writers and great books to examine the various forms of community that facilitate and sustain writing and reading, and also the kinds of communal identities that are formed *by* the practices of writing and reading'.[23]

Translated into English in 2004, Casanova's book opened up the question of why some works become so international in their reception (and thus form part of a 'world literature') as almost to slough off their national origins.[24] Other works that have not fully achieved that desirable fate will nevertheless manifest themselves differently to readers abroad. How works can be simultaneously national (or local) *and* international in their significations for readers has been explored in various transnational studies since the late 2000s.

---

[23] Pascale Casanova, *The World Republic of Letters*, trans. M. B. DeBevoise (1999; Cambridge, Mass.: Harvard University Press, 2004). Benedict Anderson, *Imagined Communities: Reflections on the Origin and Spread of Nationalism* (London: Verso, 1983). On 'local levels', see, e.g., Christine Pawley, *Reading on the Middle Border: The Culture of Print in Late-Nineteenth-Century Osage, Iowa* (Amherst: University of Massachusetts Press, 2001); Patrick Buckridge, 'Generations of Books: A Tasmanian Family Library, 1816–1994', *Library Quarterly*, 76 (2006), 388–402; and Keith Adkins, *Reading in Colonial Tasmania: The Early Years of the Evandale Subscription Library* (Clayton, Vic: Ancora Press, Monash University, 2010). The quotation is from: Peter Kirkpatrick and Robert Dixon, 'Introduction: Republics of Letters and Literary Communities', in *Republics of Letters: Literary Communities in Australia*, ed. Kirkpatrick and Dixon (Sydney: Sydney University Press, 2012), pp. v–xix [p. v].

[24] Casanova's explanation of the differentials in prestige shows the playing field to be anything but a level one. The lineage from Pierre Bourdieu's fields of cultural production is plain: see David Carter, 'Modernising Anglocentrism: *Desiderata* and Literary Time', in *Republics of Letters*, ed. Kirkpatrick and Dixon, pp. 85–98. Cf. David Damrosch, *What Is World Literature?* (Princeton: Princeton University Press, 2003).

What is the property of works that allows them to support such a variety of response? Wai Chee Dimock points to simultaneous scenes of reading – a phenomenology of reading – with its 'co-ordinates' shifting between the pre-national, the sub-national and the transnational.[25] Yet the observable fact that only some works 'travel' – whether in the original language or in translation – shows that underlying decisions of a different nature have been made in advance that permit the process to occur. Those decisions are made mainly by the book trade: the transnationalising phenomenon has a material basis. Therefore each book production, and in turn each reading, is a situated act. To ignore this is, adopting Robert Dixon's term, to sublimate the underlying materiality. This is his criticism of the universalising perspective Dimock offers. Operating from 'a less commanding point of vantage', as he puts it – in Australia rather than Britain in the 1890s, say, or rather than in the USA now – is to be acutely aware of certain disproportions.[26]

Dimock's essay of 2001, 'Literature for the Planet', is a song of praise for the capacity of literature to communicate over long reaches of time and space. Reading literary works does not require 'border patrol[s]', she says. It negates 'the inert lines of a geopolitical map', 'the static borders of the nation'. Reading evades time limits, escapes 'the biological regime of a single human being'. Ultimately, 'reading turns literature into the collective life of the planet'. Her example is Dante as read by Osip Mandelstam in Stalinist Russia. It shows that Dante is read across time and in many countries, 'parented by [the] reader' in hybridising ways. 'Dante speaks Russian, and he speaks some fifty other languages': this is the 'globalization of Dante'.[27]

---

[25] Wai Chee Dimock, *Through Other Continents: American Literature across Deep Time* (Princeton, NJ: Princeton University Press, 2006). See also Dimock, 'Scales of Aggregation: Prenational, Subnational, Transnational'. The words of her subtitle 'belong to a baseline humanity. It is only by an act of violence that we can elevate them to a national paradigm': *American Literary History*, 18.2 (2006), 219–28 [p. 227].

[26] Robert Dixon, 'Scenes of Reading: Is Australian Literature a World Literature?', in *Republics of Letters*, ed. Kirkpatrick and Dixon, pp. 71–83 [p. 81].

[27] Wai Chee Dimock, 'Literature for the Planet', *PMLA*, 116 (2001), 173–88, [pp. 181, 176, 177, 178, 179, 181].

While there is an important sense in which each of these claims is true, or at least rhetorically persuasive, the celebratory throb of the essay does not leave conceptual room for consideration of the ordinary workings of time, nor the agency of individuals (including Dante himself, his copyists and later typesetters, editors and translators), working within principalities or nation-states or colonies.[28] Nor is there room for consideration of the publishing and other institutions (including the *Società Dantesca Italiana* from 1888), the various intellectual property regimes, and the booktrade that together have copied, produced and circulated Dante's poetry for six centuries. Dimock has eyes only for the adaptive anarchy of reading and readers. What she calls 'chronological decorum' is not for her.[29]

To shift attention away from the material vehicles of textual transmission (together with the questions about agency and chronological time that they, as material objects, raise) is, in other words, to settle for only half the story. Yet to take the contrasting transnational tack of concentrating on the 'sociality' of literature brings with it its own danger of leaving literature's individuality – or whatever we are to call the operational dimension that separates one work from another in literary studies – unaddressed and theoretically unsupported.

That is why the present study is an enquiry operating at the level of the work. What can be achieved there? My hope is that this focus may ultimately generate a model able to articulate the full range of the production-consumption continuum that all literary works inhabit. The model needs firm historical articulation for any particular case so that various kinds of analysis can be spun from it and tested against it. The dynamic can perhaps be described as centrifugal whereas normally in literary studies we work, as it were, in centripetal ways: from the theory

---

[28] Cf. Ros Pesman's account of the first and only Australian translation of the *Divine Comedy* (1898, 1908) by the Queensland Premier and later Australian Chief Justice, Sir Samuel Griffith: 'Sir Samuel Griffith, Dante and the Italian Presence in Nineteenth-Century Australian Literary Culture', in *Italy under the Southern Cross*, ed. David Moss and Gino Moliterno ([Perth, WA]: Australasian Centre for Italian Studies, 2011), pp. 86–104.
[29] Dimock, 'Literature for the Planet', p. 182.

or discourse inwards to the works or texts, which are differentially enlightened (or not) by the unexpectedly energising contact. The strong gaze of the theory creates the subject matter as such. Acting in this mode entails few empirical responsibilities, which is a blessing (since much ground can be covered quickly) but can be a curse if the conclusions turn out to be fragile because of what they have left to one side.

Nevertheless, in helping us to think outside of the inherited literary-nationalist paradigm global or transnational perspectives are to be welcomed. Although the inspiration and source of my interest did not emerge from this recent debate, it was heartening to find that my conclusions about cultural nationalism in Australia are broadly consistent with its central thrust. For instance, in his study *The Global Remapping of American Literature* (2011), Paul Giles argues that the achievement of American national identity popularly supposed to have occurred in 1776 was only hesitantly negotiated during the following decades. There is, he writes,

> little to suggest [that] such a sense of national triumphalism appeared a *fait accompli* to Americans themselves in the first half of the nineteenth century, when their structures of governance and tentative moves toward political cohesion were based on what many at the time considered to be the dubious theoretical hypothesis of federal union. In the first sixty years of U.S. history, in the aftermath of the colonial period, the country's sense of national identity was as uncertain, as provisional, as its cartography ... [W]hen Ralph Waldo Emerson writes in his 1844 essay 'The Poet' about America being a 'poem in our eyes', it was precisely that: a hypothetical or imaginative conception or at least one that had not yet achieved any firm sense of territorial grounding or enclosure.[30]

Nearly sixty years after the nominal act of independence, nationhood had not come to seem real. This was partly because of the only gradual incorporation of new states and territories, and because the United States awaited the almost mystic effects of nationhood solidifying after the end of the Civil War.

---

[30] Paul Giles, *The Global Remapping of American Literature* (Princeton, NJ: Princeton University Press, 2011), p. 5.

The lesson might be applied to the Australian colonies. The geographical boundary of the island continent was conceptually organised in its being named Australia by its circumnavigator Matthew Flinders in 1804. The territorial incorporation of the whole continent under the British Crown became a reality only forty-odd years after first settlement at Port Jackson (Sydney) in 1788.[31] In the second half of the nineteenth century intercolonial rivalry, together with vested interests, delayed the colonies' Federation until 1901. Only then did something like a nation come formally into being, although some reserve powers were withheld for several decades.

After the centenary of European settlement in 1888, the sense of local or colonial (as opposed to national) identity had remained strong; and very many saw it as complementary to their British or Anglo-colonial identity.[32] During the 1890s, the sense of national identity seems to have remained a fragile thing, even after the series of constitutional conferences of that decade, the strident efforts of the *Bulletin* to conjure a nation into being, and the participation of colonial troops in the Anglo-Boer War from 1899.

Delays in imagining the change to nationhood (the American 1850s, the Australian 1950s) run parallel, together with the need to read the national present back onto the earlier period (1776 and the 1890s) when the sentiment for nationhood was taken to have become generally achieved. Close study of the 'life' of *While the Billy Boils* prompts this conclusion about the 1890s and shows why the booktrade – which one

---

[31] Annexation of the entire continent by the British Crown had been completed by 1831 when the western third of the continent was defined by letters patent as Western Australia. Its tiny Swan River Colony at Perth had been established in 1829. The eastern two-thirds of the continent was at that stage New South Wales. The borders of the other colonies were, one by one, defined later in the century as settlement expanded, and finally the present form of the Northern Territory was defined in 1931.

[32] To take the *Bulletin* at its word is to ignore the dominant class of Independent Australian Britons, as Alfred Deakin, the second Australian Prime Minister, called them. See Stuart Macintyre, 'Australia and the Empire', in *Historiography*, ed. Winks, pp. 163–81 [p. 168]: 'The men who led the process of Federation, drafted the constitution of the new Commonwealth during the 1890s, and then directed its early activities in the new century were Imperial nationalists, liberal in their sympathies, Australian in sentiment, and firm in their attachment to the Empire'.

might have thought irrelevant to literary study – proves to be anything but.

In his prose writings Lawson helped to imagine an Australian environment largely through inhabiting the idiom and tones of its people, especially those of the lower and mainly male echelons of his little-differentiated bush and city locales. Lawson naturalised the country laconically, not through reflecting on, or self-consciously or programmatically pursuing, a sense of its exceptionalism. Neither, on the other hand, did he orient his prose by overt or implicit reference to British norms as, say, his immediate predecessor Rolf Boldrewood instinctively did. Lawson's prose affords us some hundreds of sharp lights on the social condition of that late colonial moment, but no organising panopticon. The ideological formation of nation he left, by and large, to others, and most of them came later.

Empirical evidence and literary studies

Statistical methods in literary study

As another expression of the recent transnational turn, Franco Moretti's proposals for kinds of distant reading that detect statistical and geographic patterns across vast swathes of literary publication have been greeted with enthusiasm in some quarters and with horror in others.[33] This is because Moretti explicitly challenges the practice of close reading that, paradoxically, continued to be taught as a necessary training for undergraduates during the same decades in which the philosophic ground that had originally defended the practice was being stripped away or allowed to etiolate. In Moretti, the usual triumphalism is at work, and it elicits the usual responses.

Like most other scholars, however, I am grateful for enlightenment about the things I study, whatever the source. Statistical patterns derived from literary databases have great potential in bringing a new

---

[33] Franco Moretti, *Graphs, Maps, Trees: Abstract Models for a Literary History* (London: Verso, 2005). Cf. *Reading Graphs, Maps and Trees: Responses to Franco Moretti*, ed. Jonathan Goodwin and John Holbo (Anderson, SC: Parlor Press, 2011).

kind of evidence to the table. Literary-historical generalisations about the characteristics of this or that period that are themselves based on anecdote or selective sampling will be corrected by this means, and the new methods will be justified on this basis.[34] Provided the probabilistic conclusions remain open to challenge and refinement by the (sometimes disruptive) hunches of the interpreter's ordinary literary instincts and literary-historical experience, I see only gain. The same applies to the findings of computational stylistics. Authorship may have been discredited in the poststructuralist period as scarcely worth studying, yet unique authorial signatures can be located with intimidating accuracy in word-frequency patterns. The experiments are both repeatable and falsifiable.

Such conclusions have rightly begun to take their place in the literary marketplace of ideas. Their premises will be open to challenge here and there; and when sustained, the statistical techniques will probably be adjusted to cope. Their effectiveness is of course limited by the capacities of the interpreter to turn available data into evidence – but there is nothing new there. The question that all of them beg is implicitly the same broad question that underlies this book: the nature of the literary, and therefore a methodology that might address it more fully. If their answer is so far only a partial one, there is no shame in that. The methods will evolve over time.

William St Clair, book history and economic theory

The power of economic theory and market analysis as applied to the history of reading came to general attention in the mid-2000s, following publication of William St Clair's book *The Reading Nation in the Romantic Period*. He laid down a formidable gauntlet aimed at the literary-critical styles of the last twenty years. If we wish to recover the history of reading, and therefore of changing 'mentalities' as affected by reading, there is, he argued, little point applying 'exclusively text-based

---

[34] See, e.g., Katherine Bode, *Reading by Numbers: Recalibrating the Literary Field* (London: Anthem, 2012).

approaches, because they either ignore readers altogether, or they derive their readers from the texts' and are thus 'caught in a closed system'. Nor will detailed consideration of the intertextual correspondences between works of a certain period necessarily capture the experience of readers at the time since 'Not all readers had access to all newly published texts' and 'no historical reader ... read printed texts in the chronological order in which they were first published'. St Clair shows, for instance, that the Romantic poets were read far more widely, and presumably were therefore more influential, in the Victorian period than they were in their own. Furthermore, extant reports of reading, as recorded in diaries and letters, will, though valuable, always be unrepresentative 'of the far larger total acts of reception which were never even turned into words in the mind of the reader let alone recorded in writing'. The history of reading, he quips, 'is at the stage of astronomy before telescopes, economics before statistics, heavily reliant on a few commonly repeated traditional narratives and favourite anecdotes, but weak on the spade-work of basic empirical research'.[35]

One answer that he proposes is to gather sales statistics from publishers' archives. Another is to identify the changing constraints and determinants of the publishing industry over the centuries: where and how it operated monopolistically because of intellectual property regimes guaranteed by the state, and where and how it operated competitively in their absence. St Clair shows that the price and quantity of books sold respond to simple economic theories. They in turn explain why, for instance, until the late eighteenth century the reading experiences of the poor, hitherto constrained by publishers' attention to the topmost tranches of the market where new works could be sold for high profits, broadened and modernised rapidly once printer-cartels lost their comfortable control of the market. Books typically got cheaper and smaller as publishers ventured down the market levels in pursuit of much amplified sales.

[35] William St Clair, *The Reading Nation in the Romantic Period* (Cambridge: Cambridge University Press, 2004), pp. 4, 3, 5, 9.

While the extrapolation from market conditions to period 'mentalities' would be a hazardous undertaking – St Clair only gestures at it – he makes a strong case for the relevance of the production and marketing of works to the current literary debate. It is the indisputable materiality of the book form that gains him entrance to it. The present study takes that material condition for granted, and pursues its implications in relation to the late nineteenth-century colonial market in Australia, of which Lawson's *While the Billy Boils*, in its successive productions, turns out to offer a revealing cross-section. The same book-historical habit of attention continues to pay rewards as the fate of that title is traced through the twentieth century. But whereas St Clair aims at gathering the empirical knowledge-base from which to create a complex-systems model of reading over historical periods, the present study narrows the focus to a single collection of stories and sketches. There are losses and gains in such a narrowing. But in its reaching for a more specifically literary modelling of the lives of works, it does not fall victim to the strictures St Clair levels at 'closed' literary methodologies.

As described in Chapter 3, a remarkable burst of physical infrastructural development in the 1880s in the Australian colonies suddenly provided marketing conditions for the successful establishment of an Australian publishing industry, as well as for the more efficient distribution of books imported from London. Without these conditions, and his publisher's energetic exploitation of them, *While the Billy Boils* could have sunk like a stone and been forgotten within a few years, just as so many of its colonial literary predecessors that had failed to gain a London publication had done.

The new infrastructure also facilitated Lawson's own travelling. The railway line from Sydney to Bourke was completed in 1885. J. F. Archibald, co-proprietor of *The Bulletin*, famously sent Lawson there, with five pounds in his pocket, in search of 'copy' in 1892. Regular and relatively fast steamship routes allowed Lawson to travel, and in early 1896 even to shuttle, between Sydney and New Zealand. In the new subject matter that both colonies afforded him, this infrastructure granted him, we may say, the direct or indirect basis of the majority of his sketches in the published collection.

A less obvious but ultimately more significant effect of the steamship routes from Britain especially, but also from the Continent and the Pacific lines from North America, was the boost given to the international trade in intangible cultural goods. Information about the availability and reception of the latest novels was conveyed in literary gossip columns that circulated in the colonies, both in their original magazine printings in Britain brought over by ship and as cut-and-pasted into counterpart columns in the colonial dailies and weeklies. News of the wondrous new sensation or scandal could be communicated with despatch, and the slower shifts in literary taste would be duly and variously registered.

Conclusion

After so long a period of high Theory in the literary and cultural areas it was probably inevitable that more empirically sourced modes of enquiry would develop and gradually find a welcome. Older and newer forms of engagement with the texture and history of literature had been sidelined but not extinguished. They are returning, in reshaped forms; and, with them, a return to the literary may be happening. Its study will be newly modelled and defended.

This, I take it, is the situation and moment in which the present study is positioned and from which it takes its flavour and orientation. Even if the motive force differs from its more theoretically driven predecessor, no intellectual practice can be conducted innocent of theory. So it is in this case. Thus the time has not come for any display of triumphalism, since, until proved otherwise, this moment is only the most recent one one in a long, slow series. The abiding intellectual predicament remains, though inflected a little differently now. From the fact of difference, however, advances may be wrought. The important questions are: What kinds of neglected evidence can the study bring to the table? and also, What are the implications of the evidence for literary study – for the ways in which it may profitably and productively be organised and understood? A shift in explanatory paradigm from one based broadly on discourse to one grounded in the material object points to the need, I argue in Chapter 13, to re-define the concept of the work as a basis of literary study. But before the merits of that approach can be appreciated, the lives of certain works by Henry Lawson need to be explored and articulated. Together those lives make up the biography of a book.

WHILE THE BILLY BOILS

BY

HENRY LAWSON

AUTHOR OF
'IN THE DAYS WHEN THE WORLD WAS WIDE.'

With Eight Plates by Mahony

SYDNEY
ANGUS AND ROBERTSON
89 CASTLEREAGH STREET
1896

Title-page of the first impression of *While the Billy Boils* with Frank Mahony's vignette dated '96' [1896].

CHAPTER 1

A WRITING CAREER IN THE MAKING

LAWSON'S EARLY LIFE

BORN in Grenfell in 1867 and then living for the first thirteen years of his life near Gulgong, another goldmining town in inland New South Wales, Henry Lawson was to experience a childhood marked by poverty, bickering parents and only a few years of indifferent education in local bush schools. Growing deafness, first noticed when he was ten, and a tendency to depression, must have left him isolated. His school fellows called him Barmy Harry. His father Niels Larsen (later, Lawson) had arrived in Melbourne from Norway in 1855 and gone in search of gold. In this he was unlucky, but his quest led him to New Pipeclay (soon renamed Eurunderee, the Aboriginal name for the area), between Mudgee and Gulgong, where he met and in 1866 married Louisa Albury, the daughter of a local publican, himself formerly a timber-getter and bush labourer. She had been born in the colony and was eighteen.

After the Grenfell rush, the young family returned to live on her father's land. Lawson thus grew up in a tablelands farming district, itself pock-marked by abandoned diggings and shafts left by departed goldminers. The family moved to Gulgong in late 1871 when a new rush broke out there, and would experience some temporary prosperity. But by 1873 they were back in Eurunderee where Niels, a hardworking man, leased ('selected') forty acres of land from the government and set about making it productive. The farm could not support the growing family, and in 1880 Lawson was withdrawn from the Catholic school at Mudgee – where, though brought up Methodist, he had spent the previous few months – in order to help his father. Niels had begun taking on building contracts let by arms of government, at first locally and then further afield.

In his partially fictionalised 'A Fragment of Autobiography' written during 1903–06, Lawson attributed his learning to read to his mother. He remembered her reading *Robinson Crusoe* aloud to the family of an evening: 'when she'd get tired and leave off at a thrilling place, we'd get the book and try to spell our way ahead'.[1] During his brief formal education Lawson was a prize-winning student. Although at school he probably had to make do with wretchedly outmoded textbooks, there was a circulating library in Gulgong (MacDonalds, established 1872); and in Mudgee he had access to the School of Arts library. There he discovered Dickens and Marryat.[2] Gifts of books on holidays at his grandparents' place in Wallerawang near Lithgow led him to Bret Harte and *Don Quixote*; Mark Twain came later, courtesy of a friend of his mother in Mudgee.[3]

Both Harte and Twain would have afforded Lawson the insight that the rough conditions of new societies could be made the subject matter of effective storytelling.[4] Vernacular, unlettered language was the key, and in this respect it is revealing that Lawson also recalled the family reading Rolf Boldrewood's *Robbery Under Arms* in serial form in the *Sydney Mail* as it appeared during 1882–83 and also the longer serialised version of Marcus Clarke's *His Natural Life*, probably when it was re-

---

[1] *Prose Writings* 722.
[2] Cf. his poem 'The Old Bark School' (*Bulletin*, 22 May 1897):
    And we learnt the world in scraps from some ancient dingy maps
      Long discarded by the public-schools in town;
    And as nearly every book dated back to Captain Cook
      Our geography was somewhat upside-down. (*Collected Verse*, I. 331–2)
Cf. also: 'Every line that Dickens wrote/ I've read and read again', from 'With Dickens' (?1900; *ibid.*, I. 389). But the interest did not broaden. HL's close friend from 1894, John Le Gay Brereton, later recalled: '[HL] was never a great reader, and at the height of his powers, devoted more of his time to the perusal of Deadwood Dick's adventures than to anything that could be called literature. I remember his borrowing only one book from me in all the years of our friendship; it was [Rudyard Kipling's] *Barrack Room Ballads*' (1892): *Knocking Round* (Sydney: A&R, 1930), pp. 5–6.
[3] 'Men Who Did their Work: Or, The Books I Like', in *Prose Writings* 775–8.
[4] In 1917, Bertram Stevens commented: 'He had also been influenced by Poe & Bret Harte. The latter's stories made an indelible impression upon Lawson, & if he had any model for his prose sketches it was "The Luck of Roaring Camp & other Tales"': handwritten biographical essay 'Henry Lawson', dated April 1917 (ML A1889, fol. 13).

serialised in the *Australian Journal* during September 1881 – January 1883. (It had originally appeared there in the early 1870s.)[5] And in 1881 and 1882 while working with his father he was reading Poe: all would have effects on his writing.[6]

Lawson's acumen as a reader and his isolation from schoolfriends speak of a sensitising, often for him a gloomy one, for which writing would be a natural outlet. His father opposed the ambition, but it was encouraged by his mother.[7] Despite its feminine stimulus, his writing would most often be directed towards the male world of work, mateship, poverty, disappointment, sardonic humour and yarn-spinning. It must have been fed by temporary liberations from his mother's authority and domestic routine when camping with his father and other men on contracting jobs, both at this time and intermittently later in the Blue Mountains, to the west of Sydney. Partially deaf, Lawson must have listened hard. While he probably chafed at the monotony of the work, he must have internalised – so that he could later teach himself to render – the linguistic rhythms and emotional currents of that rough world of masculine work. He would become its most sensitised observer, celebrant, satirist and mourner – though, as a result, it would never be unselfconsciously *his* world.

From May 1883 he lived with his mother in Sydney, once she had broken up with her husband – at first in Marrickville, where for a few months she ran a boarding house, and then in central Sydney at 138 Phillip Street. A woman of drive and ambition (the family, according to Lawson, would call her The Chieftainess in later years),[8] Louisa Lawson had given birth to five children, four of whom survived, Henry being the eldest. All of them came to live with her in Sydney, and she needed the income from the boys' wages to maintain the household. She had successfully agitated for the creation of the Eurunderee school that Henry attended before Mudgee, had supplemented the family income

---

[5] 'Men Who Did their Work', pp. 733–4. See further, Introduction to Marcus Clarke, *His Natural Life*, ed. Lurline Stuart (St Lucia: University of Queensland Press, 2001), p. lvi.
[6] *Life* 28.
[7] 'A Fragment of Autobiography', in *Prose Writings* 731.
[8] 'Men Who Did their Work', p. 776.

by running a shop in Gulgong when they lived there, and then a post office in Niels's name at Eurunderee – and also the farm during his long absences when away contracting. But she was finally defeated by a drought in the summer of 1882–83.

Her move to Sydney effectively brought the marriage to an end; Niels would die five years later, on 31 December 1888. In 1878, before moving to Sydney, Louisa had begun publishing verse in a Mudgee newspaper. In Sydney she would quickly become involved in republican and socialist politics, and also with what often went with them at the time: free-thinking and spiritualism. In 1888 she established her feminist monthly the *Dawn* and would self-publish a volume of poetry in 1905.[9]

Sydney

Sydney in the 1880s was a rapidly expanding mercantile port and centre of population.[10] In the lead-up to the celebrations in 1888 of the centenary of European settlement, the town must have opened the young man's eyes in many ways; but the subjects he would soon be inspired to write about were poverty and politics. His walking through the early-morning streets of Sydney, 'through an army of dossers in Hyde Park', to the railway terminus at Redfern Station from where, for a few months, he caught the train to work as a coach-painter's apprentice at Clyde, and simultaneously experiencing the heady brew of red-hot republican (anti-monarchist) discussions of an evening at home, would soon have their outlet.[11]

Lawson studied at night and on weekends in 1884 and 1885, attempting but failing to gain matriculation to the University of Sydney.

---

[9] *'The Lonely Crossing' and Other Poems* (Sydney: Dawn Office, 1905, reissued 1909): see her *Collected Poems with Selected Critical Commentaries*, ed. Leonie Rutherford and Megan Roughley (Armidale, NSW: University of New England Centre for Australian Language and Literature Studies, 1996), pp. xvi–xvii. The *Dawn* ceased publication in 1905. A. G. Stephens reviewed *'The Lonely Crossing'* with her son's *When I Was King and Other Verses* (1905) on 21 December 1905 (*Bulletin* Red Page), developing the theme of what HL the writer inherited from his mother.
[10] Sydney's population was 383,333 in 1891 as against 224,939 in 1881, representing 34 per cent of the NSW population in 1891 as against 30 percent in 1881. It would grow to 481,830 by 1901 (35.6 per cent).
[11] *Life* 29.

He frequented the library of Sydney's School of Arts (and also briefly Newcastle's, north of Sydney, when sent there by his employer). For two years from the second half of 1885 he worked in the centre of Sydney as a painter for a carriage manufacturer. Next, he spent periods working with his father again, this time in the Blue Mountains, and also with his grandfather Henry Albury, with whom he got on well: 'I discovered him to be a dumb poet, a poet of the trees'.[12]

With more time on his hands in Sydney, Lawson began attending lectures and mixing with his mother's radical friends.[13] He also helped with the production of the *Republican*, whose first issue appeared on 4 July 1887, only a few weeks after the Republican Riot at the Sydney Town Hall, sparked when the meeting passed a motion of disloyalty to Queen Victoria. These must have been intense days for the idealistic young Lawson; his first contribution to the *Bulletin* – the poem 'A Song of the Republic' – was written at this time.[14] From September 1887 he began writing signed political commentary for the *Republican*; it survived for ten issues into 1888.

A trip in December 1887 to a Melbourne hospital for (as it turned out, unsuccessful) treatment for his deafness started a trend that would mark Lawson's travelling for years to come: the accidental but increasingly opportunistic pursuit of subject matter for his writing. In this first case, his side-trip to the site of the Eureka Stockade fed into a number of later works.[15] While in Melbourne, the bumper Christmas 1887 issue of the *Bulletin* – by now, a vigorous and well-established weekly – arrived, with two of his poems in it. He later recalled his reaction: 'I felt strong and proud enough to clean pig-styes, if need be, for a living for the rest of

---

[12] 'A Fragment of Autobiography', p. 730.
[13] Graeme Davison comments: 'The helplessness of the rural émigré, their exclusion from respectable society and Louisa's highly developed religious sensibility all combined to bring the Lawsons into the orbit of Sydney's radical intelligentsia': their boarding houses, offices and bookstores were clustered in central Sydney in the late 1880s: 'Sydney and the Bush: An Urban Context for the Australian Legend', *Historical Studies*, 18 (1978), 191–209 [p. 198].
[14] June 1887; published in the *Bulletin*, 1 October 1887.
[15] See further, *Life* 42.

my natural life – provided the *Bulletin* went on publishing the poetry.'[16] Lawson would continue to have to make a living with his hands; but, the meanwhile, he kept an intent eye on opportunities for pursuing what he saw as a higher calling.

When Lawson wrote the most famous of his protest poems 'Faces in the Street' in July 1888, the republican fervour was already changing direction – although the *Bulletin* would continue to promote the cause until 1894. His mother transferred her reformist energies to the *Dawn*, whose first issue appeared on 15 May 1888; and later in the year Lawson began to extend his range by writing bush ballads. His short story 'His Father's Mate' appeared in the Christmas issue of the *Bulletin* on 22 December 1888 and would be reprinted in 1890, together with his poem 'A Song of the Republic', in the first volume of what became the *Bulletin* book series: *A Golden Shanty: Australian Stories and Sketches in Prose and Verse*. This was an indicator, Brian Kiernan has commented, 'that the young Lawson was accepted immediately, even eagerly, as one who was making literature from Australian life, performing the miraculous synthesis that had been anticipated for so long'.[17]

From 1888 until 1891, Lawson was writing mainly bush ballads and political verse for the *Bulletin*, but also some prose for the *Town and Country Journal* (Sydney) from 1888, *Truth* (Sydney) from 1890, the Brisbane socialist *Boomerang* in 1891 when he was on its staff there, and the Brisbane *Worker* from 1891. During 1888–91 only six of Lawson's published writings were short stories, three of which would ultimately be selected for *While the Billy Boils*: 'His Father's Mate', 'The Story of Malachi' and 'Bogg of Geebung'.

The specifics of his stories' first publication might seem to be only background detail; but each one hints at a situation that is at once bibliographical and sociological. The stories appeared and were read in

---

[16] '"Pursuing Literature" in Australia' (21 January 1899, *Bulletin*), in *Prose Writings* 617–24 [p. 619]. The poems were 'Golden Gully' and 'The Wreck of the *Derry Castle*'.
[17] '"From Mudgee Hills to London Town": A Critical Biography of Henry Lawson', in *The Essential Henry Lawson: The Best Works of Australia's Greatest Writer*, ed. Brian Kiernan (South Yarra, Vic.: Currey O'Neil, [1982]), p. 9.

the context of a great many other contributions chosen according to the particular newspaper's agendas, themselves shaping and responding to the expectations of their (purchasing) readership.

Lawson and Socialism

Lawson's socialistic sympathies for the plight of the poor (into whose ranks he would be, until 1895, in constant danger of slipping) remained a fertile spur to his imagination. The pages of the trades unions' newspapers, especially the *Worker*, provided one of the two principal arenas in which, as a writer, he could successfully pitch his tent. Their limited space, overt sympathies and political campaigns conditioned the possibilities for his writing: both its length (he would remain a writer of *short* stories, sketches and verse)[18] and its appeal to a known readership (the men outback in the shearing sheds and on the track, union officials, and city workmen and sympathisers). His subject matter would need to centre on their experiences, while not radically departing from the tonal range nor even the narrative strategies of other reader-contributors and staff writers.

A labour movement had begun to emerge in Queensland from 1886; in New South Wales, a little later. A labour provincial press gradually sprang up (the *Boomerang* was among the first, in November 1887) dedicated to organised trades unionism, education of workers and parliamentary representation. Radical elements were sympathetic to republican separation from Britain and dedicated to violent revolution if necessary. A large-scale maritime strike in 1890 was followed by the shearers' strike of 1891; many unionists were gaoled for conspiracy. But on 9 May 1891 the first Australian Labor party members were elected to the South

---

[18] Page 1 of the *Worker* for 25 March 1893 advised: 'Editors always hate to read an article lazily long, and the general reader does not care for a couple of yards of song; so gather your wits in the smallest space if you'd win the author's crown, and every time you write, my friend, gently boil it down!' This echoed the *Bulletin*'s better known advice of 12 March 1892: 'Don't write a column on any subject if half a column will do; don't write half a column where a mere paragraph is enough. "Boil it down."' (p. 16). Approximately 1,350 words made up a column in the *Bulletin*. Two of the themes sought from *Bulletin* contributors were shared by the *Worker*: 'bush, mining, sporting, social, or dramatic themes' (*ibid.*).

Australian parliament, and on 17 June New South Wales followed suit. This was the context for Lawson's famous rallying cry 'Freedom on the Wallaby', published in the Brisbane *Worker* on 16 May 1891: '[Freedom's] goin' to light another fire/ And boil another billy . . . They needn't say the fault is ours/ If blood should stain the wattle'. That sentiment led to the poem's being mentioned in the Queensland parliament.

A quasi-spiritual appeal to mateship underwrote the politics. The title of Lawson's 1896 collection *While the Billy Boils* would aptly remember an often-repeated connection, which began to recede into the past once parliamentary representation for unionists was achieved.[19] Advocacy of republican separation from Britain evolved into an embrace of federation of the Australasian colonies on the one hand and repudiation of proposals for Imperial federation on the other.

Prior to 1896, Lawson's fictional response to the agendas of the *Worker* was sometimes close and immediate. William Lane, writing as 'John Miller' in a leading article on 16 January 1892, declared that 'Socialism . . . is the desire to be mates'. Mateship was the natural brotherhood; it required socialism to achieve its full expression. In practical terms, it meant 'to remove the pressure that now makes us hustle one another for a job'. The union was vehemently opposed to freedom of contract between squatters and shearers, which, during depressed economic times, lent increased power to the employer and effectively removed employees' bargaining capacity.

Lane was editor of the *Boomerang* until 1890, becoming editor of the new Brisbane *Worker* when it was established by the Queensland Australian Labour Federation on 1 March 1890, before subsequently organising and then leaving to found the New Australia communistic colony in Paraguay in July 1893. That same year in Australia the economic depression of the early 1890s deepened and numerous banks fell; the low point was 1895. The effects would be felt for the rest of the decade, although the discovery of gold in Western Australia in 1893 exempted it from the general downturn.

---

[19] For the title's origin, see Chapter 7.

Lane's article on socialism and mateship had appeared in the *Hummer*, the official organ of the Shearers Union, which would join with other unions to become the Australian Workers Union in May 1894. It had begun its weekly publishing in Wagga Wagga, New South Wales, on 19 October 1891, co-edited by Walter W. Head. The *Hummer* published 45 issues until mid September 1892 when it temporarily merged with the Brisbane *Worker*, which issued a New South Wales edition from 24 September.[20] By 25 March 1893 a Sydney dateline for the entire newspaper was being given. All of Lawson's contributions to this Sydney *Worker* succeed this date, but he also contributed a few pieces of political verse to the Brisbane *Worker*, starting on 16 May 1891, when working for the *Boomerang* in Brisbane.

This job, which he commenced in April 1891 at £2 a week, followed some dismal years of trying to keep writing while plying his trade as a painter in Sydney, when work was available, and with another attempt in Albany, Western Australia, from May to September 1890, where he 'wrote articles at a penny a line for the local paper'.[21] Back in Sydney, Lawson next worked as a builder's labourer, living, as he later described it, 'in a third-rate hash-house'; then he went 'Up-country again [presumably back to the Blue Mountains] ... house-painting at 8s. or 9s. a day'.[22] The job in Brisbane was his first and only break into regular employment as a journalist – a versifying journalist, in his case.[23] But, after the newspaper

---

[20] From its second issue it received its own numbering. At first the outside sheet (four pages) was that of the Brisbane *Worker*; the inside four pages were printed in Wagga; for some time from 26 November 1892, the reverse was the case. It remained under the control of the Australian Shearers Union and from 1894 of the Australian Workers Union.

[21] '"Pursuing Literature" in Australia', p. 619. HL, accompanied by his brother Peter, may have been sent by his mother to avoid Mary Cameron, later Gilmore, who was boarding with the family. She had met HL in early 1890 after moving from Silverton, near Broken Hill, where she had been a schoolteacher during 1887–89, to take up a position at Neutral Bay, Sydney. Their mothers, both journalists, had become friends. See further, W. H. Wilde, '*Courage a grace*': *A Biography of Dame Mary Gilmore* (Melbourne: Melbourne University Press, 1988), chap. 4. Wilde concludes that there was a romantic attachment, perhaps not a deep one; but there is no evidence of a love affair. He discusses 'whether Mary played a significant role in shaping Lawson the writer' and concludes that 'she did not' (p. 70).

[22] 'Pursuing Literature', p. 620. The men he worked with apparently made up the Mountain Push, who would appear in 'For Auld Lang Syne', written in early 1896 specially for *Billy Boils*.

[23] He later commemorated the newspaper in his poem 'The Cambaroora Star' (about a

got into financial difficulties, he was forced to leave on 18 September 1891, returning to Sydney where the option of staying with his aunts or mother afforded him a foothold. No doubt deeply disappointed at the frustration of his prospects as a paid writer, he wasted no time in transferring his efforts into placing work with the *Bulletin*. On 10 October 1891 a poem appeared that built on his immediate experience of return to Sydney: 'The Shame of Going Back'. Several more of his poems appeared in the *Bulletin* before year's end, and nearly thirty poems and four stories would appear there during 1892.[24] It became the other principal arena for his work. In 1893 his rate of production increased yet again, with publication divided between the *Bulletin* and (from mid-1893) the *Worker*; for the first time more were in prose than verse.

Readers of the *Worker* would have been kept in touch with Lawson's politically radical background, as well as receiving a good helping of what *Bulletin* readers were restricted to: mainly, stories and some verse set on the outback track about travelling swagmen, mateship and hardship, laced with a sobering humour. This shift in subject matter from that of the early stories resulted from the editor of the *Bulletin*, J. F. Archibald, sending Lawson west for copy.[25] In September 1892 he caught the train to its outback terminus at Bourke, on the Darling River in north-western New South Wales. Lawson had been given £5 to send back contributions; he would have to work on sheep stations and as a painter in Bourke, and go on the track with other out-of-work swagmen the meanwhile. On 21 September 1892 he wrote to his aunt Emma Brooks from Bourke: 'I got a lot of very good points for copy on the way up [from Sydney] . . . I have already found that Bushmen are the biggest liars that ever the Lord

---

radical goldfields newspaper proprietor undone by capitalist conspiracy). The *Boomerang* appeared weekly, 19 November 1887 – 9 April 1892.

[24] In April 1892, he secured letters of introduction from various Sydney editors to other editors, presumably in Western Australia. He had evidently considered going there again, but did not go: ML MSS 314/45, pp. 3–12.

[25] John Feltham Archibald (1856–1919) invented a French–Jewish ancestry for himself when he altered his forenames to Jules François in the 1870s. His early experiences in journalism led to his co-founding the *Bulletin* in 1880; he served as editor until 1903.

created. Took notes all the way up.'²⁶ The remarks suggest both that his theoretical socialism was already being tested by what he found, observed and took part in; and that he also saw himself in one sense as above the fray, as a writer and commentator on it. On the 27th he could tell her: 'I am doing a little work, *sub rosa*, for the *Western Herald*. . . . I am working up stuff for the *Bulletin*'. But alcoholic excess was all too tempting: 'Everybody shouts [i.e. buys rounds of drinks]. I must take to the bush as soon as I can'.²⁷ On 23 November he joined the General Laborers Union of Australasia and the following day, went down the Darling River for a stint of work in shearing sheds.²⁸ The sordid roughness of the shearers' living conditions left their mark on Lawson.

He was a man's man. To other men he was a reliable mate, which an instinct for humour and conviviality amidst his occasional moods and gloom, and a willingness if not a capacity for hard drinking, must have helped. But there was a sensitive man and a cultural tourist beneath, able to be touched more deeply by the Far West than, perhaps, he had anticipated. It would come out in his writing in 1893. What seems to

---

²⁶ *Letters* 49–50.
²⁷ *Letters* 50–1.
²⁸ His GLU membership ticket is in ML (MSS 314/234–236, filed at A1890–2, vol. 1, p. 40). In a letter to Arthur Parker HL gives the 24 November date; and, in a letter of 26 December 1892, HL referred to just having spent 'a month in a shearing shed on the Darling' (*Letters* 51). HL's friend James W. Gordon ('Jim Grahame') later recalled their working at the downriver Fort Bourke station (from the dates, travelling by paddle-steamer) and then at Toorale station (on foot); and later walking back to Bourke via the Warrego R. and e. along the Hungerford-Bourke road (quoted in *Life* 93). They reached Bourke for Christmas. (HL later recorded it in 'That Pretty Girl in the Army' and 'The Ghosts of Many Christmases', in *Children of the Bush*, 1902, pp. 36, 287; confirmed by a Bourke friend Billy Wood, 'Reminiscences of Henry Lawson', *Windsor and Richmond Gazette*, 24 September 1926).

HL set off for Hungerford on 27 December (*Letters* 51), accompanied probably by Gordon (see *Letters* 420–1 for conflicting evidence that it may have been Ernst de Guinney, of Russian descent). The remote passage was feasible on foot because this was a route for wool drays and swagmen looking for work (cf. HL's sketch 'Carriers': *Worker*, 24 November 1894; *Autobiographical* 355–6). There were artesian bores drilled at intervals along the road, and a few hotels. They spent New Year at the hotel at Ford's Bridge ('The Ghosts of Many Christmases', p. 258).

HL's letter to his aunt of 16 January 1893 from Hungerford specifies one 'mate' who was going on further and implies that he returned alone (*Letters* 53). He must have called in at Kerribree station owned by William Walter ('Baldy') Davis, later to appear in 'Baldy Thompson. A Sketch of a Squatter' (cf. HL's letter to his aunt from Bourke, 6 February 1893: *Letters* 54). There are useful maps in Robyn Burrows and Alan Barton, *Henry Lawson: A Stranger on the Darling* (Sydney: Angus & Robertson, 1996), pp. 349–50.

have become habitual – note-taking or rough-drafting for future use – was recorded by his friend James W. Gordon (the writer 'Jim Grahame'): '[Lawson's] deafness rather served him well, as he could lie on his bunk in a rouseabouts' hut amidst the clatter and rattle of the dish-washing and the babble of the tongues of the yarn-spinners and card-players after tea, and write until he was sleepy.'[29]

The shearing experience, and then a long and dry trek to Hungerford on the New South Wales–Queensland border, provided him with rich pickings for his future writing, and were probably entered into for that purpose. That said, he paid the price for the experience. On 16 January 1893, having walked the 140 miles from Bourke to Hungerford, he wrote to his aunt: 'You can have no idea of the horrors of the country out here. Men tramp and beg and live like dogs. It is two months since I slept in what you can call a bed. . . . But the experience will help me to live in the city for the next year or so.' Although he did not return to Sydney until about March[30] his important writing phase was in the offing.

---

[29] Jim Grahame, 'Henry Lawson on the Track', *Bulletin*, 19 February 1925, Red Page. HL's appeal to other men and their loyalty to him are amply recorded in the memoirs in *Henry Lawson by his Mates*, ed. [Bertha Lawson and John Le Gay Brereton] (1931; Sydney: Angus & Robertson, 1973).

[30] *Letters* 49–51, 53. The date of HL's return to Sydney is uncertain. Roderick (*Life* 97) claims June 1893 because of a dateline 'Bourke, June, 1893.' on a poem 'All Unyun Men', *Worker*, 23 September 1893 (copy in NLA). Roderick comments in his Introduction to *Collected Verse*: 'Most of Lawson's compositions had no date line, and the date line attached to some of them in the first printing was faked' (I. xvi). The June date is countered by a continuous stream of published material throughout 1893 from early April in Sydney (see Chronology; the first is the poem 'Saint Peter' on 8 April in *Bulletin*) and by HL's reporting that he was 'six months' away (*Letters* 91). He had originally arrived in Bourke on 21 September 1892. Jim Grahame wrote that 'We were together four or five months at that time, wool-rolling here, picking up there and tramping a good deal. . . . And then we landed back in Bourke, broke . . . It was then that Lawson met his Peter Anderson and Co. That firm secured him a drover's pass' to return by rail to Sydney for free ('Henry Lawson on the Track').

'"In a Wet Season." Along the Line' describes HL's return trip; the dominant note is rain. *Results of Rain, River and Evaporation Observations Made in New South Wales during 1893 under the Direction of H. C. Russell* (Sydney: Charles Potter, Government Printer, 1894) reports that there was no rainfall in Bourke in January or February 1893. Rain began there in mid March that year; and Dubbo, a principal town through which the railway passed, had a very wet March (3.55 inches over 7 days, as against a monthly average of 1.53 inches).

CHAPTER 2

LAWSON IN THE LITERARY MARKETPLACE

THE *WORKER*, THE *BULLETIN* AND *SHORT STORIES IN PROSE AND VERSE*

Lawson in the *Worker*

As all runs of the *Worker* held in Australian libraries are incomplete, certainty about the precise extent of Lawson's contributions is unattainable. Nevertheless the broad outlines are clear enough. He joined the General Laborers Union of Australasia on 23 November 1892 in Bourke, and his first known *Worker* pieces appeared on 10 June 1893: a poem 'The Waving of the Red', a companion piece to his article in the same issue 'A Leader of the Future', which argues that the current conditions of hardship for the working man are likely to give rise to a working-class revolutionary leader. It was followed probably on 17 June by the sketch 'The Shearing of the Cook's Dog', but no copy of the newspaper is available to confirm the date. On 24 June '"An Old Mate of your Father's"' appeared, with its nostalgic memories of the Eureka Stockade at Ballarat in Victoria. '"Some Day." A Swagman's Love Story' appeared probably on 15 July, and on the 29th, in the same issue that ran Lawson's rollicking but politically resonant poem 'The Cambaroora Star', his two-paragraph sketch appeared about the town 'Louth, on the Darling'. It was a spoof reply to an invented letter to the editor by A GOD FEARING CHRISTHEN. The letter had supposedly appeared, shockingly misspelled, in the (fictional) newspaper the *Out Back Advocate*, condemning workers who drink on Sundays.[1] Lawson

---

[1] In *Commentaries* 51–2 but missed for *Autobiographical*. HL was drawing on his experience in 1891 writing the Country Crumbs column for the *Boomerang*: verse-comment on articles in country newspapers but presented in prose format.

expresses sympathy with the drunken workers of Louth because of their struggle to survive. This sketch led Lawson to write a series of 'Darling River' sketches in the following months of 1893;[2] they showed that the line between his non-fictional sketches and his stories could be a permeable one.

In the adjacent column on 29 July 1893 was 'Squatters and Shearers' by A. E. Grace. His poem 'Swagmen of the Darling' had appeared in the *Worker* on 4 March 1893, ending with a moralistic attack on shanty-keepers who doctor the alcohol purchased by swagmen – whereas Lawson could 'even find a small place in the corner of our heart for the "hard case" who kept that shanty' at Louth. In 'Squatters and Shearers' Grace comments on a current, bitter dispute between employers and shearers over rates of pay and over union membership as against freedom of contract. Grace analyses how much a shearer can earn in comparison with his living expenses, the result typically being a difficult one for the employee. Lawson's stories are in communication with this general discourse, generated by the *Worker*'s multitude of contributors. His stories explore much the same predicament, but imaginatively and in attentive, unpredictable, less doctrinal ways.

The Christmas 1893 issue of the *Worker* claimed distribution of 15,000 copies weekly (a large proportion would have been to members of the union that owned it) and thus to be 'the most widely read in the country of any New South Wales papers'.[3] It cost 1d. Its editor liked to remind readers of the political distance between itself and the opposition:

> the *Bulletin* again barracks for the man with a 'stake' in the country. This week, in several places, it raises the well-worn bogie that a land value tax means ruin to the [small landowning] selector. As the WORKER has often remarked, the *Bulletin* has given more evidence of leaning towards the Man with the Belly than many papers which are commonly recognized as the straight-out organs of property.[4]

---

[2] He later worked them into a short story 'The Darling River' for *Over the Sliprails* (1900); see *Commentaries* 50–1 for details.
[3] *Worker*, 23 December 1893, p. 4.
[4] *Worker*, 9 September 1893, p. 2. The land value tax was the Single Tax Proposal of the American political economist Henry George (1839–97), much discussed in the Australian

Although the *Worker* attacks the *Bulletin* for its endorsement of landowner arguments against a land tax, the phrase 'the Man with the Belly' recalls the *Bulletin*'s regular cartoon-satires on property and the wealthy, suggesting that the positions of the two papers partially and often overlapped. It is not surprising, therefore, that Lawson felt comfortable writing for both. This in turn meant that overt advocacy of radical positions would find no place in his prose fiction, although political radicalism would be its nostalgically understood or mutely protested background, one clustering around the idea of mateship. It was the inheritance of 'a dying race of men who *were* men', of whom the present ones, struggling under enormous economic pressure, are only 'remnants' – thus, Lawson, at his most seer-like, in 'An Article on Man' in the *Worker*.[5]

The previous year, before heading west to Bourke, he had exposed the romanticising of the bush as false in his famous, manufactured literary duel in the *Bulletin* with A. B. ('Banjo') Paterson (1864–1941). Having gone so far, Lawson evidently soon found that, out west in Bourke later in the same year, he could retain the *Worker*'s mateship ideal only by historicising it and by plotting its sad decline. "'An Old Mate of your Father's'", published in the *Worker* on 24 June 1893, would be his best, most tonally balanced example. But there was another side to the coin. On 18 November 1893 Lawson would enumerate for the *Bulletin* 'Some Popular Australian Mistakes'. Mistake number 21 reads: 'The poetical bushman does not exist; the majority of the men out back now are from the cities. The real native [i.e. white native-born] out-back bushman is narrow-minded, densely ignorant, invulnerably thick-headed.' Lawson concludes: 'What's the good of making a heaven of a hell when by describing it as it really is we might do some good for the lost souls there?'[6]

---

colonies especially after his visit in 1890. He argued that, as private ownership of the common inheritance (land) abridged the natural right of future generations, a tax on landlords (ground rent or rates) should be levied at a level sufficient for government purposes and lead to the abolition of all other taxes.
[5] *Worker*, 16 September 1893. Cf. HL's 'Some Popular Australian Mistakes', *Bulletin*, 18 November 1893 (reprinted in *Autobiographical* 24–5).
[6] *Autobiographical* 25. In 1901 A. G. Stephens would declare 'Lawson hates the bush . . .

His stories would therefore be more concerned with social predicament than political solution. In this manner, the filiation of newspaper and writer continued. A series of letters on 'Religion and Mateship' would appear in the *Worker* in June 1894, and a series of stories by Lawson on and around the theme of mateship followed.

To New Zealand

With the collapse of a number of banks in 1893, hard times followed for small businesses, individuals whose savings were lost, and unemployed men in the cities, many of whom tried to find work in the bush, having to trudge from station to station in search of it. The euphemism for them, which Lawson often used, was *travellers*. This economic gloom also affected journalists and writers, whose opportunities were suddenly contracted. By heading west in September 1892 Lawson had been trying to make the best of what was already looming as a potentially disastrous situation. Doubtless, he was trying to hang on to the optimistic glimpse of the better life as a paid writer that the *Boomerang* had temporarily given him the previous year. His next attempt was to try his luck elsewhere. On the rebound in late 1893, after having failed to secure the editorship of the *Worker* in succession to Walter W. Head, he sailed from New South Wales to the sister colony of New Zealand.

Arriving destitute in Wellington on 27 November 1893, he was taken in by Tom Mills, the New Zealand correspondent of the Brisbane *Worker*. A journalist himself, Mills was nevertheless surprised by how hard Lawson worked at his writing, later recalling:

> I have known him at my own table occupy eight hours in writing what would fill a column in verse. The remarkable thing was that although one of such efforts was in dialect, there was neither an error nor a correction in the whole composition. He was just as laborious in prose. He used only ruled exercise books, a 'J' pen, a traveller's bottle of ink (one of those non-upsettable things), plus a shilling Routledge dictionary ... He was also his own most severe critic ... I have known him work all night on an article

Apart from those boyish memories, that single tramp, Lawson has been by choice a man of the coast and cities': 'Australian Literature', *Commonwealth Annual*, 1 (1901), 32–6 [p. 35].

– and burn it next morning. 'Not good enough, Tom.' And he needed the money it would have brought.[7]

Lawson was soon able to place some verse and sketches, at low rates of pay, with the local newspapers *Fair Play*, *New Zealand Times* and its weekly *New Zealand Mail* in December–January.[8] After some time to the north in Pahiatua, he worked timber-getting in the Hutt Valley and then for a few months on the South Island with a gang of men laying telegraph line.[9] Receiving an offer of a position on the new *Daily Worker*, which was being issued on an experimental basis for a month from 2 July 1894 in the lead-up to the New South Wales elections – a fact Lawson seems to have been unaware of at first – he set off for Sydney, arriving three days before its last issue on 1 August. He became instead the provincial editor on the weekly edition, but on 15 September 1894 lost this staff position, becoming instead an exclusive contributor at 12s.6d. a column for prose and 1d. a line for verse. During August–November 1894, he was contributing nearly every week. But, after a falling out with the *Worker* in mid-November, his rate of contribution decreased in 1895. Even so, his name, for readers, was synonymous with that newspaper. He must have been seen, and probably felt himself to be, part of the team. Reviews of his books would appear there, and the *Worker* would act as an agent for sales of each of them.[10]

---

[7] Tom L. Mills, 'Henry Lawson in Maoriland', in *Henry Lawson by his Mates*, ed. [Bertha Lawson and John Le Gay Brereton] (1931; Sydney: Angus & Robertson, 1973), pp. 52–3.
[8] The poem 'in dialect' was probably '"For'ard"', *New Zealand Mail*, 22 December 1893; in *Collected Verse*, I. 258–61.
[9] Although Colin Roderick has HL timber-getting in the Hutt Valley probably before his time in Pahiatua (*Letters* 34), HL indicated in 1899 that the job came *after* ('then went with a mate to a sawmill in the Hutt Valley', *Letters* 91: published as '"Pursuing Literature" in Australia', *Bulletin*, 21 January 1899), and that he then proceeded to Wellington. Subsequently on the South Island, HL worked for W. W. Louisson, a relative of Jack Louisson, with whom he had become friends in Wellington. Cf. Eggert and Webby 308.
[10] E.g. unsigned article 'Henry Lawson's Poems': '3000 copies [of *In the Days*] disposed of. Amongst the bush workers, however, the sale has been comparatively small ... the funds of the WORKER will be benefited by every copy sold ... cannot our members during the shearing season spend 5s. in purchasing a copy?' (*Worker*, 4 July 1896, p. 1).

Lawson in the *Bulletin*

The number of Lawson's contributions to the *Bulletin* had fallen away at the end of 1893 after he left for New Zealand and did not revive until mid-December 1894. But there he would be better paid and be in good company.[11] Although the *Bulletin*'s republican and nationalist hopes of the late 1880s had gone into abeyance,[12] the weekly nevertheless remained full of variety and vitality. A. G. Stephens, who had joined as sub-editor in February 1894, lent it some literary-critical gravitas. His assessments were often stringent, and his literary purview tended to be more international than parochial. His ingrained tendency was to weigh and measure by English and European standards; but his job as Red (literary) Page editor from 1896, essentially unhindered by Archibald, brought out a nationalism in him.[13] As Sylvia Lawson observes: 'He sermonised on the duty of writers to respond to the country's natural beauty, and to fulfil the epic possibilities of man's struggle with the

---

[11] The price HL states in 'Pursuing Literature' for the *Bulletin* was 21s. per column. That was nearly twice what the *Worker* was paying, but HL always considered himself to be, in part, working for the socialist cause. 'Touchstone', reviewing HL's *In the Days* on 9 May 1896 in the Brisbane *Worker*, commented: 'The *Bulletin* ... is one of the very few Australian journals that consider the poetic labourer worthy of his hire' (p. 4). See further, Chapter 9.

The *Worker* price seems to have been standard. Cf. G. B. Barton's comment: 'the scale of remuneration allowed by newspaper proprietors for fiction is a very low one ... [it] cannot possibly give the author any adequate return for his work': 'The Status of Literature in New South Wales: II. How the Publishers Look at It', *Centennial Magazine*, 2 (1889), 89–92 [pp. 89–90]. In 'Literature in NSW: III. How the Newspaper Proprietors Look at It', Barton gives the payment as 10s.–15s. per column: *ibid.*, 2 (1889), 238–40. Rolf Boldrewood received about 10s.–12s. per column from the *Sydney Mail* for *Robbery Under Arms* in 1882–83: see Introduction to the Academy Edition of *Robbery Under Arms*, ed. Paul Eggert and Elizabeth Webby (St Lucia: University of Queensland Press, 2006), p. xxix n. 11.

Again in 'Pursuing Literature', HL mentions receiving what he considered a miserly 5s. a column for 'some steerage sketches' in the *New Zealand Mail*. He also mentions daily rates when working as a coach and house painter in Sydney, Melbourne and at Mt Victoria as between 5s. and 9s. (the latter in 1890 before the depression). After earning £2 per week when on staff at the *Boomerang* in 1891, he went back to 5s. per day 'painting for nigger-driving bosses' in an economically depressed Sydney, while also writing for *Truth* for 5s. per column, though up to 15s.–20s. 'for special stuff' (*Prose Writings* 618–22).

[12] See *Bulletin*, 25 August 1894, p. 6.

[13] A. G. Stephens (1865–1933) was sub-editor of the *Bulletin* 1894–1906, conducted the Red Page from August 1896 and published many volumes in the *Bulletin* Books series, although only one did well (Steele Rudd's *On our Selection*). He worked under Archibald until James Edmond (1859–1933), who had been on the staff since 1886 mainly as financial editor, became editor (1903–14).

frontier.'[14] For his part, Archibald, according to the later Lawson, 'would not print the best copy (from a literary point of view) in the world, if he thought it out of the *Bulletin*'s line'. His advice to contributors was '"write in your own style" . . . Write as simply as you can. . . . Don't strain after effect. . . . Go over your copy and blot out every word you can possibly do without'.[15] This advice seemed to suit Lawson. It undoubtedly helped him to achieve, as Vance Palmer would describe it in 1954, 'a colloquial easiness of approach that gave it an effect of innovation: it had none of those stiff latinisms and journalistic clichés that cluttered the work of most of his contemporaries'.[16]

A *Bulletin* habit that did grate with Lawson, however, was Archibald's tendency to keep back contributions to suit the needs of the weekly. He had told Lawson, 'I buy while the market's open; by and by it may be closed'.[17] Although Lawson probably received immediate payment upon sale of his stories, having them quickly in print increased his popular exposure and meant they were potentially available for reprint in book form. When he could not supply promised copy to the firm that would become his principal book publisher, Angus & Robertson, Archibald's habit allowed a convenient redirection of the blame. But the complaint, to which Colin Roderick in *Commentaries on his Prose Writings* frequently appeals when explaining bibliographical anomalies, seems to have been exaggerated. After Lawson went to New Zealand on 18 November 1893, for instance, the *Bulletin* published six Lawson items up until 16 December; they must have been written and purchased before he left and presumably paid for his ticket. But then there are no more stories until after his return.

By this time Lawson had become a celebrant, not of the bush itself but, as Sylvia Lawson points out, of resistance to it, a fact that fitted

---

[14] Sylvia Lawson, *The Archibald Paradox: A Strange Case of Authorship* (1983; Melbourne: Miegunyah, 2006), p. 218.
[15] HL, 'The Sydney "Bulletin"' (1901), in *Autobiographical* 123–4.
[16] Vance Palmer, *The Legend of the Nineties* (Melbourne: Melbourne University Press, 1954), p. 114; the book includes a survey chapter on the *Bulletin*.
[17] HL, 'The Sydney "Bulletin"', p. 122.

him for the *Bulletin* stable of writers: 'The heroics of stockwhip and wattle blossom, the brightness of the open spaces, scarcely existed in the *Bulletin* outside the ballads by Paterson or less-remembered writers like Will Ogilvie'.[18] The different positions had been the subject of the staged verse-duel between Lawson and Paterson. The humour that survived the necessary stoicism and hardships of out-of-work swagmen sounded the contrasting note of Lawson's story-telling. His imagined environment extended the horizons of the *Bulletin*'s predominantly city-based readers. Lawson's writings contributed to the *Bulletin*'s 'great print circus' – Sylvia Lawson's term for the weekly's visually chaotic but energising jumble of news stories, fusillades hurled at the hypocrisies of colonial politicians and other newspapers, and anecdotes, cartoons and advertisements. All this was amplified by the weekly's successful inter-colonial reach, both in subject matter and in distribution. Events abroad were equally grist for the *Bulletin*'s mill, helping to eliminate or at least reduce the sense of exile from the cosmopolitan centre that most Australians still referred to as Home.

Lawson's prose storytelling had become technically assured and thematically confident. The late-century romantic taste for evocations, especially in verse, of deliquescent longings for, or regrets about, a love or beauty that is forever lost, was still strong, and would continue into the 1900s, both in the *Bulletin* and elsewhere. Similarly, late-century adventure novels and tales of derring-do formed a burgeoning literary commodity for publishers. But Lawson's verse and short stories, more in touch as they were with colonial living conditions, were in quietly persuasive competition. Their narrative strategies were more cunning than met the eye, and the stories were intelligently responding to shifts in taste towards realism and naturalism – as the influential English critic Edward Garnett would confirm in 'An Appreciation' of Lawson in the *Academy and Literature* on 8 March 1902. Archibald must have sensed the modernity and even sophistication of Lawson's stories, amidst their apparently 'uncooked' simplicity of approach (Garnett's term) and their

---

[18] S. Lawson, *Archibald Paradox*, p. 240, and pp. 189–90 for the following comments.

parochial subject matter. Many years later, in an essay about Archibald, Lawson touched on his growing technical prowess:

> Archibald in those days, preferred the short story to the short sketch. I thought the short story was a lazy man's game, second to 'free' verse, compared with the sketch. The sketch, to be really good, must be good in every line. But the sketch-story is best of all. I didn't know about the difficulties and 'antecedents' in writing it. Ask the shade of O. Henry.[19]

Lawson's pre-1893 stories and sketches in the Bulletin

Lawson's pre-1893 stories and sketches collected in *While the Billy Boils* are more than 'prentice work but lack the tonal balance and emotional resonance that his engagement with outback figures and conditions would give his writing. Several of the pre-1893 sketches are set in the bush. Two are amusingly even affectionately satirical – but they meander rather than conclude ('A Day on a Selection. A Sketch from Observation' and 'In a Dry Season').[20] The latter is a travel sketch of a railway journey west, probably written soon after Lawson's arrival in Bourke, and showing a city-dweller's ironic condescension to what he is newly seeing. The later stories and sketches, even the comic ones, reveal a direct sympathetic engagement that these lack. Another two are based on a practical joke prosecuted on an innocent man by the young narrator and his friends ('The Story of Malachi' and 'Bogg of Geebung').[21] These stories are saved from sentimentality, on whose brink they hover, by the counteracting guilt the persecutors finally experience; but they remain little more than anecdotal.

In other pre-1893 *Bulletin* stories that would appear in the 1896 collection Lawson resorts to a stronger sentimentality to point up significance. Two dealing with the city poor are a mixture of protest

---

[19] 'Three or Four Archibalds and the Writer' (1919), *Autobiographical* 250. O. Henry (pseudonym of W. S. Porter, 1862–1910) was an American journalist and then prolific short-story writer. Like HL, he never made the transition from collections made up of loosely connected episodes in the life of a single group of characters to more fully unified novels. See further, Chapter 10.
[20] *Bulletin*, 28 May 1892 and 5 November 1892 respectively.
[21] Respectively *Bulletin*, 22 June 1889; *Boomerang*, 23 May 1891.

and manufactured sentiment ('A Visit of Condolence: A Study from Life of a Sydney "Larrikin"' and 'Arvie Aspinall's Alarm Clock', both in the *Bulletin*: 23 April 1892 and 11 June 1892). Arvie's mother (who is from the bush) speaks a standard English despite their poverty, though her son uses the vernacular. The mother's toneless formality, however, does not work productively as a foil to Arvie's manner of speaking nor, for some of the time, to that of the street larrikin Bill. A sense of tragedy at little Arvie's death fails to materialise. When Bill's idiomatic voice is given more rein towards the end of 'A Visit of Condolence', the sentiment of loss becomes taut and restrained, and is all the more effective for it.[22]

Lawson had experimented with the Dickensian in 'His Father's Mate' (*Bulletin*, 22 December 1888), with its Smike and Nicholas Nickleby relationship between Isley and his putative father Tom Mason, until Isley topples down the mineshaft. A simpleton like Smike, Isley also dies amidst tears for his unmerited fate. This story's conventionally omniscient narrator and long short story form (after Bret Harte), with firm chapter divisions, required more dramatic scope and emotional complexity than the twenty-one-year-old Lawson could handle. He seemed to think, at least in 1888, that a suave and self-consciously literary occupying of the cultural ground would most readily satisfy his *Bulletin* readers. So he tried to write above himself in years and would-be sophistication.[23]

---

[22] In the serialised 'Jones' Alley' (*Worker*, 1, 8, and 15 June 1895; collected in *Billy Boils*), the voice of another working woman and even more persuasively that of Bill give the narrative a precise social location that warns off the would-be tragic. Mrs Aspinall, who scrubs offices and takes in washing, cannot pay her rent and will be evicted; the larrikins help her to take a minor revenge against her grasping landlord.
  Roderick misdates this story as 1, 8, and 15 June 1892. It is thematically continuous with that earlier period and succeeds it in narrative terms, but it is more confident in expression. HL had evidently hung onto some notes or an early version – one too long for the *Bulletin* perhaps – and reworked the story in 1895.

[23] Witness the literariness of: 'after the manner of Timon's "friends"', 'The "predominant note" of the scene', and '"Tis strange such people should dread disgrace so much, but the poor are often proud'; and the affected world-weariness of: 'The main army of diggers had long ago vanished to new rushes, even as its remnants are vanishing now to the old Rush where we all must go'.

The narrative strains ambitiously to cover a lot of territory in the supposed father's past. Clues are neatly laid, leading to a satisfactorily achieved twist when Isley's 'father' Tom Mason dies and his kindly real father (a simple yokel called Tom the Devil) is revealed. Lawson also peppers the prose with laboured Dickensian humour[24] and milks the story for emotional effect. (Tom Mason's real son returns – but too late, for it transpires that Mason's lifelong stoical acceptance of tragedy has finally despatched him.) Contrarily – and, in this, a sign of the future for Lawson – the action is densely located in played-out New South Wales goldfields, which Lawson was effectively annexing for his fiction. Well-observed realist detail, as well as colloquialism and dialectal spelling when Isley and Tom speak, are the vehicles, even if the latter are slightly overdone.

Mason's stoicism also looks forward to the far stronger and less conventionally well-constructed story 'The Drover's Wife' (*Bulletin*, 23 July 1892). Despite its power, even this tale does not fully escape the stricture of contrived literariness. The unrelieved harshness of the mother's overburdened plight goes unprotested until her sturdy little son, who until now has been intent on proving himself a man by chasing a snake that has come into the kitchen, has a moment of sympathetic insight into his deserted mother's state of mind, causing her to hug him to her breast at the very end of the story. The fact that Frank Mahony seized on this melodramatically heightened scene for one of his illustrations for *While the Billy Boils* in 1896 confirms the intense Dickensian note that Lawson was aiming at and striking. Yet the grim naturalism of the rest of this story links it to the city ones; it may have been essayed partly in response to Archibald's repeated hailing of the French variety, especially Zola's.[25] The containment of the necessary protest, both in the comic stories and in this one, transfers responsibility for it onto the reader: hence the added pressure to achieve a clinching ending.

[24] E.g. 'There was an unpremeditated look about Tom's "build" as he came lumbering down; he seemed as though he had been let out in several contracts to architects of very diverse views and erected without plans or specifications of any sort.'
[25] Cf. Zola 'was named in the *Bulletin* more often in those years [1880s] than any Australian writer' (S. Lawson, *The Archibald Paradox*, p. 223).

'A Christmas in the Far West; or, The Bush Undertaker', written in June 1892, is a further development and a signal of what was to come. The omniscient narration does not condescend to its more tightly focussed bush-yokel subject matter, nor does its language stray far from that range. The story is able to convey an uncensorious humour capable of liberating darker significances as it describes the grisly ritual of the burial of an old acquaintance, conducted by a mad bushman ('hatter') who has lived too long alone. He is much thwarted by a goanna tantalised by the rotting flesh of the corpse, which the hatter has unexpectedly come upon. The story-telling is a bravura tonal balancing act. Lawson contributed it to the first volume of the intended annual *Antipodean*. It was published in a richly illustrated form in London by Chatto and Windus in November 1892 but edited in Australia by the Queensland poet and public servant George Essex Evans and the journalist and (from 1897) editor of the *Catholic Press* in Sydney, John Tighe Ryan.[26]

The remaining 43 of the 52 stories and sketches in *While the Billy Boils* date from 1893 or later. They betray far less desire to push for an emotional heightening and colour, and evince less anxiety about achieving a formal neatness of ending. Lawson would more fully experiment with first-person narration, accepting the limitations that

---

[26] Ryan 1870?–1922; Evans, 1863–1909. According to Ryan in his review of *Billy Boils* in the *Gundagai Times* the story 'was refused by the Sydney papers' before being accepted by the *Antipodean* (review c. 15 September 1896; clipping in ML MSS 3269/ Angus & Robertson Ltd. Book reviews (Bound volumes) 1894–1970/1, vol. 7, with Ryan's otherwise anonymous authorship added in pencil).

The first issue of the *Antipodean* required a second printing, which appeared also under the imprint of the Melbourne George Robertson at 1s.; 13,000 copies were sold. It was reviewed in the *Bulletin* on 24 December 1892 (unsigned, p. 7), with telling mockery of the use of titled contributors. HL fared a little better: 'Henry Lawson has a story – not quite up to his standard – about "Christmas in the Far West," and about a man (whom he curiously enough calls a "solitaire") humping a corpse about.' ('Solitaire' may be a typo for 'soliloquiser': see Eggert and Webby 88.) The *Daily Telegraph* commended its 'strong and weird picture of "A Christmas in the Far West," which is perhaps the best piece of literary work in an indifferent collection'. The issue was reviewed in *Table Talk* on 23 December 1892, but without mention of the story. The illustrators were Frank Mahony, Percy Spence and G. E. Minns.

Antipodean no. 2 appeared in 1893 (and from Robertson in 1894) but the venture proved uneconomic. It was revived in 1897 (as No. 3), this time without a naming of the editors (Evans and Banjo Paterson); HL contributed a sketch 'A Daughter of Maoriland: A Sketch of Poor-Class Maoris'. See further M. D. O'Hagan, 'Evans, George Essex', in *ADB*, VIII. 446–7.

the form requires but exploiting it to annex fictional territory that would lift him well above the *Bulletin* stable of contributors. The turning point in his prose was in the offing by around mid-1892. It was confirmed by the results of Lawson's journey to Bourke in far-western New South Wales later that year.

Lawson's sketches as sequences

Lawson's development of the narrators Marsters and Mitchell dates from this period. While Lawson was still out back, these and other stories that would be collected in *While the Billy Boils* began to appear: 'Mitchell: A Character Sketch', in the *Bulletin* on 15 April 1893; and the remarkable 'The Union Buries its Dead. A Bushman's Funeral', in the Sydney *Truth* the next day. Three more were published in the *Bulletin* in May: 'On the Edge of a Plain' (a Mitchell sketch), 'Mitchell Doesn't Believe in the Sack' and '"Stragglers": A Sketch Out Back' (a shearing-shed sketch).[27] '"Rats"' appeared on 3 June 1893, once again in the *Bulletin*.

Thereafter, with the *Worker* properly under way and Lawson back in Sydney, his stories and sketches began to appear there in some number. 'The Shearing of the Cook's Dog' was the first; it probably appeared on 17 June 1893. A week later came the impressive '"An Old Mate of your Father's"'; 'Another of Mitchell's Plans for the Future' followed on 1 July. Possibly on 15 July 1893 came '"Some Day." A Swagman's Love Story', and the story that seems to develop from it stylistically, 'A Camp-fire Yarn', possibly on 5 August.[28] In both, the storyteller is Jack Marsters.

---

[27] *Bulletin*, 6, 13 and 27 May 1893 respectively.
[28] There is uncertainty about the dating of five of the stories sourced from the weekly Sydney *Worker*: 'The Shearing of the Cook's Dog', '"Some Day"', 'A Camp-fire Yarn', and also 'Macquarie's Mate' (probably 21 October 1893; reprinted Brisbane *Worker*, 28 October 1893) and '"Brummy Usen"' (probably 11 November 1893). Datings remain unconfirmed because there is no complete collection of the *Worker* for this period (ML and NLA have the best collections and were checked), and their dates do not appear on the clippings in printer's copy (ML A1867–8). Nor are four of them present in the Brisbane *Worker* microfilm; the Melbourne and Adelaide *Worker* were also spot-checked without success. Evidence for the provisional datings given here (and tabulated in Chronology) is provided in Eggert and Webby (Introduction, n. 14); the datings supersede Roderick's.
He also misdates 'Jones' Alley' (see n. 22 above) and gives 'Composed 1895' for 'For Auld Lang Syne' and 'Composed 1895–96 . . . no earlier than November 1895' for 'The Geological Speiler'

Next, Lawson diversified. 'His Colonial Oath' appeared in the *Bulletin* on 5 August 1893; on 6 August 'The Man Who Forgot' appeared in *Truth*. On 19 August 'When the Sun Went Down' was published in the *Worker* while, on 9 September, '"Tom's Selection." (A Sketch of Settling on the Land)' – entitled 'Settling on the Land' in *While the Billy Boils* – came out in the *Bulletin*. This pattern would continue, with Lawson also publishing other stories and sketches not chosen for *While the Billy Boils*, journalistic articles and verse. Lawson was in demand, and was evidently trying to make his way as a professional writer by exploiting various outlets for his work. He was writing so many individual short works that he must have always had his eye out for 'copy'. He must have spent a good deal of his waking life either thinking about what to write or writing it, then revising as he prepared fair copy, and dealing with newspaper proprietors whose payments were keeping him going. It is not to be wondered at, then, that he should experiment with repeated use of first-person storytellers (Marsters, Mitchell) and characters (Steelman, Brummy, Stiffner, Macquarie), and that intertextual relationships of theme and motif would arise between one story and another, and between his verse and stories. It was, after all, the same mind doing the thinking, the same hand doing the writing.

Lawson did not and could not, however, treat his various fictional works, even when linked, as developments of one another, even though the idea has been entertained on and off by literary critics ever since.[29] The hares were set running by A. G. Stephens's review of *While the Billy Boils* in the *Bulletin* in 1896; it has been quoted a great many times since. He criticised the arrangement, pointing out that the effect would

(*Commentaries* 147, 117). Undated in printer's copy, they are, however, recorded in the A&R Ledger at 25 April and 2 May 1896 respectively.

[29] E.g., see Brian Matthews's treatment of the Mitchell stories as an evolving sequence: *The Receding Wave: Henry Lawson's Prose* (Melbourne: Melbourne University Press, 1972), chap. 10 (see Chapter 12, below); Chris Wallace-Crabbe's literary-critical analysis of the *Joe Wilson* sequence (as published) as a proto-novel ('Lawson's *Joe Wilson*: A Skeleton Novel', *Australian Literary Studies*, 1 (1964), 147–54 [p. 148] and reprinted in *The Australian Nationalists: Modern Critical Essays*, ed. Wallace-Crabbe (Melbourne: Oxford University Press, 1971); and Colin Roderick's devastating literary-historical reply to Wallace-Crabbe: 'Henry Lawson's Joe Wilson: Skeleton Novel or Short Story Sequence?', *Overland*, 66 (1977), 35–47.

have been heightened if the stories had been grouped into 'a "Mitchell" sequence, a "Steelman" sequence, a bush sequence, a city sequence, and so on'. Then 'continuity might be unbroken and the characters might gain force and distinctness from the massing of impressions'.[30] Lawson later told Robertson to ignore the criticism, which he, Lawson, had put into Stephens's head anyway, and went on to blame the *Bulletin* for not putting the requisite stories 'through' – stories that would, once published in the magazine, have allowed the sequences to materialise in the book.[31]

Despite the wording of his criticism, Stephens was not, in any case, describing an unfolding *sequence* of planned and linked stories, but merely groupings of stories that had some character or setting in common. And in a broader reflective essay in February 1902 in the *Bookfellow* he seemed to recognise this when he commented: 'Were the whole of the Mitchell or Steelman sketches printed together, they would still remain flat silhouettes'.[32]

Stephens, in 1902, was surely right. Roderick grants Lawson his criticism of the *Bulletin*'s practice but goes on to blame the problem on Lawson's creative inability to imagine, and his lack of the self-discipline required to organise, material on the extended scale required by a novel. There is, however, a straightforward book-historical reason why Lawson's storytellers and characters do not become more coherently imagined from one story to the next. It is simply that Lawson sold and was paid for the stories individually. They had to be able to stand alone. He could offer stories to a particular proprietor if he had more than one in hand; and he might or might not be successful in selling them. But he had no control over when they would appear or in whose literary or other company they would ultimately sit, in the jumble of miscellaneous copy that characterised the multiple columns of tiny type of most 1890s newspapers – with which their habituated readers could skilfully deal.

[30] *Bulletin*, 29 August 1896 by [A. G. Stephens], Red Page.
[31] HL to GR, 9 September 1896 (*Letters* 63).
[32] A. G. Stephens, ''Lawson and Literature', *Bookfellow*, 18 February 1899, 21–4 [p. 22].

The question of one or more intended sequences of stories would arise only in late 1895 when Lawson set about selecting for *While the Billy Boils*. He then probably found that some stories were being kept back from publication by Archibald who, like many an editor, would not have wanted to swamp any issue's literary offerings with a single writer's verse and stories: the *Bulletin* aimed to be far more promiscuous than that. But that likelihood is far less remarkable than the chronological concentration of his choices. The proportion of prose sketches and stories by Lawson appearing in the *Bulletin* in 1893 had been, for him, unusually high in comparison to his verse. Since a similarly high number and percentage of stories appeared in the *Worker* from mid-1893, it can be appreciated why stories from that year would be so well represented in *While the Billy Boils*. Of the 52 stories and sketches collected, 9 precede 1893 in their date of publication, 22 come from 1893; 1894 provides 10; 1895, 8; and 1896, given the date of the gathering, selecting and revising, understandably only 3.[33] The figure for 1893 stands out. Lawson must have had a strong sense of coming into his own as a prose writer in that year. But his frustration at not receiving the editorship of the *Worker* at the end of 1893 led him, as we have seen, to leave precipitately for New Zealand and stay there for nearly eight months.

On 25 November 1893, a week after he left, '"Dossing Out" and "Camping"' appeared in the *Worker*, signed with the pseudonym 'EXILE'. A city story, it seems to tap a new vein that succeeded that of the trip to Bourke and to which he would later return in '"Board and Residence"' and 'Going Blind'.[34] But then there was nothing more in the *Worker* for quite some time. Similarly, the *Bulletin* published '"In a Wet Season." Along the Line' (an account of his trip back from Bourke) on 2 December 1893, and 'Hungerford' on 16 December, with some verse of

---

[33] Six HL stories and sketches in total appeared in 1892 (all were selected for *Billy Boils*); 1893 yielded 34 (22 selected); and a further 24 in 1894 (10 selected). There was a falling-off in 1895 (14, with 8 selected) and 1896, by the time of the collection's publication, 5, with 3 selected. A known 8 remained in manuscript form. The 1896 collection includes 2 that did not receive newspaper publication.

[34] Respectively in *Worker*, 29 September 1894 and 29 June 1895.

Lawson's. And then no more Lawson stories appeared in the *Bulletin*.[35] Both newspapers had evidently run out of copy. Lawson turned his attention to New Zealand editors and had some luck with sales: 'That There Dog o' Mine: An Australian Sketch' appeared in the *New Zealand Mail* on 8 December 1893. A Macquarie story, it presumably represents a completion of an unfinished version he had brought with him, or perhaps he brought only the idea and wrote it from scratch. This issue also announced Lawson's presence in Wellington and promised 'a short series of sketches of Australian life' by him.[36] The travel sketch 'Coming Across.—A Study in the Steerage', based on his voyage from Sydney, was definitely new.[37] 'Stiffner and Jim (Thirdly Bill)' is set in New Zealand and could well have been written there.

It appeared in the *Pahiatua Herald* on 9 March 1894. It is set in the Canterbury district of the South Island, which Lawson had not yet visited but would soon. The setting may be a localising of an already drafted Australian yarn as Roderick argues, but there is no internal or contextual evidence to support this conjecture.[38] Stiffner had previously appeared in two of Lawson's Australian stories as a shanty-keeper: 'An Incident at Stiffner's' and 'Macquarie's Mate'.[39] His character changes considerably between those two stories, and here he is quite different again. He is now violently aggressive. If some months had elapsed since

---

[35] However, two poems with outback subject matter ('"Sez You"' and 'The Paroo "River"') appeared in the *Bulletin* on 3 March and 12 May 1894 respectively: they were either the last of the material on hand before HL's departure or he submitted them from New Zealand.

[36] See *Letters* 421. The sketch was reprinted on 11 December 1893 in the *New Zealand Times*.

[37] Two instalments, respectively 15 and 29 December 1893, *New Zealand Mail*; and reprinted in its weekly *New Zealand Times*, 30 December. Its subtitle (gained in the second instalment and when reprinted) echoes an article reprinted from the *Pall Mall Gazette* in the *New Zealand Times* on 7 December 1893, 'Studies in the Steerage'. HL's poems 'Here's Luck' (about women voting there for the first time in the world on 28 November 1893) appeared in *Fair Play* (Wellington) on 16 December 1893; and '"For'ard"' (like 'Coming Across', about class distinctions on board ship from Australia) and 'The Morning of New Zealand' in the *New Zealand Mail* on 22 December 1893 and 19 January 1894 respectively.

[38] *Commentaries* 64, 67.

[39] 'An Incident at Stiffner's' (*Truth*, 23 July 1893; in *Over the Sliprails*, 1900) explains: 'They called him "Stiffner" because he used, long before, to get a living by poisoning wild dogs near the Queensland border. The name stuck'. He is mentioned as a shanty keeper (implicitly) living near Bourke in 'She Wouldn't Speak' (*Worker*, 15 December 1894). 'Macquarie's Mate', *Worker*, 21 October 1893?.

Lawson had written 'Macquarie's Mate' the change becomes more understandable: he was using Stiffner as a figure to anchor a new tale, whose lineaments may have come to him freshly in the Hutt Valley or Pahiatua. If so, the character-type had to change.

Short Stories in Prose and Verse (1894)

Returning from New Zealand in July 1894 with renewed hope, soon dashed, of a staff position on the new *Daily Worker*, Lawson was buoyed up financially by an arrangement to be provincial editor and then an exclusive contributor. A number of his stories soon appeared in the *Worker*: on 11 August 1894, 'Drifted Back'; on 25 August, 'Remailed'; on 1 September, 'Stiffner and Jim (Thirdly Bill)' again, but in a revised form;[40] on 22 September, 'Shooting the Moon'; on 29 September, '"Board and Residence"'; and, on 13 October, 'Baldy Thompson. A Sketch of a Squatter'. But by 19 November Lawson had had a falling-out with 'my feller wirkers' at the *Worker*.[41]

His commitment to the cause had been waning ever since he failed to secure the editorship of the *Worker*; his being called back from New Zealand had perhaps temporarily revived it. But publishing a sketch sympathetic to a squatter during a period of high tension – a shearers' strike was in progress, and there had been arson and violence on the part of strikers in the far west – cannot have endeared Lawson to the unionists.[42] Nor could two of his articles in the *Worker*: 'The Cant and Dirt of Labor Literature' (6 October 1894) and 'A Word in Season' (13 October). After the falling-out he went a critical step further in 'The City and the Bush' (8 December), denouncing 'wide-spread bush-union

---

[40] The very high number of changes between the versions in the *Pahiatua Herald* and the *Worker*, mainly in presentation but also in wording, suggests either a thorough revision and editing of a *Herald* clipping or the preparation of new fair copy from a draft that HL had retained.

[41] *Letters* 57.

[42] A. B. Paterson would later recall HL's saying: 'They have declared me bogus for writing a story disclosing some good points in a squatter' ('Some Reminiscences of George Robertson, Australian Publisher', *Sydney Mail*, 20 September 1933, p. 8). For the strike and unionist agitation, see Colin Roderick, 'Henry Lawson: The Middle Years 1893–6', *Journal of the Royal Australian Historical Society*, 53 (1967), 101–21 [pp. 108–9].

egotism and clannishness'.[43] Lawson was asserting his independence of the unionist cause, rejecting its claim to the moral high ground. To make matters worse, his trying to live by his pen at the *Worker*'s rate of 12s.6d. per column would have involved a deal of personal sacrifice: the better rate of remuneration at the *Bulletin* must have been hard to resist.

So, on 15 December 1894, 'He'd Come Back' and 'That Swag' [renamed 'Enter Mitchell' in *While the Billy Boils*] appeared in the *Bulletin* but 'She Wouldn't Speak' appeared in the *Worker*. Thus the exclusivity was gone but the falling-out was not complete: Lawson the columnist and sketch-writer remained a valuable asset for the *Worker*. This pattern of publication continued. On 5 January 1895, 'The Old Bark School: An Echo' ['An Echo from the Old Bark School'] was published in the *Bulletin*. A week later (12 January), 'Some Reflections on a Voyage across Cook's Straits (N.Z.)' ['Across the Straits'] appeared in the *Worker* and, on 19 January 1895, 'Steelman' came out in the *Bulletin*. This was the first signal of a new character-type, the sophisticated conman, whose flights of rhetorical fantasy would be a reliable invoker of the comic-absurd mode for Lawson once he settled it down near the end of 1895, leaving the Mitchell character-type to occupy the sadly philosophical-cynical register. Marsters, a phenomenon of mid-1893, did not reappear. Nor did Stiffner after December 1894 (in 'She Wouldn't Speak'): he is closer, in his propensity to violence, to the first Steelman of January 1895.[44]

Next there is a gap until 11 May 1895 when 'Our Pipes' (another Mitchell sketch) appeared in the *Bulletin*. On 1, 8 and 15 June 1895, 'Jones' Alley' was serialised in the *Worker*, followed by 'Going Blind' on 29 June. It would be the last story to receive authorial revisions in the printer's copy for *While the Billy Boils*. The last four of these pieces are mainly city sketches, and 'He'd Come Back' and 'That Swag' are about awkward returns to the city. The subject matter was roughly following

---

[43] In *Autobiographical* 26-7, 27-8 and 28-31 [p. 30].
[44] For 'Taking Stiffner Down', not published in HL's lifetime but extant in a holograph manuscript of uncertain date, see Chapter 3 n. 30.

Lawson's own movements, except that the Cook's Straits sketch was probably a working-up of notes he had taken at the time.[45]

'Steelman's Pupil' and 'Two Dogs and a Fence' appeared in December 1895; and, in March 1896, so too did 'An Unfinished Love Story', which was a new departure for Lawson and unlike his existing range of subject matter and approach.[46] Lawson was trying to get the stories through the press (and thus be paid for their newspaper appearance) so as to have them available for selection for the as yet unnamed volume.

At some time amidst this renewed flurry of literary activity from mid-1894 Lawson conceived the idea of publishing a selection of his work in a book. He had originally planned to do this shortly before heading off to Bourke in September 1892, when he approached the editors of various Sydney newspapers to write copyright clearances for him; but the idea came to nothing then.[47] The reason for Lawson's renewed interest in a volume collection in 1894 is suggested by the weary tone of a letter to his Wellington friend Jack Louisson: 'Am writing, by the column, for *Bulletin* and *Worker* – also some country papers – making a "living" but not contented. I'm tired of it all. . . . Am getting plenty of "orders" and some "recognition" – but what avails it?'[48] The 'country papers' must have included the Maryborough *Patriot* where 'His Country—After All' appeared on 22 December 1894. It was probably commissioned for the Christmas number by its editor Jack Perel. He was well known in the radical leftwing circles in which Lawson moved and, according to his obituarist, Perel possessed 'the ability to attract and select talent, and to

---

[45] He states in the second last paragraph that he sat down and wrote it the night (in *c.* May 1894) that the *Moa* arrived in Picton, South Island. There is little story to tell, so HL strikes the same comic tone, at his own expense mainly, as in 'Coming Across': both are travel sketches, of necessity exploiting the accidental occurrences of the voyage, not short stories.
[46] Respectively: *Bulletin*, 14 December 1895; *Worker*, 21 December 1895 (reprinted Hobart *Clipper*, 28 December 1895); and *Worker*, 21 March 1896.
[47] Signed letters to HL, 13 September 1892, from the editors of *Bulletin*, *Town & Country Journal* and *Freeman's Journal* and an undated letter from *Worker* all granted HL his copyright over his contributions (ML MSS 3269/316/Angus & Robertson Correspondence, vol. 828, pp. 7–13).
[48] 19 November 1894 (*Letters* 57–8).

inspire loyalty'.⁴⁹ This was the same day on which Lawson's first volume, *Short Stories in Prose and Verse by Henry Lawson*, was published by his mother Louisa Lawson from the office of the *Dawn* at 402 George Street, Sydney.

A paperback booklet of viii + 96 pages, retailing at 1s., it was printed with advertisements on the front and back endpapers, the front inside cover and both sides of the back cover, as well as a leaf tipped-in before page 1, an acrostic, in rhyming doggerel, spelling out through the first letter of each line 'Dr Waugh's Baking Powder'. Together with some verse, various stories were collected including several that would later be chosen for *While the Billy Boils*: 'The Drover's Wife', '"Rats"', 'The Union Buries its Dead', '[The Bush Undertaker]' (with illustrations borrowed from its first printing in the *Antipodean*) and 'Macquarie's Mate'. The standard of printing was very poor, with frequent failures of inking and unpredictable changes of font, suggesting a shortage of available type.

---

[49] Roderick refers to this publication as 'One of the mysteries of Lawsoniana', partly because few issues of the *Patriot* have survived (*Commentaries* 109); but the publication is now readily explicable. Established by Irvine ('Jack') Perel (c. 1861–1928) on 23 July 1892, the *Patriot* had a pro-Labor, anti-Chinese and anti-alien agenda, and it was studded with vigorous exposés of local corruption. According to Perel's obituarist, the Maryborough journalist and later politician William Halliwell Demaine, Perel was a 'merciless flayer of dishonesty': *Patriot*, 28 October 1928, quoted by Rod Kirkpatrick, *Purposely Parochial: One Hundred Years of the Country Press in Queensland* (Newmarket, Qld: Queensland Country Press Association, 2008), p. 160; the wording in the text above is on p. 159.

Perel's radical, almost revolutionary, style of journalism proved successful and the paper would be long-lived; it moved to Bundaberg in 1898, to Brisbane in 1903, and was not wound up until 1931. From HL's Brisbane days in 1891, HL and Perel would presumably have had mutual acquaintances. Gresley Lukin, HL's former boss at the *Boomerang*, was now a parliamentary reporter in Wellington. HL could have gone to see him when his ship the SS *Tasmania* docked in Wellington on the home voyage to Sydney from the South Island in July 1894: see *Letters* 422.

The *Patriot* would in any case have been known in radical circles in Sydney by 1894. For instance, on 27 August 1895, the *Worker* would reprint an article from '*The Patriot* (Q.)', unsigned, 'What the Workers Believe, and What They Do'. Thus the *Patriot* was reaching the office of the Sydney *Worker*. The existence of leftwing bookshops helps explain the circulation of radical newspapers. W. H. McNamara's The Socialistic Bookseller (the daughter of whose proprietor HL would marry in 1896), at 221 Castlereagh Street, Sydney, advertised in the *Worker* (including on 15 June 1895 on the same page as the third instalment of 'Jones' Alley'): 'Agent for *Reynolds*', *Lloyds*, *The Clarion*, London *Justice*, Glasgow *Mail*, &c.' (p. 4). Arthur Parker later recalled HL's taking him to the offices of the Australian Socialist League, which 'had a room upstairs with every Labour paper of the world in it': *Henry Lawson by his Mates*, p. 28.

The presence of illustrations showed some ambition, but as well as being poorly printed their positioning showed little sense of page design. The guillotining (or choice of paper stock) was little better, with some leaves left quite short.

The front matter of a book is normally typeset last, but in this case the Contents page must have been typeset before the contents of the volume were finalised because the page lacks the relevant page numbers of the fourteen items it lists, has two of them in the reverse order of their appearance and neglects to list two poems that are included towards the end of the volume. This all suggests a last-minute rush to get the booklet out for Christmas. But by 22 December 1894, the day of its publication, much of the seasonal book market would already have been satisfied.

Lawson's Preface to *Short Stories in Prose and Verse* is a manifesto, an apology and a promise:

> This is an attempt to publish, in Australia, a collection of sketches and stories at a time when everything Australian, in the shape of a book, must bear the imprint of a London publishing firm before our critics will condescend to notice it. . . . The Australian writer, until he gets a 'London hearing,' is only accepted as an imitator of some recognized English or American author . . .
>
> This pamphlet – I can scarcely call it a volume – contains some of my earliest efforts, and they are sufficiently crude and faulty. They have been collected and printed hurriedly, with an eye to Xmas, and without experienced editorial assistance, which last, I begin to think, was sadly necessary.
>
> However, we all hope to do better in future, and I shall have more confidence in my first volume of verse which will probably be published some time next year.

In fact, Lawson had laboured hard over the revision of the stories. With '[The Bush Undertaker]', for instance, where he was working from the printing in the annual *Antipodean*, his motivations were several, and overlapping as they did in practice, apt to conflict with one another. Lawson was evidently meaning to improve the unfolding of the narrative events with new or clearer details.[50] But he also wanted to

---

[50] E.g., in the annual, the hatter pulls a bag 'from under his bunk'; in *Short Stories in Prose and Verse* he pulls it 'from over a stick across the corner of the hut'. And his 'faithful friend

observe conventional standards of narration in books: his well-attested sensitivity about his poor education would have been a spur here. In the annual, the omniscient narrator is positioned closer to the hatter's level of thought and speech; there is a simple, almost childish unguardedness. Lawson pulls back from this in 1894 by repeatedly heading for the expected literary phrasing.[51] In composition, Lawson had found the hatter's voice through inhabiting the character as closely as possible; the relationship of this voice and the narrator's voices was more fluid as a result. In revision, the hatter's voice becomes (in some changes) more radically idiomatic, whereas that of the narrator becomes closer to what Lawson evidently fancied the reader's was.[52] Lawson's editor for *While the Billy Boils* would subsequently drive this wedge further: this theme is taken up in Chapter 4.

and confidante' becomes 'his four-legged mate'. (See Eggert and Webby for a recording of the textual variants. The reading text is the first periodical publication, in this case the *Antipodean*, with variants in later versions given at foot of page.)

[51] E.g., finding the corpse, the hatter says: "'Me luck's in for the day!'". *Short Stories in Prose and Verse* has "'... in, and no mistake'", losing touch with the character's idiom; HL regathers it for *Billy Boils*: "'in for the day and no mistake'". Again, as the hatter addresses the corpse, which he now recognises as Brummy, he calls it 'the fool you allers was'; *Short Stories in Prose and Verse* changes this to 'carrion', which is a logical and clarifying development, but it is not in the range of the simple hatter's idiom. Similarly, the change of 'contents' to 'precious liquor'. Again, the corpse originally 'lay on its stomach'. HL changed 'stomach' (with its direct reminder of the physicality of the corpse) to 'face' in *Short Stories in Prose and Verse*. In revising printer's copy for *Billy Boils* he must have realised he disliked it and so deleted, leaving only 'lay'.

It is possible that HL's mother had a hand in the copy-editing, but evidence that Roderick cites in support is unpersuasive. He attributes to Louisa Lawson a change in 'Macquarie's Mate' from 'By God' to 'By the Lord'. The wording reverts to 'By God' under HL's hand in the printer's copy for *Billy Boils* (ML A1867–8). But HL's mother was not in fact shy of using the word 'God' in her printed poems: 'A Birthday Wish' (*Dawn*, February 1892), uses 'God'; as do four of the first twelve poems in her *'The Lonely Crossing' and Other Poems* (1905): see her *Collected Poems with Selected Critical Commentaries*, ed. Leonie Rutherford and Megan Roughley (Armidale, NSW: University of New England Centre for Australian Language and Literature Studies, 1996).

[52] E.g. the hatter's 'spending such' becomes 'a-spendin' sech' in *Short Stories in Prose and Verse*. But a large addition near its end ('He sat down on a log near by ... back to the hut': see this story's apparatus in Eggert and Webby) widens the perspective and finds a level of disinterested sympathy or compassion for the hatter that the magazine version lacked. The distance of the narrator from Brummy is further undergirded by this move; and similarly in the change from '"Arter all," he said, leaning on his spade and wiping his brow—arter all it war Brummy!"' in the *Antipodean* to '"An' this is the last of Brummy," he said, leaning on his spade and looking away over the tops of the gaunt gums on the distant range.'

Lawson must have found the reception of his little book pleasing.[53] The *Worker* and *Bulletin* reviewed it favourably. An unsigned article in the *Bulletin* on 5 January 1895, probably by A. G. Stephens, offered a biographical introduction of Lawson to readers together with some fulsome praise, but only one work in the book was specifically referred to:

> THE BULLETIN knows plenty of clever writers, but it does not know another than Lawson who could write the sketch called 'The Drover's Wife,' which takes up twelve pages in the badly-printed little book. You can ransack the whole realm of Australian prose without finding a mate for that sketch, brim-full of the humor and pathos of the bush.... Henry Lawson is the voice of the bush, and the bush is the heart of Australia.... He lacks culture and critical insight, his sense of form is crude; but these things may come to him, for he is young – only 27 – and his work grows steadily better as he matures. Yet Art can never give him a tithe of the charm which he holds in direct fee-simple from Nature.[54]

The title of the article was significant: 'Henry Lawson: An Australian Poet'. The text assumed as a matter of course that Lawson was already known through his newspaper sketches and verse: 'HENRY LAWSON'S friends will be interested to hear that his first volume of collected work is published.' For Lawson's existing readers, the book was being cast more as a confirmation of his talent than an announcement of it. The reviewer's theme of Lawson's artlessness, unsophistication and his being directly in touch with his subject matter, would recur in later 1890s commentary.

On 12 January 1895, a whole column on page 2 of the *Worker* was devoted to the new volume of this poet of the people, as Lawson was already being called:[55] 'His sketches in prose and verse which have appeared in these columns have been read by hundreds and thousands

---

[53] It had been preceded by what was probably the first article on HL (unsigned [John Le Gay Brereton], 'Poetry in Australia', *Hermes*, 20 November 1894), which praised HL's 'intense power of sympathy ... From the ranks of the workers his voice rises up, full of comfort and of hope'. Unlike Kendall and Gordon, HL had 'elements of greatness' but needed to be treated better – e.g. by the *Worker* (cf. *Letters* 57). He was 'essentially unselfish', but 'There are signs in his work of a strong revulsion of feeling, a bitter awakening to sordid reality' (pp. 4–5).
[54] *Bulletin*, 5 January 1895, p. 15.
[55] In a letter to Jack Louisson on 19 November 1894, HL described himself as 'the unfortunate "pote" of the people' (*Letters* 57).

of bushmen throughout the colonies, as well as by the residents in our towns and cities'. The unsigned review, perhaps by the editor J. Medway Day, was positive ('His writings are photographs hardly idealized at all'); but it complained of Lawson's 'affectation of cynicism', which meant that he fell short of 'the true artistic type'. His refusal to treat of sentiment as other than a weakness would be a recurring complaint in the *Worker*. But the reviewer did find some ideological backing in Lawson's dark portraits of the typical bush worker and toiler as being exploited by the 'smug-faced plutocrat'. Suggestive, but unsubstantiated by example, was a potentially important remark: 'The dramatic style in which the stories are told requires much more skill than the ordinary reader would suppose. By one stroke firm and sure, Henry Lawson produces an effect where a less gifted writer would require to write several paragraphs of description.' A separate three-line filler advertisement appeared on page 3; it repeated the review's offer in its first paragraph and the reminder in its last that the book was 'To be obtained from this [the *Worker*'s] office' at 1s.2d. posted. The *Worker* was evidently making reparations aimed at gathering the wandering sheep back into the fold.

In the Brisbane *Worker* on 26 January 1895, on page 3, 'Prometheus' reviewed the book more positively for a whole column, implicitly taking issue with the Sydney *Worker*'s reviewer: 'The ability to produce this sense of objective reality is the surest mark of the true artist.'[56] The reviewer uses this criterion to impugn Dickens, reflecting the general critical shift towards realism that had taken place in Britain after Dickens's death in 1870 and had been gathering pace even before then. Lawson is said to possess this ability 'in an exceedingly high degree. Doubtless this is largely due to the fact that he knows what he writes about.' This theme in reviews of Lawson's prose volumes would always suit politically inspired valuations of his work; but it drew attention away from the hard-earned art of this 'true artist'. The latter was something far harder to write about and, in Lawson's case, even to detect, since the business of a realist was

---

[56] Roderick (*Criticism* 7) identifies 'Prometheus' as 'Henry E. Boote?' (see Chapter 3 n. 6), but the style suggests otherwise. Further notices appeared on 16 February and 13 April 1895.

generally taken to be to disguise the art and to eliminate the personal presence of the writer. The reviewer felt that Lawson's verse was 'not his forte' but that 'Some of his sketches of Australian bush life we regard as the truest and finest things in the whole range of Australian literature.'

If confirmation were needed that Lawson had become a sentimental favourite of the *Worker*'s readers before Angus & Robertson became his publisher in 1896, and that *Short Stories in Prose and Verse* was remembered, a rhymed verse 'To Henry Lawson's City Critics', contributed by 'J.D.' of the 'Darling River', provided it on 29 February 1896 on page 1. It was a reply to a *Bulletin* review of Lawson's first volume of verse, mentioned in his preface to *Short Stories in Prose and Verse* as forthcoming and published by Angus & Robertson in mid-February 1896: *In the Days When the World Was Wide and Other Verses*. The versifier appeals for critics to 'Let the lad sing as he likes to sing', for 'It makes our lot seem brighter again when we think of "The Drover's Wife"'. He amusingly draws into his verse many of the poems in the latest volume but also recalls 'Macquarie's Mate' from the 1894 volume.[57] Another comment of 'J.D.' links to the praise of 'Prometheus'; it casts Lawson as a city dweller who, for the bushmen, is their link between city and country:

> And we love to think as we're loafing round in the town
>   with a careless push
> That a poet who's also loafing round knows something
>   about the bush.

Lawson's Preface had predicted a better volume 'next year'. Had discussions already started with George Robertson, the active partner in Angus & Robertson, about *In the Days*? Or was the mention only reflecting secondhand reports from Banjo Paterson or John Le Gay Brereton (1871–1933), the young poet and scholar whom Lawson had befriended in August 1894, that Angus & Robertson's future plans

---

[57] The title had stuck, even if it was (as is not clear) a mistake for the poem 'Marshall's Mate' from *In the Days*.

might include him?[58] There is no evidence of an agreement in the firm's Letterbooks (preserved in the Mitchell Library), although letters before 1895 are relatively few compared to the subsequent period when the firm's publishing program was put energetically into hand. An extant letter from Brereton to Lawson suggesting he go and see George Robertson because the latter is interested in publishing his work is itself undated, although some later hand has added in lead pencil '1895'. In *The Auld Shop and the New*, Lawson's poem written in December 1910 in honour of Robertson and printed for private circulation in 1923, Robertson's notes state: 'Banjo brought the MS. of his book, "The Man from Snowy River and Other Verses," to me in April, 1895'.[59]

Paterson's collection was published on 17 October 1895. It was the first title in Angus & Robertson's new publishing venture. As many production procedures would have needed to be devised and arranged, all or most of the intervening six months would have been needed for editing, design, production and pre-promotion – even if Paterson had completely assembled the contents and finished his revisions before he submitted. But he had not. What appears to be Paterson's originally submitted manuscript is extant in the Mitchell Library. The document's Contents page shows that the sequence of poems was altered for the 1895 publication, a few poems were rejected and about a dozen added.[60] The

---

[58] For the August date, see letter, Mary Cameron [later, Gilmore] to Brereton, 16 August 1894, arranging the meeting with HL at Mrs [wife of William] Lane's in Enmore Road, Marrickville: this letter is described and quoted in Harry F. Chaplin, *Henry Lawson: His Books, Manuscripts, Autograph Letters and Association Copies* (Surry Hills, NSW: Wentworth Press, 1974), p. 80; not present in *Letters of Mary Gilmore*, ed. William Wilde and T. Inglis Moore (1980). Unaware of this, Roderick dates the meeting (*Life* 122) as not before September 1894 when Mrs Lane advertised in the *Worker* the opening of her boarding house in Newtown (evidently her next address).
[59] Page 24. James Tyrrell speculated that it was Archibald who sent both poets to see GR and states that Paterson had a letter of introduction from Archibald when he came with his manuscript in April 1895. But the Brereton letter disproves the Lawson half of the story, and Tyrrell may have been running together memory of different details into the one account: see James R. Tyrrell, *Old Books, Old Friends, Old Sydney: The Fascinating Reminiscences of a Sydney Bookseller* (1952; North Ryde, NSW: A&R, 1987), p. 101.
[60] The published Acknowledgements explains: 'A number of these verses are now published for the first time, most of the others were written for and appeared in "The Bulletin" (Sydney, N.S.W.), and are therefore already widely known to readers in Australasia' (p. [vii]).

document is mainly fair-copy autograph manuscript, but with mounted clippings and some typescript.[61] The preparation of this document could have occupied Paterson – who worked as a solicitor by day – for some months of his available time. If Paterson was acting upon Robertson's invitation, discussions some months before April 1895 would have been necessary. Perhaps Brereton had heard of the new venture from Paterson, and of Robertson's interest also in Lawson. Brereton's letter could therefore date from late 1894, and a discussion of the matter between Lawson and Robertson (who were already on friendly terms)[62] could have taken place: this is the simplest explanation for Lawson's promise in the December 1894 Preface of another volume 'next year', 1895.

Angus & Robertson was already on his horizon: the firm was a logical next step in the consolidation of a literary reputation and perhaps a career that might end the hand-to-mouth existence that he had been enduring for the previous few years.

---

[61] ML MSS 314/195. The document may have served as (apparently incomplete) printer's copy; it has the same coloured pencil or crayon kind of foliation as printer's copy of *Billy Boils* (ML A1867–8) but with extensive gaps in the numerical sequence.

[62] See letter from HL (not in *Letters*), written from 16 Thomas Street, Ashfield, on 2 December 1891, asking GR 'to lend me a couple of quid for a week or two': ML MSS 314/45, p. 1a.

CHAPTER 3

AUTHOR AND PUBLISHER

LAWSON AND ANGUS & ROBERTSON

***In the Days When the World Was Wide*: Publication and reception**

ON 26 July 1895 Lawson signed an Agreement with Angus & Robertson 'to publish a volume or volumes of verse and prose to be selected by A. & R. from the published and unpublished works of the said author, the whole of which are to be a[t] their disposal for selection, the selection to be made by the said author and J.F. Archibald and John LeGay Brereton'.[1] This cautious legal wording was cast aside in a par that appeared in the *Bulletin* the next day on the Red Page, presumably written by Archibald, who was privy to the negotiations: 'Angus and Robertson have arranged with Henry Lawson to bring out a choice edition of his works in two vols., prose and verse, at 5s. each; posted, 5s. 6d. Mrs. Louisa Lawson's 1s. edition was exhausted some time ago. The type and binding will probably be uniform with those of "The Banjo's" [Paterson's] book, to be issued by the same publishers shortly; and the four volumes (Victor Daley is also to be added) will form a substantial contribution towards a desirable library of young Australian authors.' Lawson's *In the Days*

---

[1] From a summary of contents of an A&R file of HL agreements (contracts) and assignments of rights to the firm: ML MSS 3269/Lawson, Henry – papers re 1894–1949, vol. 386, item 23 of the summary, itself in fols. 77–83. The original Agreement for *In the Days* is elsewhere (in ML MSS 3269/316/Angus & Robertson Correspondence, vol. 829, pp. 59–66). It was partially superseded by HL's signed and stamped Agreement dated 10 October 1895, to which a Schedule of poems was attached (vol. 829, pp. 81–8), selling the complete copyright for the 'volume of verse' that would become *In the Days*. This is HL's sale to A&R of his right, already negotiated in the Agreement of 26 July 1895, to a half share in any profits. Roderick reproduced the Agreement of 10 October 1895 in 'Henry Lawson: The Middle Years 1893–6', *Journal of the Royal Australian Historical Society*, 53 (1967), 101–21 [facing p. 116].

When the World Was Wide and Other Verses would appear in mid-February 1896.

Meanwhile, it was almost certainly Brereton, editor of the Sydney University undergraduates' magazine *Hermes*, who contributed its unsigned review of *The Man from Snowy River* on 6 November 1895: 'We must not come to "The Banjo" for originality of thought or depth of feeling ... [he] is a man with a good ear, a facile pen and a gift of humour. We take what he has to offer, and are thankful.' In comparison, in a separate puff for Lawson's still unnamed *In the Days*, he wrote: 'It will probably be the best collection of poems ever placed before the public by an Australian ... There is nothing mean or trivial about his songs; they are the frank expression of deep and fervent feeling'.[2]

The *Bulletin* was lending a hand with pre-publication promotion of *In the Days* as well. Reading proofs or an advance copy, Archibald reported to Robertson on 12 January 1896: 'I've been hastily over Lawson's work. It will not sell at first so readily as "Banjo", but it *will* sell and that permanently.'[3] Brereton's poem 'A Reflection on Lawson's Poems' appeared in the *Bulletin* on 18 January 1896; an announcement of the volume's availability 'next week', 'Post-free from BULLETIN office, 5s. 6d.' on 1 February 1896; and a reply to Brereton's poem by 'The Dipsomaniac', entitled 'A Reflection on Brereton's "Reflection on Lawson's Poems"', on 15 February.[4] In this same issue *In the Days* was reviewed on the Red Page and advertised on page 8 with a reproduction of Frank P. Mahony's title-page portrait of Lawson on the track. This was part of the active mythologising of Lawson – himself a city dweller – as bushman.

The *Bulletin*'s review on 15 February 1896 differentiated Paterson and Lawson from their forebears as 'the beginnings of a national school of

---

[2] Both *Hermes* items are unsigned; the review ('"The Banjo"'), p. 8; the par, p. 2.

[3] ML MSS 314/6, p. 67. Archibald was not referring to the prose: he praises a poem 'The God-Forgotten Election', to which objection had evidently been taken. It was not included.

[4] Respectively, *Bulletin*, 18 January 1896, p. 3; 1 February 1896, Red Page; 15 February, p. 3: the pseudonymous author was Henry C. Cargill, according to Walter Stone: see his *Henry Lawson: A Chronological Checklist of his Contributions to the Bulletin 1887–1924* (Sydney: Wentworth Press, 1964), p. 21.

poetry. In them, for the first time, *Australia* has found audible voice and characteristic expression.' This claim rendered more subtle the valuation of *Short Stories in Prose and Verse* from early 1895; other notes from that reception were sounded again:

> The change of note from Hope [in his early poetry] to Discontent, the change of view from impersonal to personal, have not improved Lawson's poetry. The less he broods the better he writes.... Lawson's shortcomings are obvious enough. His mental scope is narrow; he is comparatively uncultured... But how graphic he is, how natural, how true, how strong! How he feels, and makes his readers feel!... it must be remembered that his verse represents only half of his work, and perhaps not the finer half. His prose, brimming with humor and pathos, is of the best produced in Australia.
>
> Lawson's keen sympathy, his knack of observation, are characteristically feminine. His sense of humor, his talent for vivid portrayal, are as characteristically masculine.... His capacity for emotion is Lawson's best gift. It is because he feels so deeply that he writes so strongly.

While the Romantic and gender stereotypes of the critic – almost certainly A. G. Stephens[5] – struggled to deal with the mixed phenomenon he was trying to articulate, the enthusiasm was clear and the tone authoritative. Lawson had now definitely arrived.

The review by 'Touchstone' [Henry E. Boote][6] in the Brisbane *Worker* on 9 May 1896 was less positive. The reviewer accepted gladly 'the fact of [Lawson's] lines being more widely read and more widely quoted throughout the colonies than those of any other Australian writer'. But this did not mean they rose to the level of poetic art: 'He transfigures nothing with poetic fancy. He pins his muse down to plain facts.' Possessed of only 'an everyday manner', his verse has 'not one line' of 'breathing love, or admiration, or awe, in the presence of the loveliness,

---

[5] Cf. his signed 'Lawson and Literature' (*Bookfellow*, 18 February 1899, pp. 21–4: his response to HL's '"Pursuing Literature" in Australia'): 'Lawson's capacity for keen feeling – the root of his literary power – is naturally paid for by incapacities which he does not always realise ... His grammar is shaky and he has small sense of literary proportion'. Cf. also Stephens's review of *Billy Boils* in the *Bulletin*, 29 August 1896, Red Page (identified as Stephens's by HL in *Letters* 63): 'what others merely know, Lawson feels. He is indeed abnormally sensitive'.
[6] Boote was editor of the *Bundaberg Guardian* 1894–96 and then founded the Gympie *Truth*, editing it until 1902 when he became editor of the Brisbane *Worker*.

the grandeur, and the profound mystery of Nature'. Disappointed, evidently, that Lawson was no Australian Wordsworth, the reviewer diagnosed the problem as Lawson's having been trained or forced to write 'pure Bulletinese': 'Literary individualism is not permitted on its staff . . . uniformity of style and similarity of matter [are] insisted upon'. What Lawson does not lack, however, is 'Sympathy': his language 'goes straight home to the hearts of the People'. Lawson is 'content to share their poverty and champion their cause'.[7]

The tendency to collapse the distance between the writing and the life (feeling or Sympathy supposedly bridged the two), as well as to cast Lawson's intimacy with his bush subject matter as effectively annexing new geographical areas for the province of art, emerged in the criticism as themes that would apply even more readily to his prose later in the year. There was only a little attention to his narrative styles and experiments.[8] Yet the published results of these experiments were the very things that Lawson had under his eye as he got to work gathering and revising his stories for his second Angus & Robertson volume *While the Billy Boils*. His contractual partner in that process was George Robertson, whose background as a publisher needs to be understood.

George Robertson as publisher

Robertson was born in Essex in 1860, but when his father died in 1867 the family returned to Scotland, where his parents had both been born. There Robertson completed his schooling until the age of 12, when he was apprenticed to Glasgow bookseller and publisher to the University of Glasgow, James MacLehose. In 1879 Robertson migrated to New Zealand to join his brothers, spending a few years as a timber-feller. From there he went to Sydney in 1882 and worked for the Melbourne publisher and bookseller George Robertson (no relation) at his

---

[7] Page 4.
[8] A good example is the review 'A New Volume of Bush Poetry' by 'J.F.' [John Farrell] in the Sydney *Daily Telegraph*, 15 February 1896. Less wedded to the socialist cause, Farrell had difficulty with HL's espousing of revolution (as in 'The Star of Australasia').

CHAPTER 3 . AUTHOR AND PUBLISHER

Sydney branch. Four years later, he went into partnership with David Mackenzie Angus at his bookshop, established in 1882, at 110 Market Street, Sydney. In 1890 the business moved to 89 Castlereagh Street where the firm remained for 81 years. Angus's ill-health and Robertson's prodigious energy and organisational capacity saw him soon take the helm; Angus, born in 1855, would retire in 1899 and die in 1901. '[N]othing daunted Robertson', declared a man who knew from personal experience: 'Banjo' Paterson.[9] Bookselling remained at the heart of the business's profitability, despite the introduction of a successful circulating library in 1895 and a regular publishing schedule from the same year. Paterson and Lawson were Robertson's very fortunate early choices, but educational and general non-literary titles provided the necessary cash flow throughout the firm's extended existence.[10]

The conditions for efficient book distribution, and therefore potentially of regular (as against on-commission) publishing, were in place in the Australian colonies by the 1880s, and only needed someone of determination and energy to take advantage of them. The white population was increasing rapidly and becoming more literate. Free compulsory education was instituted in the 1870s, the establishment of universities occurred from the 1850s, and mechanics' institutes and schools of arts, typically with a lending library, were spreading. (There were 1,000 by 1900.)[11] With around 400,000 people in 1892, Sydney supported ten metropolitan weeklies and another ten metropolitan monthlies and fortnightlies.[12] And every country town had its local newspaper, usually a weekly: abundant venues for book reviewing were in place.

---

[9] A. B. Paterson, 'Some Reminiscences of George Robertson, Australian Publisher', *Sydney Mail*, 20 September 1933, p. 8.
[10] For a treatment of the firm's early history, heavily based on A&R correspondence collected at ML, see Alison: the source of much of the information in the next few paragraphs.
[11] Alison gives this figure (*ibid.*, p. 9). Philip Candy states over 2,000 in total (without the 1900 endpoint): '"The Light of Heaven Itself": The Contribution of the Institutes to Australia's Cultural History', in *Pioneering Culture: Mechanics' Institutes and Schools of Arts in Australia*, ed. P. C. Candy and J. Laurent (Adelaide: Auslib Press, 1994), p. 2.
[12] See Gordon & Gotch, *Australasian Newspaper Directory: Advertisers' and Subscriber's Guide* (Melbourne: Gordon & Gotch, 1892).

So too were the requisite trade and communication arrangements. By 1888, fast steamers took only 32 days to reach Sydney from London, but that was only part of the story. The radial model of business connectedness (London–colonies) was complemented by chords connecting the different parts of the colonial circumference. For a bookseller in Sydney, this meant, at first, inter- and intra-colonial steamship routes and then rail links (Sydney–Melbourne in 1883; Sydney–Bourke in 1885; Sydney–Brisbane in 1888), reliable postal services, telegraph for cabling within the colonies (from 1861 when Sydney, Melbourne, Adelaide and Brisbane were connected), and then overseas cabling when the link to London was completed in 1872. The latter was very expensive to use, but elaborate code books, which reduced the cost, were developed between Angus & Robertson and their agent in Britain Young J. Pentland, a friend and former fellow-apprentice of Angus.[13]

A network of bookshops was well established. In Melbourne Samuel Mullen and George Robertson were prominent, and E. W. Cole opened what would become a famous bookshop there in 1882, employing novel methods of attracting customers and retaining a very large stock. In Sydney, Angus & Robertson's main bookselling competitors were Turner & Henderson, William Dymock and a branch of the firm of George Robertson of Melbourne. Booksellers showed considerable enterprise running circulating libraries (for example, Samuel Mullen in Melbourne, and William Maddock in Sydney) and establishing London buying offices (for example, those of the Melbourne George Robertson and J. Walch & Sons of Hobart).

In addition, a number of Australian booksellers had a sideline in book publishing, usually on commission with the author paying the printing costs and the bookseller in effect operating only as the distributor.[14]

---

[13] A cable cost 9s.4d. per word and took six hours to reach London. A&R was connected to the first Sydney telephone exchange in 1898.
[14] Active publishers included: in Melbourne, H. T. Dwight, George Robertson (600 titles 1855–90) and F. F. Baillière; in Adelaide, E. S. Wigg. The *Bulletin* newspaper published a long series of titles from 1888; and in 1898 A. C. Rowlandson established the NSW Bookstall Company, which would become a prolific publisher of inexpensive paperbacks. See further: George Mackaness and Walter W. Stone, *The Books of the Bulletin 1880–1952: An Annotated*

Angus & Robertson had published on this basis since 1888. Consciously developing a professional publishing program on a shared-profits or royalties basis was a different and much riskier matter; but finally it was Robertson who grasped the nettle in 1895.[15] He was a man of energy. James Tyrrell, a young employee of the firm at the time, remembered him as 'an exceptionally fine-looking man ... fairly bursting with vigour and vitality, not given then to small irritations, but with no toleration for fools'.[16]

Bibliography (Sydney: A&R, 1955); and Carol Mills, *The New South Wales Bookstall Company as a Publisher* (Canberra: Mulini, 1991).

In his review of *Billy Boils* in *Gundagai Times*, c. 15 September 1896, John Tighe Ryan commented: 'In the past authors have found it useless to produce a book in Australia, and a bitter story could be written of their experiences. No matter how good the book was, the author was asked to pay the cost or at least half the cost of publishing it. Having done so he had reason to expect a return. But he was usually doomed to disappointment. The publishers managed to present a balance-sheet which showed on paper that they had suffered a severe loss. It would not be so bad if they printed the book well and circulated it. But even this they did not know how to do, consequently it has been recognised that writers to secure even Australian readers should publish in England': sourced from ML MSS 3269/Angus & Robertson Ltd. Book Reviews (Bound volumes) 1894–1970/1, vol. 7, where Ryan's otherwise anonymous authorship has been added in pencil.

[15] Reviewing *Billy Boils*, Price Warung, who had previously seen 'some advance sheets', declared that 'The publication of this volume marks a new date in the annals of Australian Literature ... Messrs. Angus & Robertson ... may be justly called the founders of Australian publishing' (*Bathurst Free Press*, 29 August 1896).

Primarily because the business records of the Melbourne George Robertson have not survived it is impossible to be definite that A&R was the first to develop a program of professional literary publishing in Australia; indeed, it is more likely there were earlier one-off experiments with profit-sharing publishing.

Cf. the comments of Mr Henderson of the longstanding Sydney bookselling and publishing firm Turner & Henderson: 'My firm has in the course of its career made strong, continuous, and persistent efforts to establish a market for the local talent which unquestionably exists amongst us, but without scoring anything better than unprofitable expenditure of labour and anxious thought, with a monetary loss at the end of it.... Speaking for my own firm, I should not care to repeat an experiment which could only result in further disappointment and loss': E. D. H.: 'What Australians Read: An Inquiry', *Sydney Mail* (12 June 1897), p. 1,244. The firm also issued *Publisher: Australian Literary News* (October 1886 – June 1889).

Searches of the AUSTLIT database readily confirm that claims for absolute priority (such as A. B. Paterson's describing him as 'almost the first man to step in on the virgin field of Australian publication') are exaggerated: 'Some Reminiscences', p. 8. Nevertheless, a leaflet issued by the Melbourne George Robertson dated January 1875 entitled 'Mr. George Robertson's Terms for Publishing Books on Commission, for Authors, Booksellers, etc.', specifies that 'All expenses of Printing, Paper, Advertising, &c.' are to be paid by the author, with a 15 per cent commission to Robertson for 'All copies sold' (leaflet in: ML A927, Sir Henry Parkes Correspondence, vol. 57, p. 23).

[16] James R. Tyrrell, *Old Books, Old Friends, Old Sydney: The Fascinating Reminiscences of a*

Part of the challenge Robertson faced was developing higher local standards of page design, typesetting and printing of letterpress, as well as efficient printing of halftone illustrations.[17] Printers in Sydney were used to newspaper rather than bookwork. Doubtless Robertson realised that continuity of dealing with the one firm would push the printer to achieve the London standards he took as his goal. The time-honoured practice of purchasing English-printed sheets, with the local bookseller's cancel title-page inserted, could gradually be superseded.

Angus & Robertson published 152 titles during 1888–1900; 48 of them appeared during 1888–1895. Most of the latter were thin volumes produced by a variety of printers. The 104 titles published during 1896–1900, on the other hand, were nearly all printed by Websdale, Shoosmith in Sydney. Robertson sometimes referred to *The Man from Snowy River* (1895) as the firm's first book. Its success – it was into its tenth thousand in October 1896 – and that of the two Lawson titles in 1896, together with solid sales from newly commissioned schoolbooks, kick-started the publishing enterprise and supported less successful literary titles.[18]

The seeming oddity of Robertson's deciding to launch his literary list with collections of verse and short stories is partly explained by their availability, which itself corresponded to the requirement for brevity of the main colonial outlets for literature in newspapers and magazines. But the option of having serialised novels adapted into book form was an available model that Robertson could have favoured but did not. The contemporary success of Rudyard Kipling, born only a couple of years before Lawson, may explain this. Certainly, Robertson's reader and copy-editor Arthur W. Jose shared the general enthusiasm for Kipling's short stories and verse. With a beguiling freshness of invention Kipling had been vigorously and amusingly carving out new territory

---

Sydney Bookseller (1952; North Ryde, NSW: A&R, 1987), p. 94.
[17] For a discussion of the illustrations in *Billy Boils*, see Appendix 2.
[18] The *Australian Lettering Book* (1898) was still available in 2007. Of the 152 titles, only 62 have authors or joint authors; A&R itself accounts for the rest – unattributed books mainly for the educational market. This policy was probably the result of their bookselling experience. Of the 152, only 29 were literary titles.

for Imperial fiction: the Anglo-Indian life of the Indian military and Civil Service, and the servant and retainer class in the towns around it. *Plain Tales from the Hills* had come out in India in 1887 and was continued in six slim volumes in A. H. Wheeler's Railway Library, Allahabad. But *Plain Tales* shot into prominence when published by Macmillan in 1890 in London. That firm's well-organised worldwide promotion and distribution methods were busily establishing Rolf Boldrewood's reputation at the same time as Kipling's. Two more short-story collections by Kipling soon appeared: *Life's Handicap* in 1891 and *Many Inventions* in 1893. Kipling's Mulvaney character became a great favourite. A private soldier, he is Kipling's adaptation of the nineteenth-century stage Irishman: his loquacious Irish brogue is captured with the usual semi-phonetic spellings.[19] *Barrack Room Ballads* had come in between, in 1892, making a new reputation as balladist for Kipling; and *The Jungle Book* beast-stories would extend his reputation remarkably from 1894.

The advent of the Kipling phenomenon from 1890 may have changed existing calculations as to the possible success in Australia of locally written ballad and short-story collections. The desirability of a parallel Australian success must have crossed minds in the book trade, and it is surely no accident that Robertson would send copies of Paterson's and Lawson's verse to Kipling as they appeared and would comment on the precedent that Kipling's *Barrack Room Ballads* had set.[20] In his reminiscences *The Romantic Nineties*, published in 1933, Jose remarked that 'the Melbourne of the Nineties . . . scoffed at our [Sydney literary Bohemia's] realism as "Kipling and Water", and stressed form and phraseology, and "the maintenance of an artistic outlook," without troubling much about what they looked out on'. In part, this was a reflection on Angus & Robertson's success; in part, it was a reflection on the *Bulletin*, which had succoured many of the firm's authors: 'About

---

[19] E.g., 'The Three Musketeers' in *Plain Tales* and 'The Incarnation of Krishna Mulvaney', the lead story in *Life's Handicap*.
[20] Letters, GR to Kipling, 21 October 1895 and 7 February 1896 (ML MSS 3269/71/4, fols. 16 and 113).

[Archibald], ready to his hand, lay Australia, then only half-apprehended even by her most devoted sons'. Only the talent to articulate the country was needed, and in this, Jose claimed, the *Bulletin* surpassed the *Age* 'as a stabilizer of national emotions and desires'. In retrospect, one could see, Jose commented, that the 'well-advertised, easily-handled, attractive volumes' of Angus & Robertson, themselves 'partly evolved from early Macmillan editions of Kipling – ensconced the output of the Nineties.'[21]

Despite Robertson's strategy of meeting the market where its tastes seemed to be tending – or where, more accurately, he was endeavouring to lead it, both in form and (Australian) subject matter – there was nevertheless a certain idealism about his ambition. When the profit figures for the various departments of the business (publishing, circulating library, retail bookselling) were compiled for the successive financial years 1895–96 to 1900–01, a hard-headed accountant would surely have wondered whether the extraordinary expenditure of energy on publishing had been worthwhile. Frank Beaumont Smith, who purchased dramatic rights of Lawson's prose fiction in 1916 was to observe some time after Lawson's death that 'Poets [i.e. creative writers in general] are not George Robertson's Business – they are his Hobby!'[22] There was some truth in the remark; it had effects on the writers, and on Lawson above all.

Extant and missing documentation

The extent of George Robertson's fastidious control over the publishing business in the period to 1901 is witnessed by various ledgers in the Angus & Robertson business archive held in the Mitchell Library as MSS 3269. As each ledger served a different function, they together recorded,

---

[21] Arthur W. Jose, *The Romantic Nineties* (Sydney: A&R, 1933), pp. 44, 52, 53, 47.
[22] Memoir, 'Henry Lawson and George Robertson' (typescript, 1 p.: ML MSS 3269/Lawson, Henry – papers re 1894–1949, vol. 386, p. 319). The bookselling division apparently absorbed salaries and wages for the publishing division as well with annual costs at £2,241.1s. in financial year 1900–01, up from £1,109.7s.6d. in 1895–96 (ML MSS 3269/6/1 from calculations on folded sheets of printed ledger paper). Bookclub salaries were £389.10s.6d. in 1900–01. This shielding of the publishing division from carrying its fair share of staffing costs again suggests it was GR's baby.

sometimes several times over, the great many transactions required to produce and sell each title. This is the case from 1897, but only one set of entries from late 1895 records charges to do with the production of *While the Billy Boils*.[23] It is unknown whether other ledgers covering 1895–96 perished in a fire in 1896 at Angus & Robertson's premises, which destroyed many of the firm's records then in existence, or whether the record-keeping became more comprehensive subsequently.[24] A second impediment for the present account is the survival of relatively few letters by Lawson, or to Lawson from Angus & Robertson, during or before the period of production of *While the Billy Boils*. The reason may simply be that Lawson was often on the premises or in personal contact while he was working on the mounted clippings of his stories and sketches, rendering letters unnecessary. He certainly was on hand when completing *In the Days*.[25] Fortunately, the correspondence between Edward Dyson (who lived in Melbourne) and George Robertson survives; Dyson's *Rhymes from the Mines and Other Verses* would appear in December 1896 and was following *While the Billy Boils* through the editing and production processes during that year. (See Appendix 1 for a detailed account.)

A third problem is the absence of a significant document. The elaborately handwritten signed Agreement for *While the Billy Boils*, dated 23 June 1896, has survived.[26] A typed Schedule listing those

[23] The entries are spread over two overlapping Publishing Ledgers, one beginning in 1894 and the other in 1896 (ML MSS 3269/11/1 and 2).
[24] 'Provenance Note' in *Guide to the Angus & Robertson Archives in the Mitchell Library, State Library of New South Wales Part I* (Sydney: Library Council of New South Wales, 1990), p. ii.
[25] As HL recalled vividly in *The Auld Shop and the New* and as GR confirmed in one of his notes to the poem on p. 27. See further *Collected Verse* I. 455–7 where the recollection of an A&R employee J. G. Lockley is quoted from an article in the *Daily Telegraph* of 21 June 1924. Speaking of the dedicatory verses to *In the Days*, which would probably have been typeset last along with the rest of the front matter, Lockley recalled: 'I saw him [HL] put those verses together in the early part of 1896, on a big work-table in an old store-room which for years was part and parcel of Angus and Robertson's establishment in Castlereagh Street. He and Mr J. Le Gay Brereton had been battling with galley proofs for weeks.' For the dates see further, Chapter 5 n. 10.
[26] (ML MSS 3269/232, Angus & Robertson Correspondence, vol. 830, pp. 89–92.) It and the 26 July 1895 Agreement also survive in typed (presumably later) unsigned carbon copies and as summarised (see n. 1 above): ML MSS 3269/316/ Angus & Robertson Correspondence, vol. 827, pp. 115–19 (26 July 1895) and 1–3 (23 June 1896).

poems (relating to *In the Days*), stories and sketches whose publication rights Lawson was selling Angus & Robertson under the Agreement was originally attached to it. This survives too, but only a handful of the contents of what became *While the Billy Boils* are listed.[27] There was also, according to Colin Roderick, a working list of inclusions for *While the Billy Boils* prepared by Walter S. Syer.[28] This is the missing document. A talented jobbing illustrator and friend of George Robertson, Syer may have been called in to advise on illustrations for the volume or to lend an organisational hand – or both. In any case, he apparently made a list of stories, presumably working from clippings that Lawson had by then already in hand and perhaps others that he was considering but could not immediately locate. Syer definitely performed such a role – making a 'preliminary selection' – in 1898 for what would become the double-volume *On the Track and Over the Sliprails* (1900).[29]

Roderick, who died in 2000, is the only scholar to have reported on the Syer list (in his *Commentaries* of 1985) but he nowhere provides a location, nor gives a physical description or transcription of the document.[30] Assuming it existed, it would have served a different

---

[27] (ML MSS 3269/316/Angus & Robertson Correspondence, vol. 828, pp. 1–5.) From *Billy Boils* are listed only: 'The Old Bark School[: An Echo]', 'The Drover's Wife' and 'When the Sun Went Down'. The handwritten statement at the top of the first of the three folios that make up the Schedules unequivocally links the typed list to the Agreement of 23 June 1896. The Agreement passed ownership to A&R of the contents of *In the Days* and *Billy Boils* 'and in all his other prose and verse works which have been printed or published in any form previous to the date of this Agreement . . . any works omitted from the said Schedules are nevertheless to be taken as included in this Assignment and Agreement'.

[28] For his signed pencil sketch 'Henry Lawson 1896', see Frontispiece. Syer (1854–1911) lived in North Sydney. He may have helped in some way with the production of A. B. Paterson's collection *The Man from Snowy River* (1895): the Dixson Library, SLNSW copy (89/568) is inscribed: 'To Walter Syer, with the Publishers' compliments & thanks'. See further http://daao.org.au/bio/walter-syer/

[29] See *Commentaries* 97, 117, 135, 145, 147.

[30] It is possible that Roderick mixed-up Syer's extant list for the double volume with the supposed one for *Billy Boils*. The extant list of stories and sketches is headed 'Bulletin ~~Selections~~ Division' (i.e. division into the two halves of the double volume). Nothing from *Billy Boils* appears on it but GR later (c. 1917) in error annotated it in ink: 'This was Walter Syers suggestions for W. the BB./ GR' (ML MSS 314/234–236, filed at A1890, p. 149).

Only *Life* lists Roderick's sources systematically (pp. 402–14). 'Transcripts of Lawson business records, copies of Lawson's agreements, assignments and authorities' are mentioned under the heading 'Angus and Robertson Ltd, Sydney', one major item in the 'Colin Roderick

purpose to that of the extant Schedule. Syer's list would have represented an 'original selection' for working purposes.[31] In contrast, the Schedule was, in relation to the prose, mainly a list of all of the other stories and sketches that Angus & Robertson was now purchasing, in addition to the contents of *While the Billy Boils*. This was pursuant to the original Agreement of 26 July 1895.[32]

Papers' – a collection that itself is not given a location, perhaps because in 1991 when *Life* appeared he was still disbursing it. Roderick consigned his papers in tranches to NLA during 1965–98 (a very large collection: principally MS 1578) and to the library of Charles Darwin University 1994–96 (uncatalogued large collection), and there is a smaller collection in ML (MSS 1221). However, a search by staff of ML (which acquired the Agreements), enquiries of HarperCollins (which took over A&R in the 1980s) and a search of Colin Roderick's papers (as above) failed to locate the missing document.

It may come to light when the cataloguing of ML MSS 3269 is completed (see n. 36 below), but several other confusions on Roderick's part reduce one's confidence. In his commentaries on the stories 'A Narrow Escape', 'Two Boys at Grinder Bros', 'Taking Stiffner Down' and 'An Oversight of Steelman's', Roderick mentions their appearance on the Schedule because they were not included in *Billy Boils*; but he does not state whether they were also on Syer's list. However, of the five items, 'Taking Stiffner Down' was in fact *not* listed in the original Schedule (see n. 27 above). Roderick also states that 'On a Good Tucker Track' [later called 'On the Tucker Track'] was 'originally intended for inclusion' (*Commentaries* 124). However, Jose's report on 'A Good Tucker Track', still in manuscript form (ML MSS 314/41, p. 205), is dated 27 October 1896, showing that it did not show up until after *Billy Boils* was published. Roderick further claims that 'Taking Stiffner Down', a manuscript in Bertha's hand never published in HL's lifetime, was 'undoubtedly written down especially for inclusion in *While the Billy Boils*' (*Commentaries* 69). The manuscript is on lined notepaper but lacks the borders on all four sides of the notepaper she used for another two stories that were incorporated ('For Auld Lang Syne' and 'The Geological Speiler'), and Roderick does not note the difference. It raises the possibility that the story was copied at a different time; so Roderick's claim remains unproven. (The manuscript is in vol. 3 of Henry Lawson, Miscellaneous Manuscripts: Prose, ML MSS 314/152–154, filed at A1862, pp. 249–56.)

'Chicken Pies' and 'It Was Awful' – both of which Roderick states appeared on the Syer list for *Billy Boils* (see Chapter 5 n. 7) – do appear on the extant Syer list for the later double volume; and, of the pieces mentioned above that Roderick states appeared on the *Billy Boils* Schedule, all except 'Taking Stiffner Down' appear on the extant Syer list.

[31] *Commentaries* 64, 124.
[32] ML MSS 3269/Lawson, Henry – papers re 1894–1949, vol. 386, fols. 77–83: this summary refers to Schedules, one of which must be the one Roderick refers to, but not to any preliminary list by Syer. Item 3 of the summary is: 'Copy of list headed LAWSON COPYRIGHTS. "Everything published serially in any newspaper prior to 23 June 1896 bought by us under agt. [agreement] of that date'. That this meant prose *and* verse is confirmed in a letter from GR to HL of 8 February 1897, occasioned by their temporarily falling-out: 'We do not intend to publish any new work of yours and of the whole of the works in prose and verse sold to us by you under the agreement of June 23rd 1896, we desire to retain the copyright only of the following [principally, the contents of *While the Billy Boils* and *In the Days*, including the versions of poems that appeared originally in newspapers]': see *Letters* 424. Further proof is that HL received £70 on 24 June 1896, only £42 of which was for *Billy Boils*. A&R performed

The final absence that the present account must attempt to bridge is that later memoirs do not help to clarify the sequence of events that led to the publication of *While the Billy Boils* on 29 August 1896. As those events, if they could be retrieved, would bear on the contents of the collection, and would show how Lawson's opportunity for revising the texts of the stories and sketches chosen was affected, an analysis of the evidence yielded by the extant printer's copy itself needs to be attempted instead. This is the subject of the next chapter.

It and subsequent chapters refer to various ledgers, letterbooks and other records maintained by Angus & Robertson in the second half of the 1890s. Appendix 4 provides an overview of them and puts into context the records that have already been mentioned in text and footnotes. One aspect requires attention here.

By the early 1930s the printer's copy used for the typesetting of *While the Billy Boils* in 1896 had been sent to London for binding into two green morocco volumes. They were to be uniform with others enclosing materials of literary and historical value selected from the firm's papers, which George Robertson – who had become highly experienced in the rare books and Australiana trade – was preparing for sale. He had begun the process of selecting by 1917; the archive would ultimately become MSS 314 at the Mitchell Library.[33] The clippings of Lawson's

---

a total buyout of HL's new copyrights from the intervening periods again on 27 August 1898 (prose only, in the Agreement for what became *On the Track and Over the Sliprails*; ML MSS 3269/316/Angus & Robertson Correspondence, vol. 828, pp. 167–81), 18 July 1899 (verse only: *ibid.* vol. 829, pp. 1–19) and 8 January 1903 (referred to, *ibid.*, vol. 829, p. 1).

[33] The collection 'of 149 bound volumes of papers, together with a substantial number of unbound letters and documents', including printer's copy in various formats of many important literary publications, was purchased in April 1933. GR had had copies of significant letters from the firm's Letterbooks copy-typed for inclusion. Using the Melbourne bookseller A. H. Spencer as an intermediary, he had first offered the collection to Sir William Dixson for £7,000 (knowing that the firm's papers would finally go to the Mitchell Library as part of the Dixson bequest) and then, when he declined, to the Mitchell Library itself, which paid £4,500: Brian Fletcher, *Magnificent Obsession: The Story of the Mitchell Library, Sydney* (Crows Nest, NSW: Allen & Unwin, 2007), pp. 119–21. See further 'Provenance Note' and 'Administrative History' in *Guide to the Angus & Robertson Archives* (a description of ML MSS 314); and the first, engaging attempt to weave a story of the firm around a selection of GR's correspondence drawn from MSS 314: Anthony Barker, *George Robertson: A Publishing Life in Letters* (1982 as *Dear Robertson*; St Lucia: University of Queensland Press, 1993).

stories in MSS 314 that would serve as printer's copy for *While the Billy Boils* (now filed as A1867–8) were originally prepared for the purpose of Lawson's revision and correction by being affixed to sheets of large paper stock, some of which were the blank verso of publishers' circulars or advertisements. These are now only partially visible when held up to the light as they were ultimately stuck down onto sturdy larger sheets of a uniform size for the binding in London.[34] A separate archive of Angus & Robertson business papers, selected by Mitchell Curator of Manuscripts Paul Brunton in late 1976 and early 1977, became MSS 3269.[35] This is the location of the ledgers, letterbooks and many of the other documents cited in this study.[36]

---

[34] A1867 consists of 89 folios and A1868 of 101. They may be viewed at http://hdl.handle.net/2123/8425 and in small formats at http://acms.sl.nsw.gov.au/item/itemDetailPaged.aspx?itemID=446554 (accessed 26 July 2012).

[35] See Paul Brunton, 'The Angus & Robertson Archives', *Bibliographical Society of Australia and New Zealand Bulletin*, 4 (1980), 191–201.

[36] MSS 3269 remains incompletely catalogued. Accordingly, the following lists were used: *(1)* a handwritten draft description by Louise Anemaat Sections I–XII (compiled before June 2002); *(2)* superseded by a typescript, 'ANGUS & ROBERTSON LTD – Business records, 1880–1974', rearranging some box numbering (watermark-dated 24 August 2007); and *(3)* supplemented by Anemaat's 'Alphabetical List of Subject Files of Correspondence' (2011).

CHAPTER 4

THE REVISION AND COPY-EDITING OF *WHILE THE BILLY BOILS*

LAWSON AND ARTHUR W. JOSE

ONE central document bears witness to the processes of revision and editing of the copy prepared for the typesetters of *While the Billy Boils*. Filed at A1867–8 in the Mitchell Library, its mounted clippings of Lawson's stories and sketches from newspapers, magazines and *Short Stories in Prose and Verse* have been marked-up by multiple hands. The most significant are those of Lawson and of his copy-editor Arthur W. Jose (1863–1934). Educated in Bristol and Oxford, Jose came to Australia as a young man. He became a teacher, poet and a university extension lecturer; and he acted as reader for Angus & Robertson over many years. His *A Short History of Australasia* (1899) would be a great success. Deeply committed to Imperial federation and said to possess a 'cocksure manner' that made him appear arrogant to some, he became a correspondent for the *Times* and would serve as editor-in-chief of the first *Australian Encyclopaedia* (Angus & Robertson, 1925, 1926).[1] In *The Romantic Nineties* he described himself as having been in 1898, when working for Angus & Robertson, 'a comparatively young and callous type of sub-editor': by 'callous', the context makes clear, he meant self-confidently interventionist.[2]

On A1867–8 the title of many of the stories whose clippings occupy more than one page was provided in pencil to avoid later confusion for the typesetters; the hand on several but not all of those that have

[1] R. Lamont, 'Jose, Arthur Wilberforce', in *ADB*, ix. 523–4 [p. 524].
[2] Arthur W. Jose, *The Romantic Nineties* (Sydney: A&R, 1933), p. 47.

the titling is George Robertson's, including the stories whose clippings come from *Short Stories in Prose and Verse*[3] as well as 'Hungerford' and '"Tom's Selection."' As Lawson changed the title of the latter to 'Settling on the Land' when he came to revise it, Robertson was evidently preparing the clippings for Lawson's use. This accords with a list of duties on folio 18 of the firm's 'Private' Letterbook, dated 12 January 1896. 'GR' is given for 'Publishing Department. Books in preparation'. 'GR & MacC [Hugh Maccallum]' are given for 'Books when published' in the same department. The newspaper sources of the clippings for *While the Billy Boils* are sometimes given in lead pencil when not a printed part of the clipping itself; but this hand is unidentified, as are the hands involved in the roughly inscribed foliations in coloured pencil or crayon and another numbering more carefully inscribed in lead pencil. (The evidence provided by these numberings is considered below.)

The majority of the clippings show an alternation of the hands of Lawson and Jose. Mostly Lawson worked first, then Jose, but occasionally the other way round. The textual note for each story in the Eggert and Webby edition of *While the Billy Boils* states the order, which is sometimes obvious when there is a series of rewordings. But, more often, establishing the order requires a search for less significant indications: for example, alternations or overrulings of punctuation and the making good of defective copy.

Sometimes the story went back to the first hand for final adjudication: usually, but not always, this was Lawson. He typically wrote first in lead pencil and confirmed in ink, usually red but occasionally black. His pen was thick-nibbed. He often then rubbed out his pencillings, but not always and not completely. Jose wrote with a very fine-nibbed black pen; his inscriptions in this medium are usually tiny but clear. He wrote with a distinctive capital *E* used in lower-case positions. The fact that he

---

[3] I.e. 'The Union Buries its Dead, 'The Drover's Wife', '[The Bush Undertaker]' and 'Macquarie's Mate'; but the pencil titling of '"Rats"' is apparently not in GR's hand. Its characteristics have been determined from the 'Private' Letterbook 1895–1906 (ML MSS 3269/71/3): his small *k* and *s* and *d*, and his capital *H* and *T* and *C*, as well as his very distinctive initials, were indicative in these comparisons.

missed some obvious typos suggests that the copy-editing was done at some speed, and in fact he would charge Angus & Robertson for only twelve hours of work for the job.

Jose as copy-editor

Jose's effect as copy-editor on the texts of the stories and sketches of *While the Billy Boils* has been the cause of some debate. In his *Commentaries* of 1985, Colin Roderick saw Jose's work as largely unwarranted, mechanistic interference, whose textual outcome, in his edition of the stories, Roderick nevertheless felt obligated to accept. In two articles in 1990 and 1991, themselves preceded by a doctoral thesis on Jose, Teresa Pagliaro presented a more nuanced view of an intelligent editor, responsive to Lawson's intentions but seeking to disarm, by astute textual changes, what he anticipated as likely objections from British reviewers. They had criticised Rudyard Kipling's successful short-story collections in the early 1890s for their tendency to include distasteful details of Anglo-Indian colonial life in the name of realism. Pagliaro also argued that, for similar reasons, Jose wanted Lawson to signal a clearer linguistic divide between the down-at-heel characters who populate his stories and the yarner–narrator that Lawson gradually developed (Marsters, Mitchell) – or, failing that, to include subtle signals of distance between the narrator and the author. She concurs with Doug Jarvis's earlier argument that there was 'an increased interest in the principles of fictional technique' at the *Bulletin*, especially those of realism.[4] Pagliaro then broadens this interest to include Jose and quotes Robertson's exasperation with it when arranging for Hugh Maccallum to work on proofs of Paterson's *Rio Grande's Last Race* (1902): 'M. has considerable knowledge of technique (an opinion isn't considered worth

---

[4] Doug Jarvis, 'Lawson, the *Bulletin* and the Short Story', *Australian Literary Studies*, 11 (1983), 58–66. Pagliaro's unpublished PhD thesis is 'Arthur Wilberforce Jose 1863–1934: An Anglo-Australian', 1990, University of Sydney. Her articles are: 'Jose's Editing of *While the Billy Boils*', *Bibliographical Society of Australia and New Zealand Bulletin*, 14 (1990), 81–93; and 'A. W. Jose: Angus & Robertson Editor', *ibid.*, 15 (1991), 11–19.

a damn unless this word is dragged in)'.[5] While this probably implicates Jose, extant evidence of his habits as a copy-editor of prose fiction suggests that he was less doctrinaire or analytical than pragmatic.

Lawson and Jose had a preliminary discussion about their common strategy for converting the clippings into a satisfactory form for the typesetters of *While the Billy Boils*. Lawson must have offered to housestyle as he went. Spellings were a particular problem, as Jose subsequently reported to Edward Dyson when Dyson was revising his *Rhymes from the Mines*, published by Angus & Robertson in December 1896:

> I believe Mr Robertson has said something about the spelling. I was talking to Henry Lawson about his, & he agreed that (a) there ought to be no *useless* mis-spelling (i.e. 'sez', because it doesn't indicate a mis-pronunciation) (b) it is simpler to leave the g's in: people will drop them in reading if they usually do so. His tales are g'd almost everywhere in the book.[6]

If the verb 'agreed' is indicative of the transaction, of who was leading the way, it was nevertheless a practice that Lawson willingly participated in. So Lawson, when revising the stories, conventionalised or toned down the dialect spellings, including his frequent, and deliberate, 'trav'lers'.[7] If he had originally been trying for a special effect in dialectal spelling, that effect would be dissipated by a resumption of the conventional form, which could draw no attention to itself. He was evidently prepared to accept that outcome.

Lawson also marked on various clippings general instructions to the typesetter to convert all double inverted commas to single, to expand all verbs ending with '—in" to '—ing', all cases of 'an" to 'and': see Illustration 1 opposite page 116. He expanded figures, monetary amounts (for example, '9s.6d.') and abbreviated initials (as in 'N. S. Wales'). Lawson

---

[5] ML MSS 314/66, p. 245, GR to R. Thomson (who succeeded Maccallum at A&R in 1898) [c. 1902].
[6] ML MSS 314/28, p. 805: this is one of Jose's four pages of notes, apparently about the first proofs of Dyson's *Rhymes from the Mines*: see further, Appendix 1.
[7] Interestingly, 'Labor' is marked to become 'Labour', one indication of a gradual shift in Australian orthography and locating it in professional *book* printing.

also crossed out nearly all lines of asterisks serving as section breaks within stories. (Often this was only a confirmation; the preparer of the clippings had usually done this in pencil already.) Lawson marked the great majority of individual examples in each of these categories; but not being a copy-editor by profession, he missed a percentage of them. Jose caught many but not all of the remainder in the stories that he worked on.

Comparative evidence of Jose's working habits is found in the printer's copy for a revised edition of *In the Days*, published in January 1900. The document is a printed copy of the 1896 first edition with markings in the hands of 'JF', Jose and Lawson.[8] Lawson has usually either erased pencillings of minor corrections or confirmed them in red ink; the pencillings must have been done prior to his stint. The pencilling hand is Jose's, who has written on page 36: 'Eng. reviews will say "Why didn't he take trouble enough to *finish* his work"', and on page 63: 'why misspelt when it doesn't represent any slang pronunciation?'. This refers to 'mustarsh' on the first line on the page. Lawson replies: 'I dunno HL.' He has then written in pencil and then red-inked over the top: 'moustache'. This shows that, even after the experience of working on *While the Billy Boils* with Jose, Lawson remained attached to his own spellings (which he also continued to use in his personal correspondence). He had evidently not accepted Jose's view that such spellings were merely 'oldfashioned'.[9] Most of the other pencilled corrections are added commas; Lawson mostly confirms them.

A letter from Robertson to Jose of 27 February 1896 about a submitted manuscript hints at the treatment Robertson and Jose had agreed was commonly needed to make a work publishable:

> The White Waratah.
> We want to know in writing

---

[8] ML C871. 'JF' is identified by Roderick (*Collected Verse* I. p. xxx) as J. F. Archibald but may be John Farrell, who reviewed the first edition for the *Daily Telegraph* on 15 February 1896 and signed the review 'J.F.'. In C871 the JF initials do not match Archibald's (as in a letter to his father, 28 June 1904: ML A3213, p. 25). The comments are usually to do with what 'JF' judges to be failures in metre and sometimes imprecisions of diction.

[9] Another example occurs on p. 194, first line, re 'bound'ry'. Jose writes 'These abbreviations are oldfashioned when they make no difference in the pronunciation'.

> 1. Do you think it would sell
> 2 Is it well enough written to go straight to the Printer without any 'fading'[10]

The term *fading* seems to imply the removal of eccentricities and the finishing-off, which books, as opposed to newspaper printings, were believed to require. The assumption is that a book decorum was needed. Jose was only doing for Angus & Robertson's authors what editors in his period and ever since have felt obliged to do: stand in as first reader and try to mediate between the intentions of the author, as best he could construe them, and such expectations of the readership, especially reviewers, as might affect the fortunes of the work in the relevant marketplace. So the question of the copy-editor's intentions and working methods becomes important to the present account.

Kipling as Jose's model

Jose would have had Kipling's stories in mind. Kipling's invention of his brash young narrator in *Plain Tales from the Hills* (1890) – implicitly of middle-class Anglo-Indian military background – solved the problem of getting rapidly into the story and getting it told, without a slow accumulation of significant detail in good, modern realist fashion or the, by then, old-fashioned, sometimes longwinded method of creating an omniscient and trustworthy narrator. Avoiding this and other dangers of omniscience is what a first-person narrator could provide. Kipling's use of casual idiomatic language and slang by such a narrator was not itself new. But Kipling's narrator's knowingness of address to the subject matter that causes each story to begin in the most abrupt way *in medias res*, and the clipped air of second-person intimacy with the reader that the narrator assumes, must have seemed fresh and welcome to contemporary readers, especially given its vigour and self-confidence. The stories in Kipling's first collection mostly deal with mad, unreasoning or frustrated love, dissipation, pig-headed pride or other behaviour that pushes the central

---

[10] In 'Authors Letter Book', 1895–97, ML MSS 3269/71/4, fol. 137. The author's name is not given and there is no record of the work being published.

character beyond the pale of Anglo-Indian and, implicitly, middle-class standards of respectability. There is plenty of room for humour and pathos in this kind of story where everything is scaled back to the brash narrator's capacity to understand. He presents himself as a compulsive storyteller, but he admits there are things he cannot explain, which must remain mysteries to him and can only be gestured at or dismissed. This provides, for readers who detect the subtlety, a satisfying handing-over of interpretative responsibility to them.

There is no class desertion signalled in the Kipling narrator's slangy language, once his character and relative youth are taken into account. Nevertheless some reviewers criticised the slanginess as a needless vulgarity;[11] and some readers would have reacted against such questionable subject matter as respectable men driven to drink, an Oxford man gone native, and British ladies becoming near-victims of adulterous passion in the hill stations of colonial India. The stories imply that isolation from Home, a debilitating climate and exotic culture can lead Britons into strange behaviours. *Robbery Under Arms* had suffered similar criticisms upon its first appearance in London in book form in 1888. There were complaints about the reader's having to keep close company with a slangy first-person narrator, who was a working man and bushranger, and having to look at 'vulgar ruffianism' through his eyes.[12]

Although the offence was a mixed one (language and subject matter) in Kipling's case, his narrator's slanginess is presented in highly conventional ways. Grammar is not compromised, nor standard spellings; and an educated class confidence communicates itself through the young narrator's brashness. Lawson's narrators lack this confidence – but neither do they need it, for they have another kind.

In 'Two Dogs and a Fence', for instance, the very choice of the subject matter presupposes the suburban life of the streets where there are fences

[11] Pagliaro quotes Quiller-Couch accusing Kipling of 'facile vulgarity' and Humphrey Ward, W. E. Henley and R. L. Stevenson criticising his style: 'Jose's Editing', p. 83.
[12] See Introduction, Rolf Boldrewood, *Robbery Under Arms* (St Lucia: University of Queensland Press, 2005), ed. Paul Eggert and Elizabeth Webby, p. liv.

both to keep dogs in and to keep other dogs out. The narrator Mitchell is only notionally present, but his appearance in the first paragraph creates the storytelling situation, which in turn strikes the tonal level, the idiomatic register, and readies us for speech-like rhythms in which observations about the typical behaviour of two dogs on either side of a fence will, in a new way, *make* sense where there was none before, and certainly not in the dogs. We are being primed, in other words, for a yarn, and this is what we get: 'The inside dog generally starts it.' We do not demand that 'it' have a grammatical antecedent since we are used to waiting for such revelations: that is the nature of the yarn. The storyteller-cum-suburban-philosopher may withhold as much as he wishes for greater effect.

When Jose came to edit this story he passed over this slightly ungrammatical sentence and did not countermand the outside dog's later intimating that the inside dog 'is worse than a flaming old slut'. But he lifted Mitchell's 'a stinkin' fuss' to 'a stinking fuss', overturned a double negative (the outside dog 'never wants to have a disagreement with nobody') and changed a comma to a semicolon – undoubtedly done as part of a change that would lend structure to what he must have judged too rambling a sentence. However, its parasyntactical form prior to the change perfectly captured Mitchell's anger at the 'sneering sort of civil way' of 'a good many peaceful men' that 'makes you want to knock their heads off, and who never start a row, but keep it going'.[13]

Lawson's experiments with presentation of wording are thus intrinsic to the narration, especially from 1893, not something that could later be harmlessly eliminated. The non-genteel world of this sketch is not – as Jose may have expected it to be – ironically or comically condescended to by a choice of language and syntax able to confirm the alliance of writer and reader in a shared educational and class superiority. This must have posed a problem for Jose, and to some extent the absent class confidence was made good by the standardisings he required. Although sympathetic to Lawson's employment of the idiom of his simple and

[13] See Eggert and Webby. Jose changed 'heads off, and' to 'heads off; men'.

outback characters, Jose evidently felt he needed to put boundaries on its use so as not to alienate reviewers and thus deter would-be purchasers.

There is no evidence, however, that Jose articulated as a conscious policy, either to Lawson or to himself, Pagliaro's subtle consideration that the Home reader might tend to identify the semi-literate yarner-narrator with the author and would, despite the contradiction, expect standard English spellings and presentation from his mouth – a conventional 'finish' – so as not to signal a class desertion or educational incapacity. According to Pagliaro, the 'author's display of skill' would, additionally or alternatively, signal a needed distance between the casual idiom of the narrator and Lawson's own.[14]

It is not clear that anyone at the time could have enunciated the supposed technical problem with this sophistication.[15] Although claims and manifestos about the artistry of realist and especially naturalist fiction were being voiced, prose fiction was not properly embedded into anglophone critical discourse as an aesthetic form until after Henry James's prefaces to the New York (revised) edition of his novels (1907–09) were gathered by R. P. Blackmur in *The Art of the Novel* (1934). The sophistication Pagliaro's case assumes is more an achievement of the New Criticism. Wayne Booth's *The Rhetoric of Fiction* (1961) was one of the more notable exercises in stylistic analysis and in the exposure and definition of narrative strategies. Kipling's narrator could henceforth be seen as an intentionally unreliable one, whereas for Kipling, 70-odd years before, it had probably been more a case of finding the glove that nicely fitted the authorial hand.

Similarly with Boldrewood. It was not until 1950 that any critic realised that the breakthrough of *Robbery Under Arms* lay in the liberating language of the first-person narrator, his 'colonial vernacular'. In the 1890s the achievement was typically seen as historical or romantic. The comment, 'Mr. Boldrewood has struck a new patch in the way of

---

[14] Pagliaro, 'Jose's Editing', p. 82.
[15] The closest Jose appears to get, and in relation to verse rather than fiction, occurs in his criticism of Edward Dyson: 'It spoils the effect of dialect pieces if [other] stories told as by you personally are badly spelt' (ML MSS 314/28, p. 809).

storytelling', was as technical as the commentary got.[16] Verse, being the older form, was far more susceptible to such commentary by the 1890s, and there Jose was certainly articulate, especially in relation to faulty metres and forced rhymes; and it is verse to which Robertson is referring in his letter about 'The White Waratah'. Objections to 'pure melodrama' and 'ultra-sentimental[ity]' – which suggest his then modern-day preference for realist approaches – also occur in Jose's notes on Dyson's *Rhymes from the Mines*.

There is no direct evidence that Lawson had read Kipling's stories, though he would have at least encountered discussions of them or references to them, and he could apparently quote from Kipling's poetry at will.[17] Even without that direct influence, there is no mystery in their both creating innovative styles of narration at much the same time: just as Twain and Boldrewood did, more or less simultaneously and in ignorance of one another, in the early 1880s in writing the first extended first-person narrations by working-class narrators in *The Adventures of Huckleberry Finn* (1884) and *Robbery Under Arms* (serialised 1882–83). The flexibilities and possibilities for humour that Bret Harte had been introducing into short-story narration since around 1870 would also have been in Lawson's mind.

Lawson's colonial vernacular

The vernacular that Lawson had been developing in the newspaper versions of his stories, especially from 1893, would be toned down during the revision and copy-editing phase. Lawson wanted success in Britain; Jose would not have had to apply much pressure to secure his agreement. Lawson had already acknowledged a need for editorial assistance in his Preface to *Short Stories in Prose and Verse*. A largely self-taught man, he

---

[16] Review, *Daily Telegraph* (Melbourne), quoted in Introduction, *Robbery Under Arms*, ed. Eggert and Webby, p. lxv; cf. pp. lxxiv–lxxix. The 1950 critic was Frank Sargeson: quoted, ibid., p. lxxx.
[17] According to Bertram Stevens in a handwritten biographical essay 'Henry Lawson', dated April 1917: in 1897 'we wd. generally walk down town, drinking at various pubs., talking about poetry, reciting snatches of Lawson or Kipling & swapping yarns ... he knew Kipling pretty well' (ML A1889, fol. 13). Cf. Chapter 1 n. 2 and *Letters* 82.

would not have wished to be dismissed as uneducated; he was vulnerable to this criticism throughout his life and never became a well-read man.

Lawson's rendering of that colonial or outback vernacular helped to provide the habitus for the events of his stories. It is clear that for him language was not only a tool, a symbolic notation of intended meaning. Language did not just convey meaning transparently. It also pointed: it was indexical. His frequent use of inverted commas around words conditioned their meaning by locating the event either within the character's habit and outlook or by pointing up the difference between the narrator's normal idiom and the linguistic expectations of the environment he finds himself beholden to: those of his landlady, for instance. The markings help to settle the reader into the story; they acclimatise us and thus create the undergirding for the disturbance to that climate that the story will enact or recount. Their deletion in printer's copy of *While the Billy Boils* tended to remove the effect at which Lawson had originally aimed.

His demotic narrator-types could make effective use of this technique. The marked terms are usually and simultaneously an expression of empathy rather than, as they might have been in the hands of another author, patronising distaste temporarily withheld for comic purposes. The same is not true of Kipling, and this is one way of defining Lawson's distinctive achievement. In the social sense, Lawson was not in Kipling's class, and tidying up his prose to give that false impression was to court the danger of dulling or even neutralising the special qualities of narration that Lawson had been developing.

In the majority of the stories in *While the Billy Boils* the narrator does not have a marked Mitchell-type personality. (Similarly, in Kipling's Mulvaney stories, the narrator figure very soon retreats into the background.) In Lawson's 'Going Blind', for instance, the first-person narrator's use of terms within inverted commas insists on the difference of the idiolect of the boarding house and then on that of the nearly blind bushman, Jack, from that of the city-slicker narrator (see Illustration 2). But the narrator's sympathy for Jack's plight intensifies as the story goes on, so that the distance between narrator and character closes. This is one of the saddest stories Lawson ever wrote. Nevertheless in revision in late 1895 he altered the narrator's ''em' to 'them' even though the former suggested a bond, at once linguistic and sympathetic, between narrator and character.

This suggests a more general consideration. Lawson knew roughly who read his stories in the *Worker*: shearers, rouseabouts, unionists, union officials, labourers and other bush workers, and sympathisers in the city. If his narrating position had to be above that of his bush characters he could nevertheless at least quote them; he could draw attention to the language habits that indexed their thinking, such as it was, and signal when they had to adjust to the habits of landladies and officialdom. (The *Worker* version of 'Remailed' – see Eggert and Webby – is a good example of the latter.) Lawson knew instinctively that his people lived *in* their language, of which he was the self-appointed chronicler. It was their language that gave him access to them.

Lawson's prose rhythms are typically speech-based, as Colin Roderick has memorably pointed out:

> traditionalists . . . resented his dislocation of their romantic idiom. Lawson, uneducated in the leisured prose of the nineteenth century, wrote in the plain, speech-based idiom of the bush and slum . . . when reading him [one feels] that he is speaking confidentially, and not to a vast anonymous public.[18]

That Lawson was innocent of the conventions of leisured prose is far from certain, for he participated in a print culture; that he did not naturalise them in his own prose is clear. It was something at which he had to work and with which he had to experiment if he was to achieve a compensating naturalness of expression. So his down-at-heel narrators' sentences are often parasyntactical rather than strictly syntactical. Then, in the next story perhaps, he will strike a self-consciously educated pose. Witness Lawson's employment of the first-person plural – as if he were

---

[18] Colin Roderick, 'Introduction' to Henry Lawson, *Short Stories and Sketches 1888–1922*, ed. Roderick (Sydney: A&R, 1972), p. xiv; and cf. *Commentaries* 106.

the newspaper itself, or the editor speaking for it as, for example, in 'Some Reflections on a Voyage across Cook's Straits (N.Z.)' and 'Remailed'. The prevailing irony is one of the medley of tones, or narrative dispositions, that he is successively striking.

In other stories an indirect free style allows him to keep in sympathetic contact with the character's thought and speech rhythms. This omniscient narrating (as in '"Dossing Out" and "Camping"') is not much different from Lawson's first-person style since, in the latter, he soon falls out of the scene: for example in dealing with the travellers' obsession of exactly where the Dunbar sank at Sydney Heads (in 'Coming Across. A Study in the Steerage') or the experience of losing a half-sovereign (in 'Some Reflections on a Voyage across Cook's Straits'), which he renders in the second person, thus drawing the reader into the narrator's conundrum. Generally, the first-person narrator prefers to look and listen rather than take part, since doing the latter takes him into a more troubling relationship with his readers. When the first-person narrator is represented as Lawson himself ('"Board and Residence"', '"In a Wet Season"') there is a touch of self-indulgent whining that he escapes only when he neutrally records what he sees.

Because the accompanying scholarly edition has the advantage of presenting the stories and sketches in chronological order and in their original newspaper texts, Lawson's unfolding experimentation with modes of narration becomes visible. Similarly, recording in foot-of-page apparatus Lawson's and Jose's alterations for *While the Billy Boils* – rather than incorporating them into the texts – exposes the veneer of book decorum that the stories received when collected. Its collaboratively achieved nature need not, the edition implies, be the end of the textual inquiry. That decorum can be newly understood in terms of what it was for.

This editorial approach has the potential to allow existing arguments to be tested and new ones in the future to be clarified as they are formulated. For instance, in his *Commentaries* volume, Colin Roderick argues that most of the *–ing* endings, the completion of contractions such as *'em*, and the standardisings were not solely at Jose's behest but relate to

Lawson's changed understanding of Mitchell in 1895 from his original one in 1893. The last in the initial, colloquial style, Roderick notes, was 'Another of Mitchell's Plans for the Future' (*Bulletin*, 1 July 1893); and the lifting in register had already started in the 1894 Mitchell stories. In 'Our Pipes' (*Bulletin*, 11 May 1895 but possibly written in 1894), Mitchell has 'settled into place as a quizzically philosophical intermediary between Lawson and the reader'; henceforth he will be more purely a narrator rather than an actor in events.[19] The regularisings for *While the Billy Boils* of 1895–96 can be seen, according to this argument, as a case of the earlier stories being made consistent with Lawson's changed style. This would help explain his acquiescence in Jose's requirements.

However, examination of A1867–8 shows the situation is not clear-cut. For instance, 'Shooting the Moon' (*Worker*, 22 September 1894 and thus supposedly after the end of the colloquial style) has, and retains in *While the Billy Boils*, Mitchell's saying 'yer', 'He seen Tom', and 'There was two beds'; but the *-in'* endings no longer occur. In regularising speech and some colloquial usages in the earlier stories Jose and Lawson were only superficially and in some cases mechanically reforming them, probably to give an appearance of homogeneity and to try to solidify the Mitchell stories into a series.

Two more Mitchell stories were created from Marsters stories. Marsters had originally come into published being in the *Worker* in July–August 1893 in '"Some Day"' and 'A Camp-fire Yarn'.[20] He is less colloquial, his speech is more educated, and he is more philosophical and serious than Mitchell. Despite these considerations, Lawson simply renamed Marsters in the printer's copy. A further Mitchell story was created by renaming 'That Swag' (*Bulletin*, 15 December 1894) as 'Enter Mitchell'. The swagman is described physically ('short, and stout, and bow-legged, and freckled, and sandy'), whereas Mitchell is nowhere described; and the swagman is not otherwise named in the story.[21]

---

[19] *Commentaries* 75–6, 79.
[20] For the dating see Chapter 2 n. 28.
[21] *Commentaries* 72. The new title 'Enter Mitchell' is inscribed in red ink but does not appear to be in HL's hand; perhaps someone sitting next to him asked whether this one could

Whether or not it was intentional, the effect of lifting Mitchell's register meant it became a little closer to that of the now renamed Marsters. Following Jose's guidelines alone could not meld the two conceptions, however, and colloquiality remained a part of Mitchell's character even after the alterations. For example, in 'Mitchell: A Character Sketch' (*Bulletin*, 15 April 1893), the opening sentence is left unchanged by Jose and Lawson: 'It was a very mean station, and Mitchell thought he had better go himself and beard the overseer for tucker.' In comparison, Jose's corrections of ''em' to 'them' and 'agen' to 'again' (but missing or leaving ''spose') look superficial. Mitchell emerges in this and a number of other sketches as the resourceful scrounger, a man of dry, sardonic humour – capacities that are not in Marsters's repertoire. Similarly, in 'A Campfire Yarn', Lawson accepts Jose's prior standardisings of the speech of Marsters's mate ('you was', 'she come'): a mechanical correction and an unthinking acceptance that do not lift the narrator's speech nearer to that of the British reader for they have the opposite effect of bringing the mate's register nearer the already near-standard one of Marsters. They call Pagliaro's defence of Jose's policy into question; he could be quite unsubtle in practice.

Surprisingly, Lawson could be too. The lifting of Mitchell's register from the 1893 stories is often unconvincing.[22] Mitchell's language is thoroughly idiomatic both early and late. As a result, having his *-in'* endings completed and his dialectal spelling ('s'posing') standardised fails to imply a lift in education or class, which is in any case not justified by the account of his youth (in 'Our Pipes'). There is insufficient re-envisioning on Lawson's part for the standardisings to take effect, and there is sometimes a loss in intimacy caused by them.

---

become another Mitchell story and picked up his pen. Roderick speculates it was Walter Syer (*Commentaries* 70), but this is unlikely; the hand more closely resembles Jose's. Syer's hand has irregular slope with untidy indistinct lettering: cf. his letter to Sir William Dixson, 6 June 1902 (tipped-in to Dixson's copy of the luxury issue of *In the Days When the World Was Wide*: SLNSW at DL 89/571). The capital *E* and *M* resemble Jose's: for the *M*, see Jose's letter to Fred Shenstone of A&R, 16 October [c. 1899], ML MSS 314/41, pp. 207–09.

[22] E.g., see the textual apparatus for 'Mitchell Doesn't Believe in the Sack' in Eggert and Webby.

Because (as described in Chapters 5 and 6) the final production stages of *While the Billy Boils* were ad hoc and scrambling, inconsistencies in the planned collaborative revision and copy-editing resulted. For example, in 'On the Edge of a Plain' – which Jose had corrected but which Lawson probably came to late in the process, revised in pencil and failed to confirm in red ink – both of them neglected to correct any of Mitchell's *-in'* endings. And they both neglected to do it in 'Another of Mitchell's Plans for the Future', while also passing over Mitchell's 'what d'yer mean'. Another doubt about the sensitivity of Lawson's discharge of Jose's copy-editorial policy arises in 'That There Dog o' Mine'. Lawson gives Macquarrie [*sic*] the shearer the same linguistic lift as Mitchell receives elsewhere, yet Macquarrie is clearly an uneducated man, often drunk. Jose queried these standardisings: 'doubt if all these ought to be inserted: it's dialogue'. Lawson's strategy is little more than mechanical copy-editing at this point, less sensitive to context than Jose's.

The latter's substantive changes – all of which are recorded in the textual apparatus in the edition – were numerous but by no means overwhelming. Most were shrewd and localised in effect; the most significant ones were requests for deletion of new endings to stories that Lawson had just added or requests for alteration of existing ones. Jose seemed to prefer terse endings, preferably in dialogue. Lawson preferred more resonant endings often achieved via a pulling back to third-person narration that nevertheless remained in touch with the tonal range of the rest of the story and was expressed within its idiomatic register.

The foregoing discussion suggests two conclusions. The first is that the commercial pressure to produce a satisfying collection required partial remouldings of the stories and sketches that inevitably, though to varying extents, compromised the intentions behind, and disguised the nature of, their original texts. The second conclusion is more surprising. The character remouldings show what relatively little resistance Mitchell's imagined character offered Lawson. Indeed, the fact that the stories could absorb them suggests that characterisation was never at their centre. Instead, what emerges as central to many of the stories from 1893 is their settling down into a shared acceptance of hardships, of youth lost, of passions put behind, of comic consolations. It is formed and re-formed in a basic communal setting, quintessentially, between a man and his mate, both of whom are down on their luck, struggling to survive. The acceptance is enacted through story: in the moment of its telling and via the mood it creates. Mitchell becomes the yarn spinner for the sad register; and Steelman for the comic-absurd, after his creation in early 1895.

Other hands evident on printer's copy

The variations in the order of Jose and Lawson's hands on printer's copy suggest a number of stints and probably the staggered receipt of clippings. In addition, there are clippings where Lawson was not involved at all and a small number of cases where hands other than Lawson's and Jose's are evident. A large hand in lead pencil has made several localised corrections in 'The Drover's Wife' and a very few corrections in each of 'A Visit of Condolence' and 'The Story of Malachi'. But no other stories seem to have been affected. It is possible that the hand is George Robertson's, although, if it is, it may seem surprising that he intervened so sparingly. However, Robertson was paying Jose to do the job and must have been a very busy man, as the firm's list of duties makes clear. In 1923, in his notes for *The Auld Shop and the New*, Robertson commented: 'My success in business was probably due to a capacity for organization, and to hard work.'[23] He would have known how and when to delegate.

Another hand – once again, large inscriptions in lead pencil – is evident in 'The Story of Malachi' and 'Our Pipes'. Although there is not much in this hand by which to judge, it has characteristics consistent with Jose's (a capital *H* and the distinctive *e*). On 'An Unfinished Love Story', which Lawson has not touched, there is a fourth, unidentified

---

[23] Page 26.

hand, also using lead pencil. But other than symbols for deletion, there is only one pencilled word in this hand, marking '"cuss"' to be changed to 'swear'. The hand may be (as Roderick affirms) Robertson's, but it is more likely someone else's as the final *r* is not in Robertson's usual shape. 'Steelman's Pupil', which is scarcely edited at all, again has nothing in Lawson's hand on it. The absence of Lawson's markings on these clippings, and the absence of Jose's hand on others – in particular on the only two stories in A1867–8 in holograph manuscript, 'The Geological Speiler' and 'For Auld Lang Syne' – help establish the overall chronology of the volume's production.[24] This is set out in the next chapter.

Another of Roderick's interpretations of the physical evidence is relevant here. He assumes that the pencilled 'CB' initials on several of the folios of A1867–8 are those of Charles Bright (1832–1903), a journalist of some distinction in Melbourne before going to Sydney in 1880. His second wife Annie, a spiritualist, ran the Freethinking literary monthly *Cosmos*, in which a poem by Lawson appeared on 31 March 1896.[25] Roderick also implicitly identifies another set of initials 'GR' as George Robertson's, concluding that Bright and Robertson 'checked' the work of Lawson and Jose before it went for typesetting.[26] However, the GR initials have no similarity to Robertson's in the firm's letterbooks. In the printer's copy (A1867–8), they appear at foot of page along with the initials on other pages of what are evidently those of the workers who typeset them – thus allowing the printer to keep track of payments for work done and (if necessary) fines for poor setting. 'CB' is only one of about sixteen sets of initials on A1867–8, not all of which are fully legible. Inspection of the archives of the New South Wales Typographical Association has allowed

---

[24] The two holograph manuscripts are in the hand of Bertha Bredt, whom HL married on 15 April 1896. The medium is black ink, and HL also revised them in black ink. In the Eggert and Webby edition, the Textual note that comes after each story gives the hands involved and their order of inscription. For the apparent misspelling 'Speiler', see the story's Textual note.
[25] 'After All' (*Collected Verse* I. 303–4).
[26] *Commentaries* 4. In addition, Robertson's sparse copy-editing demonstrably happened before, not after, HL and AJ worked on the clippings: see the Textual note and Commentary for the relevant stories in Eggert and Webby.

the identification of many of them. 'GR' was probably either G. N. Richardson or G. Robinson, and 'CB' was Cosmo Berwick.[27] Roderick's identifications must therefore be dismissed. Given that Robertson was paying Jose to do the editing at this stage, it would have made more sense to become involved later when he would have a clearer view of the contents. This, as we shall see in Chapter 6, he most decisively did – and, when he did, his considerations were scarcely literary at all.

---

[27] Collection T39 at the Noel Butlin Archives, Australian National University, Canberra. The initials on A1867-8 are: 'Hazell', 'JNK', 'RH' and 'RHB', 'CB' or 'CMB', 'G.R.', 'Buxton', 'RP', 'PC', 'CA', 'McA', 'AF', 'NR', 'Shaw', 'SA', 'hHH' and 'JBH'. The Association's mid-yearly reports contained a list of named members, organised by printing firm and 'Other Offices'. Apparently the named listing was only available if the firm had agreed to employ only union members, which a letter of 18 March 1897 from the Association to Websdale, Shoosmith, the printer of *Billy Boils*, suggests it had not.

The identified men below appear in the 'Other Offices' lists (those for 1893–95 were checked). That of 1895 lists: J. N. Kilner [JNK?]; Cosmo Berwick [CB and CMB?]; G. N. Richardson and G. Robinson [GR?]; R. H. Buxton [Buxton?] in 1893, 1895 after having 'returned from Brisbane', and 1896; R. W. Phillips [RP?]; P. Cline [PC?]; A. G. Fatzeus [AF?]; D. Shaw, G. H. Shaw or John Shaw [Shaw?]; and H. H. Hartley [hHH?]. H. B. Hazell is not listed in 1895 but appears in the Association's handwritten subscription list of 1894 with 'Websdale Shoosmith' added. RHB may have been Buxton signing differently *or* H. Breakspere, whose name appears in a Pastebook (T39/61/1) as in arrears while working at Websdale, Shoosmith in 1893.

CHAPTER 5

THE MAKING OF A BOOK
TEXTS AND ILLUSTRATIONS

THE preceding chapter examined the printer's copy for *While the Billy Boils* that has fortuitously survived (A1867–8). Special attention was paid to the revision and editing of the newspaper texts it contains. But there is also much non-textual evidence on this document. Its significance becomes plain when the document is compared to the makeup of the printed edition itself.

From printer's copy to proofs, late 1895 to mid-1896

The order of the stories and sketches in the printer's copy probably reflects their arrangement at the moment the copy went to the typesetter. Lead-pencilled paginations on the first page of each story match those of *While the Billy Boils* as published on 29 August 1896 except for two missing stories ('His Father's Mate' and 'She Wouldn't Speak', dealt with below) and also a 54-page section of the published volume where the arrangement is different. The resultant misnumbering was almost certainly occasioned by a rearrangement of the stories and sketches stemming from a desire to space the illustrations throughout the book.[1]

Because the pencilled paginations reflect an earlier arrangement of the stories than that of the published volume they must have been added to A1867-8 prior to the rearrangement. In the published volume, 'The Drover's Wife' occupies pages 127–38 (see Table 1), but the pencilled pagination on its first page in A1867-8 is 'p169'. Evidently it was not

[1] Printer's copy of *The Man from Snowy River* (ML MSS 314/195, filed at A1909) also has a few pencilled paginations that match the pagination of the published volume of 1895.

TABLE 1: CONTENTS OF THE 1896 EDITION OF *WHILE THE BILLY BOILS*

1	An Old Mate of Your Father's	*pages*	1–6
2	Settling on the Land		7–14
3	Enter Mitchell		15–17
4	Stiffner and Jim (Thirdly, Bill)		18–27
5	When the Sun Went Down		28–31
6	The Man Who Forgot		32–39
7	Hungerford		40–44
8	A Camp-Fire Yarn		45–49
9	His Country—After All		50–56
10	A Day on a Selection		57–65
11	That There Dog o' Mine		66–69
12	Going Blind		70–77
13	Arvie Aspinall's Alarm Clock		78–82
14	Stragglers		83–90
15	The Union Buries Its Dead		91–97
16	On the Edge of a Plain		98–100
17	In a Dry Season		101–105
18	He'd Come Back		106–109
19	Another of Mitchell's Plans for the Future		110–112
20	Steelman		113–116
21	Drifted Back		117–120
22	Remailed		121–126
23	The Drover's Wife		127–138
24	Mitchell Doesn't Believe in the Sack		139–141
25	Shooting the Moon		142–145
26	His Father's Mate		146–160

originally intended to go in between 'Remailed' and 'Mitchell Doesn't Believe in the Sack'. It would have occupied the same page-extent, but at pages 169–80. The reason 'The Drover's Wife' was moved back to page 127 in the volume was probably that, without the move, its illustration and that of '"Dossing Out" and "Camping"' would have been quite close to one another, at pages 160 and 172. In the finished volume, on the other hand, the illustrations (which are placed opposite the text from

27	An Echo from the Old Bark School	161–162
28	The Shearing of the Cook's Dog	163–167
29	'Dossing Out' and 'Camping'	168–172
30	Across the Straits	173–180
31	Steelman's Pupil	181–187
32	An Unfinished Love Story	188–194
33	'Board and Residence'	195–202
34	His Colonial Oath	203–204
35	'Some Day'	205–208
36	A Visit of Condolence	209–215
37	In a Wet Season	216–221
38	'Rats'	222–225
39	Mitchell: a Character Sketch	226–228
40	The Bush Undertaker	229–239
41	Our Pipes	240–244
42	Coming Across—a Study in the Steerage	245–262
43	The Story of Malachi	263–269
44	Two Dogs and a Fence	270–272
45	Jones's Alley	273–289
46	'Brummy Usen'	290–295
47	Bogg of Geebung	296–300
48	She Wouldn't Speak	301–304
49	The Geological Spieler	305–316
50	Macquarie's Mate	317–323
51	Baldy Thompson	324–327
52	For Auld Lang Syne	328–333

Item numbers have been added.

which their captions are taken) are fairly well spaced: the nearest are 34 pages apart and the furthest 60 pages apart.[2]

This is the reason for something that Colin Roderick noticed, without being able to explain it bibliographically: that 'Mitchell Doesn't Believe in the Sack' 'is not so well placed . . . it incongruously follows

---

[2] The first illustration is designated in the Illustrations list as opposite p. 2 (where the text of its caption occurs) and the second as opposite p. 62. But the first one was shifted to serve as a frontispiece. Thereafter the illustrations occur opposite pages 98, 138, 172, 210, 270 and 322.

"The Drover's Wife" . . . and precedes the comic sketch "Shooting the Moon"'.[3] The Mitchell story did not at first do so. Up until the end of 'Remailed' (page 126 in *While the Billy Boils* as published) and from 'Steelman's Pupil' onwards (from page 181), the pencil pagination in A1867–8 matches that of the published volume. The change affected only pages 127–80. The direct link between the pencilled pagination and the volume pagination, together with the requirements of the illustrations necessitating the shift, show that the pencilling was not added by a later collector but during the production process. Determining exactly *when* will better explain why.

The missing stories

Although 'His Father's Mate' and 'She Wouldn't Speak' are not present in A1867–8, they cannot simply have been a late addition intended to make up 'the desired number of pages', as Colin Roderick claims they were.[4] 'His Father's Mate' makes 19 pages in *While the Billy Boils*; once the 19 pages are factored in there is no pagination hiccup either in the published volume or in the pencilled pagination in A1867–8. The story had originally appeared in the *Bulletin* on 22 December 1888 and was collected in *A Golden Shanty: Australian Stories and Sketches in Prose and Verse*, published by the Bulletin Book Company, Sydney, in 1890.

The loss of 'His Father's Mate' from the printer's copy can be explained. If it had been a mounted clipping like the rest it could have been lost or accidentally discarded, particularly if it appeared late in the typesetting process after the rest of the copy had been returned. But the lack of a gap in the pencil pagination means that it almost certainly did not appear late. Probably Lawson marked up an actual copy of *A Golden Shanty* perhaps because it had conveniently wide margins or because the *Bulletin* printing of the story was borrowed and had to be returned. Comparing the two as he went along would have enabled Lawson to retrieve what he considered superior wordings from the *Bulletin* version

[3] *Commentaries* 75.
[4] *Commentaries* 4, 63–4.

and to unpick some of the formalising that the *Golden Shanty* version had received in production. Collation of these two versions with that in *While the Billy Boils* confirms that contamination of the two texts did occur. The book would have easily become dissociated from the rest of the copy in later years, especially when Robertson sent the printer's copy to London for binding. The situation is unique in the volume; it points to the likely source of printer's copy and explains its loss.[5]

'She Wouldn't Speak' is a different case. Roderick points out that the story was not on the preliminary list of contents of the volume apparently prepared by Walter Syer for Angus & Robertson and that some other stories, which do appear on the list, are not in the published volume.[6] But again there is no pagination hiccup in A1867–8, once the story is allowed for. It occupies four pages of *While the Billy Boils*. 'Chicken Pies' and 'It Was Awful' – both of which Roderick states appeared on the Syer list – are quite short but would have occupied five printed pages, so there was not a simple substitution.[7] The clipping of 'She Wouldn't Speak' probably came to hand late, was typeset but then lost.[8] Collation of the newspaper version of 'She Wouldn't Speak' and that in the published

---

[5] Two alternative explanations are less compelling: HL's preparation of a new handwritten fair copy of 'His Father's Mate'; or his markup of *Bulletin* clippings pasted onto larger sheets – except that he did not restore from the *Bulletin* sections deleted in *GS* (e.g., the last three paragraphs of Chapter I): see further, Commentary for the story in Eggert and Webby.

[6] If a contents list prepared by Walter Syer for *Billy Boils* actually existed (see Chapter 3 pp. 84–5), containing the titles of stories subsequently rejected, this would explain how 'The Geological Speiler' (number 49 in the published volume) came to have a lead-pencilled and circled '62' on its first folio, and how 'For Auld Lang Syne' (number 52) came to bear '61'. The third folio of 'An Unfinished Love Story' has, similarly, '56' and 'Bogg of Geebung' is '57'. The numbering could have been copying a list of available contents.

[7] They would have made two pages and just over two pages respectively, once the latter's two lines of asterisks were deleted as the copy-editing policy required. Cf. *Commentaries* 63–4: Roderick appears to imply that there must have been a swap of 'She Wouldn't Speak' *and* 'His Father's Mate' for 'Chicken Pies' and 'It Was Awful', but this cannot be so because of the differing page-extents. (They appear in *Prose Writings* 114 and 111–12.)

[8] 'Baldy Thompson' was at some later stage slotted into the gap left by the absence of 'She Wouldn't Speak', between 'Bogg of Geebung' and 'The Geological Speiler': this is the position it occupies in A1867–8, the binding of which dates to 1917 or later. So this left it in the wrong position apropos the printed volume, but its correct pencil pagination shows there was no change such as there was for 'The Drover's Wife'. This may mean a mix-up of some kind with the return of printer's copy, an attempt to make good when the gap was noticed or an attempt at some stage to disguise it.

volume shows no compelling evidence of authorial revision, which tends to confirm the likelihood of late arrival. Moreover, as we shall see, there was ample time available for these changes to be effected, as well as for the consideration and rejection of other stories.

The sequence of events in production

The sequence of events in the production of *While the Billy Boils*, so far as they can be reconstructed, seems to have been as follows. As we have seen, on 26 July 1895 Lawson had signed an Agreement with Angus & Robertson that quickly consolidated into two volumes: *In the Days When the World Was Wide*, which appeared on 14–15 February 1896, and the still unnamed volume of 'Prose Sketches' advertised at the back of copies of *In the Days* as to appear 'Shortly'. (The advertising section is dated January 1896.) On 23 October 1895 Lawson wrote to a friend: 'My book [*In the Days*] will be out in about two weeks'.[9] He had evidently finished correcting its proofs by then. It had been hard work, and we know from later recollections that the business of writing and especially revising 'The Star of Australasia' with his friend and fellow poet John Le Gay Brereton had been particularly fraught.[10] But at least Lawson was now available to work fulltime on collecting and revising stories for *While the Billy Boils*.

The Agreement of July 1895 had stipulated that the stories would be 'selected by A. & R.' with advice from Brereton and J. F. Archibald. In practice, Robertson's own role in the choice would have been paramount. In due course he would be paying the printer – and would have expected to call the tune in the lead-up to publication. For his part, Lawson, doubtless with help from others, would have to try to locate those stories already printed (or at least those he favoured for the collection), have them mounted for revision, and encourage editors to publish immediately those accepted for publication that had not yet appeared. Archibald and A. G. Stephens at the *Bulletin* were, as we have

---

[9] *Letters* 59.
[10] GR later recalled seeing 'a rough draft of ['The Star of Australasia'] shortly after "When the World Was Wide" agreement was signed' – on 10 October 1895, a successor to the more general Agreement of 26 July (*Collected Verse*, I. 456). See further, Chapter 3 n. 25.

CHAPTER 5 . THE MAKING OF A BOOK

seen, dilatory in this respect, sometimes keeping back stories to balance out the contents of future issues.

It would have made sense for Lawson to keep a copy of his writings. As early as 1892 he had it in mind to produce a collection of his stories, and it was easier to collect and retain clippings than retrieve his bulkier manuscripts from editors of magazines and newspapers and to store them. Being discarded after publication would doubtless have been the usual fate of such manuscripts: both the fair copy used by the publisher and the rough copy by the author, if he had retained it until then. On the other hand, a number of the clippings in A1867–8, and in the Lawson scrapbooks that Angus & Robertson maintained (A1890–A1892), have tears and gaps that Lawson has made good (suggesting that the text was still visible to him somewhere else) – signs of the clippings having been previously affixed to another surface from which they were lifted for the new purpose. Brereton later recalled that, after Lawson got an advance on his new contract (of 26 July 1895), he helped him move out of a cheap boarding house into McGrath's Edinburgh Hotel: 'His worldly goods were in a large sack, and I was rather surprised at its weight . . . togs, scraps of copy, photographs, and a general miscellany'.[11] But even if Lawson aimed to keep a copy of each work, his circumstances and his alcoholic sprees meant that such an archive would have been far from complete.

It is more likely that what Brereton saw were notes and drafts for items that had not yet been published. When the contents of what became *While the Billy Boils* are read in the chronological order of their first printing (as in the Eggert and Webby edition), it can be seen that the subject matter roughly follows Lawson's wanderings and is usually in some way based on his current or recent experience. But occasionally a sketch or story that mines material from an earlier phase will intervene

---

[11] John Le Gay Brereton, 'Henry Lawson', *Art in Australia*, 3rd series, no. 2 (1 November 1922), p. [3] of unpaginated issue. Cf. A. G. Stephens's letter to Arthur Hoey Davis ('Steele Rudd') of 20 July 1897, informing him that the reprinting in volume form of his *Bulletin* stories was being considered: 'Probably you have clippings of your work: if so, I should be glad if you would go over them and mark any improvements you can . . . it would save a little trouble in collection' – and *this* from the publisher of them (Fryer Library, Hayes Papers, UQFL 2/2771).

between others that can only have been written later. For example, '"An Old Mate of your Father's"' reverts to Lawson's earlier years at Eurunderee; it comes amongst a series of outback sketches in mid-1893 following his return from Bourke, probably in March that year (see further, Eggert and Webby xxxix). '"In a Wet Season"', an account of his return, did not appear until December, many months afterwards. While the possibility of deliberate delay at the *Bulletin* office in bringing this and other such sketches immediately forward to publication cannot be ruled out, the simpler explanation that Lawson typically had many items simultaneously in preparation, and that he brought them individually to completion as inspiration struck or material necessity required, is an attractive one. It is underscored by the ending of 'Some Reflections on a Voyage across Cook's Straits (N.Z.)'. In this travel sketch, writing in the (ironic) Royal plural of the newspaper editorial, Lawson recounts:

> Then we crossed the street to a pub and asked for a room, and they told us to go up to No. 8. We went up, struck a match, lit the candle, put our bag in a corner, cleared the looking-glass, &c., off the toilet table, got some paper and a pencil out of our portmanteau, and sat down and wrote this sketch.
> But the candle is going out.

That voyage happened around May 1894; the sketch was published in January 1895 nearly six months after his return to Sydney from New Zealand.

Brereton himself collected Lawson's writings from the newspapers from the day he first came across a Lawson poem in the *Bulletin*, 'The Wreck of the *Derry Castle*', as a Grammar School boy; it appeared on 24 December 1887.[12] When the same problem of tracking down his publications recurred during the gathering of stories and sketches for *On the Track and Over the Sliprails*, Lawson told Angus & Robertson: 'I believe a good few scrap-books containing my work are in existence', but '[I] may have to advertise as a last recourse.'[13] At least one newspaper clipping

---

[12] Brereton, 'Henry Lawson', *Art in Australia*, p. [1].
[13] 1 August 1899 (*Letters* 105). Arthur Parker later recalled: 'I began to cut out his poems as they appeared in the *Bulletin* and other papers, and paste them in a book. He said he had never seen anyone so careful. And for long after he would come to see me with a big roll of

service existed in Sydney at the time and was a possible source of supply.[14] More likely, it would have been a hit-and-miss affair of trying to find a supply of the relevant old copies of magazines and newspapers amongst friends and business acquaintances, including the offices of the *Worker* and the *Bulletin*. In their Preface to *While the Billy Boils*, 'THE PUBLISHERS' single out for acknowledgement the 'proprietors of the Sydney *Bulletin* who have in many ways assisted us'. It is dated 14 August 1896.

Lawson, as we will see below, would have finished his main round of revision, for which he was available from October 1895, by around mid December. Assuming that Syer's list was compiled partly to guide him, then it would have been in existence at latest by December 1895 and as early as October – or even earlier if Syer was preparing it while Lawson was still busy with *In the Days*. From its date of compilation (and perhaps rolling revision), Syer's list could have been used as a way of keeping track of the printer's copy that was gradually accumulating or was yet to be published in the *Bulletin* and *Worker*, and those stories that were still under consideration.

The illustrations

The Angus & Robertson ledgers record an order on 30 December 1895 for eight illustrations for *While the Billy Boils*. This entry does not prove that the illustrations were chosen by then; but it does show that Frank P. Mahony, an artist and illustrator of high repute, had come

---

papers under his arm. Those three albums of mine were used to assemble his first published books': *Henry Lawson by his Mates*, ed. [Bertha Lawson and John Le Gay Brereton] (1931; Sydney: Angus & Robertson, 1973), p. 20. Nevertheless, HL's letter to James W. Gordon ('Jim Grahame') of 22 March 1920 suggests the wisdom of hard-won experience: 'above all, save all your clippings and original copies with a view of submitting to A & R or someone for book publication' (*Letters* 380).

[14] None appears in Sands directories of the period for Sydney, but the A&R business archive contains a cyclostyled copy of a handwritten letterhead-advertisement (effectively, a With Compliments slip) of the 'Australasian & International Press Agency/74 York Street, Sydney/W. B. Melville, representing:—/[then three columns of 51 newspaper titles, all from suburban Sydney and country NSW]'. This document is attached to two press notices of *In the Days*: in ML MSS 3269/Angus & Robertson Ltd. Book reviews (Bound volumes) 1894–1970/1, vol. 7. This press agency was probably one of several supplying A&R, since the exercise book (vol. 7) contains reviews from other colonies, from some country NSW newspapers and the main Sydney city newspapers, which the agency apparently did not represent.

to an agreement with Robertson about their number and cost.[15] Some discussion of the work involved is likely to have occurred. Syer's list could have served as a reference for all concerned in production. Mahony would have needed guidance about contents and their proposed order, even if only provisional, so that he did not bunch up his illustrations in any one part of the volume. He definitely consulted part of the printer's copy. His initialled note next to the clipping of 'A Visit of Condolence' ('Something might be done here,/ old Sydney [unclear word]/ Woman at door/ FPM') matches one of his illustrations; and, next to 'Macquarie's Mate', there is the word 'Illustration'. Again this corresponds with an illustration in the published volume.[16]

Neither is it clear when these inscriptions were made. The two processes (typesetting and drawing) would ideally have happened at the same time. The illustrator would preferably have read printer's copy first. But if Mahony's work was delayed then Syer's list would become superseded by the production of the proofs themselves. As it turned out, there was no urgency for Mahony. After 30 December 1895, there would be a considerable production delay, partly because not all of the stories were yet to hand. And the pressure of work, for Robertson and Hugh Maccallum (the manager and only employee of the Angus & Robertson publishing division) in promoting *In the Days*, which came out on 14–15 February 1896, together with the need to allow some breathing space in the marketplace between this Lawson volume and his next one, would have tended to slow down progress on the production of *While the Billy Boils*.

Mahony may have looked at the accumulating revised and still unrevised copy and gained an idea for one or two illustrations. This is one explanation of the fact that his illustration for 'On the Edge of

[15] Melbourne-born Francis Prout Mahony (1862–1916) had contributed two acclaimed illustrations of explorers to the *Picturesque Atlas of Australasia* (1886), and oil paintings by him were in the collection of the National Art Gallery of New South Wales: see further, B. G. Andrews, 'Mahony, Francis', in *ADB*, x. 381. His original illustrations for *Billy Boils* are extant; they are reproduced here as Illustrations 3–11: see further, Appendix 2.
[16] The hand could be Mahony's, but it is not distinctive enough to allow attribution. It is not in Syer's hand. The illustrations occur opposite pp. 210 and 322 in the published volume.

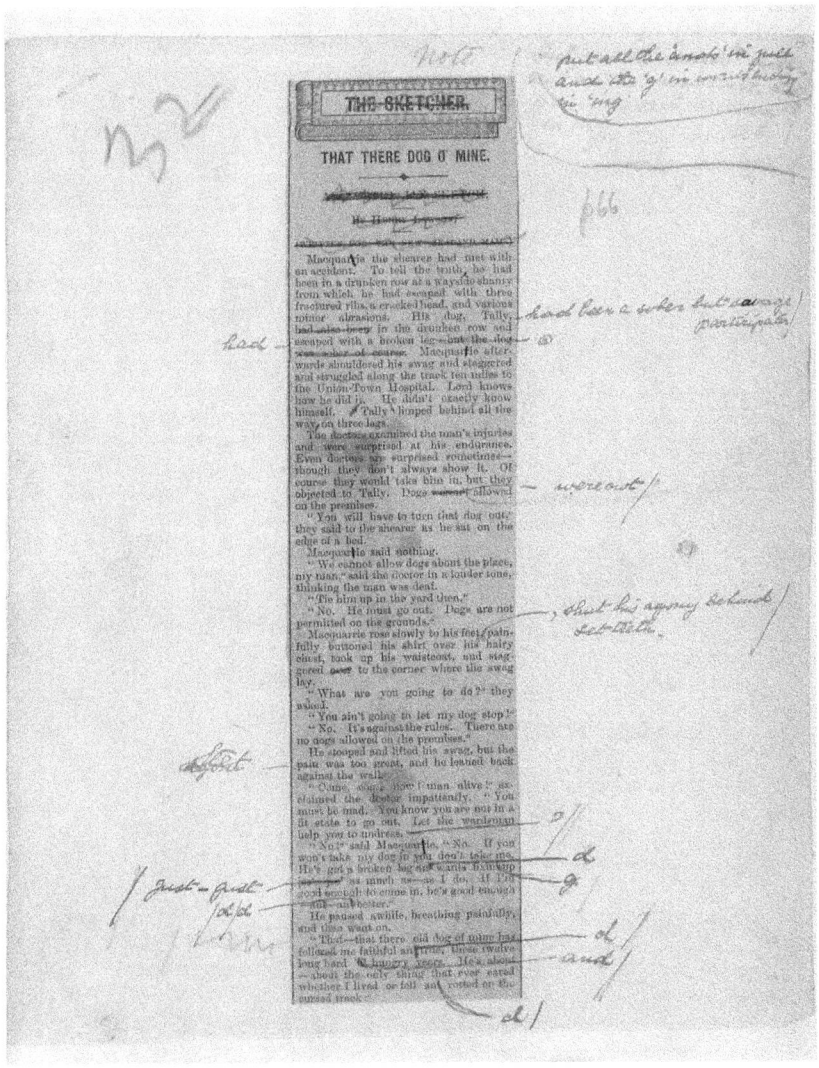

1. Printer's copy for 'That There Dog o' Mine'

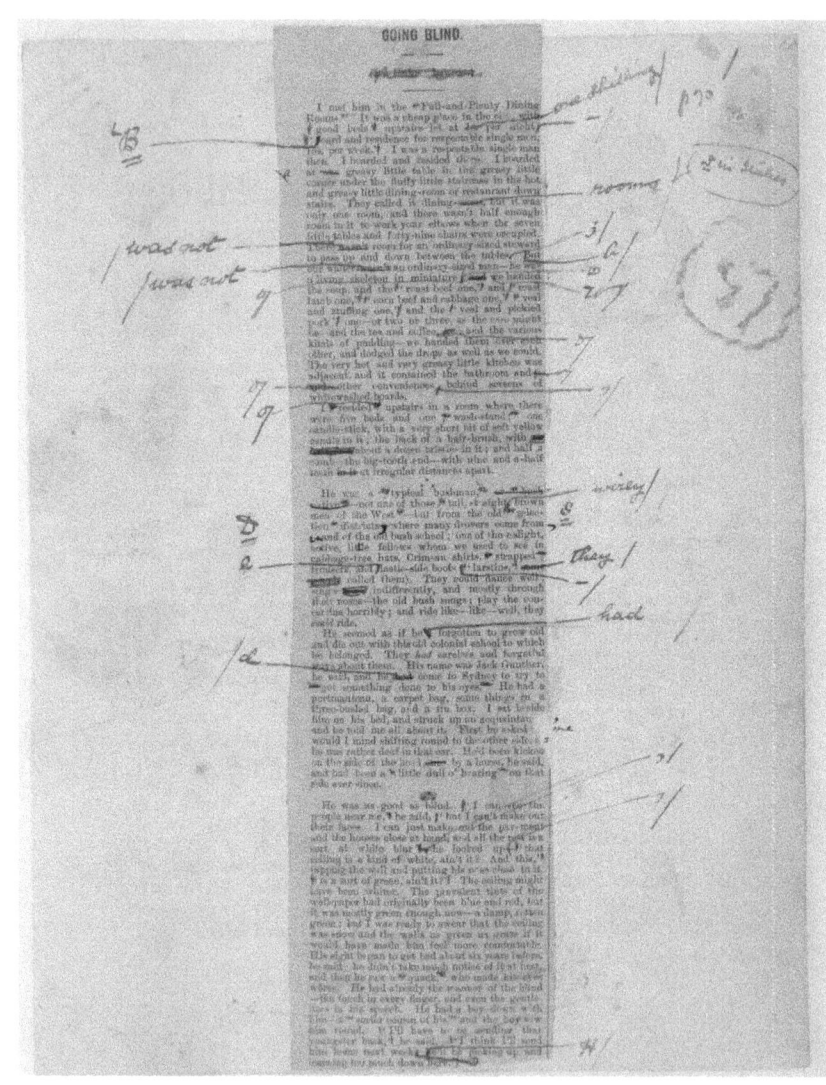

2. (*above*) Printer's copy for 'Going Blind'
3. (*right*) Frank Mahony's illustration for '"An Old Mate of your Father's"': 'They would talk of some old lead.'

4. Frank Mahony's illustration used in the first impression of *While the Billy Boils* for 'On the Edge of a Plain': 'Poured some water into the hollow.'

5. Frank Mahony's illustration used in the second impression of *While the Billy Boils* for 'On the Edge of a Plain': 'Poured some water into the hollow.'

6. Frank Mahony's illustration for 'The Drover's Wife': 'Mother, I won't never go drovin'; blast me if I do!'

7. Frank Mahony's re-drawn illustration for 'The Drover's Wife' for 1900 cheap edition of *While the Billy Boils*

8. Frank Mahony's illustration for '"Dossing Out" and "Camping"': 'Tenderly examining the seat of the trousers.'

9. Frank Mahony's illustration for 'A Visit of Condolence': 'I'm sorry mum. I didn't know.'

10. Frank Mahony's illustration for 'Two Dogs and a Fence': 'The inside dog generally starts it.'

11. Frank Mahony's illustration for 'Macquarie's Mate':
'His mate's alive.'

12. Walter Syer's (uncaptioned) illustration for the inside front boards of the trial issue (1896) of *While the Billy Boils*.

a Plain' (opposite page 98 in the published volume) assumes the text of the *Bulletin* printing, not that of the version as revised by Lawson. The *Bulletin* text had read: 'said Mitchell, as he dropped his swag in the mulga shade and sat down'. This implicitly left Mitchell's mate standing, which is the attitude in which Mahony portrayed him with the seated Mitchell. Lawson changed the wording to 'said Mitchell to his mate, as they dropped his swags in the mulga shade and sat down'. Only in proofs was 'his' altered to the now necessary 'their'.

It may be that Mahony took the clipping away after Jose had corrected it but before Lawson had revised it and that he returned it with a request to alter the text to fit the new illustration. Certainly, Lawson's revisions to this sketch were only three in number, all in pencil in the first paragraph and not confirmed in ink, as was his habit in nearly all of the stories and sketches that he revised. The new grammatical mistake ('his') suggests he was rushing and perhaps that there was some confusion about what he was to do. His three revisions were probably inscribed after Jose's work on the story (in Jose's characteristic thin-nibbed pen in black ink), since it is likely Jose would have caught the obvious error. Although there can be no certainty on the matter, this all suggests some last-minute work by Lawson, perhaps just before a batch of copy was sent to the printer for typesetting. However, because there are no markings relating to illustrations on any story in A1867–8 other than the two mentioned, and because it is very likely that the submission of the second half of the printer's copy (where the two markings appear) was delayed, Mahony probably got to work by consulting proofs of the first batch when they became available and such printer's copy as was waiting to be finalised – including 'On the Edge of a Plain'. (There is other evidence pointing to at least a two- or three-tranche, perhaps a multiple-tranche, submission of copy; it is given below.)

The foliation of printer's copy

At some stage in the preparation of copy a foliation was roughly applied in very thick coloured pencil or crayon. The blue foliation was 1–34 and

55–75. A red foliation, perhaps signalling the finalising of a second batch of printer's copy, covered the gap 35–40 and 43–54. The red 41 and 42 are not in A1867–8; evidently these two folios were at first in the count but later deleted. They may have been the clippings for 'Chicken Pies' and 'It Was Awful', mentioned above.[17] The resumed blue foliation 55–75 may have represented a third batch. There is also a red foliation 1–3 on 'An Unfinished Love Story' that can have come to hand only after its appearance on 21 March 1896. It has no markings by Lawson or Jose on it: so this is clearly a foliation inscribed after that (or those) of the red-and-blue 1–75.

A1867–8 and therefore the published volume mostly follow the order of the foliation – but with rearrangements. If we respect the foliation strictly it becomes possible to specify the original order of the stories and sketches up to the point where the foliation runs out. (See Table 2.) Some stories thereafter have no foliation at all; others are linked by what is a subsequent foliation in green 1–23 ('Our Pipes' to the first page only of '"Brummy Usen"', in the same sequence as the published volume) and another in green 1–4 ('A Visit of Condolence' and the first folio of '"In a Wet Season"'). These green foliations have no breaks in their sequences; they indicate an attempt to keep copy in the determined order for the printer. Because the original ordering of the stories indicated by the red-and-blue 1–75 foliation was rearranged in A1867–8, and because the altered order corresponds with that of the published volume (with the exception of 'The Drover's Wife'), and further because, as described above, someone recorded the published volume's pagination on the first folio of each story but with 'The Drover's Wife' in its original position, the lead-pencil pagination must register a stage during production not afterwards.

But which stage exactly? The textual apparatus in the Eggert and Webby edition shows that Lawson made revisions in proof that were long enough to create an extra page in the second story in the volume but in no other; and the pagination recording takes this into account.

[17] See n. 7: they would have needed only one folio-length clipping each in A1867–8.

CHAPTER 5 . THE MAKING OF A BOOK

Evidently, galleys were returned to Angus & Robertson with the first tranche of printer's copy; Lawson and Jose made their revisions and corrections; page proofs were then produced, incorporating them, and were returned.[18]

Printer's copy of the second half of the volume was later sent off in one or more batches (which was normal practice), and returned with galleys.[19] The pagination could have been added to A1867–8 at that

---

[18] It is possible that no galley proofs were actually sent to A&R because the mounted clippings might have been thought to serve the purpose of galleys. Under this scenario, the type would have been set in galley trays, and proofs produced for a visual inspection by the printer; the type would have then been paged and locked, and page proofs produced. Correction would have been carried out directly on page proofs; and HL's and Jose's revisions and corrections incorporated into a second round of page proofs. However, if this were the case, it is likely that HL would have been more restricted in his proof alterations than he was. The pagination of the page proofs would have required alteration nearly throughout because of his additions to the second story and GR's shifting of stories, which he would have foreseen. This relative fluidity of content is more consistent with galleys. Furthermore, marks indicating the end of typesetters' stints on the longer pieces of continuous prose in A1867–8 do not match page endings in the published edition – as they might be expected to have done in the absence of galleys. (Such markings appear on the two stories in Bertha's holograph, 'The Drover's Wife', '[The Bush Undertaker]' and 'Jones' Alley'.)

Roderick's reasoning that galleys were used is, however, faulty. He claims, in error (*Commentaries* 77–8), that a roughly cut galley proof of a 16-line story in ML (MSS 314/236, filed at A1892) was 'set up with the intention of including it in *While the Billy Boils*' but not used then nor in later collections. The story is entitled 'A Light That Failed' in the proofs, with a new title added in pencil 'An Old Sweetheart'; it is a revision of 'A Love Story' from the *Bulletin* of 25 November 1893. In the same scrapbook, there is a galley proof with identical page design of a story of 19 lines, 'A Typical Bush Yarn', overlooked by Roderick. It was first published in the *Bulletin* on 11 November 1893 and rewritten for *Short Stories in Prose and Verse*, whose text is the source of the galley version. The proof as typeset shows one development only: a 2-em dash has become 'devil' on the proof. HL has then changed the same line in handwriting from 'The devil you did!' to 'Well Im xxx!!!' [*sic*] and added double quotation marks around the whole story. This allowed it to become a tale told by a character in another, longer story that also incorporates material from other previous pars and sketches: this thrifty reworking produced 'Two Sundowners' for HL's collection *Children of the Bush* (London: Methuen, 1902). Both galleys employ double inverted commas in their typesetting; *Billy Boils* – crucially – used single forms. The double volume *On the Track and Over the Sliprails* (A&R, 1900) had the same page design as *Billy Boils* but used double inverted commas: thus these proofs would appear to be overset matter for the latter volume but not used in it. This also explains the rough scissoring and co-location of the proofs in a scrapbook, which A&R was evidently using to keep track of the HL stories whose rights the firm had acquired.

[19] The Angus & Robertson Publishing Progress Register confirms the practice as the norm (ML MSS 3269/12/2). Cf. the letter from Hugh Maccallum to Mrs Creed [Louise Mack] of 23 August 1897: 'Re your request for the copy of "Girls Together" we beg to state that when we have only one copy of the MS of any book our rule is not to allow it outside the house *until it*

point, as part of the effort to settle on the remaining illustrations and their position within the volume. It is an easy matter to determine final pagination from galley proofs. The number of typeset lines per page was known and would have provided a reliable ruler-measurement to run over the galleys. Under this scenario, Robertson would next have made his final decision to shift 'The Drover's Wife'.[20]

Some sense can be made of the original ordering of the stories. Table 1 gives the Contents of 1896, to which the numerical sequence of the stories and sketches (1–52) has been added. Table 2 gives the original ordering of those stories and sketches covered by the red-and-blue foliation of A1867–8.

The order of stories established by this numbering probably registers a finished stage of the work of revision and correction during the October–December 1895 stint. They would produce the equivalent in galley proofs of about 164 printed pages.[21] All of these stories in A1867–8 bear markings by both Lawson and Jose, with the exception of folios 68 and 69 ('"Dossing Out" and "Camping"'), which Lawson clearly overlooked as Jose's markings include an instruction to him for an alteration or deletion to which he did not respond. Several other stories that were definitely available in late 1895 and that also bear Lawson's and Jose's alterations are not part of the original foliation. They were evidently set aside to await the publication or receipt of clippings of other stories that together would make up the remainder of the printer's copy.

When the original arrangement is considered it is clear that Lawson was not trying to order, or had already determined that he could not satisfactorily order, the stories into those strict thematic or narrator-

---

goes in detachments to the Printer.... If however you care to send anyone to copy the parts you want we shall be pleased to put our "copy" at your disposal' (ML MSS 3269/72/1, fol. 103); italics added.

[20] Cf. the sequence of production events for Edward Dyson's *Rhymes from the Mines* set out in Appendix 1.

[21] I.e., counting the full extent of 'A Day on a Selection' (the foliation would not have needed to proceed past its first folio if it was the last of its batch), allowing five pages for the missing folios, and deducting one page for the material later added in proof to '"Tom's Selection" ['Settling on the Land']: see Chapter 6 pp. 138–9.

TABLE 2. THE (INCOMPLETE) STORIES ORDERED BY THE ORIGINAL FOLIATION IN A1867–8

A1867–8 FOLIATION IN A1867–8		1896 collection as published ITEM NUMBER AND TITLE IN 1896	1896 PAGINATION
(blue foliation 1–28)	1	An Old Mate of Your Father's	1–6
(blue 1–28)	2	Settling on the Land	7–14
(blue 1–28)	3	Enter Mitchell	15–17
(blue 1–28)	4	Stiffner and Jim (Thirdly, Bill)	18–27
(blue 1–28)	5	When the Sun Went Down	28–31
(blue 1–28)	6	The Man Who Forgot	32–39
(blue 1–28)	7	Hungerford	40–44
(blue 1–28)	8	A Camp-Fire Yarn	45–49
(blue 1–28)	9	His Country—After All	50–56
(blue 29–31)	30	Across the Straits	173–180
(blue 32–3)	11	That There Dog o' Mine	66–69
(blue 34, red 35–6)	28	The Shearing of the Cook's Dog	163–167
(red 37–9)	12	Going Blind	70–77
(red 40)	27	An Echo from the Old Bark School	161–162
[missing folios 41–2]	—	[*possibly* Chicken Peas *and* It Was Awful]	—
(red 43–53)	13	Arvie Aspinall's Alarm Clock	78–82
(red 43–53)	14	Stragglers	83–90
(red 43–53)	15	The Union Buries Its Dead	91–97
(red 54)	34	His Colonial Oath	203–204
(blue 55–7)	33	'Board and Residence'	195–202
(blue 58–62)	16	On the Edge of a Plain	98–100
(blue 58–62)	17	In a Dry Season	101–105
(blue 58–62)	18	He'd Come Back	106–109
(blue 63–4)	35	'Some Day'	205–208
(blue 65–7)	19	Another of Mitchell's Plans for the Future	110–112
(blue 65–7)	20	Steelman	113–116
(blue 68–9)	29	'Dossing Out' and 'Camping'	168–172
(blue 70–4)	21	Drifted Back	117–120
(blue 70–4)	22	Remailed	121–126
(blue 75)[22]	10	A Day on a Selection	57–65

[22] Only the first page of 'A Day on a Selection' is foliated. Folio '74', a short clipping, was

based clusters that he later claimed he had aimed at doing, when stung by A. G. Stephens's review of the published collection, criticising him for failing to do so.[23] In comparison to the published sequence, the first ordering was merely a different medley of themes, settings and narrators.

The account now becomes complicated, but close attention to the detail permits a decisive clarification to be reached. Folios 1–75 include all items up to number 35, except for 23–6 and 31–2. Number 23 is 'The Drover's Wife'. It would have been available for the first stint of revision because it had appeared in *Short Stories in Prose and Verse*, and it bears Lawson's, Jose's and possibly Robertson's markings. Number 26 is 'His Father's Mate', which had appeared in *A Golden Shanty*, as already explained. Both were presumably set aside for later selection in the second compilation of printer's copy. The existence of unfoliated stories in A1867–8 after those gathered in 1–75, and the multiple foliations after the 1–75 foliation, suggest that the second half of the volume was, however, not sent off for typesetting as a single unit.

Number 24 is 'Mitchell Doesn't Believe in the Sack'; it bears both Lawson's and Jose's markings, as does 25, 'Shooting the Moon'. The former seems to have been sent for typesetting separately from the 1–75 sequence because it has a pencilled reminder above the clipping 'Note All G's and 'ings in full'.

Item 31, 'Steelman's Pupil', did not appear in the *Bulletin* until 14 December 1895; Lawson did not revise its clipping, and the three, pencilled copy-editorial markings on the clipping cannot be attributed with any confidence to Jose. The story's non-appearance in the 1–75

---

mounted beneath 73 on the same sheet in A1867–8.
  There are a few other hints of preceding experiments with ordering: 'The Drover's Wife' (item 23) has a circled '1' on its first folio and 'A Day on a Selection' (10) has a circled '2'; but there is no continuation of this sequence. On the first folio of 'That Swag' ['Enter Mitchell'] HL wrote in pencil, and later partially erased, the titles of four items in the left margin: 'Macquarie's Mate/ Old Mate of Your Father's/ Day on a Selection/ Settling on the Land'. The first folio of the clippings for 'Hungerford', which is item 7, has '7' in red ink and its blue foliation ('18') is a mistaken duplication (actually it is 18 bis); this suggests a recommencing of the ordering on HL's part.

[23] Stephens's review is quoted in Chapter 8 p. 173.

foliation suggests the terminal date for Lawson and Jose's initial stint of revision and correction. Again, Lawson and Jose played no part in the correction of story 32, 'An Unfinished Love Story', which appeared on 21 March 1896 in the *Worker*. Its red foliation 1–3 is quite distinct from that of 1–75. That leaves items 36–52.

Of them, numbers 36 and 37 ('A Visit of Condolence' and '"In a Wet Season"') bear the first green foliation 1–4. The former bears Jose's and (possibly) George Robertson's markings; the latter Jose's and Lawson's: so it may have been temporarily set aside in December, as was (probably) story 39 'Mitchell: A Character Sketch', which received Jose's and Lawson's attention. Stories 38, 40 and 50 (along with 23) had appeared in *Short Stories in Prose and Verse* and were also presumably waiting for the compilation of the second half of printer's copy.

Items 41–6 bear the green foliation 1–23, with only the first folio of 46 being numbered. Four of these six (41, 44, 45 and 46) lack Lawson's markings, so their receipt and preparation as printer's copy presumably postdate the initial stint, and the other two may have been worked on but set aside. Number 48 ('She Wouldn't Speak') is not present in A1867-8, but, as we have seen, was apparently on Syer's preliminary list and probably arrived late in proceedings. It may simply have been misplaced after or during production since the lead-pencil pagination on A1867-8 correctly allows for it. Items 49 and 52 are holograph manuscripts. The clipping of 'Bogg of Geebung' (47) bears no textual alterations; it is the story about whose inclusion Lawson later said he was dubious (see Chapter 6, page 132). The only remaining one (number 51), 'Baldy Thompson', is another with Jose's and Lawson's markings that was presumably set aside for later selection.

In summary, it seems that Lawson was only involved in a concentrated way in the initial stint in late 1895; that an ordering was probably then established, witnessed by the blue-and-red foliation 1–75 and perhaps sent to the printer in more than one batch; that some other stories not thus represented were revised and copy-edited at the same stage but set aside for ordering when the rest of the contents came to hand; that others (but not Lawson) corrected clippings for this remainder as they came to hand; that Robertson made some final decisions about inclusions and exclusions (of at least the item or items represented by the missing folios 41 and 42) but probably more; and that he reordered the sequence of the stories in the 1–75 foliation. His reasons for the reordering are considered below; but first the assumption of the submission of copy to the printer in at least two main tranches, which the scenario assumes, needs testing against other available evidence.

Despatch of printer's copy in two or more tranches

Jose's copy-editing would not have slowed things down as he was obviously working in tandem with Lawson during October–December 1895: queries and unresolved wordings, anticipating the other's response, appear on many stories in A1867–8. Nevertheless, this still left some work unfinished, especially in relation to those stories and sketches that would ultimately appear in the volume but had not yet appeared in magazine or newspaper form. Because none of the first half of the volume (up to 'Steelman's Pupil') would have been affected by this factor, its printer's copy could have gone to be typeset in advance of the second half.

If the printer's copy was divided in this sensible manner, its second half (including 'An Unfinished Love Story') cannot have been sent for typesetting until 21 March 1896 when that story appeared in the *Worker*. It was the last of the stories in the volume to appear in newspaper or magazine form, and the pencil paginations in A1867–8 suggest that the printer's copy already in hand was not set or at least paged independently of the delayed story.

Reinforcing this likelihood is the fact that all the volume's irregularities in documentary supply occur in this second half. These are:

'FOR AULD LANG SYNE' and 'THE GEOLOGICAL SPEILER'. The fact that these stories in printer's copy are holograph manuscripts in the hand of the woman Lawson had just married on 15 April 1896, Bertha Bredt, implies a late decision to typeset from holograph once it became plain that they would not appear in magazine or newspaper form before the volume appeared. 'For Auld Lang Syne' has a pencilled note on its first page: 'Send to Jose & then to H.L.' As Lawson had already revised the manuscript in ink until page 7 and thereafter in lead pencil, including adding some alternative wordings, and as Jose's hand does not appear – thus leaving the alternatives unresolved – the instruction probably refers to expected proofs rather than (or in addition to) the manuscript. The typesetters took the easy route of ignoring the pencilled alternatives, which were thereby lost. These two stories were probably prepared and typeset very late in the production process. Because, in the holographs, numerous false starts were deleted by Bertha after having just written them, and because the text continues with new wordings that equally make sense, she must have been taking down the story from Lawson's dictation, perhaps to hurry things along. She left every second line blank for him to use later for corrections and revisions. 'The Geological Speiler' is paginated in Bertha's hand 1–19; page 16 has only three lines of her handwriting. She must have been instructed to leave the rest blank and continue at page 17. This suggests the existence of a rough copy or notes (identified below) whose text Lawson could not for the moment resolve for the fair-copy version. He later wrote out the remainder of page 16 with two false starts rather like hers, and page 17 continues from it with a new paragraph.

'SHE WOULDN'T SPEAK'. As its copy is not present in A1867–8, it probably turned up fortuitously, late in proceedings, but before the typesetting and paging was finished (since, as we have seen, the pencil pagination is correct around the pagination gap that the story filled).

'AN UNFINISHED LOVE STORY'. This story was not published until 21 March 1896 (in the *Worker*). It has pencil corrections only, and they are too big and looping to be Lawson's; the hand is unidentified.

'OUR PIPES' and 'THE STORY OF MALACHI'. They bear corrections in what is probably but not certainly Jose's hand (the corrections are uncharacteristically large and in lead pencil). There is another, unidentified hand on the clipping of 'The Story of Malachi'. Prior to this work Lawson made good in pencil the ends of a few defective lines, suggesting it had been damaged when lifted from a scrapbook. But he did not return to revise or correct it; and he had no part at all in the preparation of 'Our Pipes'. These facts suggest that, although published in the *Bulletin* in good time (11 May 1895), 'Our Pipes' had only just come to hand and 'The Story of Malachi' (published 22 June 1889) received some initial attention from Lawson in October–December 1895 but was initially rejected.

'STEELMAN'S PUPIL' and 'TWO DOGS AND A FENCE' had only recently appeared in the *Bulletin*, on 14 and 21 December 1895 respectively. Their clippings in A1867–8 bear no revisions by Lawson.

Thus Lawson could well have finished his main preparation of printer's copy by 14 December 1895. He would not have needed to return to it beyond arranging for Bertha's fair copying. Roderick dates 'For Auld Lang Syne' as 1895 without giving evidence, but April 1896 is more likely. From the 15th, when they married at Weldon's Matrimonial Agency in Sydney, Lawson and Bertha would have been free to spend all their time together. The fact that the Angus & Robertson ledgers record a payment for this sketch on 25 April 1896 suggest they put the time to productive use – and helps explain why they married so precipitately and privately in the first place, evidently putting off a honeymoon (to Perth) until the book that would settle Lawson's literary affairs was itself put to bed.

Payment for 'The Geological Speiler' is recorded on 2 May 1896.[24] Roderick argues that it is a second version of 'The Geological Spielers', a story that would ultimately find independent publication in the *Bulletin* on 24 December 1898.[25] This is not strictly true. 'The Geological Spielers' of 1898 gives the impression of having been written first, and the 1896 story extracted from it, leaving the long introduction and some later reflections that would make up the later sketch. After the appearance

---

[24] ML MSS 3269/11/1, fol. 46.
[25] *Commentaries* 117–18.

of *While the Billy Boils*, HL would have had little reason to write of the same events afresh: thus a draft of or notes towards an omnibus version from which both stories would be developed must have pre-existed the 1896 story.[26]

The various pieces of evidence, when taken together, strongly suggest that printer's copy of the second half of the volume was being finalised while the setting of the first half was in train. Thus Lawson's intensive phase of involvement in the preparation of copy for *While the Billy Boils* almost certainly did not continue into 1896. But since there was still a lot more work to do, someone else had to take responsibility. Enter George Robertson – whose motives, as the next chapter explains, were not identical with Lawson's. Robertson would probably have seen his role, once the volume had been contracted, as to be exercised mainly towards the end of the production process, a time when the prospect of success or failure in the marketplace would have come decidedly into focus for him: after all, it was the firm's money he was investing in the stories of this wayward writer.

---

[26] As HL dictated to Bertha, he was presumably working from it, but it cannot have been in a final state: see further, Commentary for 'The Geological Speiler' in Eggert and Webby. In HL's letter to A&R, 24 March 1899, attached to the Agreement for what became *On the Track and Over the Sliprails*, HL refers to '"Geological Speilers" (Prelude to Sketch in "W.B.B.")': ML MSS 3269/316/Angus & Robertson Correspondence, vol. 828, pp. 169–71 [p. 169].

CHAPTER 6

RESPECTING THE MARKETPLACE
THE PUBLISHERS' NATURAL WISH
TO MAKE A FAT 5S. VOLUME

COLIN Roderick's brief explanation in his *Commentaries* volume of the inclusion in *While the Billy Boils* of 'His Father's Mate' and 'She Wouldn't Speak' revolves around Robertson's wanting to bulk out the volume in order to make it comparable with Kipling's collections of short stories published in the early 1890s.[1] Although Roderick does not cite his source, he is echoing Jose's memory of events as recorded in *The Romantic Nineties* and has linked it causally to the absence of these two stories from the printer's copy (A1867–8). In Roderick's account, they are both late inclusions. Although their absence is, as we saw in Chapter 5, otherwise explicable as a problem of documentary supply, the nexus between retail price and page-extent nevertheless needs to be explored. The bookselling marketplace had its own imperatives, of which George Robertson would have been all too aware.

In the 1890s, poetry volumes seem to have required a page-extent of around 200 pages to justify a 5s. price: Kipling's *Barrack Room Ballads* was 208 pages; *The Man from Snowy River* made 184 pages; and *In the Days* 234 pages. Edward Dyson assured Robertson on 17 February 1896 that his submitted manuscript for *Rhymes from the Mines*, together with two 'sets of verse' and a third piece he would shortly be sending, would now make a volume of 200 pages.[2] Jose's selection of the poems submitted to Angus & Robertson by Will Ogilvie (published as *Fair Girls and Gray*

---
[1] *Commentaries* 4.
[2] ML MSS 314/28, p. 748.

Horses, 1898) would amount, he predicted, to 205 printed pages: 'I don't see much chance of enlarging this. A few of the poems might be spread over more pp.'³ Clearly, page-extent was a crucial consideration.

Macmillan's successful editions of Kipling's short-story collections *Plain Tales from the Hills* (1890), *Life's Handicap* (1892) and *Many Inventions* (1893) made 312, 352 and 366 pages respectively.⁴ In comparison, *While the Billy Boils* would make 336 pages.⁵ As an attractively produced prose-fiction volume of the requisite length, Lawson's stories would implicitly invite comparison, on the retail bookseller's shelves, with Kipling's, whose short-story collections sold at 6s. As a successful bookseller, Robertson undoubtedly knew the price points of the local market intimately and had determined that 6s. was too high for fiction titles, even those with production standards that would match those of Macmillan's 6s. series. A reviewer of *While the Billy Boils* would note the shrewdness of the move: 'so far as we know this is the first book which has been produced in Australia exactly on the lines of the standard English six-shilling novel, to which in typography, paper, and binding, it is fully equal although less in price.'⁶ In comparison, but with lower production standards, Boldrewood's *Robbery Under Arms* had been available in Macmillan's hardback 3s.6d. series from 1889, with a colonial library issue on cheaper paper and limp binding at 2s.6d. Angus & Robertson would have to lower its sights eventually, but George Robertson was, for now, keen to establish a fiction and poetry library that would match comparable English volumes in production standards and that would undercut them in price.⁷

---

³ ML MSS 314/41, p. 183.
⁴ Respectively, 19.5, 22 and 23 crown octavo gatherings; these figures take into account any final blank pages. Cf. the cheap A. H. Wheeler Indian Railway volumes of Kipling's stories that continued the original *Plain Tales* (1887): they were 6–6.5 octavo sections (96–104 pages). The Wheeler copies at ML were issued in London by Sampson Low, Marston, Searle and Rivington and printed by the Aberdeen University Press.
⁵ (21 octavo sections). *Billy Boils*'s text ends on page 333, the printer's colophon appears by itself on page 334 and the last leaf (two pages) is blank. A 16-page advertising section on cheaper stock follows. For the first impression, the tipped-in illustrations needed separate printing, so they had no effect on the pagination: see further, Appendix 2.
⁶ Anon., review of *Billy Boils*, in *Town and Country Journal*, 29 August 1896.
⁷ Cf. the comments of an unnamed commercial traveller interviewed upon his return to England for 'The Australian Colonies As They Are To-day' in the *British Weekly* (anon., 21

It must have been against this background that Robertson asked Websdale, Shoosmith to quote for printing a volume of 300 pages. More pages meant higher costs of production, but there was a necessary minimum to achieve. So Robertson would have been pressuring Lawson to put more stories on the table for consideration. The printer submitted an estimate dated 6 March 1896; and on 7 April Robertson made various calculations in preparation for determining the size of the actual printing and the formats for binding. Robertson was already committed to Lawson, so the question at issue was not whether to go ahead with the title but what format or formats to choose. Robertson was evidently also already committed to Websdale, Shoosmith: a trial page design (discussed below) had been prepared in early February 1896. Thus the typesetting could have begun soon after, before the complete contents and therefore the exact page-extent were settled. If this meant that some stories were set but not finally selected (what Angus & Robertson later routinely referred to as 'overset matter'), little would be lost: this would explain the listing of stories in the Schedule that were not used in *While the Billy Boils*.[8]

Various options, each of which would have different effects on likely profit or loss, had to be canvassed in view of the anticipated demand. Robertson's conclusion in his calculations of 7 April 1896 was that the total production cost to Angus & Robertson (paper, printing, illustrations and binding) per 300-page volume would be 'say 1/8 [1s.8d.] per copy' for hardbacks and 1s.2d. for paperbacks. On 2 February 1896, he had informed his trade connection in Glasgow, James MacLehose & Sons, that it would be 'a 3/6 book with 8 plates. bound in cloth ... and in paper cards at 2/6'.[9] In the event, he did not immediately proceed with the latter

October 1897). To the question 'How did you find the book trade in Australia?', he answered: 'Much better than it was two years ago. The colonies will, of course, take some time to get back into a healthy state, but business is decidedly mending. ... The people of Australia care little for six-shilling novels. Indeed it would be no exaggeration to say that the sale for the six-shilling novel is over in the colonies, the cheap colonial editions having become so popular. Among the most successful booksellers in Australia are Messrs. Angus and Robertson, of Sydney. They have lately taken to publishing, and at the time of my visit had thirteen books in the press.'

[8] See Chapter 3 pp. 83–4.
[9] ML MSS 3269/71/3, fols. 30–1.

format, but the calculation confirms his interest in serving the market's demand for cheap publications.[10] He would have reasoned, however, that a starting retail price of 5s., later reduced to 3s.6d. after initial demand wore off (but with the initial costs of typesetting and preparation of the illustrations already amortised, thus reducing the costs of reprinting) would make a tidy profit for the firm and for Lawson, even after the discount to retailers was taken into account. Turning these matters over in his mind after having made his calculations, Robertson seems to have hit on an even better solution, one that Macmillan did not pursue with Kipling. If the page-extent could be increased from 300 to 336 pages, a third, cheaper publishing format (two slim volumes at 1s. each) would become available once demand at 3s.6d. fell away.

That this was a conscious intention can be substantiated. As we saw in the preceding chapter, 'The Drover's Wife' was at first placed to begin at page 169 in *While the Billy Boils*; but on the proofs, probably because of the need to space out the illustrations, its position was changed to start at page 127. When the title was divided into a cheap First Series and Second Series (two volumes) in 1900, 'The Drover's Wife' resumed its original position so that it could occupy the prominent position, important for sales, of being the first story in the Second Series. It seems unlikely that this was a happy coincidence.[11]

---

[10] ML MSS 3269/71/4, fol. 299, dated 7 April 1896: 'Estimate of cost of Lawsons prose based on Dble. Deckle Edge Dble. crown 35 lb. 17/- per ream landed, and on W.S &Co. estimate of March 6th '96.' Sixty reams at 17s. per ream 'prints 3072 copies of 300pp each'. The paper cost would thus be £51 and the printing (including the typesetting) £83.9s. This worked out at approximately 11d. per copy.

Next GR calculated binding costs for 1,000 copies in cloth (£29.17s.6d. or 7d. per copy) and 2,000 in paper (£8.7s.6d. or 1d. per copy). The engraved illustrations would work out at 1½d. per copy (£19.8s. in total, of which the artist would receive £1 for each of the eight illustrations and the engraver 9d. per square inch, making £6 in total for the engraving). In the event, (photographic) process engraving was used for reproducing the eight illustrations.

(There is a typed copy of these calculations in ML MSS 314/45, p. 47: evidently, GR later thought it significant enough to have it copied, along with a selection of the firm's letters, for the archive he would sell – now MSS 314.)

[11] The decision to shift 'The Drover's Wife' to that of first story of the Second Series had the effect of transferring its illustration too. The nearness of two illustrations to one another – the likely cause of the shift for the 1896 volume – was now no longer a problem. The new shift arrangement left both Series with four illustrations each.

Print-shop supervisors had, as a matter of course, to be able to estimate likely page-extents to given page designs: the process was called *casting off* (and ultimately it would lead to division of the job among the available typesetters – the term's older meaning). This was necessary if the publisher was to be able to estimate paper requirements (Angus & Robertson ordered their own) and thus overall costs. Provided the printer could tell Robertson the relationship of already printed newspaper columns to the volume's pages, Robertson would have been able to estimate roughly how many columns he needed. That would explain why he could ask, in good time, for Lawson to bring what were probably existing rough drafts or at least notes for two new stories into fair-copy manuscript form ('For Auld Lang Syne' and 'The Geological Speiler') and to revise them. Even so, assuming that Robertson was aiming at the 336 page-extent, he would probably have needed to have more material on hand for the volume than was used, just in case, to be slipped in at the last minute if the printer's copy came up significantly short. A large blue-pencil or crayon cross through the opening section of 'Bogg of Geebung' suggests it was initially rejected but held back for possible use in the second half of the printer's copy. When Lawson received his first printed copy of *While the Billy Boils* in September 1896 in Perth, he told Robertson that he remained 'doubtful about "Bogg of Geebung" and one or two others'.[12] It appears immediately before 'She Wouldn't Speak', which is missing from A1867–8 and also seems to have been a late addition.[13]

While printer's copy was being prepared in late 1895, Robertson would not have known that 'The Drover's Wife', an already acclaimed

---

[12] *Letters* 63.
[13] A surplus of copy is confirmed in HL's undated letter to GR of probably January 1897 where he was seeking to interest GR in his next volume of prose, evidently in the face of GR's expressed preference for a volume of verse or a novel as likely to sell better: 'The sketches you have in hand, including "Darling River Sketches", which contain many entirely new pictures, would give the second volume a brighter tone than the first: see "The Mystery of Dave Reagan", for instance' (*Letters* 66). The latter (published originally in the *Worker* of 4 November 1893) was definitely available for *Billy Boils* as it had been republished in *Short Stories in Prose and Verse* in 1894. The Darling River sketches, which had appeared in the *Worker* from July to October 1893, would later be combined to form 'The Darling River' in *Over the Sliprails*.

story, would start exactly at page 169. But both publisher and printer would have known that a volume of 336 pages could later be divided neatly into two saleable units of 168 pages (plus front matter) each. Short story collections opened up this possibility in a way that novels did not conventionally, and 168 pages was a handy number for flat-sheet printing in octavo or (later, when the format became common) sixteenmo. Division into two volumes was what Robertson would engineer for *On the Track and Over the Sliprails* in 1900, except this time *On the Track* and *Over the Sliprails* were produced separately from the beginning and with separate paginations (viii + 160, the last leaf being blank; and viii + 168, the last page having advertisements). But, in hardback form only, they were available bound together as one volume. Lawson's next collection *Joe Wilson and his Mates*, produced in Edinburgh in 1901 and reprinted for Angus & Robertson by S. T. Leigh in Sydney in 1902, reflected the same printing necessities; it made viii + 336 pages, with the last leaf carrying advertisements on its first page. In due course it was also split into two shorter volumes. It is hard to believe, therefore, that the shrewd George Robertson did not, in 1896, foresee the possibility for *While the Billy Boils* of its future exploitation in cheaper formats. Expensive forms such as the traditional three-volume novel were manifestly failing by the mid-1890s, and the general move was to cheaper initial, and then even cheaper reprinted, one-volume forms of publication. Short-story collections, Robertson must have realised in 1896, opened up a further possibility in formatting that could potentially extend the sales life of the title.

His desire in a general way to emulate Kipling's collections would not have been as important to him as the need to maximise returns on his investment; elsewhere he refers to the 'publishers' natural wish to make a fat 5/ volume'.[14] The lower the retail price the more copies had to be sold to achieve the same return. It was far better to start at 5s.

In these early years of his publishing venture, Robertson must frequently have had to choose between establishing the firm as a

[14] GR to R. Thomson, n.d. [1902]: ML MSS 314/66, p. 244.

literary publisher of significant, lasting but not necessarily immediately successful works, and publishing predictably popular fiction and verse that would ensure the firm's financial stability and ultimate success. Certainly, he prided himself on a capacity to read the market. In the same letter as the one just quoted, he goes on: 'Curiously enough both Jose and Maccallum thought very little of Snowy [*The Man from Snowy River and Other Verses*] as it was passing through the press. Jose preferred Dyson! But they were wrong because ABP has gained not only cash but fame'.

The illustrations and the chronology of production

As noted in Chapter 5, the safest moment for Mahony to have started work in earnest would have been after the contents were finalised and the sequence was set. But becoming involved when some of the book was typeset and the rest was in final printer's copy would also have seemed a reasonable procedure since it would expedite the production of the volume. He could first have made decisions using the printer's copy of whatever was waiting to go to the printer, thus accounting for the two (the only two) annotations in A1867–8 about illustrations. This would have slowed down its despatch to the printer only by a little; and then he could have (less urgently) turned to the proofs of the first batch or batches, now in hand. That would soon have produced the need to shift 'The Drover's Wife', a decision that would have been marked on the (lost) proofs. Mahony could have then got on with preparing the illustration for this story and the other seven.

There were fifteen weeks between 'soon after 21 March 1896' – the time given provisionally in Chapter 5 when the start of the second main tranche of the printer's copy was sent off in batches for typesetting – and 10 July 1896, the date a charge for printing blocks for the illustrations was entered in the Ledger.[15] This is a plausible length of time for Mahony to have completed the eight illustrations and a simple vignette for the

---

[15] ML MSS 3269/11/1, fol. 46.

title-page, and so tends to support the proposed earlier date. However, as further outlined in Appendix 2, some local experimentation with reproduction soon proved unsatisfactory and, for the printing of the plates, Robertson had to resort to his old connections in Glasgow. The job would have been ordered by April, or early May at the latest, because, by 6 June he was expecting the job to be already in hand in Glasgow or completed.

The printed illustrations would have been re-machined in Sydney, this time with the letterpress of the captions, ready to be finally tipped-in during binding. The printing of 24,000 illustrations (8 illustrations for 3,000 copies) is charged in the Ledger at 1 August 1896, the same date that the stereos and matrices for the text were charged.[16] (The printing of the volume itself would not be charged until 23 September, well after the volume had been released.) The illustrations would be placed, not between the volume's octavo gatherings, but opposite the appropriate point where the caption occurred in the text.

Other ledger entries and some letters support this rough chronology. An entry for the charge for a sample typesetting of two folios of "'An Old Mate of your Father's'" is dated 4 February 1896.[17] This corresponds with the (undated) pencilled instruction on the first leaf of A1867–8 to return the sample 'today before 12.30', suggesting that a decision was about to be made. It must soon have been, for, as we have seen, on 6 March Websdale, Shoosmith (who had printed *The Man from Snowy River* and *In the Days*) prepared their quotation for the printing costs of *While the Billy Boils*. This suggests that the work on *While the Billy Boils*, although virtually finished, as far as Lawson was concerned, by about mid-December, was

---

[16] ML MSS 3269/11/1, fol. 46.

[17] ML MSS 3269/11/1, fol. 46: 'To Setting up 2 pp in L/p [Long primer] & pica (An Old Mate)' costing 7s. The terms apparently refer to the common 1890s design for fiction: 10-point capitals for the running headlines and pica (12-point type) for the text. (This entry is not a misplaced charge actually relating to the dedication to *In the Days*, 'To an Old Mate', as the latter is set in italic in a smaller typeface but leaded to approximate a 12-point body.) The entry of 4 February records what was must have been the second page design. The same folio records for 30 November 1895: 'To 1 Copy Gaunt's Moving Finger (sample of type)', 1s.9d. This novel had recently appeared in Methuen's Colonial Library. An evidently related charge is then recorded for 21 December 1895: 'To Setting up 3pp. in pica (Drover's Wife)'.

put aside for the rest of that month and January. Since there was a well established commercial relationship between publisher and printer, work on typesetting the first half of the volume could have begun in advance of the printer's quotation of costs of 6 March and, as we shall see, must have done so before Robertson's calculations of 7 April.

The typesetting

On 19 February 1896, with *In the Days* only just published, Lawson took himself off to New Zealand – his final period of freedom as a bachelor. He arrived back in Sydney on 10 March. He had promised his New Zealand friends in October 1895 that he would come and see them before Christmas, but he scarcely gave himself time to step ashore there before heading back. This suggests the pressure of looming deadlines, which Tom Mills in Wellington confirmed in an undated letter, probably of March 1896, to W. A. Woods: 'Last week Lawson dropped in here ... he'd promised R. & A. [i.e. Angus & Robertson] to come back in three weeks to bring out his prose'. Lawson had left the manuscript of 'An Unfinished Love Story' with Mills on his previous visit to New Zealand in 1893–94, having borrowed £1 from Mills and asking him to place it in a New Zealand newspaper or magazine and keep the first pound in payment of the loan. '[J]ust as the boat was leaving', Mills later wrote to Angus & Robertson, 'he mentioned the story, and asked me to send it on to you for his book of sketches. This I did by the following boat'; 'he would have *missed the boat* had I not held him to his duty to you'. This was surely another reason for the trip: retrieving needed content for the volume.[18]

---

[18] Both letters in *Letters* 423, 422. Mills was asking for the £1 now that A&R had published the story in *Billy Boils*. In *My Henry Lawson* (1943), Bertha implies that the trip was cut short because of HL's urgent desire to return to her (quoted in *Collected Verse*, I. 458). 'Thin Lips and False Teeth' is the sequel of 'An Unfinished Love Story' and was originally published in the *Worker* on 10 November 1894 (see *Commentaries* 135: the story appeared only in a special issue of *Over the Sliprails*, where the statement about its being a sequel occurs.) It develops implications, present in the first story, as the main character – the hard-hearted and self-indulgent Brook – trifles with the affections of Lizzie Drew only to break her heart. A silent sufferer, she now emerges as the epicentre of both stories. The relationship of the two stories suggests that 'An Unfinished Love Story' – completed by 20 July 1894 when HL left Wellington for Sydney – was probably not revised in 1896 prior to its appearance in the *Worker* on 21 March 1896.

CHAPTER 6 . RESPECTING THE MARKETPLACE

If any galley proofs were ready by 10 March upon his return, Lawson could have immediately set to work on them. He probably did, for at least some page proofs (the next stage) were ready by 9 April 1896, when Robertson sent off 'a few page proofs of Lawsons Stories' to a bookseller friend in Melbourne, Henry Hyde Champion, editor of the eponymous literary magazine the *Champion*, in the hope that he would give the forthcoming collection 'a sentence or two' in the review of *In the Days* that Champion was writing for the *Age*.[19] Robertson adds that the new title 'will be over 300 pp we think'. This shows that the typesetting was still proceeding at that date.

The letter to Champion suggests a probable date for the completion of the two stories in holograph in A1867-8. Their appearance – first one, then the other – on Robertson's desk may have been what tipped the scales towards achieving something like a 336 page-extent. Between them, 'The Geological Speiler' and 'For Auld Lang Syne' made eighteen printed pages. Neither has an illustration, and at twelve pages the former is the second longest story in the volume. Only the originally serialised 'Jones' Alley' is longer (by one printed page).

The typesetting must soon have concluded. On 5 May 1896 Jose was paid £2.2s. in relation to *While the Billy Boils* for 'Reading'. It seems that this was for his work on printer's copy. His only subsequent income from this title was 6s.6d., recorded in the ledgers on 30 October 1896; this may relate to the proofs of the two stories written out by Bertha, which, as we have seen, were to be sent to him.[20] The total amount that Jose received is only half what he got in the same year for his work on Dyson's *Rhymes from the Mines* and two-thirds of his receipts for Louis Becke and Walter Jeffrey's *The Mutineers*. His hourly rate is given in an

---

[19] ML MSS 3269/71/4, fol. 180.
[20] For another possible explanation of the charge, see Chapter 7 p. 157. Gertrude Townshend Mayer received £7.12s. from the London publisher Bentley in 1886 for abridging and editing Caroline Leakey's *Broad Arrow*, and Royal Gettmann gives the range £5–£25 as typical of Bentley's payments to such editors: *A Victorian Publisher: A Study of the Bentley Papers* (Cambridge: Cambridge University Press, 1960), pp. 227–8. A slightly unclear entry in the Publication Ledger ('To Sending [illegible] Edit') gives the £7.12s. amount (Richard Bentley & Son Archive, British Library, vol. 40, p. 107).

autograph manuscript statement for Angus & Robertson of his work completed to date and of what remained.[21] At the stated rate, he can only have worked on *While the Billy Boils* for fourteen hours in total; so he can have done very little work – paid work at least – on the proofs, even though he definitely worked on proofs of Dyson's volume (see Appendix 1). Perhaps George Robertson or Hugh Maccallum filled the gap; and, as we shall see, Lawson must have as well. No charges would need entering in the Ledgers in either case. Robertson had certainly read proof of at least some parts of *In the Days* and had written to Lawson requesting he make changes to two poems to help sales.[22] But there is no corresponding letter in the firm's Letterbooks in relation to *While the Billy Boils*.

Only one story received additions in proofs large enough to alter the pagination: '"Tom's Selection"' ['Settling on the Land']. This, the second

---

[21] ML MSS 314/41, p. 179, where his rates for various kinds of work are also itemised. His hourly rate for the £2.2s. payment was 3s.6d. Against 'Lawson's verse' is charged £2.2s. (this, completed) and against Lawson's stories ('Unfinished'), 12 hours for the same amount. The Ledgers give the two amounts for *Billy Boils*: ML MSS 3269/11/1, fols. 46 and 78. The two charges for Jose's work on Dyson's *Rhymes from the Mines* are recorded at 5 May 1896, 'Mr. Jose Reading' 17s.6d., and 3 November 1896, 'Mr Jose's Reading & Correcting' £3.8s. (MSS 3269/11/1, fol. 55); and a charge against Louis Becke and Walter Jeffrey's *The Mutineers* at 26 November 1896, 'Paid to Mr Jose as reader' £3.3s. (MSS 3269/11/1, fol. 57).

Cf. a letter to Jose from GR, 30 October 1916: 'I am sending you forty-six galleys of prose by Banjo Paterson. . . . It has the makings of a "seller", but after giving it about an hour of my precious time I have come to the conclusion that it *needs attention*. So I send it along. It may be a £10 (cash) job, or it may be only a £5 one . . . Hack it about just as if its author were dead, instead of being merely in Egypt. I'll say I did it': quoted in Barker, *George Robertson*, p. 14. The galleys were probably those of a short-story collection *Three Elephant Power* (1917).

[22] Letter, GR to HL, 1 December 1895 from Blackheath in the Blue Mountains where GR had his weekend retreat: ML MSS 3269/44/4, fol. 67 but 'omitted from microfilm due to poor condition of original material'. When inspected in 2008 the original was crumbling badly but parts were legible:

Here are some notes from a bookselling point of view on your proofs. Literary criticism I don't pretend to but I *can* booksellerize. If you can alter any of the lines objected to take my word for it the book will have a much bigger sale. Without a doubt a 5/ vol of Poetry can have but a small sale outside the Shearer of the Shearers class [and the] shorn will buy mighty few. I am sure of this as [I am] of any point in my trade – *and I know it well*. The shorn will wait for a cheap edition for a certainty in 99 cases out of a hundred, and then mostly forget to buy it. [The lines to alter] are nearly all out of Faces [in the Street] & Forward, & possibly a hundred years hence when the conditions are changed that suggested them they might [not] hurt – but [you] may take my word for it that und[er pres]ent day conditions they will.

The letter goes on to discuss the objectionable lines in both poems at some length.

story in the volume, gained about 260 words, enough to force a new page and thus end the volume on page 333 rather than page 332, a little closer to the ideal 336 pages and leaving only one blank leaf. The wording is definitely Lawson's.[23] Conversely, there is no evidence of trimming at proof stage having an effect on pagination.

Had Lawson been asked to make a page? Such a request would make sense. When typeset, folios 1–75 would have created the equivalent of about 164 pages; more copy would presumably have been already sent for typesetting; and rearrangement of the contents was still to happen, as Table 2 in Chapter 5 shows. When Robertson was finally in a position to do what he thought was the final arranging he could then have noticed that 'The Drover's Wife' was starting one page short of 169. Asking Lawson to make a page would have been an obvious recourse. Only then, under this scenario, did Robertson realise the problem with the illustrations. His first two volumes, Paterson's *The Man from Snowy River* and Lawson's *In the Days When the World Was Wide*, had not contained illustrations, so perhaps he was not as alert to this contingency as he might have been.

The production in summary

The likely series of events can now be summarised. Lawson experimented with the sequence of at least a handful of the stories when revising in late 1895.[24] The aim of having 336 printed pages may have looked unachievable to him, assuming he knew of it. It may, indeed, have seemed hard enough to gather sufficient copy for the 300 pages that Robertson initially wanted. Lawson took himself off to New Zealand on 19 February and was back on 10 March. His last-minute request to his friend Tom Mills on the docks in Wellington as he left was to send on 'An Unfinished Love Story' via the next mailboat. This makes perfect sense if the initial target was out of reach when he started for New Zealand. Had he hoped for inspiration on the trip – just as his last voyage to New

---

[23] Recorded in foot-of-page apparatus (pp. 176, 179) in Eggert and Webby.
[24] See Chapter 5 n. 22.

Zealand had produced 'Coming Across.—A Study in the Steerage' and his trip from the North Island to the South Island 'Some Reflections on a Voyage across Cook's Straits (N.Z.)' ['Across the Straits']? If so, nothing came of it for the collection.

In the interim, Robertson evidently finalised the sequence of the first main tranche of printer's copy (folios 1–75 of A1867–8) and sent it off, perhaps in batches, for typesetting. He held back 'The Drover's Wife' from this first tranche, even though it was available for selection, perhaps already hoping that this strong, already well known story could start a second volume if it later became possible and desirable to stimulate market demand by dividing the contents into two cheap series.

After Lawson returned to Sydney on 10 March he must have immediately arranged for the newly unearthed story to be published in newspaper form so that it could be included in the volume. It appeared in the *Worker* on 21 March. This would become the last previously published story to be included in the collection, but in the second half; and neither Lawson's nor Jose's correcting hand appears on its printer's copy for the collection.

With the proofs about to arrive or newly on hand, Robertson made a costing calculation on the basis of a 300-page volume on 7 April 1896, and by 9 April he was able to send a section of page proofs to a bookseller in Melbourne. Perhaps only then noticing that the proofs in hand came out at around 164 pages, his course of action became clear. He evidently told Lawson that more stories would be needed to make up a second lot of 168 pages. Hence Lawson's now having to write two more afresh; in this, he would have the assistance of an amanuensis who was now conveniently on hand and continuously available.

On 15 April Lawson married her, Bertha Bredt the step-daughter of a Sydney bookseller, at a matrimonial agency in Sydney. He was paid for the two new stories as compensation for their not appearing in newspaper or magazine before the volume's appearance. The payments were recorded on 25 April and 2 May, for 'Auld Lang Syne' and 'The Geological Speiler' respectively, suggesting that the longer story came in last.[25] Robertson had then to finalise the sequence of stories and sketches in the first half of the volume and to arrange the contents of the second half: its multiple foliations suggest it went off in more than one batch. Part of it had perhaps gone off already. Finally, Lawson needed to and, as we shall see, did read their proofs. It was while doing so that Robertson was finalising the arrangement of the volume's contents and saw the need for Lawson to add a page of new text in the first half so that 'The Drover's Wife' would start – temporarily as it turned out – on page 169. This desideratum was only sacrificed to a competing one – advantageous placement of the illustrations – when Robertson saw the results of Mahony's labour.

Lawson's final stint: Revising the proofs

Proof correction was the next step in the production chain. The nature of Lawson's intervention in the typeset texts in proof can be partially retrieved and characterised. There is no documentary evidence to show he corrected the proofs, but collation of the printer's copy and the 1896 first edition show very many changes that can only be his as well as very many that are probably not.

The full evidence may be found in the accompanying edition of *While the Billy Boils*; the foot-of-page textual apparatus records the changes. Apart from the extra page of material added to '"Tom's Selection"', the following examples are indicative. In 'A Visit of Condolence' the spelling 'duz' survived Jose's work on the printer's copy (Lawson did not participate in correction of this story). But, given his agreement with Jose when preparing printer's copy, he may well have been responsible for the change at proof stage to 'does'. This supposition proposes itself when one notes, elsewhere in the story, subtle changes of 'Govermint' to 'Guvmint' and 'onest' to 'wunst', which are very unlikely to be the responsibility of George Robertson (or of Jose). On the other hand, Lawson would have had no reason to change 'that covered the coffin' to

---

[25] See further, Chapter 5 n. 6.

'with which the coffin was covered' (in 'The Union Buries its Dead'): this reads like a formalising hand imposing a grammatical nicety. Again, it is difficult not to attribute to Lawson a change such as this in 'The Drover's Wife': 'his brother, who lives on the main road' to 'his brother, who keeps a shanty . . .', especially when one notes in the same story the addition of two new sentences about Black Mary: 'Or, at least, God sent "Jimmy" first, and he sent Black Mary. He put his black face round the door post, took in the situation at a glance, and said cheerfully: "All right Missis—I bring my old woman, she down alonga creek."'

Such extended intervention is unusual. Lawson's proof changes are more usually tinkerings, either continuing to implement the policy agreed with Jose, or small local interventions or clarifications, or polishing or reducing the last paragraph of stories.[26] The lifting of Mitchell's register may be noted in 'On the Edge of a Plain' and probably represents a formalising that is not Lawson's: 'the old folks was alive' and 'his feet is very sore' are corrected to plural usages, and 'watchin'' gains a *g*. But the addition of '—you're smart—' in the same sketch introduces a momentary, sharp counter-note that almost certainly comes from an author who was attending intently to the dialogue as he read:

'. . . they kept watching me, and hardly let me go outside for fear I'd'—
'Get drunk?'
'No,—you're smart—for fear I'd clear.'

On the other hand, Lawson seems to have been either unable to remember or to have lacked the confidence to retrieve his earlier wordings and presentations, some of which were originally quite delicate but had been insensitively formalised by Jose. For example, in the *Bulletin* version

---

[26] E.g. 'The Union Buries its Dead': see Eggert and Webby. Cf. the ending of '"Dossing Out" and "Camping"', where the deletion of the last sentence for *Billy Boils* removes a reminder of the original version's 1893 present; and of 'For Auld Lang Syne' where the two-sentence last paragraph is removed. As Jose had been critical of several of the endings in printer's copy these surgical removals may have been at his suggestion or instigation. But in 'Remailed', it must have been HL who added to Dowell, Esq,'s address 'Munnigrubb Station'; and two new sentences and a clause to 'Shooting the Moon'. In 'Steelman' it was probably HL who changed 'said the utterly defeated Brown' to 'said Brown, wearily'; and in 'Jones' Alley' it was perhaps HL who simplified the mouthful, 'is often superior and more ready than that of many educated men-of-the-world', to '. . . superior to many educated . . .'.

of '"Stragglers": A Sketch Out Back', we read: 'They are all shearers, or, at least, they say they are. Some might be "only rousers"'. In printer's copy in Jose's hand, the opening inverted commas before 'only' were shifted to come before 'rousers', thus converting Lawson's trademark use of the quotation to locate a story within the linguistic world of the shearers to a self-conscious, defensive even fussy acknowledgement that the word was, to the envisaged reader, non-standard. Jose's re-marking got through proofs of *While the Billy Boils* unscathed. Similarly, there are several cases, including one in the same sketch, of Lawson allowing Jose's correction of 'o' ' to 'of' to proceed to print, even though it removed some of the colloquiality of setting and expectation.

'Another of Mitchell's Plans for the Future' gained other bluntings of Lawson's original presentations in proofs: 'd'yer' became 'd'you'; 'There's some grand girls' became 'There are . . .', and so on. It is not inconceivable that Lawson, if still seized of the force of his agreement with Jose, perpetrated them himself. '"Some Day": A Swagman's Love Story' is especially afflicted with such regularisations but also contains a new single-sentence paragraph that must be Lawson's: 'He smoked for awhile in savage silence; then he knocked the ashes out of his pipe, felt for his tobacco with a sigh, and said:'.

Despite the likelihood that at least two sets of eyes corrected proofs some typesetting errors were newly introduced. For instance in '"Rats"', the exclamation mark after 'gullet' in the newspaper version became, wrongly, a question mark: '". . . The hook's half way down his blessed gullet?"' Again, a typesetter might be responsible for the expected comma instead of the newspaper's full-stop in 'A Camp-fire Yarn'. An 'old maid', who has followed a young carpenter to Albany in Western Australia, thus forcing him to acknowledge their promised marriage from which he has fled, is speaking: '"That isn't our room: *this* is our room. Bobbie! Come back at once! . . ."'. *While the Billy Boils* reads '. . . room, Bobbie! . . .', thus eliminating the implicit stage-play of Bobbie's trying to slink away from his unwelcome fate.

The evidence of the printer's copy, in-house correspondence and proofs shows that the 'Lawson' who stood as author on the title-page of the Angus & Robertson version of the stories was supported by a far more collective set of writing, editing and publishing processes than the one whose signature stood at the bottom of the newspaper versions of those same stories and sketches.

With the proof stage completed, the volume could go to print. But the printing trades in Sydney were simply not geared up for the sudden demand, as Robertson would complain in a letter to Young J. Pentland, a former fellow bookseller's apprentice of Angus's Edinburgh days and now Angus & Robertson's agent in London and Edinburgh:[27]

> The trouble we have had in reaching the stage we are at (we are by no means satisfied with it) has been enormous. Only one firm in Sydney has enough small pica to set up 150pp. & stereotyping as you go along is awkward. . . . In order to turn 150 copies per day out the binders have to go at it from 8 am till 10 pm.[28]

The letter's reference to the shortage of type sounds general in its application even though Robertson was presumably expressing a very recent frustration – the letter is dated 12 September 1896 – and thus about a production subsequent to that of *While the Billy Boils*. Nevertheless, it is a reminder of one further likely lack of authorial control over the collection: its proofs were probably checked in batches (since the volume made 333 pages) without any opportunity of altering the batches already checked and then stereotyped. Once this was done the standing type could be distributed, allowing it to be reused for the next section of typesetting. This limitation may well have affected *While the Billy Boils*.

If so, the approximately 164 printed pages produced by the original foliation may have been an attempt to send enough copy to exhaust the

---

[27] The complaint is confirmed by a series of letters to booksellers earlier that month: see ML MSS 3269/71/4.
[28] Letter, GR to Young J. Pentland, 12 September 1896 (ML MSS 3269 71/3, fols. 117–18). Binding is nearly always a separate order from printing in the A&R ledgers of the second half of the 1890s. It was done only upon orders from the firm; the printer held the sheets and even the bound copies in stock until needed: see Chapter 7 n. 15.

available type. Table 2 in Chapter 5 covers only stories and sketches up to number 35; of them, only 23–6 and 31–2 were not covered by this initial foliation. 'The Drover's Wife' is number 23. 'Mitchell Doesn't Believe in the Sack', 'Shooting the Moon' and 'His Father's Mate' are 24, 25 and 26. If Robertson found himself constrained to settle the sequence of contents so as to allow distribution of the type for re-use, then he could have done so for, say, the first 120 pages ('The Drover's Wife' begins on page 127 in the published edition), moving stories 27–30 and 33–5 to later in the volume, thus allowing stories 1–22 to fall into their final position. He must then have ordered the typesetting of the remainder of printer's copy, probably sent in batches. At some stage in this latter process the necessary relocation of 'The Drover's Wife' must have been settled by reference to Mahony's drawings, whether completed or semi-completed. Once this had happened, neither Robertson nor Lawson would have been able to consider the sequence of stories as a whole, nor have been in a position to call for their re-sequencing.

Conclusion

In the face of this bibliographical reasoning about the archival evidence one irresistible conclusion emerges. Whatever the author's wishes as to the number and sequencing of stories, they came a distant second to his publisher's production constraints and marketing considerations. The initial unavailability of some stories, either awaiting publication in the *Bulletin* or unable to be found, would have been a further frustrating factor. This in turn meant that Lawson's late 1895 burst of effort in the revision, which was not repeated for the later stories as they came to hand, was inconsistently applied across the volume as a whole. At best, the revision of the stories, their number and sequence seem to have been the outcome of a number of pressures of which Lawson was only in partial control.

This conclusion complements what the analysis of the evidence in Chapter 5 showed of the process of revision and copy-editing of printer's copy: that, whatever texts for the book publication Lawson might have arrived at undirected, he became caught up in a collaboration that inevitably affected and to a significant extent dictated the terms of his engagement with his own newspaper texts. The traditional definition of the literary work as the text of the author, to which the scholarly editor's 'text of final authorial intention' responds, becomes impossibly distended under this bibliographical and book-historical gaze. Nevertheless, it is possible and practicable to retrieve the earliest published forms of Lawson's stories, to complement this editorial act with documentation of the textual changes effected along the way to book publication in 1896, and to attribute individual responsibility for those changes. This, in a nutshell, is the approach of the accompanying edition.[29]

It is equally possible as an editor to understand the work-as-published *un*critically as a historical fact: as the destination point of the various people involved in its production, and to acknowledge additionally that that text became the one encountered by its readers. For that reason a study of the series of publication events of *While the Billy Boils* and its contents is necessary, not only prior to 1896, as has been done so far, but also after 1896. This, and the collection's reception from that time, are the subject of the next two chapters.

---

[29] The Introduction in Eggert and Webby contains a full discussion.

CHAPTER 7

LAWSON'S NO LONGER

PUBLICATION OF *WHILE THE BILLY BOILS*

Printing and publication

While the Billy Boils was given over to its public on 29 August 1896.[1] It contained a Preface by 'THE PUBLISHERS' dated 14 August. Lawson had written his own Preface for *In the Days When the World Was Wide* but, as the new one explained:

> IN the absence of the author, who is now resident in Western Australia, it devolves upon us to make the customary acknowledgments to the various journals from which these stories are reprinted. Most of them first appeared in the Sydney *Bulletin*, a number of them in the Sydney *Worker*, and others in the *New Zealand Mail*, the *New Zealand Times*, Sydney *Truth*, the Brisbane *Boomerang*, the *Maryborough Patriot*, and *The Antipodean*, while two are now published for the first time.
>
> We may rightly be deemed ungrateful did we not take this opportunity of thanking the Press of Australia and New Zealand for the aid they have given us in our effort to publish here, and in a presentable form, the works of some of our living writers. Especially are our thanks due to the proprietors of the Sydney *Bulletin* who have in many ways assisted us.

The Preface positions the volume not within the *oeuvre* of an established writer, nor within the biography of an emerging one, but within a print culture (the first paragraph) and a publishing business (the second), one built upon good will and co-operation. This was a completion of what

---

[1] The date is established from a letter from GR to Pentland, 12 September 1896: '*While the Billy Boils* . . . is a fortnight old today and 1900 have been sold' (ML MSS 3269/71/3, fol. 117). For a quasi-facsimile description of the volume, see Mackaness 13–14.

might be dubbed a logic of book decorum – or fittingness for the new purpose – quite different from that of the newspapers. A standardising had been imposed visually and textually on the stories and sketches during their design, editing and typesetting. Part of that decorum was (and still is) to draw no attention to the printed volume's calm and reassuring resolution of the very many niggling issues, all in need of decision, that arose, as we have seen, during its production. A restrained page design lent the illusion of transparency to the textual contents. It was rhetorically powerful without having uttered a single word.

Given the trying circumstances surveyed in the last three chapters, Robertson's reference to the volume's 'presentable form' in the second paragraph was wonderfully mild – but also purposeful. He was evidently hoping that the good response in the press to the firm's first two volumes (Paterson's and Lawson's verse collections) would continue for its third. The details of the first paragraph are not precisely accurate. For instance, the Sydney *Worker*'s contribution to the contents is far more important than stated thus initiating an appropriation of Lawson to the *Bulletin* that has misled generations of critics. Again, five of the stories were sourced from their already revised versions in *Short Stories in Prose and Verse*, not from their original newspaper or magazine versions. But, of course, Robertson would have sensed that the less said in these ways the better. His firm was the publisher of a literary property whose now stabilised and permanent material form would once and for all supersede the many earlier, scattered appearances of its contents in miscellaneous and ephemeral publications. With two impressively produced collections now published, Henry Lawson as Author had decisively arrived on the print-cultural scene in Australia; and so had Angus & Robertson as Publisher.

The writing of the Preface had been preceded by a general clearing-up of the financial indebtedness; and the collection received – at last – its title. Thus, as we saw in Chapter 3, on 23 June 1896 the overall contractual arrangement was clarified in a new agreement for the volume, pursuant to the original one of 26 July 1895, with Angus & Robertson purchasing '[e]verything published serially in any newspaper prior to 23 June 1896 bought by us under agt. of that date.'[2] The Copyright payment of £42 for *While the Billy Boils* was made the next day, Lawson having decided he could not wait for the receipt of profits, of which Robertson had originally offered him a half share. On 30 June Lawson and his new wife left for Western Australia.

Settling on a title

In Angus & Robertson's first eight-page catalogue of their own publications dated November 1895, Lawson's volume of stories was described only as 'Prose Sketches'; they would be available '*Shortly*'. This was repeated in the advertisement section, dated January 1896, that appeared at the end of copies of *In the Days* when it was released in February. In a letter of 20 March 1896, Robertson told Jose: 'I have a letter from the Editor of Review of Reviews asking me to ask Professor MacCallum to review Lawsons volume of Prose when it appears.'[3] And Robertson's calculation of the costs of printing *While the Billy Boils*, dated 7 April 1896, referred to it only as 'Lawsons prose'. In correspondence in 1919 Robertson would recall that Jose had thought of the title,[4] which nowhere appears on printer's copy for the collection (A1867–8). Instead, only '1 H.L.' and '2 HL' are given as identifiers for the first and second stories, and nothing thereafter.

---

[2] The payment (for 'Copyright £42') is entered in the Ledger (ML MSS 3269/11/1, fol. 46), and dated 24 June 1896. ML MSS 314/246 is a card catalogue of HL works owned by A&R, prepared at a later date. Card 71 is for 'The Geological Spieler': 'c'right phd [purchased] 26/3/96': this date is repeated on the cards for all other stories in *Billy Boils*. On the first page of 'The Geological Spieler' in A1867–8 there is a lead-pencilled annotation: 'Estimated 2½ cols/ 2-10-0': hence the payment to HL for the story recorded on 2 May 1896 (see Chapter 6 p. 140). Thus '26/3/96' seems to be a consistent mistake, a transposition, for 23 June 1896.

Evidently the agreed rate was £1 per newspaper column in 1896; but by 1898, recognising HL's success in the interim, the rate had risen to four guineas: the Agreement for *On the Track and Over the Sliprails*, dated 27 August 1898 but signed on 1 September, contained provision for HL to be paid £25 for six unpublished stories at £4.4s. each (ML MSS 3269/316/Angus & Robertson Correspondence, vol. 828, pp. 167–81).

[3] ML MSS 3269/71/4, fol. 156.

[4] Letters between GR and Hugh Wright of A&R, 13 February, 21 March and 26 March 1919 (ML MSS 314/47, pp. 1, 7, 11). Teresa Pagliaro first noted this: 'Jose's Editing', p. 82.

On 4 May, by which time the proof reading may have been nearly completed, Robertson mentioned 'Lawsons Prose volume' in a letter to an Adelaide bookseller, E. S. Wigg & Co., adding that he hoped to have it ready 'in June'.[5] On 20 June the prediction became 'in July'; and while the degraded condition of the letterbooks rules out certainty on the matter, this appears to be Robertson's first extant letter to note the new title, 'While the Billy Boils'.[6] Yet Lawson apparently did not yet know of it.

Jose's source of the title is an interesting matter. The meaning of *billy* as a vessel in which to boil water to make tea had long been a colloquial usage in the Australasian colonies.[7] As we have seen, in 1891 Lawson had invoked what was evidently already a traditional association in leftwing circles in his poem 'Freedom on the Wallaby': '[Freedom's] goin' to light another fire/ And boil another billy'. Despite being a committed (and therefore, in the politics of the day, rightwing) Imperial Federationist, Jose evidently felt he could safely invoke the alternative, sentimental meaning of male camaraderie and yarn-spinning around the campfire. Its literary form went at least as far back as Garnet Walch's *The 'Fireflash': Four Oars and a Coxswain* (1867), in which a group of male friends goes on a rowing and sailing excursion on Sydney Harbour. They finally land at The Spit and camp for the night: 'beneath the overspreading branches of a large tree our noble selves are grouped "waiting for the billy to boil"'.[8] Each man takes his turn to tell a tale. Susan Nugent Woods's series of two short stories 'Beside the Billy' in the *Australian Journal* in 1870 adopted the trope. In her stories, the first-person narrator, a goldfields Commissioner, recollects the rough living conditions and bitter winter weather of the goldmining districts in Otago in New Zealand, where the male society around the billy at night would prompt the storytelling instinct: 'it boiled in no time, and

---

[5] 'Authors Letterbook', 1895–97, ML MSS3269/71/4, fol. 195 (letter to E. S. Wigg & Co., Adelaide).
[6] *Ibid.*, fols. 220–1 (letter to E. S. Wigg & Co., Adelaide).
[7] First recorded in 1839 from a New Zealand source (*Australian National Dictionary*, 1988).
[8] Garnet Walch, *The 'Fireflash,' Four Oars and a Coxswain: Where They Went, How They Went, and Why They Went and the Stories They Told Last Christmas Eve* (Sydney: Gordon & Gotch, 1867), p. 13.

its very breath, as it floated out in odorous steam, lifting the lid for its own convenience, gave us heart for the present and hope for the future'.[9] Though concerned with poor workingmen, these two tales of death in the snow, and of murder, consciously cultivate mid-Victorian middle-class sentiment.

More recently and directly in 1888 (and thus Jose's more likely source), the billy motif had been used in an influential collection in a poem by Keighley Goodchild entitled 'While the Billy Boils': 'In calm content by the fire we lie,/ And watch while the billy boils.' It is a time when 'We can revel in tea and talk'. This apolitical inflection, Jose may have felt, would help defend the apparent artlessness and the compromised sequencing of Lawson's collection of yarns.[10]

The delay in publication until August 1896

As we have seen, George Robertson's change of mind in April–May 1896 about the desirable page-extent of Lawson's prose collection would have been one factor in its delayed appearance. The firm's other unexpected demands on the printer may also have been slowing things down during 1896: the need for reprints of the Paterson and Lawson verse collections; and the productions of a midwifery textbook (on commission) and Edward Dyson's *Rhymes from the Mines*.[11] On 11 July Robertson informed James MacLehose & Sons, which acted as Angus

---

[9] Woods's stories 'Beside the Billy', *Australian Journal*, 5, no. 61 (June 1870), 584–5 [p. 584]; and 'Beside the Billy No. II', *ibid.*, 6, no. 64 (September 1870), 34–5.

[10] For the leftwing inflection, cf. 'Australia's on the Wallaby', a poem by 'H. C.': 'We're bound for New Australia, and the billy's on the boil' (line 4: *Worker*, 26 August 1893, p. 3, reprinted from *New Australia*). 'H. C.' meant Head Central, i.e. Walter W. Head, editor of the association's journal from its establishment in November 1892.

Goodchild's ballad 'While the Billy Boils' appeared in two of the three centennial collections of Australian poetry edited by the entrepreneurial Douglas Sladen: in *Australian Ballads and Rhymes* and in its 'enlarged' edition *A Century of Australian Song* (both: London: Walter Scott Company, 1888); originally in Goodchild's privately published *Who Are You?* (Echuca, Vic., 1883). See n. 4 above: Wright informed GR of the Goodchild precedent.

David McKee Wright submitted a ballad 'While the Billy Boils' dated 'August 6' to the *Otago Witness* as number IX in a series that had commenced in June 1896. It appeared on 27 August 1896. Given that advance copies of HL's collection were probably not available in Sydney until 12 August, the common use of the title must be a coincidence.

[11] See Appendix 1.

& Robertson's Glasgow distributor, that the collection would 'be out in about a fortnight'; and on 23 July Robertson told the Hobart booksellers Propsting and Cockhead that it was 'being printed now and there can be no doubt it is the best looking vol of prose ever done out here – and we think the best stuff too'.[12] This sounds as if advance copies were imminent.

There would soon be frustrations, however. Robertson's post-publication complaint, quoted in Chapter 6, about the shortage of type in Sydney, is from the heart. The other likely cause of delay was the illustrations. They did not need to observe the same production deadlines as the typesetting and printing. The two processes only needed to come together at the end, when the letterpress captions were added. The title-page vignette by Mahony used in the published volume was not charged in the Ledgers until 18 May and the charge for the blocks of the illustrations not until July. As we saw in Chapter 6, Robertson had to resort to his Glasgow connections to get the illustrations printed to a satisfactory standard. This volume's production values were to be much higher than the Sydney trade was used to. Robertson wanted it to look handsome, with deckle-edged pages, gilt top edge and good-quality illustrations – what various reviewers called a good 'get-up', one that would more than hold its own in the London or Scottish book trade, from which Robertson himself had come. Achieving this in a Sydney printing industry used mainly to newspaper and jobbing work would have been an uphill battle.

The ledger records payment for printing the illustrations on 1 August 1896 (£6.7s.), and on the same day a charge of nearly £4 for 'Author's Corrections', confirming that a fairly thorough proof reading had indeed been done, as well as a charge of £21.12s.6d. for the making of 'Stereos & Matrices'. These would allow the typesetting to be reproduced (stereotyped) and printed cheaply into the future: but the charge represented yet another investment in that future. As far as Angus & Robertson was concerned, this volume had much financial work

[12] Respectively, ML MSS 3269/71/3, fol. 79 and MSS 3269/71/4, fol. 238.

to do. The printing cost, which would have included the typesetting, is recorded on 23 September 1896 for 3,000 copies at £93.10s. and the binding of the same number as £114.10s. Charges for paper and cloth are recorded separately because separately sourced, much having to be imported via Pentland, the firm's agent in Britain.[13]

The 'Thousands' of *While the Billy Boils*

Robertson soon adopted the idea, which he had used for his first two titles, of recording sales progress on the title-page, doubtless as a promotion tool. Thus the first thousand copies of the first edition simply record '1896' on the title-page (see page 32 above), but thereafter the issues were labelled 'Second Thousand', 'Third Thousand', and so on, even though the first two impressions were of 3,000 each. The first impression was printed by Websdale, Shoosmith but the second one was printed late in 1896 by McCarron, Stewart & Co. of Pitt Street, Sydney at the much-reduced cost of £26.15s. for the 3,000 (since the cost of typesetting had already been met) with the binding of the fourth thousand at £21.13s.4d. The pressure of sales and the production delays had evidently caused Robertson to engage a new printer to cope with the demand.[14]

In Angus & Robertson's Publishing Progress Register – which records by date the movement of goods to and from printers, and proofs to and from authors – stereotyped plates of *While the Billy Boils* are recorded as sent to McCarron, Stewart on 8 October 1896 with first bound copies received on 24 October (the Fourth Thousand).

Sales remained fairly brisk, for this issue was exhausted by the end of the following January and the Fifth Thousand were supplied as 567

---

[13] ML MSS 3269/11/1, fol. 46.
[14] ML MSS 3269/11/3, fol. 78. GR was negotiating details of binding by 6 November 1896 and the charges are booked at 4 January 1897: see letter, GR to McCarron, Stewart & Co., 6 November 1896 (ML MSS 3269/71/4, fol. 409). He had first approached Websdale, Shoosmith for a quote and would return to them thereafter: see letter, GR to Websdale, Shoosmith, 10 September 1896 (ML MSS 3269/71/4, fol. 337). Without changing the signature names (A, B, C, etc.) McCarron, Stewart printed in sixteenmo format (evident in the gathering and sewing), presumably on a larger press than had been available to Websdale, Shoosmith, who had printed (and would subsequently print) in octavo.

'quires' on 10, 13 and 18 March 1897, and the remainder in book form in instalments until 30 June. Copies of the Sixth Thousand were received from 11 September 1897; the last copies came into stock on 10 March 1898.[15]

The English issue of While the Billy Boils

The Fourth Thousand was issued normally for the local market, as was, presumably, part of the Fifth.[16] From the latter, however, 'quires' (either in the form of gathered or gathered-and-sewn sheets, perhaps made up into sewn book blocks) were sent to England for binding and publication there by Simpkin, Marshall, Hamilton, Kent & Co. of London. This issue was given a reset title-page dated '1897'. Without the usual sixteen-page Angus & Robertson catalogue at the back, the Simpkin, Marshall issue appeared in early July.[17] Copies of the Sixth Thousand inspected in Australian libraries have catalogues dated September or December 1897.[18]

The special English issue of 1897 was, in the event, a compromise; it was not what Robertson had originally aimed for. He had busied

[15] ML MSS 3269/12/1, fol. 6. As stereos had been returned on 10 September 1897 the printer must have been warehousing copies or sheets for A&R awaiting binding, since the number of copies received is usually only 24 or 48, often repeated every second day.

[16] There is a copy in the Baillieu Library, University of Melbourne.

[17] The 'Simpkin' issue of *Billy Boils* is noted as among 'THIS WEEK'S BOOKS', *Saturday Review* (3 July 1897), p. 22. The British Museum copy is stamped '24AU97'.

Elaine Zinkhan kindly provided me with photocopies of front matter from copies of the London issue she inspected in the Cambridge University Library, the Bodleian, the National Library of Scotland, the British Library, the Widener Library at Harvard and the library of the University of Texas at Austin. Copies inspected in Australia showed no variation. All are dated 1897. Mentioned in copies of *Billy Boils*, A&R's Canadian distributor was Hart & Riddell – booksellers, publishers, stationers and binders – established in 1892 in Toronto (originally as Hart & Co. from 1873). S. R. Hart was a Canadian; M. Riddell was a Scot who had worked with the publisher William Collins in Glasgow. A&R also had distributors in Cape Town (J. C. Juta & Co.), Bombay (Thacker & Co.), Calcutta (Thacker, Spink & Co.) and Glasgow (James MacLehose & Sons).

Another 514 copies (from the Sixth Thousand) are recorded separately as one (undated) indent. Since GR informed HL on 8 May 1898 that Simpkin, Marshall had been supplied with 1,000 copies to date (*Letters* 429), the 514 must have been a second shipment to England, despite an earlier intention to have the volume printed there (see Appendix 2 n. 4). They were issued with the title-page of Simpkin, Marshall, Hamilton and dated 1898 as the 'Seventh Edition' (copy at NLA; it has both Simpkin, Marshall and ordinary A&R advertising endmatter: the latter is dated April 1901, so the title evidently sold slowly in London after 1898).

[18] Respectively, Tom Collins House, Perth, and ADFA Library Special Collections, Canberra.

himself in the days immediately after publication in Sydney to achieve a similar result in London with a 'Home' issue brought out by a well known publisher. The traditional flow of books from London published in colonial editions series offered a model: surely, Robertson must have reasoned, it would work in reverse so long as the books were of high quality. Even though reviews of the English issue would inevitably be delayed they would, as the magazines that carried them filtered back to Australia, give a second boost to sales there as well as establishing a bridgehead for Lawson and the firm in the British market.

The resistance Robertson encountered amongst the trade in London as he tried to secure regular publication for the collection and also for *In the Days When the World Was Wide* came as a shock to him. Robertson at first asked his old Glasgow employer James MacLehose & Sons to place the collection with a publisher. Having already failed to do so with Paterson's *The Man from Snowy River and Other Verses* (1895) and Lawson's *In the Days When the World Was Wide and Other Verses*, on 8 October 1896 the Glasgow firm appointed the literary agency A. P. Watt in London to act on Angus & Robertson's behalf with the two Lawson titles. Although dilatory at first and then unsuccessful with various firms, the agency at length managed to secure an agreement for *While the Billy Boils* with Methuen. On 2 March 1897 Watt advised acceptance despite the offer being considered low by MacLehose, since the only present alternative, Simpkin, Marshall, 'are principally a distributing house, and not publishers in the sense in which Messrs. Methuen & co. are'.[19]

Methuen or Watt must have already written separately to Angus & Robertson (or cabling occurred) because less than three weeks later, on 22 March 1897, the firm formally accepted Methuen's offer. But when the 500-odd quires were received Methuen rejected them because they

---

[19] Methuen's offer of 1s.8d. per quire was considered low and was not immediately accepted: MacLehose to GR, 22 January 1897 (ML MSS 314/57, pp. 431–3); Watt to MacLehose, 2 March 1897 (ML MSS 314/87, pp. 355–7). Watt found HL's verse title impossible to place. On 10 December 1896 MacLehose had proposed Simpkin, Marshall to GR as a fallback when A. P. Watt was initially reporting failure to secure a placement for the HL titles (ML MSS 314/57, pp. 427–9); Watt's letter to MacLehose was 8 December 1896 (*ibid.*, pp. 425–6).

had been printed on an inferior wove paper stock: not the antique deckle-edged laid stock, trimmed only at the top edge for the application of gilt, used for the first impression of 3,000 that Methuen had been shown.[20] Robertson later explained in a letter to Lawson of 8 May 1898 that the requisite paper had not been obtainable in Sydney and so he probably anticipated that, as the quality of the goods delivered fell short of those promised at an agreed price, there was every chance they would be rejected.[21] In another letter dated 22 March 1897, to MacLehose, Robertson advises that: 'If by any chance Methuen retracts, print Simpkin Marshall's name on titlepage, bind and offer to them at 2/6 a copy, sending out 75 for review. Keep 5th Thousand at foot of titlepage. Should the alternative arrangement be necessary, subscribe to some press-cutting agency and send us all reviews.'[22]

Like all Australian writers of his time Lawson understood where literary recognition needed to be achieved if commercial success, on a scale far larger than the colonies could afford, was to follow. So he was understandably anxious in a letter to Robertson of 3 September 1896

---

[20] Elaine Zinkhan provides a highly detailed and reliable account in 'Early British Publication of *While the Billy Boils*: The A. P. Watt Connection', *Bibliographical Society of Australia and New Zealand Bulletin*, 21 (1997), 165–82. Zinkhan's sources are predominantly ML MSS 314 (GR's selection from the firm's archive) and the A. P. Watt Records, collection no. 11036, at the Wilson Library, University of North Carolina, Chapel Hill. The present account also uses documents from ML MSS 3269, some of which (letters of 22 March 1897) are letter-book copies of correspondence from GR whose originals are preserved at Chapel Hill: ML MSS 3269/125/72, on fols. 117 (to Methuen) and 123 (to James MacLehose & Sons), which are placed at the beginning of this Letterbook, out of sequence and physically crumbling.

[21] *Letters* 429. When arranging for the second impression of 3,000 to be printed GR had originally approached Websdale, Shoosmith on 10 September 1896 for a quote on the basis of '48 lb double Crown' paper stock whereas GR had calculated the first impression on the basis of 'Dble Deckle Edge Dble crown 35 lb 17/[shillings] per ream landed' (ML MSS 3269/71/4, fols. 337 and 299 [7 April 1896] respectively.) The same request for a quote includes the binding with 'the cloth (not buckram this time) to be supplied by us'. This suggests that GR was deliberately trying to cut costs, although the unavailability could well have been true and known to him when he sought the quote on the basis of an alternative.

[22] Letter reproduced from the A. P. Watt Records in Zinkhan, 'A. P. Watt Connection', p. 176. The facts that GR specifically asked for '5th Thousand' to be added to any title-pages printed in Britain, that the initial quires sent are recorded as being from the Fifth Thousand in the Publishing Progress Register, and that all the Simpkin, Marshall copies sighted have '*Sixth Thousand*' on their title-page suggest that some mix-up in the numbering occurred in Britain.

from Western Australia upon first seeing a copy of his book that we 'Must have English edition of "Billy Boils" perfect. I'll see to that'.[23] In his next letter, having now looked more closely at the volume, he pointed out a couple of textual errors he had noticed; and in his next letter he suggested that Robertson had 'Better get a reliable reader to go through a copy, copy his corrections into another, and send to me'.[24] Lawson seemed to think that a new typesetting would be feasible but, given that stereotypes had been made and that resetting was expensive and unnecessary, only a very few corrections would be feasible. Each one would need to be effected by sweating the replacement characters of cold type into the exact position in the lead plates. Although, as mentioned in Chapter 6, the Publishing Ledger records a charge against *While the Billy Boils* of 6s.6d. on 30 October 1896 for 'Mr Jose – Reading', and although, in addition, another charge for 'Alteration to Stereos' is recorded on 30 December 1896, there is no textual evidence that any correction actually occurred until the printing of the third impression in late 1897, and even then it involved only one isolated case.[25]

After Methuen's withdrawal, Blackwood in Scotland expressed interest in publishing the collection, writing to Lawson and Angus & Robertson. George Robertson replied on 15 June 1897:

> We have yours of May 3 re "While the Billy Boils" the copyright of which, as well as of "In the days when the World was Wide & other verses belongs to us. Stereos of both books are in the hands of Messrs James MacLehose & Sons with instructions to print a British edition if one can be arranged for by Messrs A P Watt [&] Son. So far as we know nothing has yet been done and we are writing to our General Agent, Mr Pentland asking him to try to arrange the matter. The stereos we wish to remain

---

[23] *Letters* 63.
[24] *Letters* 63, 64. *Billy Boils* reads 'Lizzie shoved' instead of 'Lizzie shovelled' (HL's letter actually has '"shovel"') in 'An Unfinished Love Story'; and 'dread of daily resurrection' instead of 'daily dread of resurrection' in 'Jones' Alley': see the Commentary to the two stories in Eggert and Webby.
[25] ML MSS 3269/11/1, fol. 78. The revision, probably made at HL's direction, deletes a passage from 'An Unfinished Love Story' of a few lines describing the 'poddying' of a calf to wean it from its mother. The aim was clearly to eliminate a near repetition of much the same description, with very similar wording, in 'A Day on a Selection'. For an explanation, see Introduction to Eggert and Webby.

our property & MacLehose will print & deliver in quires to the publisher. The verses are now in their sixth thousand & While the Billy Boils in its fifth thousand here.[26]

Unfortunately MacLehose, 'knowing nothing of Blackwood', as Robertson later explained to Lawson, 'arranged with Simpkin & Co.',[27] in accordance with the instructions Robertson had already given.

Cheaper prices and divided formats

Sales had been gradually slowing down, and it was not until March 1898 that the Sixth Thousand was nearly exhausted. The retail price of 5s. had probably been proving a barrier once the first, carefully stimulated rush was over and the subsequent sales effects of the English reviews of the Simpkin, Marshall special issue were digested in the colonies. It was decision time for Robertson. He wisely decided to cut the price to the same level as colonial editions locally: 3s.6d. for the cloth-covered copies and 2s.6d. for paper and to order a new impression of 3,000 copies for the latter.

Printed by Websdale, Shoosmith, once again on the cheaper wove paper, copies began coming into stock from 29 November 1897, in time for the Christmas market. More than 1,200 were received by 24 December and last copies by the end of May 1898, whereupon another thousand was ordered and received between 9 July and 20 September 1898.[28]

In this way, the Thousands continued to appear, though at reduced prices. Hardbacks in the standard green cloth continued to be produced too, and by 1898 the Twelfth Thousand (counting both forms) had appeared, even though sales of the hardbacks continued to be slow. The Websdale, Shoosmith 'OFFICE COPY' (personal collection), a hardback Twelfth Thousand, has a catalogue dated June 1900 while the Thirteenth

---

[26] ML MSS 3269/72/1, fol. 45; Zinkhan's 'A. P. Watt Connection' overlooks this letter, which continues: 'Your letter to Mr Lawson has been sent on to New Zealand where he now resides and we feel sure he will be pleased with your request to send something for "Maga". No higher compliment could have been paid him.'

[27] GR to HL, 8 May 1898 (*Letters* 429).

[28] Publishing Progress Register (ML MSS 3269/12/2, fols. 24, 44).

Thousand did not appear until 1902.[29] There were 3,733 sales between 1905 and 1922, an average of a little over 200 copies per year,[30] and as late as 1923 this edition continued to be issued in hardback form.[31] Always on the lookout for more ways of exploiting the intellectual property represented by Lawson's collection, Robertson prepared a special issue, gilt with portrait, in 1903 in conjunction with Humphrey Milford, publisher for Oxford University Press, London.[32]

In 1900 Angus & Robertson published *While the Billy Boils* divided into two volumes (called First and Second Series) of 168 pages each and with 'The Drover's Wife' moved to become the lead story of the Second Series – the marketing ploy that, as explained in Chapter 6, Robertson must have had in mind since 1896. Adjustments were entailed, but a single pagination (to page 333) was continuous across the two volumes. New front matter was printed but the typesetting of the 52 stories and sketches otherwise remained the same: thus, bibliographically, these impressions and issues are part of the first edition. In paperback at 1s. the volumes had wrappers with a vignette by Frank Mahony, the same as that used on the original title-page of *While the Billy Boils*. Copies noted by Lawson's bibliographer George Mackaness have catalogues dated October 1899 (First Series) and March 1900 (Second Series). Thicker paper-stock bulked out the volumes. The illustrations remained but the inkwash originals had been redrawn for cheaper (line) reproduction than photographic process engraving.[33] They formed part of what the

[29] Personal copy (3s.6d. hardback). In this copy's advertising section dated May 1902, the title is said to be in its Twenty-third Thousand: the total claimed must include the cheap 1s. Commonwealth Series issues (see next paragraph).
[30] Typed list of sales of various HL titles, 1905–22, perhaps made at HL's death as part of the review that led to a shift in sales strategy in 1923 (ML MSS 3269/Lawson, Henry – papers re 1894–1949, vol. 386, fol. 51).
In an A&R catalogue dated July 1908 – in a 1908 paperback First Series (personal copy) that lacks any title-page statement about which Thousand it is – the advertising of the 3s.6d. hardback title refers to the title as being in its Twenty-Eighth Thousand. It was in its Thirty-Second Thousand in 1916 (Mackaness 15). These figures evidently include sales of the cheap formats.
[31] ML copy sighted. The printer was Marchant & Co., Sydney.
[32] Information in Mackaness 16; no copy sighted. It retailed at 5s.6d., later reduced to 4s.6d.
[33] See Appendix 2. The printer was F. Cunninghame & Co. of Pitt Street, Sydney. Catalogues show that the Australian Book Co. was the London distributor. By 1913 the printer of the

firm now referred to as its (cheap) Commonwealth Series, consisting mainly but not exclusively of Lawson titles, doubtless to take advantage of the approaching Federation of the colonies into the Commonwealth of Australia on 1 January 1901 and to hitch the firm's publishing program in Australian literature and history to that notable event. A special issue was prepared for the bookseller E. W. Cole of Melbourne. It appeared in paperback in 1901 and 1903 with the title-page and front cover adjusted to substitute Cole's name for Angus & Robertson's. In 1906 the two volumes were refreshed with new wrappers illustrated by Norman Lindsay; Cole also released this issue in 1908. These productions are recorded with great particularity in the firm's ledgers and Publishing Progress Register.

At the same time a newly announced series, 'The Billy Boils Edition', was created to promote the continuing one-volume normal trade (cloth) format. Trimmed smaller than earlier printings but still produced by Websdale, Shoosmith, the Thirteenth Thousand was the first of these issues, appearing in 1902. The use of line illustrations and a cheaper paperstock, which started with the Commonwealth Series, are evident in this issue too, and 'The Drover's Wife' is in its new position at page 169.[34] This positioning became standard.[35] Thus the hardback two-series-as-one had now become the derivative format, with printings aimed at covering both formats in different bindings. By 1913 it was being issued, along with some other Lawson titles, in a flexible lighter

hardbacks was W. C. Penfold of Pitt Street, Sydney, but Marchant & Co. of Sydney is given for the First and Second Series. The London distributor is given in a March 1913 catalogue (copy at Fryer Library, University of Queensland) as Oxford University Press.

[34] In this 1902 (personal) copy the Illustrations list is adjusted to reflect the shifted story but it still lists, just as it had since 1896, the first one as being opposite p. 2 (or, at least, as referring to text on p. 2) rather than mentioning its actual place in the volume as frontispiece. Other experiments with presentation continued up to the last minute in 1896, as witnessed by the existence of two states of the front matter of the First Thousand (hitherto unidentified: not in Mackaness). The earlier state is a quarto gathering (four leaves). Adding a leaf for the Illustrations list meant adding a conjugate leaf at the beginning of the front matter; this became the half-title page. This is the second state of the First Thousand. (These two states – both are personal copies – were preceded by the trial issue of 12 copies: see Appendix 2 n. 3.)

[35] Copies sighted where 'The Drover's Wife' begins at p. 169: 1902 ('Thirteenth Thousand'), 1907 and 1923 (no 'Thousands' statement): all at ML.

green hardback cover with elaborate tooling (gold on the spine) in an Art Nouveau style.[36]

'The Billy Boils Edition' series became the home also for some semi-luxury issues of various titles over the years. In 1905 Angus & Robertson also gathered the firm's six Lawson volumes to date under the series title 'The Works of Henry Lawson' at 25s. per set, boxed, and with special bindings in French or Rutland morocco available for an additional outlay.[37]

The publishing life of the collection involved the production and distribution of successive issues that were answered by successive phases of reception. The initial phase represents an especially important and revealing expression of that life of *While the Billy Boils*; it is dealt with in the next chapter. Chapter 9 then deals with Lawson's fortunes while in Britain during 1899–1902, a period in which a selection of the stories and sketches would be revised for publication by a mainstream British publisher, Blackwood.

---

[36] Oxley Library, State Library of Queensland (1913); personal copy and ADFA Library (1915).
[37] See Mackaness 9.

CHAPTER 8

EARLY RECEPTION OF *WHILE THE BILLY BOILS*

THE FIRST FIVE YEARS

A reviewing campaign

REVIEWS do not just happen. They are typically elicited by careful planning on the part of the publisher, whose investment is now most acutely at risk. *While the Billy Boils* received more than 250 reviews, the bulk of them upon first publication, in newspapers and magazines from around the Australasian colonies.[1] A very significant number also appeared in Britain, especially after the release of the Simpkin, Marshall issue in 1897; as did a sprinkling in South Africa after Angus & Robertson arranged for J. C. Juta of Port Elizabeth and Cape Town to act as agent for its books there, also in 1897. The reviews, now preserved in the Mitchell Library, were collected for the Sydney firm by one or more press cutting agencies, and the firm's British agent Young J. Pentland also forwarded others.[2]

Such a bounty of reviews was the result of a careful campaign. Fourteen

---

[1] Alison (p. 261) counted 265. Other A&R titles received fewer, largely because fewer review copies were distributed. Victor Daley's *At Dawn and Dusk* received 118 reviews, Louis Becke and Walter Jeffery's *The Mutineer* 110, Paterson's *The Man from Snowy River* 151 but HL's *In the Days* only 59 (Alison 161).

[2] Only one North American review is known (*Indianapolis Journal*, 2 August 1897), and it is only an excerpt from a review in the London *Academy* (17 July 1897; see below), but other reprintings of British reviews may well have happened. Because, in the late 1890s, A&R had no distribution arrangements in the USA or Canada it is unlikely that books were forwarded there for review. A handwritten brochure for the Australasian and International Press Agency (see Chapter 5 n. 14) is inside the large exercise book containing the reviews of *Billy Boils* from 1896: ML MSS 3269/Angus & Robertson Ltd. Book Reviews (Bound volumes) 1894–1970/1, vol. 7. All reviews mentioned in this chapter are from this source and are unsigned, unless otherwise indicated.

CHAPTER 8 . EARLY RECEPTION 163

of them appeared on the publication date, 29 August 1896 – a Saturday, doubtless chosen to take advantage of the day of issue of the weekly newspapers that were sent throughout the colonies. The reviewers must have been supplied with advance copies. Angus & Robertson, indeed, was generous with them, sending, as the firm's Ledger records, '221 Review Copies as per Jl [Journal]'.[3] These mainly went to bookseller-customers in the cities and country towns, securing advance orders at a discounted price by this means, and with instructions to send the volume on to the local newspaper for review.[4] Orders for special-purpose 'wrappers' and 'postcards' also appear in the Ledger as a charge against *While the Billy Boils*.[5] The wrappers seem to have served not as dust jackets (none appears to have survived) but for postal purposes, and probably had a blurb printed on them or on the postcards.

The circulation of such advertising copy is suggested by the constant refrain in the reviews of the collection's mix of 'pathos' and 'humour'. Also frequently repeated were the facts that the collection contained 333 pages of stories and sketches sourced from newspapers in Australia and New Zealand; that the copy in hand was an advance copy sourced via the local bookseller, through whom it had come from Angus & Robertson; that its 'get-up' showed a new sophistication that amounted to the

---

[3] ML MSS 3269/11/1, fol. 46. The Journal for this period has not survived but a counterpart for 1897 (ML MSS 3269/23/2: 'Publishing Review and Complimentary Copies') shows that copies of the 2s.6d. issue of *Billy Boils* of 12 November 1897 were sent out to 74 newspapers, another 9 used as travellers' samples within Australia, and a further 14 review copies sent to New Zealand newspapers. In 1899–1900 over 40 booksellers and almost 30 newspapers were sent copies of the 1s. *Billy Boils* (either or both of the First and Second Series) with another '12 for Canvassing Ads', which the cheap paperbacks carried, and '42 to Australian Bookstalls' (ML MSS 3269/13/1, fols. 115–18).

[4] A subscription form for *Billy Boils,* dated 25 August 1896, is extant (ML MSS 314/45, pp. 67–8). This last-minute gathering up of subscriptions was a way to give the firm's bookseller-customers the idea that they got in ahead of the rest, with a 5d. discount per copy and copies supplied to be charged to the following month's account. Cole's Book Arcade, Melbourne, subscribed for 72 copies; Ward, Lock and Bowden [Melbourne] 150; E. S. Wigg of Adelaide and Perth 100; Edwards, Dunlop & Co. [the firm's Sydney headquarters presumably] 200; George Robertson & Co. of Melbourne 50; Dymocks [Sydney] 50; Turner & Henderson [Sydney] 50; Cole's an additional 175; Melville, Mullen and Slade of Melbourne 50; Cassell & Co. of Melbourne 50; Edwards, Dunlop ['Brisbane' office] 50; and so on.

[5] ML MSS 3269/11/1, fol. 46. Other entries concern 'Showcards' for use in the bookshops, and a 'Strawboard for showcards'.

birth of an Australian publishing industry (a forgivable hyperbole, as we saw in Chapter 3); that there were eight good-quality illustrations by Frank Mahony (who, as one reviewer commented, 'appears to have . . . derived his inspiration direct from the force and feeling of the stories themselves');[6] that the collection showed bush life 'in all its phases' with a 'photographic fidelity', and that it was based on Lawson's actual experience 'on the wallaby track'. One of the shorter reviews, after some rambling paraphrase and quotation from the collection, suddenly changes register with text that may have come directly from the advertising matter:

> Almost every phase of bush and station life is described by Mr. Lawson with a fidelity only possible to one who knows it thoroughly. Although many of these sketches are very short – not more than three or four pages – there is scarcely one that does not present us with some salient episode, phase of character, or description. There is both humour and pathos in the volume, which deserves to be read not only for the amusement it contains but also for its faithful delineation of some characteristic aspects of Australian life.[7]

Robertson had evidently decided to make things easier for the editors of small newspaper concerns by helping them to write their couple of paragraphs.

The new book, coming so soon after Paterson's *The Man from Snowy River* and Lawson's *In the Days When the World Was Wide*, and now exceeding their production values, seems to have created a genuine pride in the success of a local publishing venture, one which had opened up a new avenue for local writers. The publisher is warmly commended in nearly every review. Getting the book into the hands of the reviewer was the key. A couple of hundred near-simultaneous reviews across the Australasian colonies, Robertson must have thought, would set everyone talking about the new arrival on the literary and publishing

---

[6] Fred J. Broomfield, 'A Pantheon of Bush Types', *Australian Workman*, 24 October 1896. The claim, as we have seen, is literally true. Broomfield, who mixed in the same circles as HL, may well have had inside knowledge.

[7] *Australasian*, 5 September 1896. The source does not appear to have been a *circular* from A&R since charges against *Billy Boils* for circulars do not appear in the Ledger until 1897.

scene. The arrangement was in everyone's interest, even though it meant that the majority of the reviews and mentions amounted to little more than unpaid advertisements. As A. G. Stephens would observe in his review in the *Bulletin*: 'the rolling snowball of [Lawson's] fame has been kicked onward by a thousand eager feet' (29 August 1896).[8]

Robertson's guiding of the reception process extended to arranging and paying for a review which, when completed, was sent to the monthly *Review of Reviews for Australasia* (Melbourne).[9] According to a letter of 12 August 1896 from Robertson to the 'Manager' of this monthly, Banjo Paterson had agreed to write the review but J. F. Archibald had now convinced him it would be improper to do so. Robertson then refers, by way of explanation, to 'the feeling that exists, not so much between the two poets as between their followings'. He then arranged for David G. Ferguson, a Sydney barrister, to take on the review; the firm's Ledger shows a payment of £3 for 'Ferguson's Review in Rev. of Reviews'.[10] The review came back through Robertson who forwarded it to the *Review of Reviews* on 14 August with a request that something be added about 'the get up of the book'.[11]

Again, on 24 August 1896, Robertson sent Henry Hyde Champion, editor of the *Champion* in Melbourne, an advance copy of *While the Billy Boils* with the request that he help get the *Argus* to review it. On 18 September Robertson also sent a copy to the editor of *The Times* (London), adding that copies had been sent also to 'Messrs Kipling, [Andrew] Lang and Le Gallienne'.[12] Richard Le Gallienne went on to write a fine review for the *Idler* and a short review appeared in *The Times*

---

[8] The *Worker*, which had an arrangement to sell copies to its readers, helped to beat the drum with advertisements. And the *Bulletin* followed up its review with an interview with Louisa Lawson on 24 October 1896 on its Red Page: 'A Poet's Mother – Louisa Lawson'.

[9] The dateline of the review is 20 August 1896 but its position in the exercise book housing the collection of reviews for *Billy Boils* places it as received in early September 1896. Each review was evidently stuck down upon receipt, depending upon available space, thus creating a rough chronological order.

[10] 23 September 1896 (ML MSS 3269/11/1, fol. 46).

[11] The editor was W. H. Fitchett; letters (ML MSS 3269/71/4, fols. 263, 264). No reference to the 'get up' was added.

[12] ML MSS 3269/71/4, fols. 288, 350.

on 26 February 1897.[13] As the Ledger shows a charge against *While the Billy Boils* for an advertisement in the *Australian Medical Gazette*, and as a very favourable review appeared in it in October 1896, it is likely that Robertson was not above promising a *quid pro quo*.[14] In late-colonial New South Wales, lawyers and doctors were among his best clients, and many were serious book collectors.

Lawson's pessimism and his realism

What was the result of all this effort? A great many short reviews and notices appeared, but far fewer long or considered ones. And a number of the long reviews took the easy route of quoting one or more of the stories at length, usually after some brief but plodding remarks that sounded much the same notes as in most of the short reviews. Nevertheless, the range of responses in the longer reviews and in some of the shorter ones is revealing, and the high standard of many of those from newspapers in country towns is another notable aspect of the early reception.

Although a leading article in 1898 in an Otago newspaper reported comments by Bishop Thornton of Ballarat about 'the low tone of life in the cities and in the bush of Australia' – and although the writer went on, by way of illustration, to point out the applicability of his remarks to some stories in *While the Billy Boils*[15] – almost none of the reviews during 1896–97 condemned the collection outright. The reviewers were nearly all struggling to measure Lawson's prose against the literary categories or expectations they brought to it, and having to adjust them in the process. Even those tempted to sneer at the texts found themselves having to admire the production qualities of the material book itself, which served as a reassuring passport into the homes of the middle classes. The occasional coarseness of language was often touched on as a

---

[13] *Idler*, 10 (1896), 114–16.
[14] Charge dated 23 September 1896: ML MSS 3269/11/1, fol. 46.
[15] E.g. those stories that 'owe their point to the circumstance that some debtor has successfully outwitted a creditor' (as in 'Jones' Alley'): leading article, *Otago Daily Times*, 5 December 1898. Thornton's comments were made during his inaugural address to the Church of England Congress, 22 November 1898, reported widely in Victorian newspapers.

concern, though usually explained as endemic to the realist treatment of its subject matter; or, failing that, as counterbalanced by the reviewer's linguistic interest in the slang of the bushmen.

A class division, expressed as taste, emerged, however, around the issue of Lawson's exploring 'the lowest depths of respectable poverty' in the city sketches and the squalor of some of the bush sketches (*Town and Country Journal*, 29 August 1896). For later commentators such as Turner and Sutherland (in 1898, see below), this was a warning signal that Lawson was following the prescriptions of the French naturalists; but few of the first reviewers made the connection.[16] In 1895, in a review of *Short Stories in Prose and Verse*, the *Worker* had complained that Lawson's cynicism was an affectation (12 January), and on 20 July asked: 'Could not friend Harry give us a glimpse of the coming carnival, when the warriors shall be rewarded; when the social martyrs shall be set free'?

The milder form of the objection, which clearly touched 1890s colonial sensibilities across the spectrum, was reviewers' difficulty in dealing with Lawson's 'pessimism'. It was 'very unhealthy', according to the Sydney *Evening News* (29 August 1896), and the *Catholic Press* found his philosophy 'somewhat stern' (29 August 1896). The *Block* (Sydney) offered a diagnosis: 'through all his prose, as well as his poems, runs that half-hearted sort of pessimism; and that half-declared revolt against the pain of the world, so characteristic of the man himself'. Others chimed in. Price Warung mentioned Lawson's 'keen sympathy, his susceptibility to what is delicate beneath the more rugged surfaces of life'. The *Worker* expressed relief that the 'undercurrent of hopelessness, not to say despair, which is so marked a characteristic of his verse, is not so strong in his prose sketches' (29 August 1896). But the reviewer for the *Goulburn Evening Penny Post* registered a recklessness in the pessimism before acknowledging that it 'does not detract in any way from the undoubted power displayed' by Lawson's 'quiet, powerful realism' (3 September 1896).

---

[16] The reviewer for the *Block* implicitly did: 'To some, human nature is always worth reproducing, in whatever guise it comes to the artist; and the clearer you make your picture, slurring nothing, extenuating nothing, so much the better. Other people think quite otherwise. These may perhaps as well leave *While the Billy Boils* alone' (29 August 1896).

The objection to the pessimism was probably in part a disappointment that the contemporary appetite for stories of romance and adventure was not being satisfied, after the hopes raised by the outback setting. The stories and sketches' 'utter hopelessness', according to the *Freeman's Journal* (5 September 1896), 'must destroy any idea of romance that the reader may have associated with the Australian bush'. In an allied vein, Ferguson noted, in the *Review of Reviews*, the absence of 'landscape with colour' and his surprise that 'There is not a horse in the book, from title-page to imprint – not one horse'. It would have been more accurate to say that, although a dozen of the stories and sketches mention horses, there is no celebration of heroic, wild or otherwise romantic riding to be found, nor even any overt admiration of horseflesh. Just the opposite is true: the horses are more likely to be broken-down hacks. Lawson was challenging his middle-class readers' expectations with what they were finding, at once a dispiriting but also an eye-opening form of realism. The struggle to reconcile these responses is a notable feature of the whole phase of the collection's early reception.

There was some continuity between the reviews of Lawson's earlier two volumes and this one: the sense of a break with the past, of a genuinely Australian prose voice at last (as opposed to those of Henry Kingsley and Marcus Clarke, though, curiously, with Rolf Boldrewood seldom mentioned), of Lawson's being intimate with the conditions of life that his writing described, and as a result, so far as comments on style went, there being little if any distance between writer and subject matter. That the quality was a result of his unusually skilled command of idiomatic language; that he must have schooled himself to incorporate the varieties of register he had imbibed as a child in the Bush and, though partially deaf, still heard around him; that he had been merely confirmed in his inclination by the stories of Bret Harte and later Mark Twain; that he was not temperamentally inclined to employ the more ironic and archer tones in some of the higher journalism he was doubtless reading – none of this was recognised at first, nor could it be said.

Generally the reviewers who touched on his style, used epithets such as 'natural', or declared that there was no style (which is virtually the same thing), or that it was photographic and that they could therefore commend 'its thoroughness of treatment' (*Lithgow Mercury*, 4 September 1896). 'P.M.' went a little further with the comment: 'All the sketches, with one or two trifling exceptions, seem to be just naked, native-born suggestions arising from actual things, and to have been garbed in just sufficient language to make them presentable and assimilative to readers. These qualities make Lawson's volume of prose of exceptional value' (*Champion*, 5 September 1896).

In a review in the *Bulletin* that has since achieved a currency of its own and effectively fossilised commentary on Lawson's style, A. G. Stephens claimed of Lawson that: 'Art he has none; his artifices are of the feeblest ... His quaint simple style suits his themes and mode of thought ... The happy word and phrase come to him easily: the incidents fall without effort into place: his picture is made before he knows' (29 August 1896). This would have been news to Lawson who, in 1899, would recall how he learned to write his sketches: 'I sought out my characters and studied them; I wrote of nothing that I had not myself seen or experienced; I wrote and re-wrote painfully, and believed that every line was true and for the right'.[17] When A. G. Stephens responded: 'I believe he feels an editorial cut in his copy as keenly as if it were a cut in his flesh', he put this down to Lawson's over-sensitive nature, not acknowledging the care and thoughtfulness that must have been brought to bear in order to refine the kind of realism for which he would be remembered.[18]

Readjusting the question of style by broadening it to the question of Lawson's realism, the reviewer for the *Otago Witness* commented: 'He never sacrifices truth to sentiment; he makes no points of artistic licence for the sake of picturesque effects; he never sacrifices the real to the ideal.' The reviewer went hastily on, with one eye on the anticipated reaction: 'Not that his style is either callous or cold; there is plenty of

---

[17] *Letters* 94, published as '"Pursuing Literature" in Australia', *Bulletin*, 21 January 1899.
[18] *Criticism* 79: 'Lawson and Literature', *Bookfellow*, 18 February 1899, pp. 21–4.

pathos in these brief sketches, there are exquisite touches of tenderness, but they are the unrehearsed pathos and tenderness of real life – not the beautiful but unreal conception of the artist' (17 September 1896). But whichever way the argument inclined, either to the bracing (unfamiliar but healthy) or to the pathetic (familiar and consoling), there was little room left to analyse how Lawson achieved his realist technique.

However, in a sharp insight in the *Bathurst National Advocate*[19] the unnamed reviewer noted the consequence of Lawson's approach to his sketches: 'The prime defect of Lawson is in his want of power to create character; he sees and feels as but one man in a hundred thousand can see and feel – and therefore he is a genius – but his work is still pure narrative, and description; his men and women do not live apart from his text. If there be one exception in this book to this judgment it is to be found in "An Unfinished Love Story"'. There was otherwise no available rhetoric in which to conceptualise the radical newness. Appeals to the metaphor of photographic fidelity offered a shortcut by changing the medium and lending an up-to-dateness; but in doing so they obscured the verbal achievement for which Lawson had sweated and striven.

John Farrell, in his review for the Sydney *Telegraph*, changed tack slightly in trying to define Lawson's characteristic mode: 'The sketches have in them the quality of concise and exact statement, of sufficient description, and of suggestiveness, which continually reminds one of how far Rudyard Kipling can make language go in serving his ends. Mitchell, the ordinary human swagman, . . . is almost as perfect a portrait as [Kipling's] Mulvaney' (29 August 1896). This is as far as the technical commentary stretched.

Comparisons with Bret Harte's accounts of 'life on the Pacific Slope forty years ago' and Rudyard Kipling's accounts of Anglo-Indian society were many. They were employed to try to define what it was that was decisively new in Lawson's creation of Australian types (*Adelaide Advertiser*, 1 September 1896). This tack shaded off into the politics of

---

[19] The date given in handwriting in the reviews book (see n. 2 above) is 31 September 1896 [*sic*].

affiliation with Home and thus of what was and what was not 'Australian'. So, for instance, the *Braidwood Dispatch* claimed that 'the author of this book [has] distinctly stamped the character ... of an Australian type and the style [is] purely that of a colonial author'. Though 'He depicts in terribly graphic terms and with the unsparing hand of one using the dissecting knife, the miserable existence of ... all the flotsam and jetsam strewn about the country which are such a trouble to society and such a burden on the Government ... there is not a word of politics to be found in the whole of the work' (2 September 1896).

In contrast to this politically conservative response, other reviewers drew purposeful attention to the mateship displayed in the sketches and stories, to Lawson's depiction of

> men of weary limbs, and thin and sun-browned faces, full of a stubborn sadness relieved by a grim humour of the Stoic order; men who are profane, usually penniless, mostly thirsty, often drunk, often scarcely honest, and full of the original Esau. But they are men, who live, who are true to their mates, ready to undauntedly face life and accept its scourgings with set teeth or even with a defiant smile.... The whole book smacks of its unconventional, open-air, democratic, irreligious vigor ... We should like to hear more about the wanderings of Mitchell.

This is from the *Ballarat Evening Post* (3 September 1896): some of the spirit of Eureka evidently lived on, for which Lawson's stories were a convenient focus and inspiration.

Avoiding the political inflection, Farrell staked a higher claim in stating that 'hardly anything can be found here which is not actual and, in some degree, representative'. Fred Broomfield's review in the *Australian Workman* is entitled 'A Pantheon of Bush Types'. He entrenched Farrell's claim by observing, and going on to demonstrate at some length, that even 'Lawson's dogs are types, no less than their masters' (24 October 1896). This general claim for representativeness would prove to be one of the dominant notes of the critical debate for the next century.

Another tack in this debate – one that had been taken more frequently in the reviewing of Rolf Boldrewood's *Robbery Under Arms* in the late

1880s – was Lawson's historical significance. The claim was that the stories and sketches were destined to become 'a historical reference of pioneering settlement in the colonies' (*Mount Alexander Mail*, 8 September 1896). On 17 September 1896 the *Otago Witness* took this further: 'such writers as Henry Lawson will be the social historians which future generations will rely upon. In these pages, "the heir of all the ages," the future product of free education, technical schools, university extension, universal suffrage, and old-age pensions will find portraits ... of types which will then be as extinct as the dodo.' This was a somewhat reduced claim than national representativeness; and it did not retain currency even in the case of Boldrewood, despite his broader canvas. It would have been an even slenderer reed for Lawson's reputation to rest on; but in the event it proved unnecessary. Its principal interest is its serving as another index of contemporary expectations and assumptions.

Response to the 'sequences'

Price Warung, writing in the *Bathurst Free Press* on the day of publication, raised an issue that would become a common one: the variable quality of the sketches and stories. There would be little agreement on which were the bad ones. But Warung went further, saying the volume would have better served Lawson's literary reputation had it been one half or one-third the length. As we have seen, this was commercially out of the question because of the nexus in the literary marketplace between length and price. But where did the criticism come from, given that it often went contradictorily together, as here, with commendation that Lawson had given us as never before 'Australia in a hundred phases of character, of episode and of scenery ... [T]aking the volume as a transcript of things Australian, there is scarcely a passage of ten consecutive lines which I would like to see expunged.' In a two-page spread in the monthly *Review of Reviews* that featured a reproduction of Mahony's illustration for 'The Drover's Wife', David G. Ferguson followed suit: 'a really uninteresting one it would be hard to find'.

The criticism received a defining inflection from A. G. Stephens. He said he would have preferred Lawson to rewrite the contents of the collection 'into a single plotted, climaxed story' or, failing that, to have 'contrived a set of characters to pass from chapter to chapter, as Mark Twain manages, and hung his matter on their pegs'. Instead, the scattering of the possible sequences throughout the volume ('there is a "Mitchell" sequence, a "Steelman" sequence, a bush sequence, a city sequence, and so on') dispersed their force:

> They should have been classified and put in sections, so that continuity might be unbroken and the characters might gain force and distinctness from the massing of impressions. Exactly the opposite course has been followed. . . . Not only is power lost, but the haphazard mixture jolts the mind like an unexpected bottom-step. . . . As it is, the reader is perpetually getting-up steam for a five-minutes' journey which brings him back to [the] starting-point.[20]

When Lawson read this review he reacted angrily in a letter to George Robertson, saying that the idea Stephens was now putting forward as a principle of organisation was actually his own original one, that he had told Stephens of it, and that Stephens was now using it as a stick to beat him with, when Stephens knew very well that the stories needed to complete the various series were not available. They had been bought by the *Bulletin*, which had not published them, meaning they were not available for reprinting in the Angus & Robertson collection.[21]

As we saw in Chapter 2, this was only partly true, but it has been uncritically accepted ever since. Certainly it was a convenient self-justification for Lawson. The real problem lay in the expectations that a high-quality book format raised at the time for fiction (though not

---

[20] The *Maitland Daily Mercury* similarly expressed its regret that HL 'has not concentrated his powers upon the production of a lengthened story of Australian life and character' (29 August 1896). The *Bendigo Advertiser* noted the absence of 'that continuity which might have been observed, and which would have led to greater appreciation on the part of the reader' (31 August 1896). And the *Toowoomba Chronicle* wished for 'a better arrangement of the series, for the reader is taken from a scene in the back blocks to the heart of Sydney, and from there to New Zealand, and back again to the Australian interior with a suddenness that is startling, to say the least' (3 September 1896).
[21] HL to GR, 9 September 1896 (*Letters* 63).

for collections of verse): that there would be a single work of literature, or interrelated works, within it. However, the original circumstances of publication mandated otherwise. Unless Lawson had the desire and capacity to reconceive the stories and sketches completely, there was no chance that they would form sequences – in the sense of being sequential, one leading on with seeming naturalness to the next. They might be made, in a more loosely connected way, to form series as Stephens suggested ('classified and put in sections'). But that would have only drawn attention to the overlaps, repetitions and contradictions, and to the fact that the characters did not develop, story by story.[22] Instead Robertson evidently persuaded Lawson that it would be better to scatter the various sketch and story types throughout the volume to give, instead, a sense of variety and freshness.[23]

This was a sensible decision. Although the sketches and stories had been professionally edited, and also revised by the author, there was no disguising their origins and what they in fact were: short pieces for weekly newspapers and magazines that needed to stand on their own, without the support of others of related theme or approach. This is, after all, what Lawson had mastered in the previous few years. The conversion into permanent book form raised for Stephens what for him were the higher criteria appropriate to *literature*. He mentions the distinction between it and 'occasional publication' several times in his review.

To some extent the distinction has shaped the thinking of literary critics ever since. Certainly, many of the reviewers cited 'Going Blind' as

---

[22] 'Lawson often repeats himself in his ideas in the same words and phrases. This may suit in perishable newspaper literature, but not in a book' (*Gulgong Advertiser*, c. early September 1896: cf. Chapter 7 n. 25). Fred Broomfield pointed out in the *Australian Workman* that Mitchell is 'James' [or 'Jim'] in 'Remailed' but 'Jack' in the other Mitchell sketches (24 October 1896). Again, 'Jones' Alley' starts: 'SHE lived in Jones's Alley. She cleaned offices . . .'. If the stories are to be read as a sequence then the background is unnecessary.

[23] This would be GR's explicit agenda with *Selected Poems* (1918), whose proof sheets he enclosed with a letter to HL of 30 January 1917: 'The selection and arrangement are mine. Some good poems have been left out because of their similarity to poems included. In arranging them I have alternated happy poems and sad ones. The Star of Australasia is first because of its prophecy, For'ard is last because of its ending' (ML 314/48, filed at A1875, p. 39). The last detail probably explains the position of 'For Auld Lang Syne' in *Billy Boils*.

a highlight of the collection. It is a *story*, more recognisably literary, and thus would in due course be able to respond to New Critical analysis. But at the time the preference more probably indicated a preference for the 'pathetic' over the 'squalid' – terms used to differentiate subject matter in the review in the *Block*. Stung by Stephens's criticism, one echoed in other reviews, and by the wish of his publisher for a novel, Lawson would try to satisfy the organic precept; but he never fully succeeded in doing so.[24]

In the Sydney *Telegraph*, John Farrell nominated his preference of a half dozen of the pieces that were 'fit to rank with the best short tales ever written'. Each of them is a story rather than a sketch. Three of them were 'The Drover's Wife' ('perhaps the best'), '[The Bush Undertaker'] and 'An Unfinished Love Story'.[25] The fact that the other three ('Arvie Aspinall's Alarm Clock', 'His Father's Mate' and 'A Visit of Condolence') share a common dependence on sentimentality – the taste for which would not long survive Farrell's generation – shows the ingrained preference that Lawson's sketches of bush life were up against and how fragilely based post-World War II assumptions about the new literary taste of the 1890s actually were. (This argument is pursued in Chapter 12.) Similarly, the assumption that Stephens's objection to 'those stories in which the pathos is deliberately manufactured, like "Arvie Aspinall's Alarm Clock"' was widely shared at the time is a straightforward mistake.

The reviewer for the Melbourne *Argus* came up with a similar list of preferences to Farrell's, but substituting 'Going Blind' for 'The Drover's Wife' (a story that was very frequently commended in the reviews), and clearly preferring Lawson's stories to his sketches – some of which are of 'so fragmentary a character that, barring their terseness and abrupt unconventionality of expression, there is little to recommend them to a reader. These scarcely deserve more than the ephemeral notice gained for them by newspaper publication' (3 October 1896). It is thus a noteworthy fact that far more enthusiasm was expressed by reviewers

---

[24] The Joe Wilson series of short stories would be the closest he got: see Chapter 10.
[25] The *Melbourne Sportsman* (1 September 1896) added 'When the Sun Went Down' to the list, for the same reason, after having differentiated them from the outback sketches.

for Lawson's pre-1893 writings than for those that succeeded his trip to Bourke – including the Mitchell and Steelman sketches – that is to say, before he got into the stride that subsequent critics have considered to be his major period.

Other reviewers were able to make the transition that Stephens could not. Some noted that the implication of the collection's title was that the contents were not meant for continuous reading (even if punctilious reviewers had no choice), but rather that they were suitable for reading individually at odd moments, figuratively in the time it took the billy to boil – or else for reading aloud after a meal as a form of social or family entertainment.[26] The author of the 'Books, and Other Things' column in the *Barrier Miner* specifically answered Stephens's criticism that the collection 'lacks arrangement . . . We confess to liking this book of Australian sketches precisely as it is'.[27] Also answering Stephens, 'P.M.' in the *Champion* pointed out that there was precedent in Kipling's stories, where 'the "Mulvaney" series are sprinkled through the volumes, just as the Mitchell and Steelman yarns are scattered in Lawson's book'. 'P.M.' added that:

> If a man talked all Mitchell and all Steelman for a stretch his mate on the track would grow very weary, and would probably cut the series short with an expressive, 'Blast yer, stow it.' Readers would feel very much the same, whereas now if they are sorry to leave Mitchell, their regret only increases the pleasure with which they come up with him again. Such an effect is good and is artistic. It seems only carping and mere conventionality to object anything to the contrary. (5 September 1896)

Given that Robertson sent a copy of *While the Billy Boils* to Kipling

---

[26] E.g. in the 'Scribblers and Screed' column in the *Freelance* (Melbourne), 3 October 1896: 'Lawson's idea was evidently to reproduce in his book the casual inconsequential way in which stories crop up around a camp-fire'. In August 1898 in *Leisure Hour* (London), C. H. Irwin explained the meaning of *billy* in 'Australian Sketches: The English Language in Australia', a review-article of E. E. Morris's *Austral English: A Dictionary of Australasian Words, Phrases and Usages* (1898): 'Henry Lawson's book "While the Billy Boils" suggests the "yarns" that may be told around a camp-fire, or at a picnic, while the tea is being prepared' (pp. 652–5 [p. 653]).

[27] *Barrier Miner*, 5 September 1896. Other reviews or literary columns also carried on debates started in the first reviews. E.g., the *Macleay Argus* argued with 'Some city critics [who] complain of the depressing effect of the stories' (5 September 1896).

upon its publication and that his collections served, at least in a general way as we saw in Chapter 6, as a model in his thinking about the book's design and production, it is quite possible, indeed likely, that the sequencing can be traced back to the same source. It was a strategy that had, after all, most definitely succeeded in the marketplace.

In Chapter 5 we saw that, even if the original ordering of the contents of printer's copy for *While the Billy Boils* were substituted for the published sequence, Stephens's criterion cannot have been at the forefront of Lawson's mind. He was demonstrably not trying to order, or had already determined that he could not satisfactorily order, the stories and sketches into strict thematic or narrator-based sequences. In comparison to the published sequence, the first ordering was merely a different medley of themes, settings and narrators. Perhaps, in this, he was already influenced by Robertson; and perhaps he had realised the inevitability himself.

The critical stalemate around this issue has never been resolved except by successive editorial selections chosen from Lawson's many volumes.[28] They have tended to canonise only a small selection from *While the Billy Boils* of what are in fact quite varied writings, placing the favoured few with similar ones from other volumes. It is one reason why the edition of *While the Billy Boils* that accompanies this book strips away the accretions, intentions and sequencing of the 1896 book rather than treating them as the inevitable climax of a literary evolution.

The British reviews, and their effect in Australia

The Australian reviews were finished by early November 1896; but starting from late July 1897 many excerpts appeared in Australian newspapers' literary columns taken from the review in the London

[28] A recent critical response by Brian Matthews is more promising but ignores the material circumstances: HL 'was conducting a revolution in the nature of the short story in this country, eschewing models with formal neatness, a twist in the tale, a beginning, a middle and an end and an identifiable climax, in favour of a kind of pre-modernist reticence, a withdrawing from the idea of conventional order, and a quality of observation that endowed the external world with a sense of eerie, symbolic possibility without ever finally endorsing it': 'A Lawson for our Times', *Australia Book Review* (May 2009), 11–14 [p. 13].

Spectator. This single review gave another lease of life to the reception of *While the Billy Boils* in Australasia.[29] Unsigned, but attributed in pencil in the Angus & Robertson collection of reviews to A. W. Jose who was by then in England, the *Spectator* review described the collection:

> [as] biting into the very heart of the bushman's life, ruthless in truth, extraordinarily dramatic, and pathetically uneven . . . He is apparently content to let what he has to say drift through the sheets of Australian and New Zealand newspapers . . . Kipling began his literary career in the same track, and perhaps it has its advantages. At any rate, both men have somehow gained that power of concentration which by a few strong strokes can set place and people before you with amazing force.
> (8 May 1897)

This review, which preceded the Simpkin, Marshall issue of *While the Billy Boils* in London in July 1897, was probably designed as a boost for it. The *Glasgow Weekly Herald* of 22 May 1897 had in fact already noticed the Sydney publication with a long quotation from '[The Bush Undertaker]'. This came after the *Times* had announced that 'the Kipling of Australia is still to be waited for' but granted that the Lawson collection 'is depressingly instructive, and has an air of veracity' (26 February 1897). The *Spectator* review, however, was far more substantial and was taken by Australian newspapers as a palpable sign of Lawson's acknowledged success at Home.

From July 1897 the British newspapers were reviewing the London issue, though most reviews were short and many felt the need to explain what a billy was.[30] Some linked Lawson's collection to the growing political agenda of the new Imperialism – the Greater Britain that would consist of the mother country and the colonies as a federated entity.[31]

---

[29] Reports of the *Spectator* review appeared in the *Sydney Morning Herald* on 26 June 1897 and in the *Town and Country Journal*, 24 July 1897. Large sections were reprinted, unattributed, in the *Coonamble Independent*, 9 July 1897; the *Windsor and Richmond Gazette*, 17 July 1897; and the *Mount Wycheproof Ensign*, 9 July 1897.

[30] There were at least 30 reviews and mentions in Britain: e.g. *Black and White*, 17 July 1897; *Glasgow Herald*, 15 July 1897; *Belfast News*, 15 July 1897; *Birmingham Gazette*, 29 July 1897; *Yorkshire Herald*, 28 July 1897; *Paisley and Renfrewshire Gazette*, 3 July 1897; *Bookman*, August 1897; and the *Rocket*, 5 August 1897.

[31] E.g., the *North British Advertiser*, 3 July 1897; and *Academy* (London), 17 July 1897.

E. V. Lucas's unsigned review in the *Academy* stands out, but it struck much the same notes about Lawson's realism and style as the better Australian reviews had done:

> Mr Lawson's passion for unadorned veracity, and his genuine feeling for character, make him more trustworthy [than Boldrewood and Louis Becke] ... The result is a real book, a book in a hundred ... Mr Lawson has gone direct to facts. He does nothing himself but arrange and present; that done, he stands aside. You cannot find his own opinion on anything. His feeling for style in his own person is poor, but when he makes another speak, his language is terse, supple and richly idiomatic. He can tell a yarn with the best ... *While the Billy Boils* can be recommended to every one who likes full-blooded, man-to-man writing.[32]

Literature's reviewer made an advance in the understanding of Lawson's style by concluding that 'the simplicity of the narrative gives it almost the effect of a story that is told by word of mouth' (20 November 1897). But this was only spelling out what other reviewers had implied when they talked of Lawson's sketches as yarns. In a review evidently written by somebody with Australian experience, the *Manchester Guardian* pointed to the nurturing role of the Sydney *Bulletin* and made an unusually perceptive evaluation:

> Mr. Lawson seems to us to be on the whole more successful with what one might call his sketches than with his short stories ... there is a deep vein of tenderness and kindly observation that is wholly pleasing in such sketches as 'An Old Mate of your Father's' ... In men like Mr. Lawson and Mr. Paterson – another contributor to the 'Bulletin' – we have the promise of really excellent work which shall be distinctively Australian if only they will consent to develop naturally both in prose and verse along their own lines, and not persist in the amiable but somewhat stunting conviction, which is almost universal in Australia, that a sort of finality was attained by Adam Lindsay Gordon in the philosophy of Australian life. (27 July 1897)

As the reviews came in, someone at Angus & Robertson was reading them and marking passages for quotation in the advertisements that would in due course appear in the back of copies of the firm's

---

[32] The review (17 July 1897) is attributed to Lucas in handwriting in the Reviews book: ML MSS 3269/Angus & Robertson Ltd. Book Reviews (Bound volumes) 1894–1970/1, vol. 7.

publications, including of course those of *While the Billy Boils*. This process had started by the Third Thousand; the advertising section is dated September 1896 and contains extracts from eleven Australian reviews. The Simpkin, Marshall issue in London had no advertising section; but a (personal) copy of the Twelfth Thousand (1898), with an advertising section dated June 1900, replaced all of the Australian reviews with four from London counterparts: the *Academy*, *The Times*, *Literature* and the *Spectator*.³³ Clearly these authorities from Home were felt to be more persuasive for Australian book purchasers than their local counterparts. Ledger entries for printing '2000 Spectator Reviews 1500 8vo [Trade] Circulars' in June 1897, a further 8,000 *Spectator* reviews on 3 July and 'Academy reviews' in August show that Robertson was putting the Imperial endorsements to good use in the local trade.³⁴ As I have had occasion to remark once before, in the book trade the colonial tail could sometimes wag the Imperial dog.³⁵

South African reception of *While the Billy Boils* – of the Sydney publication not the Simpkin, Marshall issue from London – commenced in August 1897. The *Port Elizabeth Telegraph* drew the moral that colonists in the two countries shared 'something like affinity of incident' and declared that although the volume's contents had 'not much literary merit . . . the narratives have the impress of reality about them'. The *Cape Times* went a little further ('nothing stilted or strained to gain effect'), but little new emerged by way of commentary.³⁶ The book could be purchased from J. C. Juta's bookshops in Port Elizabeth and Cape Town at the same price as in Sydney, 5s.³⁷

---

³³ The advertisement identified the reviewer in *Literature* as A. Patchett Martin (1851–1902), former editor of the *Melbourne Review*. He returned to England in 1882, edited *Oak-bough and Wattle-blossom* in 1888, and was part of the movement, which notably included Douglas Sladen, to introduce Australian literature to British readers around the time of the Australian Centennial.

³⁴ ML MSS 3269/11/1, fol. 78.

³⁵ Paul Eggert, '*Robbery Under Arms*: The Colonial Market, Imperial Publishers and the Demise of the Three-Decker Novel', *Book History*, 6 (2003), 127–46.

³⁶ *Cape Times*, 25 August 1897. Mentions appeared in the *Cape Argus* on 18 and 25 July 1897. A review (c. May 1898) appeared in the *Transvaal Critic* comparing *Billy Boils* to 'Percy Fitzpatrick's collection of South African "yarns" entitled *The Outspan*'.

³⁷ South African distribution commenced after Lothian sent a traveller there in mid-1897. A

A curious addition to the South African reception is the fact that, doubtless as a patriotic gesture, Angus & Robertson gave a dozen copies each of the 1s. Commonwealth edition of the two-Series *While the Billy Boils* to the colonial Bushmen's Contingent sent to South Africa from Australia in 1900.[38] Presumably the copies were read there, but no response has been traced. While there is a temptation to draw the obvious ideological link between whatever Lawson may be fancied to stand for in the 1890s and the colonials who volunteered in far greater numbers than could be accommodated and who, as mounted bushmen, would soon prove to be a potent weapon in fighting against the Boers, it needs to be remembered that one reviewer had come away with the impression that there was not a single horse in the whole volume. Apart from the exploits of the conman, there is very little sense of triumph, national or otherwise, to be found in *While the Billy Boils*.

The ongoing discussion

The beginnings of the long debate about the relative superiority of Lawson's verse or of his prose may be traced to the early reviews, though in fact only a small minority of reviewers raised the question. The Melbourne *Leader* 'was inclined to give the preference to his prose' (12 September 1896); but the *Freelance* (Melbourne) wanted to leave them equal, only that in the verse Lawson 'inclines to optimism, in prose to pessimism'. Other reviewers, including A. G. Stephens, went out of their way to suggest that 'The charm of Lawson's prose is essentially that of his poetry' – even though, in his review of *In the Days*, he had written: 'it must be remembered that his verse represents only half of his work, and perhaps not the finer half' (*Bulletin*, 15 February 1896). Stephens was still undecided.

letter (A&R to John Lothian of Melbourne, 25 June 1897) shows the traveller took A&R books, sold mostly at half retail price to Lothian. But GR states he wishes to open up communication with Juta directly: 'If they take 500 copies of the Snowy River Series within one year we shall do them at half price' – otherwise at the standard 3s. (ML MSS 3269/125/72/1, fol. 51).

[38] The Ledger records the charge for the copies against *Billy Boils* at 20 April 1900 (ML MSS 3269/13/1, fol. 118). The Citizens' Bushmen Contingent sailed on 28 February 1900; the Imperial Bushmen on 23 April 1900.

By 1899, Walter Murdoch went further than Stephens in his article, 'The New School of Australian Poets' in the Melbourne *Argus*. At first satirical about the clumping verse contained in the various Angus & Robertson volumes that had appeared since 1895, and the 'undiscriminating praise' they had received, Murdoch changes tack with an unsuspected acknowledgement: 'The kind of truth presented in their verse has been far more artistically presented in a volume of prose sketches – I mean Mr Lawson's *While the Billy Boils* – which, I take it, is the most distinct achievement in art that our younger writers have yet produced'.[39] This is the firmest early registration of the superiority of Lawson's prose over his verse, and indeed over everything else going around in the other capital; it was a patrician Melbourne comment about a Sydney phenomenon – of which, more below.

Another refusal to make an anticipated distinction occurred in the *Otago Witness*, which concluded with the sentiment that 'it is a book of which all Australasian readers should feel proud to think it was written by a compatriot'. This identification of the colonial reader as uniformly Australasian – as undivided by the two future nationhoods – is a revealing cultural note. The Wellington *Evening Post* confirmed it with its hospitable comment: 'The name of Henry Lawson is becoming a household word throughout Australasia. He has touched our hearts through the pages of the Sydney Bulletin, the Brisbane Boomerang, and many another paper, north, south, east, and west' (28 September 1896). The fact that *While the Billy Boils* received at least 30 reviews and

---

[39] 6 May 1899 (reprinted in *Criticism* 82–90: pp. 86, 87). Stephen Murray-Smith quotes an older Murdoch recalling his undergraduate years at Ormond College at the University of Melbourne (he received his BA in 1895): 'When I was an undergraduate, he was our one Australian hero as a far as literature was concerned. The Sydney *Bulletin* came into our common-room at Ormond College, and there was a group of us who opened it mainly in the hope of finding a short story by Lawson. Not a poem; in verse, we thought Banjo Paterson's vivacious and fluent jingles better than anything Lawson did': *Henry Lawson* (Melbourne, Lansdowne Press, 1962), p. 37.

Rolf Boldrewood, whose tastes had been formed in an earlier era, answered Murdoch, defending the poets and adding: 'Without disparaging Mr. Lawson's realistic prose sketches, and who knows every hint of the "local colour" if not he? I must affirm that his ballads in "The Days when the World Was Wide" are to be preferred as artistic presentments' ('The New School of Australian Poets', *Argus*, 3 June 1899, p. 3).

mentions in New Zealand newspapers is further testimony to a cultural commonality that has since been to some extent obscured.

When Angus & Robertson released *While the Billy Boils* in late 1897 at the cheaper prices of 3s.6d. in cloth and 2s.6d. in paperback, a trade circular from the firm evidently made its way in excerpted form into various colonial newspapers. The *Sydney Mail* reported that: 'The new editions have the fine type and illustrations of the 5s edition, and have been issued at the solicitation of the trade. This is the sixth thousand. The issue is practically the inauguration of a new Colonial Library, the first to be written, printed, and published within the colonies themselves' (20 November 1897). Many other newspapers, including in New Zealand, commended the publisher warmly for issuing the cheap edition, and some took the trouble to review the book as if it were a new title.[40] Most reviews remained positive, although the *Catholic Press* commented that 'the style is bad, the method poor, and in a word they are only a species of curt and rugged journalism for readers who have no time for reflection and no desire to read save to break the moments in a tram car' (15 October 1898). The contrast between the literary work (which required leisure because it called for reflection) and the occasional newspaper publication continued to divide the reviewers and commentators. Nevertheless, Lawson's name and that of his publisher had become synonymous, and 'the thousand eager feet' that Stephens described as propelling the snowball of Lawson's fame continued to contribute simultaneously to Angus & Robertson's commercial success. The gap between the bookselling trade and the press remained surprisingly small. There was evidently a common sense of purpose, a shared pride in colonial success.

A. G. Stephens was an outsider in this; and when he replied in 1899 to Lawson's '"Pursuing Literature" in Australia', his view was firm and unforgivingly upright:

[40] E.g. *Otago Witness*, 25 November 1897; Wellington *Evening Star*, 27 November 1897.

Lawson's pre-eminent Australian appeal lessens the force of his universal appeal. He is splendidly parochial. That increases his claim upon his country, but decreases his claim upon literature ... His work is crowded with intimate detail. But as Art it lacks perspective: Lawson is too close to his subject ... This objection is not at all concerned with the omission or inclusion of any items in his sketch-series; as Lawson seems to think. Were the whole Mitchell or Steelman sketches printed together, they would still remain flat silhouettes.[41]

In his 'Introductory' note to *The Bulletin Story Book: A Selection of Stories and Literary Sketches from 'The Bulletin' [1881–1901]*, which included 'The Drover's Wife', A. G. Stephens acknowledged that 'It has not been attempted to choose the best examples of literary style.' In saying this, Stephens was deferring to the preferences that the *Bulletin* circle by now identified with the Melbourne literary scene (and which Murdoch had enforced satirically in 'The New School of Australian Poets').[42] In his note, Stephens goes on next to confound the (Sydney) expectation that 'it has not been attempted to choose examples of work characteristically Australian. The literary work which is Australian in spirit, as well as in scene or incident, is only beginning to be written. ... Australia is still a suburb of Cosmopolis, where men from many lands perpetuate in a new environment the ideas and habits acquired far away.' Nevertheless, he acknowledged the collection contained 'a few examples of Australian work – of work that could not have been conceived or written anywhere but in Australia'. The country itself contained, he believed, 'a wealth of novel inspiration for the writers who will live Australia's life and utter her message. And when those writers come, let us tell them that we will never rest contented until Australian authors reach the highest standards

---

[41] *Criticism* 80: 'Lawson and Literature', *Bookfellow*, 18 February 1899, pp. 21–4.
[42] Commitment to an overt literary style was in fact no less prevalent in Sydney, as for instance in John Le Gay Brereton's *The Song of Brotherhood and Other Verses* (London: George Allen, 1896). In 1907 in the first number of *Bush Companion*, Bertram Stevens numbered Brereton among 'an independent group whose work shows hardly any local influences at all'. This was not exactly the case, but Stevens's point that 'the Bush school' was only one of others is true: quoted in H. P. Heseltine, *John Le Gay Brereton* (Melbourne: Lansdowne Press, 1965). In 1921 Brereton became the first Challis Professor of English Literature at the University of Sydney.

set in literature.'⁴³ This shows that the 1950s sense of the achievement of the 1890s was not shared even by so central an 1890s figure as Stephens. Even though there is understandably something defensive about his introduction to a book – with the literary pretensions *of* a book – this *Bulletin* Red Page editor emerges as an uncompromising critic who was inflexible when it came to what he took to be the higher sphere of literature. The convergence of his desiderata – Australian subject matter and high art – would not be fully identified with the 1890s until that later decade: Chapter 12 returns to this theme.⁴⁴

Later discussions

Later issues of *While the Billy Boils* attracted further reviewing, as of course did his new titles from 1900.⁴⁵ Following the now familiar

---

⁴³ A. G. Stephens, 'Introductory', *The Bulletin Story Book: A Selection of Stories and Literary Sketches from 'The Bulletin' [1881–1901]* (Sydney: Bulletin Newspaper Co., 1901), pp. v, vi, viii.

⁴⁴ Stephens's eighth and last essay on HL appeared at his death: 'in its way, to its degree, Lawson's style is unsurpassed. No writer in English has used words to picture people and things and emotions more vividly and forcibly than Lawson at his best'. But 'His womanish wail often needs a sturdy Australian backbone'; 'he read few books; his mind was not widened by literature'. 'Even [in] the years of his prime, from 1890 to 1900, [he] produced only a selection of splendid fragments . . . he never justified, in the aspect of literature, his rare gifts of observation, insight, and description, often made golden by sympathy and compassion and idealistic fervour. Much of his work remains to Australia; very little to the world': 'Henry Lawson', *Art in Australia*, 3rd series, no. 2, 1 November 1922, 10 pages, unpaginated. Stephens's first essay on HL (a review of *Short Stories in Prose and Verse*, 1894) is discussed in Chapter 2; his successive reviews are reprinted in *Criticism*.

⁴⁵ The *Stock and Station Journal* greeted the Commonwealth two-series 1s. issue of *Billy Boils* with a lengthy unsigned personal memoir, 'Mostly about Lawson', evidently written by a fellow member of the Sydney bohemian Dawn and Dusk Club. The four-part article stretched over four issues, 10 August – 14 September 1900. It gauged HL's success nicely: 'While his work was appearing almost every week, and we could meet him every other day and hear him tell the "basis" of his next "story," it was difficult to realise the size of man he really was. We saw too much of him, we knew he could write, but we knew so many other things that he could not do . . . and we failed to estimate him at his true value' (Part I). Part II responded to HL's decision to go to London: 'Lawson may live in the "big smoke," but he is too tender an exotic to flower generously in a foreign soil. And even if he sticks to his Australian *metier* he is bound to lose color and feeling in the land of fog and dirt'. Part III added: 'Certainly his best work to date is in "While the Billy Boils," and a few lyrics in the method of Burns . . . I reckon "Mitchell" has as much of the real Lawson in him as can be got. Cynically sanguine, prone on occasion to throw care and caution to the winds, subject to brief fits of the blues, but a good fellow all through.' From Part IV: HL 'never writes anything that is not redolent of sweat and of sin; of the dust of the track, or the thirst of the dry season. And through it all is the grim comedy of life . . . Lawson has no Fancy, and most of his poetry is merely verse.'

pattern, reviews throughout Australasia and in Britain recalled the earlier collection, usually favourably. Lawson's *The Country I Come From* – a selection from *While the Billy Boils* and *On the Track and Over the Sliprails*, published by Blackwood of Edinburgh in 1901 – received at least a dozen reviews, mostly appreciative.[46]

As the years went by, the opportunity for more broad-ranging reviews was occasionally seized. Reviewing *The Country I Come From*, the *Birmingham Post* described the sketches and short stories as 'written in a Kiplingesque style, and some of them are not unworthy imitations of the master' (30 August 1901). But the *Athenaeum* went further, in a review considering Lawson alongside Louis Becke's *Tessa: The Trader's Wife* (published by Fisher Unwin). Obtuse and condescending at once, it sounded a variation on a familiar theme in commenting that Lawson's 'literary development appears to have reached that irritating stage in which a writer feels that to be realistic he must confine himself to the blemishes and foul spots of his subject. Mr Lawson will grow out of this, and the sooner the better . . . The better half of the traditions of the *Sydney Bulletin* have in their way been to young Australian writers an education. The poorer half Mr. Lawson must slough and put from him utterly' – especially his 'raw Americanisms', with which he makes 'wearisome play', such as 'biled rag' and 'chawing-up apparatus' (17 August 1901). (The latter objection had also been made in some of the early Australian reviews.)

On 21 July 1902 the *Speaker* (London) ran an unsigned wide-ranging discussion, 'Australian Literature', that also served as another review of *The Country I Come From*:

---

[46] The best was probably the one in *Lady's Pictorial* (23 November 1901): 'There is rough power, humour, and pathos in Mr. Lawson's book which will delight readers who do not object to be taken from the conventionalities and stupidities of "smart" society, or the *tame* audacities of modern Bohemia'. The stories picked out as the best were all from *Billy Boils*. The *Pilot* (17 August 1901) reviewed the collection together with Miles Franklin's *My Brilliant Career*, also from Blackwood, whose publication HL had helped bring about. The earliest known review of *The Country I Come From* is dated 4 July 1901, in the *Scotsman* ('a fine, natural freedom') – a note picked up in *Literary World* (London): 'The strange solitude of bush life, its struggles with Nature, its freedom from conventionality, its untrammelled, highly-spiced speech, its rough humour, and its real and constant pathos are here in these vivid, strongly-drawn sketches' (11 October 1901).

The school of writers fostered by the *Bulletin*, men like Paterson, Lawson, Daly, Dyson, Quinn, Brady, and Ogilvie – all of whom made their name through this journal, and most of whose volumes were published by it – are genuinely Australian; of that there can be no doubt. Paterson is an Australian as Gordon or Kendall was not: in his absence of the higher notes of poetry, in his contempt for romance and for philosophic thought ... Lawson is also representatively Australian, but represents the views of those Australians to whom fate has assigned an inferior seat at the theatre of life. Like Mr Thomas Hardy, he has been accused of holding a brief for the devil; certainly he describes the gloomier aspects of existence in the "back-blocks" with an ironic pathos, a stern economy of emotions and morals, a pitiless realism.

This was yet another of the early British reception pieces probably written by an Australian, resident in Britain.[47] Its overt agenda is to sweep away the idea that the better known Adam Lindsay Gordon, Henry Kendall and Marcus Clarke between them bore the Australian literary banner. The definition of what it was to be an Australian writer was being rewritten. It was a memorable intervention, and it developed a theme present in a number of the early reviews. In the process it elided the fact that Lawson was as much a product of the *Worker* as the *Bulletin*, forgot that Stephens's missionising for this new Australian literature had nevertheless included a *Bulletin* review of *While the Billy Boils* that was particularly severe, and more especially consigned to a footnote (literally, in this case) the fact that Angus & Robertson had anything to do with his rise.

The 'academic critic' and Edward Garnett

We may naturally assume, from this summary of the reviews, especially from the confidently argumentative ones, that a new consensus had formed concerning 'the beginnings of a national school of poetry', as A. G. Stephens had bravely put it when reviewing Lawson's *In the Days*

---

[47] Cf. the review-article of *The Country I Come From* in *Literature*: 'Over here he is principally known by his volume "While the Billy Boils" ... The newspaper in Australia is the chief patron of literature, and Mr Lawson's fiction, which has many of the qualities of his poetry, comes also from the Press' (6 July 1901).

(*Bulletin*, 15 February 1896), and more broadly of an Australian literature. Looking, however, at Henry Gyles Turner and Alexander Sutherland's *The Development of Australian Literature* (1898) calls a sobering halt to any temptation to claim a widespread acceptance beyond *Bulletin* circles that the achievement of Lawson and his fellow writers had in fact either established a flourishing 'Australian' literature or even provided the dominant thematic note to it. The book also exposes to our view the existing cultural momentum that the 1902 essay in the *Speaker* was trying to turn. In his celebration of the Australian subject matter being imaginatively created by local writers, A. G. Stephens had been, in 1895–96, probably not so much recording a change in the literary scene as trying, entrepreneurially, to conjure one up. His defensive remarks in 1901 (in *The Bulletin Story Book*) show how little success had been achieved.

In the Turner and Sutherland book, Lawson is treated only as a poet and Gordon, Clarke and Kendall are the only writers treated at length. The book has some remarkable lacunae, but is otherwise a careful and often perceptive work. In particular, it takes account of the possibilities of the bookselling and reading marketplace, the economic advances of the period, the 'absence' in Britain 'of a desire to know anything about it [Australia]' until about 1875, the effect of international visitors to 'the first great International Exhibition held in Melbourne in 1880–81', the promotion of Australian writing in London in the late 1880s by Douglas Sladen, A. Patchett Martin and others, the stimulation of an appetite for colonial things via the Colonial and Indian Exhibition at South Kensington in 1886, and even the effect of the successful exploits of visiting Australian cricket teams. The net result was that 'The weekly and monthly periodicals [in London] began to canvass for Australian tales and sketches, and found that quite a number of colonists, resident in England, could provide them with excellent copy'.

In the Australian colonies, however, less advance had been made because:

> outside the large army of active and generally very capable journalists, we have not yet got any men or women in Australia living exclusively by the

product of their pens. And when it is considered with what redundancy the vast output of European literature finds its way to our shores; how even a rigid selection of the very best of the magazines would absorb far more time in their perusal than the average intelligent colonist can possibly spare, it ceases to be a surprise that no one is willing to devote labour and talents to the production of what the community may decide it has not time to look at.

The background to A. G. Stephens's defensive remarks is given by Turner and Sutherland's conclusion:

> Until such a national spirit is developed ... we must be content with the production of a local literature, essentially English in its characteristics, but moulded by climatic and scenic surroundings into a form that gives it sufficient distinctiveness to justify the term Australian. If we are content to dismiss the influential part which the nobility and aristocracy play in English fiction, the social material for the ordinary novel is much the same in Melbourne as in London. And it is greatly to the credit of Australian fiction that, so far, it has generally been healthy, clean, and optimistic.

When they deal with Lawson's *In the Days* in their general survey of Australian poetry they object to his profound 'pessimism' and his tone of 'cynical discontent – a sustained denunciation of the classes as opposed to the masses'. Of the *Bulletin*'s cultivation of short stories they have nothing to say; but their comments about Australian novelists' lack of reverence for French naturalism are indicative: 'Nor have they, for lack of material, yet descended to the depths wherein Grant Allen and Sarah Grand are groping, or to the unclean realism of George Moore, and the many English imitators of Zola's earlier writings.'[48]

Was this expression of taste (more or less standard in England during the 1880s and 1890s) also a coded signal of a Sydney–Melbourne divide, a response to the satirical jabs that the *Bulletin* had been making about the Melbourne literary scene?[49] Or was it more fundamentally an expression

---

[48] Turner and Sutherland, *The Development of Australian Literature* (London: Longmans, Green; and Melbourne: George Robertson, 1898), pp. 18, 21, 25, 26, 47, 26.
[49] For some jabs, see Ken Stewart, 'The Colonial Literati in Sydney and Melbourne', in *Nellie Melba, Ginger Meggs and Friends*, ed. Susan Dermody, John Docker and Drusilla Modjeska (Malmsbury, Vic.: Kibble Books, 1982), pp. 176–91 [pp. 183, 189].

of class affiliation? The *Bulletin*'s loud commitment to republicanism during the 1880s, as against Establishment loyalty to Imperial ties in Melbourne, would have been sufficient cause for division. Definitive answers to these social-political questions are probably unattainable, but a print-culture explanation at least broadens the terms of reference. Although, as Geoffrey Serle points out, Melbourne had no equivalent of the *Bulletin* around which a literary circle might form,[50] the southern city had been the Australian headquarters of the book trade for a few decades. It was the largest centre for the importation of British books in the world, possessed its own publishing industry, which supplemented the dominant import trade, had an impressive Public Library (where Marcus Clarke had worked), and through its prestigious weekly and (until the mid-1880s) quarterly and monthly magazines had been used to setting cultural agendas.

Nevertheless, the literary book-publishing impetus was gradually shifting to Sydney, and in the period 1890–99 Sydney publishers moved ahead of Melbourne in terms of the number of literary titles published.[51] The *Bulletin*, as a Sydney-based national newspaper, had been energetically attempting to drive new cultural and political agendas since 1880. Its first decade had gained for it a reputation as being bohemian, inconoclastic, irreverent – as only borderline-respectable – and thus as the reading matter, on the stations, better suited for the workmen than the squatter and his family. The *Shepparton News*, for instance, reported in 1891 that the nearby Tatura Mechanics Institute had refused it entry

---

[50] But Edward Dyson's *Bull-Ant* (then *Ant*) was a short-lived Melbourne imitator (May 1890 – June 1892). Geoffrey Serle, 'Victorian Writers in the Nineties', in *The 1890s: Australian Literature and Literary Culture*, ed. Ken Stewart (St Lucia: University of Queensland Press, 1996), pp. 32–65 [p. 57].

[51] The AustLit database (www.austlit.edu.au) as at 28 November 2010 listed 157 literary titles first published in Melbourne during 1890–99 plus another 22 reprints or new editions that had been first published elsewhere, for a total of 179. The Sydney figures are 219 plus 8, making a total of 227. Both numbers include reissues of British-originated or earlier titles, and genres include science fiction, crime, romance, historical fiction and travel writing. These figures do not encompass other (e.g., educational, religious and scientific) publications. However, George Robertson of Melbourne published more than twice as many Australian literary titles during 1890–99 than did A&R: 79 as against 33. I thank Katherine Bode for alerting me to this phenomenon.

and, although otherwise defending the *Bulletin* for its international outlook, conceded that it was 'not a paper we should commend to the young ladies of a select boarding school'.[52] Rolf Boldrewood, whose notion of Australia was born of the experience of an earlier colonial generation, would have little to do with the Sydney paper. And when the professor of English at the University of Melbourne, E. E. Morris reviewed Lawson's *In the Days When the World Was Wide* for the (Melbourne) *Review of Reviews* in 1896 he implied that he had never before heard of Lawson. If so, he cannot have been reading the *Bulletin*. Given his background, this would probably have been a deliberate policy.[53]

The reviewing in Sydney of the Turner and Sutherland book (co-published by George Robertson of Melbourne, from whom the review copies had come) was not enthusiastic. The *Sydney Mail* reviewed it dutifully judging it 'conscientious and interesting' and granting its arguments ample paraphrase, but added that 'we might have wished the space more equitably distributed' and noted the overlooking of Lawson's humour in *While the Billy Boils*. The *Town and Country Journal* followed suit: 'everyone who reads the book will think of names who ought to have received recognition'.[54] And in 1903 in the Red Page of the *Bulletin*, 'F.M.' would refer to 'that fool book' in quarrelling with the biographical chapter on Clarke – who, according to Turner, had '"impressed the seal of truthfulness on his description of the Australian bush to an extent unequalled by any other author who has essayed the theme." And

---

[52] *Shepparton News*, 10 November 1891: quoted in, and see further, John Barnes, *The Order of Things: A Life of Joseph Furphy* (Melbourne: Oxford University Press, 1990), p. 161.
[53] E. E. Morris, 'More Australian Poetry', *Review of Reviews*, 20 April 1896 (in *Criticism* 28–34). Without naming him, Arthur W. Jose describes Morris in *The Romantic Nineties* (1933), quoting from his own papers, as 'a radical anti-socialist, an Imperial Federationist who hates Kipling, an anti-*Bulletin*, anti-Ruskin, founder of Shakespeare, Home Reading, and Charity Organization societies' (Sydney: A&R), p. 39. See further, the entry for Edward Ellis Morris (1843–1902) by Olive Wykes, *ADB*, v. 293–4. Jose's still-active 'healthily boyish' prejudice (p. vi) probably gives the flavour (though doubtless further entrenched or romanticised over the intervening period) of the late 1890s Sydney view of literary Melbourne: 'Its literary circles were obsessed with respectability, the respectability which they believed fervently to be of the ruling English type, for which Ada Cambridge wrote her polite and soothing novels' (p. 40).
[54] *Sydney Mail*, 12 March 1898, p. 543; *Town and Country Journal*, 19 March 1898, p. 43 (both unsigned).

this', comments F.M., 'in 189[7], when some others who did know had essayed.'⁵⁵ Resentment of the Melburnian overlooking of the Sydney achievement is plain.

While, figuratively from this point of view, most of the early reviewers of *While the Billy Boils* might be said to have taken up their positions on one side of the Murray or the other, many of them, as we have seen, did not simply plump for the home team. When the Melbourne-based politician, ardent proponent of colonial Federation and future prime minister Alfred Deakin read *While the Billy Boils* in early November 1896 the notes he made betray a real enthusiasm: Lawson 'paints the sombre side of bush life with unsurpassable fidelity'; his sketches 'are absolutely living in their burning reality'.⁵⁶

Moreover, the objection to Lawson's 'pessimism' (of which Turner and Sutherland's 'unclean realism' was a variant complaint) had been there from the start, including in the Sydney *Worker*. It was an existing tide of expectation about the literary that Lawson was having to push back, a resistance that he was but slowly dislodging. His rejection – in dwelling on the experience of the struggling bushman – of a more stylised and sentimental form of prose writing was the nub of the offence. Joseph Conrad saw the daring achievement straight away when he read some of the Joe Wilson stories in 1901: 'Lawson's sketches are beyond praise – the more so that in such a subject it takes a first rate man not to break through the thin ice of sentimentalism'.⁵⁷

Boldrewood's biographer, Paul de Serville, has surveyed the cultural

---

[55] The date is given as '1892' – presumably a typo for 1897, the date of the volume's Dedication: F.M., memoir 'Of Marcus Clarke (and Some Others)', *Bulletin*, 26 November 1903, Red Page.

[56] In *Walter Murdoch and Alfred Deakin on Books and Men: Letters and Comments 1900–1918*, ed. J. A. La Nauze and Elizabeth Nurser (Melbourne: Melbourne University Press, 1974), p. 93. Deakin made notes on his reading, mini-essays; this one is dated 7 November 1896.

[57] Letter to William Blackwood, 3 June 1901: *The Collected Letters of Joseph Conrad*, ed. Frederick R. Karl and Laurence Davies, 9 vols., *Volume 2 1898–1902* (Cambridge: Cambridge University Press, 1986), p. 329. The stories appeared in *Blackwood's Magazine* in 1900–01. Conrad's reference, in the plural, seems to comprehend 'Brighten's Sister-in-law' (*Blackwood's*, November 1900; the last instalment of *Lord Jim* appeared in the same issue), 'A Double Buggy at Lahey's Creek' (February 1901), as well as 'Past Carin'' in the issue he had just read (May 1901).

stereotypes that have become associated with the 1890s *Bulletin* and, with his own subject foremost in mind, concluded that it is a mistake to assume that 'there was only one form of Australian identity in the 1890s and that the *Bulletin* embodied that form . . . There were more Australias than the *Bulletin* cared to admit.'[58] While granting that the *Bulletin*'s 'targets were not confined to the Melbourne literary scene, but they were conspicuous there', Ken Stewart had already shown that the case was more variegated:

> the *Bulletin* was eclectic in its tastes and criticism, devoting about as much space to commentary on Shakespeare and on overseas writers as to criticism of Australian literature; and the original literature it published represented, contrary to the stereotype, a variety of styles, genres, and subject matter. Support for Australian literature, in principle, was as universal among Sydney and Melbourne literati as the recognition that, in Stephens' words, 'Australian literature is today insignificant'.[59]

The present survey of the reviewing of *While the Billy Boils* demonstrates that the universality of the latter belief was gradually giving way before Stephens's pronouncement, which dates from 1901.[60] But the change can only have been gradual and partial: there was no sudden revolution in taste in the 1890s towards things Australian, no matter how hard George Robertson worked to stir the cultural pot through his publishing initiatives. A series of articles that appeared in the *Sydney Mail* in mid-1897 called 'What Australians Read: An Inquiry' shows what the consensus to which Stephens referred was based on. The series, written by 'E. D. H.', evidently a staff journalist, was based on interviews with leading librarians and booksellers, at first from Sydney and then, as the series gathered steam, from Hobart and Melbourne. Most of the interviewees put down their reflections on their patrons' or customers' book-borrowing and book-buying habits in writing; and these documents were liberally quoted. Adam Graham Melville

[58] Paul de Serville, *Rolf Boldrewood: A Life* (Melbourne: Melbourne University Press, 2000), p. 259: the context was a campaign by Archibald to force Boldrewood to acknowledge publicly that, in *A Modern Buccaneer* (1894), he had used material bought from Louis Becke.
[59] Stewart, 'Colonial Literati', pp. 188–9.
[60] A. G. Stephens, 'Australian Literature', *Commonwealth*, no. [1] (1901), 32–6.

(1842–1921), of the principal Melbourne bookseller and lending library – formerly Mullen's but from 1889 Melville, Mullen and Slade – had read the reflections of his Sydney counterparts, and observed that: 'The conditions of the public taste regarding recent literature and new books are the same in Melbourne as they are in Sydney.' E. D. H. further explained that the 'difference sometimes noticed between the taste of Melbourne and Sydney theatre-goers' is not replicated with literature since 'all drink at the same founts, the sources of supply are the same, and a book which is a success in one colony will almost necessarily succeed in another'.[61]

Melville had (selectively) affirmed one strand of the Sydney booksellers' testimony by stating that in Melbourne also there is 'the same preference for wholesome novels ... [and] the same objection to impure or suggestive literature'.[62] However, J. G. Lockley, who had spent ten years working for Maddocks's Library (which had become Dymock's) and who was now manager of the Angus & Robertson Book Club (the firm's lending library), was less inhibited:

> The first rush for an author which Mr. Lockley remembers in Sydney was for Haggard, and especially for 'King Solomon's Mines.' Then came the period of the theological novel. 'Robert Elsmere,' 'John Ward, Preacher,' and 'O'Donovan' each had a run. The reading public, however, soon seemed to tire of theology, and as a reaction became rather wicked and rushed for the sex problem stories of the 'Heavenly Twins' type. The more wicked the more rushed. But now they have surfeited with *outré* renderings of the matrimonial tie, and are seeking relief in romance and bloodshed.[63]

Despite the publishing efforts of his employer and his personal acquaintance with Lawson and probably Paterson, Lockley does not mention any Australian writer, whether as the object of a 'rush' or, indeed, at all.

The variety of reading experiences that Australian readers were

---

[61] In E. D. H.: 'What Australians Read: An Inquiry', *Sydney Mail* (17 July 1897), p. 122.
[62] *Ibid.*
[63] *Ibid.*, 29 May 1897, p. 1,131.

enjoying in the 1890s is also testified to by the lists of successful books (mostly British, some American and with Boldrewood also appearing) given in the articles; and also noted are the broadening in reading habits caused by the University Extension Scheme lectures, the ever-cheaper publication of out-of-copyright classics and the beneficial effects in Australia of the Colonial Library series of various British publishers in bringing down the price of in-copyright and new literature. The very small role that Australian literature was playing in this variety and broadening is evident; and it was in any case a phenomenon that, according to Mr Kettlewell (a Dymocks representative), had only started 'during the last 18 months', concurrently with Angus & Robertson's new publishing initiative.[64]

Lawson as prose writer is mentioned in Kettlewell's ordering of popularity, but only because Kettlewell, unlike the others, gives a separate list of Australian writers who are 'all in current sale'.[65] Only Mr Martin of the Sydney Mechanics' School of Arts lending library reports Lawson as poet as being among the most popular borrowings: 'Kipling, Tennyson, Browning, Lawson, and Paterson easily distance every other poet in the order given.'[66] A recent survey of extant records of several 1890s reading groups in Sydney, Hobart and elsewhere comes to much the same conclusion: that Australian literature was only minimally represented in the discussions, which heavily favoured English writers; and, when the local product made an appearance, rarely did discussion extend beyond a tiny handful of poets, Adam Lindsay Gordon and Henry Kendall being the chief of them. Lawson was recognised as a poet but not as a writer of sketches and short stories. Evidently they fell below the literary purview, or had not been encountered at all. One participant in Hobart, Rose Scott, 'deplored the excessive praise of Australian poets, as showing a lowering standard of excellence' and noted that 'The first literature of this country, like the American, was merely an echo of the

---

[64] *Ibid.*, 5 June 1897, p. 1,192.
[65] *Ibid.*
[66] *Ibid.*

old.'⁶⁷ So, clearly in 1901, Stephens was right, even if the ground had been very gradually shifting.

The shift would continue. Although not directly answering Turner and Sutherland, an essay appeared in the *Academy and Literature* in London in 1902 that called into question the standards they were invoking: 'An Appreciation' by Edward Garnett.⁶⁸ Like the other main participants in the debate over Lawson's prose he wanted to change the tenor of the literary debate, in his case in Britain. Already an influential publisher's reader, Garnett had read *While the Billy Boils* after its publication in London in 1897, had been in touch with Lawson in 1898 before he left Australia and had been helping him with practical advice during his stay in England. (Garnett is treated at more length in Chapter 10.) In the essay Garnett refers to 'the academic critics'. Turner and Sutherland had more varied credentials than that but possessed considerable authority. Turner (1831–1920) was a prominent banker, essayist and, later, historian of Victoria. Sutherland (1852–1902) was a graduate of the University of Melbourne, a retired headmaster and, in the 1890s, became a leader-writer for the *Argus* and *Australasian* in Melbourne. With Turner and others he had founded the *Melbourne Review* in 1875, had edited Kendall's works, and would briefly become an academic in English at Melbourne University in 1902.

---

⁶⁷ Quoted in Elizabeth Webby, 'Not Reading the Nation: Australian Readers of the 1890s', *Australian Literary Studies*, 22 (2006), 308–18 [pp. 313–14]. A reader in South Australia, Herbert Solomon, a university graduate, argued: 'We cannot yet be said to have a national literature – we are not even a nation', adding 'In this busy age we have not much leisure for reading, and we are content, as a rule, to limit our poetical excursions to the field of English poets of renown' (quoted, p. 316).

⁶⁸ Garnett, 'An Appreciation', *Academy and Literature*, 42 (8 March 1902), 250–1: it appeared the month before HL left England (see Chapter 10) but there was further reference to HL in Garnett's 'Classes of Novelists', *ibid.* (17 May 1902), 510–11, a reply to G. S. Street's, 'Novelists and Classes', *ibid.* (5 April 1902), 365–6. All this was grist to the mill of HL's acknowledgement in Britain.

Another British reception is recorded in a letter from the travel writer and novelist W. H. Hudson to Garnett on 16 June 1902: 'Since Saturday I have been staying at Itchen Abbas with my friends the Greys – and last evening we discussed Lawson's book which Lady Grey has just read. She likes the sketches you marked and one besides – "A Visit of Condolence" – but doesn't think as much of Lawson as you do' (*Letters from W. H. Hudson to Edward Garnett*, London, Dent, 1923). 'Lawson's book' must have been *Billy Boils* since *The Country I Come From* does not contain 'A Visit of Condolence'.

CHAPTER 8 . EARLY RECEPTION

Garnett's objection to the academic critic had doubtless been formed closer to home:

> no doubt with the highest standards of the great masters constantly before them, and with keen eyes for the relative planes of fine art, [they] may affirm that Lawson's work really falls within the province of those ephemeral story-tellers who serve only to amuse their generation. The answering argument is that Lawson through these journalistic tales *interprets* the life of the Australian people, typifies the average life for us, and takes us beneath the surface . . . Nothing is more difficult to find in this generation than an English writer who identifies himself successfully with the life of the working democracy, a writer who does not stand aloof from and patronise the bulk of the people who labour with their hands. This no doubt is because nearly all our writers have a middle-class bias and training, and so either write down to or write up to their subject when it leads them outside their own class, and accordingly their valuations thereof are in general falsified.

Having explained why he believes 'Lawson's verse is that of a third–rate writer' Garnett goes on to hazard some explanations about why his prose comes to be 'that of a writer who represents a continent'. He refers to Lawson's 'apparently artless art', his 'racy language and an extremely delicate observation of those tiny details which reveal situation and character'. He has a capacity to capture 'the gesture of the living man'. 'It isn't great art', Garnett notes, 'but it is near to great art'. He criticises Lawson's 'temptation to introduce sentimental touches that mar his realism': a firm, modern stance that not even the better reviewers in 1896–97 could unambiguously embrace. His only other criticism returns us to the dilemma that other commentators had faced without much clarification:

> If Lawson's tales fail to live in another fifty years – and where will be most of Kipling's, Stevenson's, Hardy's, and even Henry James's work then? – it will be because they have too little beauty of form, and there is too much crudity, roughness, and uncookedness in the matter.

Since they have all survived as classics, the objection, urged conditionally, must be false. It derives, I suspect, from the very position Garnett believed he was undermining, which he called the 'academic'. This returns us to

Stephens. He had glints of insight when it came to Lawson as well as an entrepreneurial streak. Some of his agenda-setting apothegms – such as 'Lawson is the poet of the bush, and the bush is the heart of Australia' – are still quoted. But he also had the conscience of an academic critic whose business it was to uphold standards. Between the two positions there was a chasm into which Lawson's reputation, at Stephens's hands, fell. In this situation and although Stephens had the inside knowledge, Garnett emerges as the surer guide to what Lawson had achieved. He was the more substantial, more balanced, less blinkered critic.

In these various ways, both in Australia and in Britain, *While the Billy Boils* was being used to advance cultural agendas, just as it had forced attentive reviewers to reconsider the expectations they brought to their reading of it. Its attraction to reviewers brought many new literary considerations to bear and put existing ones under some strain. It would prove to be an evolving dialogue, in which *While the Billy Boils* would evolve along with the commentary on it. Its reception history in the twentieth century would weave in and around its changing material-bibliographic forms. Chapter 11 takes up this theme – but first there is the question of money.

CHAPTER 9

WHO MADE THE MONEY, AND HOW MUCH?

OR, WHY LAWSON WENT TO ENGLAND

THE period between publication of *While the Billy Boils* and Lawson's departure for England in 1900 seems to have been an alternation of shiftlessness and hard work for Lawson. His departure for Perth on 30 June 1896 with his new wife Bertha was probably an attempt on her part to get him away from his drinking pals and, on his, to find subject matter to write about – what he called, in the journalist's way, 'copy'. The trip was a fulfilment of his plan to go to the western colony in April 1892, aborted when he was sent to Bourke by Archibald. During their stay, the newly published author would have to work as a house painter, and he and Bertha would be forced to live in a tent. They lasted a few months in Perth and then returned to Sydney, arriving on 13 October 1896.

By November Lawson was drinking heavily again and apparently got into the habit of coming to ask George Robertson for money. The latter wrote to Bertha on the 28th:

> It cannot be helped I suppose but it is awkward before ones customers. I am sending you a couple of pounds towards the second weeks 'screw' promised him. Had I given him more money yesterday afternoon he would have gone away, but in the state he was in it would not have been right.

This answers her undated letter sent from 91 Redfern Street, Redfern, in Sydney, in which she apologises for her husband's insulting Robertson in his shop ('He was mad with drink'). She talks of their need to go to New Zealand to break the habits he was falling into once again.[1] The second

---

[1] ML MSS 314/45, p. 83: a typescript copy of a letter dated 28 November 1896, GR to Bertha Lawson; her letter to him is at p. 113a.

week's 'screw' might be related to a steady stream of copy Lawson was submitting at this time: the firm's Manuscripts Register records three Lawson stories received by 23 October 1896; by 15 November two had been declined, and one accepted – but it is not clear for what.[2]

Lawson had been making overtures to Robertson in a letter from Western Australia about putting together another collection, and Robertson's letter to Bertha suggests that some tentative understanding had been reached.[3] In another undated letter to Robertson of around this period Lawson writes: 'There are several things I wish to speak to you about, but we have no opportunity for conversation in the shop in business hours. I think the best thing we could do would be to hurry out a second volume of prose in a cheaper form. It would perhaps create a demand for the first. I cannot understand why *While the Billy Boils* didn't go better'.[4] But Angus & Robertson would not in fact publish new Lawson titles until 1900, when it would produce four: two collections of stories and sketches: *On the Track* (17 April 1900) and *Over the Sliprails* (9 June); and two of verse: *Popular Verses* (August) and *Humorous Verses* (September). The four were soon also issued as two combined volumes.[5]

The long delay is explained by a serious falling-out between Robertson

---

[2] ML MSS 3269/23/1, fol. 1: the three stories were all returned by the reader: 'Mitchell on Matrimony': 'Too pious. Decline' (published in the *Bulletin*, 11 December 1897, and *On the Track* in 1900); 'Good Tucker Track': 'accept' (developed as 'On the Tucker Track' for *Children of the Bush*, 1902); and 'Case for the Oracle': 'Decline' (*Bulletin*, 21 November 1896; *Over the Sliprails*, 1900).

[3] HL to GR, 3 September 1896: 'I am saving copy for the East. Country is rather barren of material. I am working up a couple of novels – also got some decent verse since in my later style . . . will send you copy of my W.A. notes and sketches' (*Letters* 61–2). The Perth journalist Andrée Hayward, writing in 1904 and recalling a conversation of 1896, stated that HL took a trip to the goldfields: 'Men I Ha' Met', *Spectator* (Perth), 18 June 1904, p. 3 – reported by Charles McLaughlin, 'Adventures in AustLit: The Goldfields Bards of Western Australia', *Westerly*, 54.1 (2009), 133–7 [p. 135]. However, a more immediate report contradicts Hayward's recollection and should be given more weight. HL was interviewed when returning from the same WA trip when passing through Melbourne en route to Sydney: 'Strange to say, he didn't go beyond Perth. A trip [to] the goldfields has to be deferred . . . He made plenty of notes' (*Champion*, 17 October 1896, p. 452).

[4] *Letters* 66, dated by Roderick as '[January 1897]'.

[5] As *On the Track and Over the Sliprails*, a double volume with two internal title-pages and paginations, with only the spine (a publisher's binding) giving the joint title (July 1900); and as *Verses, Popular and Humorous* with one pagination (7 December 1900): dates from *Life* 195, 229 and Mackaness 24.

and Lawson that soon occurred, and that Bertha, in her letter, had evidently been trying to stave off. On 8 February 1897 Robertson wrote tartly to Lawson: 'We do not intend to publish any new work of yours' and stated what copyright the firm retained: *In the Days* and *While the Billy Boils* in their entirety, 'Skeleton Flat' 'which was printed in the first edition only of that volume [*In the Days*]', and a few other poems cut down for *In the Days* where the firm claimed copyright both in the cut down form and the original magazine form.⁶

This letter may be a reply to an undated letter of Lawson's to Robertson that Roderick dates as [February 1897]:

> When I spoke to you *re* sketches yesterday morning I thought you didn't want sketches and it would only waste your time and mine bringing them in. The merit or worthlessness, acceptance or rejection of the last sketch had nothing to do with it. That was for *you* to decide. I spoke without any ill feeling whatever. I'm very sorry that you adopted such a tone in reply to me in the presence of Mr Angus; and you can't blame me for resenting it.⁷

Thereafter Lawson wrote to Hugh Maccallum at Angus & Robertson rather than to Robertson himself. Lawson was writing from New Zealand as he had in the meanwhile secured a position as a school teacher at a Maori ('Native') school at Mangamaunu and would remain until late October 1897. The day he began there, 6 May 1897, was the same day as his commercial fate was being sealed in London – the day when, unknown to Lawson and as we saw in Chapter 7, the probability of a mainstream publisher taking up *While the Billy Boils* slipped from Angus & Robertson's grasp. For now, writing on 25 June 1897, Lawson's mind turned to a book that 'will be mostly New Zealand character sketches, personal reflections, some old debts paid to one or two unfair critics, literary and otherwise, and scenery – with the Native School as a peg to hang on'. In the letter he mocks his own tendency to depression and consequently his resentfulness at 'the world's apparent ingratitude

---

⁶ ML MSS 3269/71/4, fol. 471.
⁷ *Letters* 67: the mention of the rejection could plausibly date the letter as November 1896 (see n. 2 above). But HL's going on to report that he was told by 'Mr Maccallum that you have not got your money back for the books' repeats a note in his letter of [January 1897].

and treachery' and vows for the sake of 'true friends, bushmen and others, who trusted and believed in me through it all' to 'write myself up to the top of the Australian gum'.[8]

The same day, upon receipt of some letters from England, he wrote a second letter to the firm: 'Blackwood offers £2 2s. per thousand words and all the usual rights, and says that his attention has been directed to *While the Billy Boils* by one of his contributors'.[9] This was for *Blackwood's Magazine*; and there were similar requests from the editor of *Chambers' Journal* and from a fiction syndicating agency, the Northern Newspaper Syndicate, also in England. Next, a rumour that *Short Stories in Prose and Verse* had been reprinted or was again being offered for sale reached Lawson via Angus & Robertson, who would have been rightly concerned that the value of their intellectual property – material from that 1894 volume reprinted in their two Lawson volumes – was being undermined. Lawson vigorously rejected the idea that he had anything to do with it, but the incident cannot have helped relations with Robertson.[10]

A typescript copy of an undated letter from Robertson to Lawson, writing in the voice of the firm in the plural, is indicative of the state of feeling. It probably dates from 1 March 1898, only about a fortnight before Lawson would return to Sydney from New Zealand. On 1 March the Publishing Ledger records a £30 payment as 'Royalty H Lawson',[11] and the letter reads: 'We have much pleasure in sending you the enclosed draft for thirty pounds', which, Robertson states, he hopes to repeat at the end of 1898. 'But our personal contact with you led to so much unpleasantness that we are obliged to impose a condition upon you. Should you ever enter our place of business again, or in any way attempt to see us personally, no further payment will be made to you.'[12] Nevertheless, Robertson was a businessman above all; and a series of

[8] *Letters* 68–72.
[9] *Letters* 72.
[10] Letter, HL to A&R, 26 July 1897 (*Letters* 75–6).
[11] ML MSS 3269/11/1, fol. 118, the opening for *In the Days*. The Private Ledger (ML MSS 3269/12/1) records a royalty payment of £5 in relation to *Billy Boils* on 3 August 1898 (fol. 23).
[12] ML MSS 314/45, p. 113. Why GR was within his rights to withhold payment at will is explained below.

payments to Lawson that started the following month seems to signal the beginnings of an agreement for Lawson's next volume with Angus & Robertson.[13] Acting for Lawson at Robertson's request Banjo Paterson (who was also a lawyer) made a list of stories by Lawson sold to various editors that would be available for the new volume.[14] Thus for a while things settled down, with Lawson securing a temporary position for April–June 1898 as a clerk in the Government Statistician's Office, Sydney.

The series of addresses recorded in Lawson's correspondence until April 1900 nevertheless shows that his financial difficulties continued.[15] Given the ongoing frosty climate at his Sydney publishers, and in view of the interest from overseas publishers that he had received in 1897, the hope that he had expressed to his Aunt Emma on 19 September that year, while still at the Native School, of going to England 'next year', must have begun to feel like an increasingly attractive proposition.[16] By the end of 1898 the decision had become irrevocable; and on 21 January 1899 his rationale, '"Pursuing Literature" in Australia', appeared in the *Bulletin*.

It is effectively an apologia for the intended departure of the same man who had written a defiant Preface, full of nationalist literary sentiment, to *Short Stories in Prose and Verse* (quoted above in Chapter 2). It had turned out that defiance was not enough, that achieving recognition in England was unavoidable, after all. It was a struggle to find the money to go, but Lawson and Bertha, with their first child Joseph Henry Lawson,

---

[13] The Private Ledger records five payments from the firm's Copyright Account from 28 April to 1 June 1898 (no title given, ML MSS 3269/12/1, fol. 35).
[14] An agreement in the form of an assignment of copyright 'in all the published prose work of him the said Henry Lawson' was effected on 27 August 1898 (ML MSS 3269/316/Angus & Robertson Correspondence, vol. 828, pp. 173-7). The payment on signing the agreement is given as £30 (duly recorded as paid at ML MSS 3269/12/1, fol. 23) and the final total as £75 (see below).
[15] They lived at 1 Regent Street, Newtown (Sydney), March–July 1898; then with HL's brother-in-law J. T. Lang during August–September; then HL lived at Courtenay Smith's Rest Haven for alcoholics, North Willoughby; and then with Bertha at various North Sydney addresses until April 1900.
[16] *Letters* 78.

now two, and their second, Bertha, aged two months, finally left on 20 April 1900.[17] Various figures, including the Governor of New South Wales, had contributed to their travel costs.[18]

The cost of 'Pursuing Literature'

The garnering of a literary income in the Australasian colonies was a precarious business. An unsigned article in the *Sydney Mail* in July 1898 pointed to the substantially greater number and the generally higher quality of the books read in the colonies proportionate to Britain. The article nevertheless conceded: 'With a limited population, we cannot, of course, give the rewards to our writers which London, as a platform facing the whole English-speaking peoples, offers, and so English publication must for long to come be the ambition of the local author.' The writer goes on to accept the verdict that '"an author who can make his living by writing Australian books is at present unknown". That is so. So far the weekly press has occupied the place of magazines, and the Australian literary man, so long as he keeps to Australia, has hitherto had to look on literature as a recreation more than a pursuit.'[19] Whether Lawson read this article is unknown, but the generally accepted piece of wisdom, which it was retailing, would have been well known to him.

His essay, '"Pursuing Literature" in Australia' appeared six months later. Lawson complains about the paltry rewards he had achieved from his writing in what he understood as a national cause. In 1893 he was receiving, he writes, 12s.6d. a column for his sketches for the *Worker*, a miserly 5s. a column for 'some steerage sketches' in the *New Zealand*

---

[17] Joseph Henry Lawson had been born on 10 February 1898 in Wellington (*Letters* 83), and the family left for Sydney on 12 March. Bertha was born on 11 February 1900.

[18] David Scott Mitchell lent him £25 (*Letters* 119, 437). The Governor of New South Wales, Earl Beauchamp, was his other main benefactor, along with, at the last minute at the wharf, GR: see HL, '"Succeeding": A Sequel to "Pursuing Literature"', in *The Essential Henry Lawson*, ed. Brian Kiernan (South Yarra, Vic.: Currey O'Neil, [1982]), pp. 363–70 [p. 364].

[19] *Sydney Mail*, 'Books and their Makers', on 9 July 1898, p. 103. This was a response to a report on Australian writing in *Literature* (London) – the source of the quoted text – that relied on the recently published *Development of Australian Literature* by Henry Gyles Turner and Alexander Sutherland (1898): see further, Chapter 8 pp. 188–92.

Mail and 'an occasional guinea' from the higher-paying *Bulletin*.[20] He calculates that he had received £700 for 12 years of literary work since he began to be published in 1887, of which 'considerably less than a third' had come from the two Angus & Robertson books.

The *Bulletin* had turned out to be his most generous income stream. He was not the only writer of the period to realise that the mass circulation weeklies could bring in a more reliable and often better income than books, even if recognition as a literary author did not necessarily go with it.[21]

In his article, Lawson goes on to make some further calculations. He says that by selling his copyrights to *In the Days* and *While the Billy Boils* (his only Angus & Robertson books published to date), and taking into account other advances, he had ended up with only £190 for 'the cream of ten years' literary work'.[22] On the other hand, he reports, the 'publishers and printers and booksellers' must have made between them £2,750, given a 5s. retail price for *In the Days* and the first impressions of *Billy Boils* before it dropped to 2s.6d. and sales by the end of 1898 of 6,000 and 7,000 respectively.

His conclusion, which follows some sentences that flirt with self-pity without fully embracing it, is forcefully sardonic:

> My advice to any young Australian writer whose talents have been recognized would be to go steerage, stow away, swim, and seek London, Yankeeland, or Timbuctoo – rather than stay in Australia till his genius turned to gall, or beer. Or, failing this – and still in the interests of human nature and literature – to study elementary anatomy, especially as applies to the cranium, and then shoot himself carefully with the aid of a looking-glass.[23]

---

[20] It is likely that this was a rate for a single poem or story of at least a column in length: see Chapter 2 n. 11.

[21] Boldrewood is an example (see Chapter 2 n. 11, and cf. G. B. Barton's 'The Status of Literature in New South Wales', quoted there), as is Edward Dyson (see n. 49 below).

[22] HL must have been brooding on this for some time. An article in the *North Coast Beacon* of 19 January 1898 by 'Miss A. Gillies, Tintenbar', and apparently based on a letter from him from Kaikoura ('he is leaving New Zealand'), states: 'Lawson, under pressure of circumstances, relinquished the right to both of his books for about £170, a very small remuneration for the best of his work for the last ten years.'

[23] The article in its earliest state before editing is given in *Letters* 87–94. The title in the

How accurate was Lawson's reporting of his income that led him to this conclusion? The editor of the Red Page where the essay appeared, A. G. Stephens, answered Lawson in the *Bookfellow* on 18 February 1899. He was evidently privy to inside information from Angus & Robertson, and he questioned the legitimacy of Lawson's complaint:

> Plainly, this young man does not know when he is well off.... I understand that for his book of verses he received some £56: whereas, had he been able to hold on [i.e. not sell his copyright and instead stick to the originally offered half-share of profits] ... he would have received some £187 on a 6,000 sale. For his prose Lawson received upwards of twice as much as for his verse ... *And in each case he would still be entitled to his half-share of profits for the remainder of the term of copyright – some 39 or 40 years.*[24]

Lawson's article received a sympathetic report in London in the *Athenaeum* but it galled some readers of the *Bulletin*'s Red Page. A number of replies were printed in the issues of 11 February and 11 March 1899. The sea-shanty poet E. J. Brady grew indignant on patriotic grounds ('This our native country is good enough for some of us still'), and distanced himself from the 'pessimistic Australian literature, this unlucky melancholy of Kendall, and Gordon, and Clarke', which he felt would in due course be seen as more descriptive of those writers than of the country of which they wrote. He saw Lawson as continuing in the same pessimistic vein. Others were impatient with Lawson's 'howling over his hardships'.[25] 'Why should the writer assume Providence will be on his side; it is only one form of honest graft.' And, 'Can't a machine shearer make his £100 in the one season – say three months'?[26] Another writer wished he had earned as much as Lawson had from his writing; and so it went. But one Harry Stockdale touched on the quality of Lawson's confessional, mood-driven piece: 'the simplicity and force of the language is delightful', he wrote.[27] And, in London, the *Academy*

Bulletin, by which it became known, is editorial; HL wrote it in the form of a long letter to the editor.
[24] *Bulletin*, 22 July 1900, pp. 23–4.
[25] 'M. O'K', *Bulletin*, 11 March 1899, Red Page.
[26] '7 x 7', *Bulletin*, 11 February 1899, Red Page.
[27] Stockdale, *Bulletin*, 11 February 1899, Red Page.

ran the unsigned 'The Case of Henry Lawson'. It discussed the article at length and in a sympathetic manner, repeating without disputing Lawson's assessments of the relatively low payments available in Australia: 'he is a good writer, a shrewd and humorous observer, and his sympathies are all with the weak and noble; but he has failed altogether to measure his fellow man and act accordingly'.[28]

So how much *did* Lawson earn? Was his article merely special pleading or not?

What Lawson earned

In his 1991 biography of Lawson, Colin Roderick describes Lawson's essay as a 'public exhibition of petulance', and the physical document, the manuscript that Lawson submitted to the *Bulletin*, as having 'all the marks of an author far gone in his cups'. Finally, he states that Lawson's calculations of his income in the essay cannot be trusted because, according to Roderick's calculations, Lawson's earnings 'could not have been less than £1,200 for the three years from April 1897 to April 1900', and *this* when the annual rent for a two-storey six-bedroom home was £100 per annum.[29] This evidence forms part of Roderick's picture of an unbalanced man, an ungrateful author who was being looked after by a generous publisher, George Robertson. In his 2007 article, 'The Pinker of Literary Agents', John Barnes – who is an otherwise careful and reliable scholar – simply agrees with Roderick, but without offering any further evidence. Also noting A. G. Stephens's comments, he concludes 'that, comparatively speaking, at times Lawson earned substantial sums as a writer'.[30]

---

[28] The author was apparently E. V. Lucas, since the article notes 'our review of *While the Billy Boils*' (*Academy*, 8 April 1899, p. 409); the review is attributed to Lucas in handwriting in the Reviews Book (ML MSS 3269/Angus & Robertson Ltd. Book Reviews (Bound volumes) 1894–1970/1, vol. 7).
[29] *Life* 200–01.
[30] John Barnes, 'Henry Lawson and the "Pinker of Literary Agents"', *Australian Literary Studies*, special issue *New Reckonings: Australian Literature Past, Present, Future*, ed. Leigh Dale and Brigid Rooney, 23.2 (2007), 89–105 [p. 92]; Barnes refers to A. G. Stephens, 'Lawson and Literature', *Bookfellow*, 18 February 1899, 21–4.

Despite this concurrence, what does the available evidence show? Unfortunately Roderick's biography of Lawson suffers from a chronic under-documentation of its factual claims. Relying on memory rather than stopping to check the documentary evidence can be a hazardous exercise, particularly when one's work on the subject matter stretches back some decades. Perhaps Roderick was under pressure from his publisher to reduce the documentation. Whatever the case, citation of evidence is a necessary discipline if later scholars are to build on one's work. Roderick does not substantiate his calculations and seems, indeed, to have allowed himself to be more decisive in his judgement of Lawson than the evidence permits.[31]

In the Angus & Robertson archive at the Mitchell Library, there is a Lawson folder containing some Memorandums of Agreement (contracts), correspondence with other publishers about the sale or

---

[31] In his entry for '"Pursuing Literature" in Australia', Roderick says he had 'computed the moneys received by Lawson from all sources for all of his literary work sold from 1 October 1887 to 4 April 1900' as totalling £999. He then oddly refers to 'Lawson's income over those ten years' without acknowledging that he had changed the year span (*Commentaries* 274–5). The amount from periodical printings of prose and verse he gives as £775 in total. In view of the typical payments from the *Bulletin* and *Worker* cited above, if we nominate £1 per item as a generous average, then HL is supposed to have received payment for 775 periodical printings, (representing, say, 650 works and allowing, generously, for reprintings in other periodicals and assuming he was actually paid for them). His output up to 1900 is nowhere near 650, as a count from the Contents pages of Roderick's various editions reveals (fewer than 450 works).

Odder still, in *Life*, Roderick quotes the same figure of £999 as received 'from 1 October 1897 to 4 April 1900 ... these two and a half years' (p. 201); and he does not refer back to *Commentaries* information about year-span as being now corrected. The figure of £1,200 quoted above (from *Life*) derives from adding to the figure of £999 HL's salary of £2 per week for not quite six months while working for the Brisbane *Boomerang* in 1891 (thus, about £50) and a presumably similar weekly wage while provincial editor for the *Worker* for a few months in 1894 until there was a falling out (so probably less than £50). This leaves a shortfall of £100. Whichever way one looks, there is confusion abounding here. The conclusion that Roderick's information about HL's income cannot be trusted is difficult to resist.

Even if Roderick's calculations were correct (£1,200 for 1897–1900), HL would have received £400 p.a. (= A$40,000 p.a. in 2001 terms: see n. 38, below, for this official calculation). But his earnings cannot have been anywhere near this amount, given that a longer period is at issue. A less generous calculation for the period up to 1900 yields: 450 works in periodicals plus 50 reprintings, creating income of say (generously) £500; plus income from documented sales of rights to A&R for copyrights (£224 in total for *In the Days* and *Billy Boils* and *On the Track and Over the Sliprails*). Thus one reaches a figure (£724 in total) not far removed from HL's own in '"Pursuing Literature" in Australia': i.e. 'about £700' over the extended period.

purchase of Lawson rights, and some calculations about payments made to Lawson.[32] The last is a summary of entries mainly registered in the firm's Royalty and Copyright ledgers. It was evidently put together when Lawson died in 1922.

In this folder, Item 3 is a 'Copy of list headed LAWSON COPYRIGHTS. "Everything published serially in any newspaper prior to 23 June 1896 bought by us under ag[reemen]t. of that date."' 'Everything' covered prose and verse, which is why the Agreement is given as for both *In the Days When the World Was Wide* and *While the Billy Boils*, even though the volume of verse had already been published. The amount stated is £70. As Item 4 gives the copyright payment for the volume of prose as £42, evidently £28 was for *In the Days*. This agreement may have been to further formalise an earlier one for a volume of verse by Lawson, dated 26 July 1895 and then called 'Faces in the Street & Other Poems', with the remuneration arrangement envisaged as 'Half profits' – that is, an equal sharing of the profits between publisher and author after expenses. But Lawson received £54 on 10 October 1895 when, preferring the money immediately, he sold the copyright of the poetry volume to his publisher. Robertson was careful to record in various places that he restored Lawson's half-profit right to him once the volume began to sell well (that is, when half-profits reached £54),[33] but that a feckless Lawson soon sold it back to him again: hence, presumably, the extra £28.

With the agreement of 23 June 1896 Robertson was evidently acting to clear things up. He would do so again in further assignments of copyright for later work on 27 August 1898 (£75 was paid for 'All Prose to date'), 18 July 1899 and 9 January 1903.[34] In relation specifically to *While the Billy Boils*, Item 4 itemises the following payments:

---

[32] ML MSS 3269/Lawson, Henry – papers re 1894–1949, vol. 386.
[33] E.g., in his notes to HL's *The Old Shop and the New*, p. 25 n. 5. At MSS 314/45, p. 83 there is a draft of a letter to HL attributed in pencil as 'A B Patersons wording 1896' (notation presumably added in c. 1917) where GR offers to pay HL half-profits in *In the Days* once the £54 already paid to HL is reached.
[34] Part of the 1898 payment was an outright sale of newspaper and magazine stories and sketches, some only fragments and some yet to appear, but intended for HL's next volume of prose with A&R.

2/5/96	Geological Spieler 2-10-0
24/6/96[35]	Copyright 42-0-0
10/6/96	Advance 2-0-0
Dec. '96	Petty Cash to Lawson 8-2-1

This makes a total of £54.12s.1d. for 1896. Despite having sold his copyrights, Lawson got into the habit of dropping by the shop and asking for small sums to keep him going. The last amount in the list would have incorporated these, but his falling-out with Robertson by early 1897 probably put an end to it. Nevertheless, the Publishing Ledgers to 1903 itemise another £53.10s. in respect of this title,[36] so that the total paid to Lawson to 30 June 1903, over a period of seven years since payments began, was £108.2s.1d. Robertson had evidently decided that he had a moral if not a legal obligation to reward Lawson for the success of the firm's sales strategy as it changed over the years.

Item 4 refers to a 'List (in Mr Shenstone's handwriting) of agreements and payments made to Lawson'. This List is probably the document present in the folder as pages 73–75 in blue pencil. It gives the total payments of Angus & Robertson to Lawson for all titles from 1895 to 1922 as £748.10s.6d. Of this, £200 is noted as being paid at 1 December 1919 for moving picture rights. This was money received from Beaumont Smith, who had staged a play called *While the Billy Boils* in 1916 and would in due course make a film drawn from several of Lawson's volumes.[37]

This is the last payment before Lawson's death. Because the rights to Lawson's other volumes of prose published elsewhere had been carefully

---

[35] 24 June 1896, the day after the date of the contract, is the date of payment recorded in the Ledgers (ML MSS 3269/11/1, fol. 46).

[36] 25 April 1896, £1.10s. for 'For Auld Lang Syne' (ML MSS 3269/11/1, fol. 46); 3 August 1898, £5 'royalty' (MSS 3269/12/1, fol. 23), but called a 'Loan' at MSS 3269/11/3, fol. 30; 12 January 1899, £15 cheque to HL (ML MSS 3269/11/2, fol. 82); 2 September 1899, £25 (ML MSS 3269/12/3, fol. 119); and 5 August 1902, £7 ('Part of £25') (MSS 3269/12/3, fol. 120: presumably this £25 was in respect of multiple titles).

[37] An extra payment is recorded at 6 July 1923 to the Public Trustee (which was appointed to control HL's estate) for £6.6s. The music by Felix Le Roy and lyrics by Tom Kelly for a song called 'While the Billy Boils', bound-in with 'Down in the Trenches' and evidently a World War I publication (Sydney: Joe Slater Publishing, n.d; copy at NLA), does not refer to HL but co-opts the popularity of his title into the sentimental evocation of a communal identity.

acquired by the firm over the years, Robertson would presumably have felt morally as well as legally entitled to keep all profits now that Lawson was dead.

Thus Lawson's lifetime earnings from book sales totalled around £550 from Angus & Robertson, £108 of which was for *While the Billy Boils*.[38] Banjo Paterson did better from Angus & Robertson than Lawson because he did not immediately sell his copyrights and instead continued to enjoy half-profits from *The Man from Snowy River* and other titles for many years.[39]

The publisher's profits

There seems to have been no final reckoning of the firm's profits from publishing Lawson since the exploitation of the intellectual property was and would continue to be an ongoing matter. Nevertheless the ledgers afford rolling, year-by-year snapshots, broken down into title by title, and those usually into format by format; some calculations are extant that record the basis on which cheques were paid to Lawson; and there are some illuminating summaries in the archive of the overall profits of

---

[38] The value of these amounts in 2001 prices needs to be multiplied by a factor of fifty to take general inflation into account: thus £100 (where £1 became $2 upon decimalisation in 1966) becomes (in Australian dollars) $10,000 in 2001 terms. In 1901 a 50-hour week produced an average male wage of £2.3s.6d.; the equivalent in May 2000 was $830 for a 37-hour week. In 1901, £100 could be earned in the equivalent of 46 weeks. See Australian Bureau of Statistics, 'Prices in Australia at the Beginning and End of the 20th Century', at www.abs.gov.au, accessed 7 June 2010.

Payments to HL from other firms are dealt with in Chapter 11: there were two, high initial advances of £200 from British firms but no reprints to create a following cash flow for him. In the absence of well-organised British book publication, sale of magazine rights in the best outlets seems to have provided the most lucrative income. Yet the typical payment per item was too small to make up the difference: 30s. per column seems to have been the very best *Bulletin* rate HL could achieve in the 1890s when, according to Geoffrey Serle, the *Bulletin* (selling into all the Australasian colonies) and, next, the newspaper weeklies were the highest paying outlets. Rates were always in danger of being undercut from the heavy importation of very cheap US and British weeklies, the widespread use by editors of literary matter lifted from British and other magazines and newspapers, and from the importing of moulds. Serle comments: 'If ever there was a sweated trade it was journalism and writing in general': 'Victorian Writers in the Nineties', in *The 1890s: Australian Literature and Literary Culture*, ed. Ken Stewart (St Lucia: University of Queensland Press, 1996), pp. 32–65 [pp. 56, 60].

[39] For each new 'Thousand' Paterson received payments ranging from £21 to £31: ML MSS 3269/12/1, fol. 22. He finally sold the copyright to A&R in 1908 (see Alison 123).

the firm and of its publishing division over the relevant period.

In the Days When the World Was Wide netted Angus & Robertson nearly £265 up to the end of its Sixth Thousand by 1 March 1898 and a further £150 profit for its Seventh and Eight Thousand by 28 August 1899. The profit for *While the Billy Boils* 'from commencement to date' (that is, to the end of the Tenth Thousand and probably into the Eleventh) is 'Estimated' in the latter calculation as £250 – presumably only a guess since the Ledgers suggest nearly £305 to 30 June 1899.[40] Both calculations led to a decision about what to pay Lawson. As Jennifer Alison shrewdly points out, the wording of Robertson's letters to Lawson make it clear that the payments were strictly *ex gratia* – a 'gift'. Perhaps he was maintaining, with characteristic decisiveness, his original determination to keep the literary publishing on a professional basis by paying his authors half-profits, even when, as with the feckless Lawson, it worked against the firm's financial interest.[41]

We have seen that Lawson had earned £108 in total from Angus & Robertson for *While the Billy Boils* in its various formats by 30 June 1903. The firm had done well, despite the purchase of copyrights and the *ex gratia* payments. About 12,000 copies of the first edition had been printed, with about 7,500 (less complimentary and review copies) being bound in cloth and sold at 5s. and then, from 1898, at 3s.6d. The remainder were the paperbound copies at 2s.6d., with nearly all sold. About 11,000 copies each of the division of the work into two volumes

[40] The Publishing Ledgers carry forward credit and debit balances on the successive openings recording transactions, allowing profits for the first 6,000 (in the 5s. format) of *Billy Boils* to be identified as £160 (ML MSS 3269/11/1, fol. 119) and the cheaper format (3s.6d. and 2s.6d.) as £144.8s.1d. (The latter is an addition of credit balances separately itemised on ML MSS 3269/11/2, fol. 82 as £130.3s.9d. and £14.4s.5d.) Note that such abstractions of absolute profit lend a false sense of completion to what was an ongoing series of investments in the present against expected sales in the future. Note also that charges against individual titles for a percentage of the overheads (premises and staffing) do not seem to have been made.

[41] See Alison 126; GR's letter to HL ('gift'), 2 March 1898 (ML MSS 3269/72/1, p. 342). Alison's concern that the calculated profits per copy for *In the Days* cannot be right (10½d. per copy for the first 6,000 but 1s.6d. for the next 2,000) ignores the fact that setting-up costs (typically, editing, typesetting and stereotyping) were charged against the initial print runs, costs from which the next 2,000 copies were exempt. Reprints only involved costs for printing, binding, advertising and sundries; provided sales continued, they would normally return a higher profit.

as First and Second Series had been printed, making 22,000 copies in all. Nearly 15,500 had sold at the retail price of 1s. at a net profit of just over £200.[42]

Roughly estimating £300 as the profits for the Ninth to Twelfth Thousands,[43] adding it to the £305 already noted, and then adding the £200 for the sales to date of the First and Second Series, we arrive at a rough figure of £800 – more than seven times what Lawson had earned from the title. Additionally the firm had in stock 1,315 copies in total of bound copies of the First and Second Series, worth approximately £37 when and if sold. The firm had already paid for the printing of about 5,000 copies not yet bound worth about £50 after binding was paid for. The profit per copy had fallen radically to less than 7d., although Robertson's cunningly foreseen division of the collection into two series doubled the returns. But this was the story of publishing in the 1890s and after: the drive to cheaper and cheaper forms of publication. Nevertheless, the copyright for future exclusive exploitation – until (as it turned out) 1973 – was in the possession of the firm, and it owned the stereos, matrices and blocks, whose costs had been fully amortised.

Figures for the profitability of the firm as a whole and of its respective divisions were also calculated, probably in 1901, and are preserved in the Angus & Robertson archive. Over the six financial years (July–June) from July 1895 to June 1901, sales from publishing at Angus & Robertson lifted from £2,166 to £7,466; but net profit rose from £674 to only £1,142, with the four intervening years showing less profit than the first. In comparison, the Book Club, once it got properly going in 1896–97, made the firm more profit than did publishing in each year except the last, including 1898–99 when it made considerably more than double. The retail bookselling business made more than the other two departments combined for four of the six years. They nevertheless played a significant role in the expansion of the business, together

---

[42] The sales income, valued in the Ledgers at 6¾d. per copy, would be about £436, less binding charges of about £15 per thousand: thus £203.
[43] At £75 per thousand, which is what *In the Days When the World Was Wide* had returned.

making up 48 per cent of the net profit in 1900–01. The overall net profit rose from £1,984 in 1895–96 to £4,540 in 1900–01, an increase of 229 per cent.[44]

Lawson's contribution to the profits of the firm did not go unnoticed: in July 1899, he received a payment of £75 for the copyright of his next verse collection, *Verses, Popular and Humorous* (1900), a significant improvement on the £42 that he was given for *While the Billy Boils*.[45]

The value of the latter title to the firm is also registered in an indirect, almost bizarre way in a typed two-page document, headed REJECTED MSS., signed with Robertson's initials and stuck into the back endpapers of the firm's Manuscripts Register. It specifies nineteen reasons to be chosen from and quoted in full when rejecting manuscripts submitted to Angus & Robertson for publication. Numbers 8 and 9 are intended to be applied to collections of short stories that are 'not hopeless':

> 8. Short stories are absolutely tabu. Neither the public nor the trade will buy them in book form. If they have not already appeared in any magazine or weekly newspaper you should submit them at once. We understand that good money is made by some short-story writers, but our experience with volumes of short stories has been anything but satisfactory.
>
> 9. Volumes of short stories cannot be made to pay except when by authors of well-established reputation. Since Henry Lawson we have published none that have returned the cost of printing.[46]

Profit comparison: *While the Billy Boils* and *Robbery Under Arms*

In the standard literary accounts of the 1890s in the Australian colonies Lawson is accorded prime position. For H. M. Green, writing in the early 1950s, Lawson was 'not only the most notable but the most representative

---

[44] These calculations are at ML MSS 3269/6/1. There are also separate summaries of results for trading, profit and loss, and capital accounts, financial year by financial year, given from 1888 to 1909. July–June financial years began in 1893; earlier results are by calendar year. The firm's net profit for 1890 was £1,452.

[45] Two payments in July 1899, totalling £75, for a volume of 'New Verse' are recorded in the Private Ledger (ML MSS 3269/12/1, fol. 37).

[46] ML MSS 3269/23/1. This document bears no date but, judging from its reference to May Gibbs's fairy stories published by the firm (1916), must have been prepared some time between then and GR's death in 1933.

writer of his age, in prose or verse'.⁴⁷ In the index of the latest literary history of Australia (2009) Lawson has far more entries than any other author of any period.⁴⁸ Despite the anti-nationalist revisionism of the 1970s–80s feminist case about the 1890s, Lawson remains a figure by which commentators orient their thinking about Australian literary history. But how important was Lawson to readers of the time?

The standard assumption is, first, that he was a far more significant presence than say John Farrell, Victor Daley, Edward Dyson and Barcroft Boake (all were Angus & Robertson authors, and the Ledgers confirm their relative insignificance); and, secondly, that Lawson's rising star effectively displaced Rolf Boldrewood's, whose best days as a writer of prose fiction (the early 1880s) were long gone.⁴⁹ Born in 1826, he is generally seen as a precursor to the literary 1890s, although he did continue to publish through that decade into his sixties and then seventies.

An empirical comparison between the two is possible because of the survival of the printing, sales and royalty figures for Boldrewood's classic *Robbery Under Arms*, preserved in the Macmillan archives at the British Library and at Reading University. Though originally serialised in Sydney during 1882–83 this adventure novel first achieved book publication in three-volume form in London in 1888 and then in a cheaper one-volume form the following year in Macmillan's Colonial Library series published at 2s.6d. in the sober dark-green covers for the

---

⁴⁷ H. M. Green, *A History of Australian Literature: Pure and Applied*, 2 vols (Sydney: A&R, 1961), I. 532; the publication of this *History* was long delayed.

⁴⁸ Gregory Kratzmann pointed this out in his review of *The Cambridge History of Australian Literature*, ed. Peter Pierce (2009) in the *Australian Book Review* (February 2010), pp. 7–8. A count reveals that Rolf Boldrewood, for instance, has 10 mentions; Henry Handel Richardson has 26; Patrick White has 33; but HL has 50.

⁴⁹ Cf. Leon Cantrell: 'his talent had spent itself by the nineties', Introduction, *The 1890s: Stories, Verse and Essays*, ed. Cantrell, Portable Australian Authors (St Lucia: University of Queensland Press, 1977), p. xxiv. A. G. Stephens had long since struck the note: 'In kind [HL's] work is like the sketch-work of T. A. Browne; but the writers move in different spheres, and Lawson is on a higher plane of literary force': 'Australian Literature', *Commonwealth Annual*, 1 (1901), 32–6 [p. 35].

From sheer industry rather than quality, Dyson managed to make £600 p.a. after the mid-1890s; and he claimed to have been the only freelance writer of his time to make a living from writing: see further, Graeme Davison's entry on Dyson, *ADB*, VIII. 395–6.

colonial market and at 3s.6d. in red cloth and on slightly better stock for the Home market. It was this pricing and respectable appearance that set expectations for literary book publishing in Australia and that Robertson needed to match or exceed.

We have seen that Lawson earned £108 in the seven years after 1896 from *While the Billy Boils*. While the following is unavoidably a comparison of sales of a novel as against a collection of short stories and sketches, it is nevertheless illuminating. In comparison to Lawson's prose collection, Boldrewood earned, in his first seven years after the Macmillan publication of *Robbery Under Arms* in 1889, 22 times as much from that title: £2,367.[50] This was off the back of far higher sales than Robertson managed to achieve for *While the Billy Boils*: 46,000 copies of *Robbery Under Arms* at 3s.6d. and 52,000 at 2s.6d. were printed by 1896. As we have seen, Robertson reduced to this pricing only after two years of marketing. Both titles ultimately went into very cheap formats: *Robbery Under Arms* in 1898, nine years after its first Macmillan release, in a double-column format with tiny type at 6d.; and *While the Billy Boils* in 1900, four years after release, at 1s. each for the two Series. In 1902 Boldrewood did a calculation for that year for sales of *Robbery Under Arms*. The return to him was £73, not including returns from the cheap 6d. edition, which was being reprinted initially in runs of 30,000.[51] The eighth printing of this size occurred in 1911 and the total reached 320,000 in 1916, a year after Boldrewood's death. He received £100 for the first of these cheap printings and presumably comparable amounts thereafter.[52]

---

[50] Boldrewood's contract stipulated 4d. per copy on all copies sold in either market; this was raised to 6d. from June 1890. By then, 5,000 copies of the 3s.6d. issue had already been printed (and presumably sold, since more printings were ordered in June and then August 1890). Calculating the sales of the Colonial issue as the same as the Home issue, this gives a figure for the initial period of £167. With the higher royalty for the remaining 41,000 copies of the Home issue until 1896 and 47,000 Colonials, the result is £2,200, thus £2,367 in total for 1889–96 in respect of *Robbery Under Arms*. For details, see the Introduction to the Academy Edition of *Robbery Under Arms*, ed. Paul Eggert and Elizabeth Webby (St Lucia: University of Queensland Press, 2006), pp. lviii and lxx–lxxii. Print runs were recorded individually for the Home issues but the Colonials total is only a composite up to 1896.
[51] See *ibid.*, p. lxx n. 127.
[52] Cf. Boldrewood's 'Private Journal' for 1898 (at 23 March): 'Letter from Macmillan & Co. offering £100 for 6d. Edition of Robbery Under Arms. To cable "Yes." (NLA MS 3208). That

A final comparison is perhaps the most revealing: during the twenty-six years after 1896 until Lawson's death in 1922 he received from book sales of his various titles about £550 from Angus & Robertson, and an unknown amount but almost certainly a smaller one from his other publishers, none of whose ventures with Lawson titles was particularly successful (principally Blackwood, Methuen, Lothian, Tyrrells). In comparison, in the seven years from 1889–96 Boldrewood received from Macmillan £6,600.[53]

The disparity in income is only partly explained by the better terms that Boldrewood was gradually able to extract from his publisher in London than Lawson could from Angus & Robertson in Sydney. Boldrewood's far greater success depended on the superior sales and distribution capacities of the well-placed Macmillan. It was all very well to order print runs of 30,000; it was another thing to sell them. But, sell them, Macmillan could and did. The firm was a successful Imperial publisher. In the 1880s it had pioneered the Colonial Library publishing arrangements for Empire sales, and it had offices in the USA. The firm was thus in a position to release the same title simultaneously around the anglophone world, usually with advance copies and publicity.[54]

Angus & Robertson could not. As we have seen, Robertson's attempts to place *While the Billy Boils* with a mainstream British publisher failed, and *In the Days* did not even achieve the limited British distribution via Simpkin, Marshall that the stories did.

Sales of the prose collection in London to 30 June 1903 were moderate. Of the two initial consignments in 1897–98, about 900 seem to have

---

this was the first printing only is confirmed by a letter of 15 February 1898 from Frederick Macmillan to A. P. Watt, Boldrewood's agent since 1895: in return for £100, the author would give the publisher the right 'to print a certain number of copies (probably 30,000) and sell them right out, not reprinting after the first Edition was exhausted' so that the 'permanent sale' of the ordinary issues would not be impaired (A. P. Watt Papers, Wilson Library, University of North Carolina at Chapel Hill, 26.18: I thank Elaine Zinkhan for this latter information). See further, Paul Eggert, 'The Bibliographic Life of an Australian Classic: *Robbery Under Arms*', *Script & Print*, 29 (2005), 73–92.

[53] See *Robbery Under Arms*, ed. Eggert and Webby, p. lxx n. 127.
[54] See further, Paul Eggert, '*Robbery Under Arms*: The Colonial Market, Imperial Publishers and the Demise of the Three-Decker Novel', *Book History*, 6 (2003), 127–46.

been sold in the first year but sales fell away markedly thereafter.[55] Cloth copies sold at 5s. retail. The collection was however taken by W. H. Smith's Subscription Library (188 Strand, London, and at railway bookstalls).[56] In total, this initial sale amounted to a modest rather than a notable success, and thus provided little challenge to existing Imperial bookselling arrangements.

About four years later, by 30 June 1901, another 500 copies were consigned to the Australian Book Company in London and the price was dropped to 3s.6d.[57] On 30 June 1903, there were still nearly 350 copies in stock, and on 29 October 1903, 200 were marked for return to Sydney. As an ongoing sales proposition *While the Billy Boils* had failed in London, despite the push that Blackwood's publication of *The Country I Come From* (1901) would have given Lawson's name. In addition, 250 copies of *On the Track and Over the Sliprails* and 300 copies of *Verses, Popular and Humorous* were returned.[58]

Why was Robertson unsuccessful in London? He would not be the last Australian publisher to learn that the trade was normally one-way – and not the way he wanted. Clearly the situation made no sense at first to those in Sydney. The first two Angus & Robertson titles had been doing surprisingly well in the colonies, which was a novelty. Why would they not perform at least as solidly in the much larger and well organised Home market? Just before the third title in the series, *While the Billy*

---

[55] The consignment in March 1897 to Simpkin, Marshall (575 copies but with 81 complimentaries left a maximum of 494 for sale) was apparently not an outright sale: some reporting of sales as credits appears in the Ledgers, whose sales information is incomplete. See Chapter 7 n. 17 for the second consignment of 514 from the Sixth Thousand. Only 38 copies were sold in the second half (or possibly all) of 1898 (ML MSS 3269/11/2, fol. 81), 25 copies in all of 1899 (ML MSS 3269/12/3, fol. 119).

[56] Witnessed by the firm's sticker in a personal copy.

[57] ML MSS 3269/12/3, fols. 120, 92, 227. The cheap 1s. First and Second Series were apparently not for sale in London.

[58] ML MSS 3269/12/3, fol. 227. Of the London sales of Victor Daley's *At Dawn and Dusk* (July 1898), their agent James Bowden wrote to A&R on 25 May 1899: 'there has practically been no sale whatever' (ML MSS 314/13, p. 49). Paterson's *The Man from Snowy River* did best: see Alison 120 (a table of print-runs taken from a Macmillan edition of 1917). Macmillan took up the volume by 1904 as publisher, whereupon Home sales lifted; but the printings for the Australian market easily outstripped British during 1902–08 (14,500 vs 3,500). There were steady sales in the Home market during 1910–17.

Boils, was published, Robertson's business partner David Angus tried a combination of enthusiasm for the series and commercial shaming to get his old friend Young J. Pentland (the firm's agent in London and Edinburgh) to take the crucial next step:

> I feel as if I can not forgive you for not acting as our Publisher at home. it is of no use your saying they are outside your line . . . nothing ought to be outside your line if there is money in it & there is money in these. think over it & if you make up your mind to act. Cable the word *Published* & we will understand you are the publisher of Lawson & all our future publications.[59]

Pentland did not.

The sort of gratified curiosity at the emergence of a new Australian publishing venture of high standard that Robertson was able to whip up amongst the Australian booksellers and reviewers could not be replicated in England because of the nationalist card that he repeatedly played in his colonial correspondence. In this he was materially assisted, as we have seen, by the *Bulletin* and the *Worker*. Robertson was willing to admit, privately at least, that there may have been something meretricious in the campaign. He wrote to an Australian bookseller, J. Kevin, on 2 August 1900: 'The fact is that Paterson and Lawson who are "Bulletin" pets have been so boomed that the Bookselling trade all over the Colonies believe in them and push them – & this is the secret of their great success'.[60] Is there any wonder that the London trade was unimpressed? Perhaps word about this upstart colonial competitor got around in the trade in Britain, where the allure of Australian subject matter would have seemed thinner. In London the books' adoption was less automatic; and cutting a figure there must have been far harder.

Purchasing only Home-market rights for a literary work when a major likely source of sales was in the colonial market had become less attractive since the spread of the Colonial Library series from the mid-1880s. Neither Angus nor Robertson seems to have grasped the

---

[59] 27 July 1896: ML MSS 3269/71/3, p. 84.
[60] ML MSS 3269/72/3, fols. 195–6.

meaning for them of this significant change in the Home market, to which both had originally been apprenticed. Lawson had grasped it, at least temporarily. In a letter to Hugh Maccallum at Angus & Robertson on 15 November 1897, answering their cable of the 13th, he wrote that he would not 'dispose of Australian *and* English rights' to his next book because 'Methuen and others say [they would want to purchase] both English and Colonial rights'.[61] On 28 June 1899 Lawson replied to a letter sent him by Edward Garnett; he had been reader for Fisher Unwin in London until about 1897. The letter, addressed to T. Fisher Unwin, acknowledges Garnett's letter of 'Some time ago', enclosing 'a letter and circular from you'. Fisher Unwin must have been one of the publishers Lawson mentioned in his letter to Maccallum. Lawson proceeds:

> My second volume of prose, was, perhaps unfortunately, disposed of in Australia nearly a year ago.
>
> I have another verse volume which, I think, will be much stronger than the first; also a good deal of prose copy on hand. When I have got proofs of new vol. off my hands, and the order of arrangement of new prose work has developed itself a little more in my mind, I will be glad to negotiate with you for English AND COLONIAL publication.[62]

The fact that Lawson was unable to come to terms with any British publisher for a book at this stage is probably the result of his having too little material to send them, and also the need for organisation and planning on a scale he could not manage. Once back in Sydney and after his stint in the Government Statistican's Office that he threw over after three months, and with a wife and child to support, he had little choice but to return to his old hand-to-mouth habits, writing for immediate sale to the local weeklies. In this situation, the easiest thing to do was to stay with Angus & Robertson for the book collections, on the offered terms. This he did until 1900. When at length he left for England it was to pursue a literary career there. As John Barnes has pointed out, 'he

---

[61] *Letters* 81.
[62] HL to T. Fisher Unwin, 28 June 1899, carbon-copy typescript, University of Sydney Library. The approach from Fisher Unwin is also referred to by HL in a letter to David Scott Mitchell, 4 February 1900 (*Letters* 119). See further, Chapter 10 pp. 227–9.

probably thought of the move as permanent'.[63] The anonymous reviewer of *While the Billy Boils* in the *Spectator* must have reinforced the idea with the comment:

> That [his stories] should not be read on this side of the world seems to point either to a contemptuous indifference to European opinion or to an unusual ignorance on the part of the writer as to his own merit.[64]

Lawson was gradually determining to put that to rights; the next chapter shows what steps he took.

---

[63] Barnes, 'Henry Lawson in London', *Quadrant*, 23.7 (July 1979), 24–35 [p. 26]. He adds on p. 34: 'There was never any chance of his taking on the character of an expatriate or losing his affection for Australia or his sense of being an Australian; but in England he had had opportunities to discover his capacities as a writer, opportunities such as he did not have in Australia'.

[64] 'An Australian Story-Teller', *Spectator*, 8 May 1897.

CHAPTER 10

'PURSUING LITERATURE'

LAWSON'S STORIES IN BRITAIN 1900–1902

SALES figures and income from literary writing, discussed in the preceding chapter, are not, of course, the same thing as aesthetic significance. But they do give a measure of a writer's presence in the minds of readers of the period. This question of presence raises the broader and more pervasive question of when and by what means it is registered.

When Joseph Furphy famously complained in chapter 4 of *Such Is Life* (1901) about the influence of Henry Kingsley's kind of fictional Romance in *The Recollections of Geoffry Hamlyn* he probably had in mind a present-day fact rather than – what in another important sense it was – a novel first published in 1859. Because of its initially high prices in both three-volume and then one-volume form, it had a restricted circulation in the Australian colonies, despite being highly praised for its treatment of life there. (Kingsley was a visitor during the 1850s.) But it became cheaply and continuously available throughout the 1890s.[1]

For any writer of the period it was not a case, as T. S. Eliot would famously generalise it in 1919, of the whole literary tradition being available to and re-enriched by the individual talent in the moment of writing. Less grandly, it can be understood as a matter of those books from earlier periods, as well as from the present one, that have been influencing the way readerships think and in response to which

---

[1] See Paul Eggert, 'Australian Classics and the Price of Books: The Puzzle of the 1890s', *Journal of the Association for the Study of Australian Literature* (special issue *The Colonial Present*, ed. Gillian Whitlock), 8 (2008), 130–57 and the Introduction to the Academy Edition of the novel, ed. Stanton Mellick, Patrick Morgan and Paul Eggert (St Lucia, Qld: University of Queensland Press, 1996), pp. xxi.

new writers have to orient themselves. Those books that have been influencing readerships are the ones that the publishing industry has made available. Availability and circulation in the writing present are the key. In the Introduction we saw that, in the literary field, commentators are used to thinking either *synchronically* (the circulation of discourses in a particular era, which individual texts absorb and express) or *diachronically* (the change of literary tastes and the rise and demise of successive literary movements, plotted out over time). But in truth, looking out from where one is at any one moment of time – as Furphy was doing – the situation is heterochronic.[2]

In the 1890s, various factors relevant to the book trade worked together to guarantee this heterochronicity. It was an era when titles were still kept in stock for extended periods, when, because of stereotype printing, frequent short-run reprints made financial sense once the initial set-up costs had been amortised, when transportation of goods had become efficient and relatively fast, and when, for a variety of reasons, cheaper retail prices for new literary titles, not only those from the publisher's backlist, had become feasible. Simultaneous availability makes a heterochronic explanation of the Australian 1890s more or less compulsory now. The colonial decade was a literary-historical moment not only of the *Bulletin* writers and of Ada Cambridge and Tasma and Catherine Martin and Guy Boothby. The 1890s was just as importantly in Australia the moment of Dickens and Emerson and Bret Harte and Longfellow and Mark Twain, of Trollope and Kipling, of Shakespeare and the Bible, as well as a host of others who clattered around in the minds and imaginations of readers and writers of the decade. Their formative currency is still apparent in faded nineteenth-century volumes in Australian secondhand bookshops, and in extant catalogues of the circulating libraries and literary institutes.[3]

---

[2] I thank John Gouws, for putting this term into my lexicon and, even better, forcing me to think about it.
[3] I am unable to deal here with the role of the lending libraries of Schools of Arts, Athenaeums and Mechanics Institutes. Partly it is for reasons of space but also because much more fundamental research on book-borrowing patterns remains to be done, not only at

Availability of influential books in the heterochronic present depends upon distribution capacity and price. That is why, especially in respect of a colonial periphery at considerable distance from the metropolitan centre, the writing of literary history must be inflected by book history. It is under this purview that it makes sense to argue that, for instance, throughout the 1890s Rolf Boldrewood was a more significant presence than the fine new realist talent, Henry Lawson – even though Boldrewood's mix of colonial-adventure tale, historical account and stereotyped Romance is seen now, and was seen by some forward-thinking literary journalists and others at the time, as of a past era that needed to be superseded. The information given in the preceding chapter about the relative seven-year sales figures of *Robbery Under Arms* and *While the Billy Boils*, and the very different incomes received by Boldrewood and Lawson, bear this out. Lawson really belongs to what may be called the Long 1890s, a period which, it can be argued, was not fully achieved until the 1950s and did not end until the late twentieth century. (The next chapter, about the afterlife of *While the Billy Boils*, examines and finds support for this claim by following its publishing history over a very extended period.) It follows that when critics talk about, say, the nationalist ideology to be found in Lawson's or other *Bulletin* writings they are just as likely to be referring to a formation of the 1950s as of the decade they believe themselves to be discussing. Furphy's complaint simply brings the matter out into the open.

The other side of the availability coin for colonial authors published locally is that while, as George Robertson had proved, money and reputation for an author could be earned locally, the same did not extend to the Home market where the infrastructure and the most influential taste-forming institutions (the quarterly, monthly and other magazines, the larger subscription libraries, the critics, the publishers' readers) were predominantly in London and, to a lesser extent, in Edinburgh. The book trade was, for better or worse, mainly an Imperial one: so that

---

title-level – as is traditional in library-history research – but at the crucial format-level as well. The bibliographical distinction follows from my analysis of price and formats.

when Lawson left Sydney on 20 April 1900 to try to establish himself in England he knew that what he was doing was a gamble that could pay off handsomely. He had the talent. That was already affirmed locally. He needed to throw the dice.

Lawson at work in England: The first year

The biographical picture of Lawson and his family in England after they arrived about late May 1900 has become fairly clear because of work carried out by various scholars across several decades: Colin Roderick in his edition of Lawson's letters in 1970, an article of 1977 and his biography of Lawson in 1991; and John Barnes in articles of 1979, 1983, 1984 and 2007, making use of Lawson correspondence in the Blackwood Papers, National Library of Scotland, and the papers of the literary agent J. B. Pinker in the Berg Collection at the New York Public Library and at Northwestern University Library, Chicago. Roderick's account in the *Life* brings much new information to bear; but, intent as its author is on pursuing a psychiatric account of Lawson's decline (depressive, bipolar), the account lacks the judicious balance of the literary-historical and literary-critical, as well as the helpfully full citation of evidence of Barnes's pieces. More recently, in 2007, Lucy Sussex and Meg Tasker returned to the biographical questions with relevant information from the British census of 1901, Bertha Lawson's medical records and evidence from literary gossip columns.[4] Together they have given us a fairly clear picture of where the family lived, their dire financial straits after Bertha's difficulties developed

---

[4] Roderick, *Letters*; 'Henry Lawson's Joe Wilson', *Overland*, 66 (1977), 35–47; and *Life*. Barnes, 'Henry Lawson in London', *Quadrant*, 23.7 (July 1979), 24–35; 'Henry Lawson in England: The "High Tide": A Revelation', *Quadrant*, 27.8 (August 1983), 60–9; 'Edward Garnett and Australian Literature', *Quadrant*, 28.6 (June 1984), 38–43; and 'Henry Lawson and the "Pinker of Literary Agents"', in *New Reckonings: Australian Literature Past, Present, Future; Essays in Honour of Elizabeth Webby*, ed. Leigh Dale and Brigid Rooney, pp. 89–105 (special issue of *Australian Literary Studies*, 23.2 (2007)). Tasker and Sussex, '"That Wild Run to London": Henry and Bertha Lawson in England', *ibid.*, pp. 168–86. Tasker and Sussex show that a liaison on HL's part with a 26 year-old servant during his wife's hospitalisation cannot be ruled out. Lizzie Humphrey came to live in his small rented flat (or at least is recorded by the Census as being there on 31 March 1901), presumably to look after his daughter, who is also recorded as in residence: see Chronology for details of his living arrangements and movements.

into a psychiatric illness necessitating her (expensive) hospitalisation and then commitment to an asylum, and Lawson's literary contacts during this period as he worked hard to write and sell stories. The shift in approach was registered nicely by Barnes in 2007:

> Contemporaries and later commentators have emphasised the incoherence of Lawson's personality leading to his inability to manage his own affairs, but have given little attention to the material conditions under which he was trying to establish himself as a full-time writer.[5]

The previous assumption – that because the obvious, marked decline in the quality of Lawson's writing from 1902 followed his sojourn in England it must therefore in some way have been caused by it – has been decisively superseded by the realisation that some of Lawson's finest writing, the stories that would make up the first half of the collection *Joe Wilson and his Mates*, were either freshly written in England or adapted there from earlier material or ideas. Among the literary jobs Lawson undertook in England was the selection and revision of a number of stories from *While the Billy Boils* for a new collection drawn from that volume and *On the Track and over the Sliprails*. Published in June 1901 as *The Country I Come From* by the same firm, Blackwood, as had corresponded with Lawson in 1897, work on it came in between his preparation of two new volumes, *Joe Wilson and his Mates* from Blackwood (November 1901) and *Children of the Bush* from Methuen (July 1902). *The Country I Come From* is the focus of my interest here.

Looked at in the sum, the two periods of twelve months or so on either side of his departure from Australia were peculiarly productive for Lawson. His first volume in four years, *On the Track*, was published on 7 April 1900, only a fortnight before he left Sydney; and he was working on proofs of *Verses, Popular and Humorous* and *Over the Sliprails* up until the day before he left.[6] *Over the Sliprails* was published on 9 June and would soon, in July, become a companion collection of prose to

---

[5] Barnes, 'Pinker of Literary Agents', p. 92.
[6] See *Letters* 437. *Verses, Popular and Humorous* as a double volume was delayed until 7 December 1900, the individual volumes having been available a few months earlier.

On the Track, available with it in a single volume.[7] Robertson did not bother with an initial 5s. retail price this time. Market conditions had evidently changed. Most British firms exported their colonial editions retailing at 3s.6d. and 2s.6d., and this set a price in the colonial market for literary titles, lower than that still achievable in the Home market (where the standard price for single-volume titles of new fiction was still 6s.), though even there the market pressure was downwards.

Lawson was on the lookout for 'copy' on board ship and declared at first that he had found 'oceans' of it; but little of significance came of the journey.[8] In England, however, he was able to make a fresh start, and he arrived as a successful author, in the colonies at least. Living outside of London from July to mid October 1900 in Harpenden, Hertfordshire, Lawson was soon 'full of work', as he told Miles Franklin on 6 September 1900.[9] He had by that date already written two of the Joe Wilson stories ('Brighten's Sister-in-Law' and 'A Double Buggy at Lahey's Creek') and was finishing, or had very recently finished, '"Water Them Geraniums"'. Extraordinary stories, they would anchor Part I of *Joe Wilson and his Mates*.[10] Lawson had corresponded with Fred Shenstone at Angus & Robertson before he left about whether any of the stories he had assigned to the firm for *On the Track* and *Over the Sliprails* would not be used and therefore whether he could have permission to rework them.[11]

Edward Garnett had written to Lawson in 1897, and proposed his work for inclusion in Fisher Unwin's Over-Seas Library series. George Jefferson, Garnett's biographer, quotes one of Garnett's undated reader's reports on Lawson urging Unwin 'to bespeak any further work Lawson

---

[7] See further, Chapter 9 n. 5.
[8] A letter to the *Australian Star* from near Albany, WA in [April] 1900 (reprinted in *Letters* 126; cf. *Life* 220–1) and the arrival in England in the first of the 'Letters to Jack Cornstalk' (see n. 17, below).
[9] *Letters* 128.
[10] Blackwood accepted 'Brighten's Sister-in-Law' on 13 August 1900 (Blackwood to HL, 13 August 1900: *Letters* 440); it was published in *Blackwood's Magazine* in the same issue as the last instalment of Joseph Conrad's *Lord Jim*: see n. 44 below for publication details.
[11] A few would ultimately be adapted for the second volume he would write or prepare in England, *Children of the Bush*; and 'Jimmy Grimshaw's Wooing' would be used unchanged in *Joe Wilson and his Mates*. See *Letters* 438–9 and *Commentaries* for its entries on the relevant stories.

does and commission him' for this series. Garnett had described the series to the travel and short story writer, and anti-Imperialist, R. B. Cunninghame Graham (1852–1936) as:

> Tales and Sketches about Colonial Life and English Colonial Settlers, Emigrants, Travellers' life all the world over. The note of this series would be *not* Imperialism but the inclusion of any work sufficiently artistic to give to local life atmosphere and point of view of the new countries. Such a series would be experimental and probably its volumes would be rather suggestive than be finished artistic work.[12]

This letter dates from 16 May 1898, and a begging letter Lawson wrote to David Scott Mitchell before he left Sydney states that he was enclosing 'letters from Garnett'. The editorial desideratum ('suggestive' rather than 'finished artistic work') probably accounts for an otherwise mysterious reference by Lawson in an essay he wrote in 1903, '"Succeeding": A Sequel to "Pursuing Literature"'. As later in the same essay he names Blackwood and Methuen, the implication here must be that he is not referring to them but very probably to Fisher Unwin:

> I had a box full of old printed matter and copy, finished and fragmentary, which I'd humped about the world for years . . . But when in Herts I had that copy, and I put some of it together and sent it to one of the publishers who had written to me – the worst of the lot, I couldn't have picked out a worse publisher for my purpose, or sent him a more unsuitable book if I'd tried on purpose. But he wanted me for the sake of my Australian success and the work I might do in England; but, while he was writing and asking me to come and see him and avoiding a definite proposal – and while I was writing long and most unbusinesslike letters back, explaining things that had no bearing on the case and giving myself away properly, and getting into a net – I got a letter from an Australian in London.[13]

Nothing eventuated. Unluckily, Garnett – who could have defended

---

[12] Quoted in George Jefferson, *Edward Garnett: A Life in Literature* (London: Cape, 1982), pp. 46–7. See further, Paul Eggert, 'Publisher's Reader: Edward Garnett', *Meridian*, 2 (1983), 163–5. Garnett's letter to Cunninghame Graham, 16 May 1898, is at the Humanities Research Center, University of Texas at Austin. His book was intended to inaugurate the series.

[13] HL, '"Succeeding": A Sequel to "Pursuing Literature"', in *The Essential Henry Lawson*, ed. Brian Kiernan (South Yarra, Vic.: Currey O'Neil, [1982]), pp. 363–70 [p. 365]. John Barnes was the first to link the 'worst' epithet to Unwin ('Pinker of Literary Agents', p. 94 n. 13). My evidence here strengthens the identification.

the submission and guided Lawson, as he did so many other writers when reshaping their writing for publication – had left Fisher Unwin's employ at the end of 1899. Jefferson describes Unwin as a publisher who 'found it difficult to come to a decision', and Lawson's opinion of him by 1903 (as 'the worst') may well reflect Garnett's: as one of those publishers who 'see horrible pictures of capital sweating its uphill way drawing faint behind it the triumphal car of the proletariat author'.[14] Garnett would nevertheless prove a useful contact. Lawson visited him at his house on the Kent–Sussex border, the Cearne, at least once; in January and February 1902 they were in constant contact; and Garnett would, on 8 March 1902, publish an appreciative and perceptive essay on Lawson in an influential magazine.[15]

The Australian in London was Arthur Frank Maquarie (1874–1955), who looked Lawson up soon after he arrived in England and whom Lawson describes as being 'quite mad on the higher poetry ideal and had starved himself for it.'[16] Maquarie took him to lunch with Herbert Morrah, the editor of the *Argosy*, who commissioned and would soon publish Lawson's impressions of London as his 'Letters to Jack Cornstalk'.[17] On Morrah's advice, Maquarie next took Lawson to the office of James Brand Pinker (1863–1922). This was in the first half of July 1900.[18]

[14] Jefferson, *Edward Garnett*, p. 72. Garnett's opinion of Unwin is in a letter to Cunninghame Graham of 4 July 1898.
[15] See Chapter 8 pp. 196–8. HL's letter to Garnett of 18 February 1902 thanks him for sending a copy of his essay ('An Appreciation', *Academy and Literature*, 42 (8 March 1902), 250–1) prior to its acceptance for publication, and adds: 'Am grafting hard at new book – present title "As Far As I'm Concerned" . . . I could have sent you a lot of disconnected matter, but I want my books to be as complete as possible now', thus differentiating this material from the 'copy' he had (probably) sent Fisher Unwin in 1900 soon after arriving in England. This and other HL letters to Garnett whose originals are in the Humanities Research Center, University of Texas at Austin, are excerpted in Bernard Hickey, 'Some Henry Lawson Letters to Edward Garnett', *Australian Literary Studies*, 12 (1985), 128–31 [p. 129].
[16] HL, 'Succeeding', p. 365. This essay and Barnes ('Pinker of Literary Agents') are the sources of the information in this paragraph.
[17] In *Argosy*, October 1900 and January–February 1901 (reprinted in *Autobiographical* 141–64). Maquarie also heralded HL's arrival in London with two puffs in the *Argosy*, one on HL as poet and the other as prose writer (August and September 1900).
[18] The July appointment date is established by their Agreement dated 13 July 1900 (Thomas Lothian Papers, State Library of Victoria, MS 6026) and by Pinker's accounts: see n. 20

Pinker had set up in business as a literary agent in 1896 and by 1901 was representing Henry James, Joseph Conrad and Stephen Crane. Later he would add D. H. Lawrence to his list. He would nurture the careers of many writers, even being prepared to lend some of his authors money against future royalties. Lawson benefitted from this (perhaps shrewd) generosity for a few months, at one stage to the extent of £200,[19] as did Conrad for most of the 1900s decade.[20]

Lawson immediately wrote to Robertson to tell him of the development.[21] This was not just a courtesy to a man who had treated him well. It was purposeful. Pinker had already got to work and on 21 August 1900 wrote to the *Bulletin*:

> Mr Henry Lawson has now arranged for permanent residence in England. He has placed his business affairs in my hands, and I am writing to say that I shall be very pleased to hear from you if there is a possibility of our arranging the Australian rights in some of his works.[22]

Pinker meant, of course, works published in Britain. He was seeking cooperation from the holder of magazine rights in the orderly progression of Lawson's periodical writings to book form. He may also have been seeking advice as to how to proceed in Australia. As a letter of the following day to Angus & Robertson makes clear, he had in mind offering to the Sydney firm the role of second fiddle: that is, offering colonial rights for Australia (or Australasia, since New Zealand was, from a London point of view, simply another part of the same market)

below. Maquarie's poetry would be well represented in Walter Murdoch's *Oxford Book of Australasian Verse* (1918).

[19] Barnes, 'Lawson in London', p. 28.
[20] Pinker's holograph statement of account for HL, 24 July 1900 – 14 June 1901 shows all sales of his writings, cost of typing, commissions deducted and payments to HL. By the end of 1900 HL was £31 in debit to Pinker: see *Henry Lawson: His Books, Manuscripts, Autograph Letters and Association Copies Together with Publications by Louisa Lawson*, collected and annotated by Harry F. Chaplin (Surry Hills: Wentworth Press, 1974), pp. 66–7. Yet, as John Barnes comments of the HL letters to Pinker preserved in the Pinker papers in the Berg Collection at the New York Public Library: 'Given Lawson's difficulty in managing his affairs, what strikes one about his relationship with Pinker is his effort to keep his indebtedness under control' and that, 'In spite of all the troubles that had beset him, Lawson was in credit when he left England' ('Pinker of Literary Agents', p. 101).
[21] HL to GR, [August 1900] (*Letters* 127).
[22] ML MSS 314/45, pp. 297–8.

for new Lawson books to be published in Britain. Surprisingly, this offer also applied to those already published in Australia:

> I am writing to you on behalf of my client Mr Henry Lawson to ask if we cannot arrange for a fresh edition in England of his various books? I think Messrs Blackwood would be willing to take up the books in this country, and they would certainly stand a very much better chance if issued by a firm of that standing. It occurred to me that you might be disposed to come to some arrangement to this effect. Mr Lawson is working steadily at a new book, and if you are agreeable, I should propose to him that we arrange for you to publish this and further books in Australia.[23]

Pinker's proposal for a 'fresh edition' would have been no surprise to Robertson, but it was Anglo-centric. It reflected the ideas of Blackwood's letter to Lawson, a letter that Lawson passed on to Robertson when informing him of Pinker's appointment. Blackwood in that letter wondered aloud: 'Might it not be well now to bring out an entirely new edition of *While the Billy Boils*?'; and he also asked to see *In the Days When the World Was Wide*.[24] The 'fresh edition' did not materialise, but a more practical alternative soon presented itself.

Given the August date of the above letters and the fact that an entry in an Angus & Robertson 'Publishing' journal records the sending of a copy of the First and Second Series of *While the Billy Boils* to Pinker, presumably for Blackwood, on 9 September 1900, either Lawson's undated letter had put the idea to do so into Robertson's head or Blackwood had requested the two volumes independently.[25] Copies of *On the Track* and *Over the Sliprails* must also have found their way to the Edinburgh firm for it was from these two volumes and *While the Billy Boils* that the material for Blackwood's first Lawson volume came. As Angus & Robertson was the copyright owner of all three an assignment of Home-market rights and royalty arrangements was necessary. Once apprised of this fact, Blackwood concluded in a letter to Pinker in late November: 'My endeavour will be to arrange for such a selection of Mr

---

[23] Pinker to A&R, 22 August 1900 (ML MSS 314/45, pp. 298–9).
[24] Blackwood to HL, 13 August 1900 (*Letters* 440).
[25] ML MSS 3269/13/1, fol. 121; and, for 'two volumes', cf. n. 27, below.

Lawson's stories as will enhance his reputation here, which seems the only way in which he can profit by the transaction.'²⁶

The Blackwood letter that sealed the arrangement is in the Angus & Robertson archive at the Mitchell Library. Dated 9 January 1901 (and annotated by hand: 'answered 5/3/01'), it sought permission to publish a selection of Lawson's stories: 'I have selected the stories which I think it should contain. This selection, a list of which I enclose, has been approved by Mr Lawson . . . the volume will contain no new matter'.²⁷ Angus & Robertson would receive ten per cent royalty on a 6s. retail price. Putting business propositions in an unambiguous way was and is an efficient way of proceeding, and that is the nature of this letter. However, there are two indications that it may not simply have been a matter of Blackwood proposing the contents and Lawson approving the choice.

The first indication is that, in June 1899 when his relations with Angus & Robertson were at one of their periodic lows, Lawson declared he was 'decidedly against the idea of a "dainty" selection to be made by a cultured outsider' and he demanded 'a voice in the future selections, arrangements or editing of his works'.²⁸ The second indication is that four of the five stories that had appeared in *Short Stories in Prose and Verse* – 'The Union Buries its Dead', 'The Drover's Wife', '"Rats"', '[The Bush Undertaker]' and 'Macquarie's Mate' – were selected. '"Rats"' was the exception, amounting to an early narrowing of what has since

---

[26] Blackwood to Pinker, 30 November 1900, Blackwood Papers, National Library of Scotland, quoted in Barnes, 'Lawson in London', p. 31.

[27] The sixteen items from *Billy Boils* that were listed (and ultimately included) are: '"An Old Mate of your Father's"', '[Settling on the Land]', 'Stiffner and Jim (Thirdly, Bill)', 'The Man Who Forgot', 'His Country—After All', 'The Union Buries its Dead', 'Mitchell Doesn't Believe in the Sack', 'His Father's Mate', 'The Drover's Wife', '[The Bush Undertaker]', 'Coming Across.—A Study in the Steerage', 'The Story of Malachi', 'Steelman's Pupil', '"Board and Residence"', 'Two Dogs and a Fence' and 'Macquarie's Mate' (ML MSS 3269/ Lawson, Henry – papers re 1894–1949, vol. 386, fol. 241; the list is fol. 243). It is clear from the list that the copy consulted was *Billy Boils* in its First and Second Series, not the single sequence of 1896.

[28] Letter, HL to A&R, 24 June 1899 (*Letters* 103). Hence the postscript on a HL letter of c. 16 August 1899 to Fred Shenstone (Hugh Maccallum's successor at A&R): 'Saw Jose today re arrangement of work' – i.e. of *On the Track*, then in production (*Letters* 434).

been confirmed in Lawson selections since World War II as central representatives of the Lawson prose canon.[29]

As Lawson was involved in the selection for his mother's production of his volume of 1894 the recurrence of four of the five stories in the Blackwood volume strongly suggests his hand at work. Of the other twelve stories and sketches chosen from *While the Billy Boils*, only two of them are Mitchell stories: 'The Man Who Forgot' and 'Mitchell Doesn't Believe in the Sack'. Four are set in New Zealand or en route there and were perhaps chosen partly to give geographic and generic range: 'Coming Across', 'Stiffner and Jim (Thirdly Bill)', 'Steelman's Pupil' and 'His Country—After All'. The last of these attractively confirms the taciturn main character's intention to return to Australia rather than try California. The rest, with the two exceptions of '"Board and Residence"', set in Sydney and 'Two Dogs and a Fence', set in an unnamed urban location, are from what had emerged as standard Lawson territory – the bush, although more the up-country region than the outback: '"An Old Mate of your Father's"', '[Settling on the Land]' and 'His Father's Mate'. This last one, a sentimental favourite from 1888, was Lawson's earliest published story. The only other early story (from 1889), 'The Story of Malachi', is a surprise, for this is not the mature Lawson even though it is another bush tale. Both have failed to be confirmed by the postwar anthologists.

Blackwood would have received the '5/3/01' reply from Angus & Robertson in April 1901, in time to make the spring publishing season in

---

[29] Because there was only one printing of *The Country I Come From* (and only of 1,050 copies: Mackaness 26), copies are unusual in Australian libraries and only rarely come onto the secondhand market. As a result the selection in *Short Stories in Prose and Verse* itself was probably – directly or indirectly – more influential on postwar editors making their selections, nearly all of whom were Australia-based. As is the way with these things, selections tend to become perpetuated, with only the brave editor failing to include the already established favourites. Of the five stories only 'Macquarie's Mate' has failed to make the cut, for instance in the selections by Colin Roderick (1970), Brian Kiernan (1976) and John Barnes (1986). The other four stories, including '"Rats"', have been consistently confirmed. See further, the last listing in Appendix 3.

The Country I Come From has not been input for Project Gutenberg (http://gutenberg.net.au/pages/lawson.html) even though nearly everything else of HL's has been. Neither is it available at the fulltext database setis.library.usyd.edu.au/oztexts or on the AustLit database (austlit.edu.au): all accessed 26 July 2012.

June. The volume's production seems to have been entirely concentrated in the two months or so before its appearance in June. The selected copy went to the printer's for typesetting and the pulling of proofs for the author. In an undated letter to Blackwood, Lawson wrote: 'No doubt you will send me proofs of my selected volume. I want to make it as perfect as possible. There are a few ugly sentences I want to straighten up.'[30] By mid-May, according to a letter he wrote to Angus & Robertson, he had very recently finished that task:

> Blackwood's selected edition of prose, under the title of 'The Country I Come From' is being pushed on. I have revised carefully and will send you a list of pages containing corrections which you may like to make in your future Australian editions.[31]

There is no evidence that they followed through, and in a letter in 1917, written while he was revising for Angus & Robertson's publication of his *Selected Poems* in 1918 and envisaging a new edition of his prose (which did not materialise), Lawson recalled:

> An educated young Australian friend of mine took days and nights correcting and restoring *While the Billy Boils*, &c., &c., in London for Blackwood's *Country I Come From*. I sent sheets of list of pages, pars, and lines corrected out to you, but heard no more of them, and a new edition of *While the Billy Boils* came out without them. Better start the hunt for that letter and list now. If unsuccessful, we can simply get two good readers to go through *The Country I Come From* and the stories selected for it together. The prose will give us no trouble at all. The matter referred to above was simply restored. Old Wm Blackwood was rather surprised that I wanted proofs. It was too late for galleys. But he sent me the pages and helped in every way: held back the book.[32]

---

[30] Blackwood Papers, National Library of Scotland; and in Chaplin, *Henry Lawson*, p. 67.
[31] Letter, HL to A&R, 15 May 1901 (*Letters* 129).
[32] Letter, HL to GR, 15 February 1917 (*Letters* 279).
It seems to have been the custom at Blackwood to check second (revise) proofs in-house: cf. an undated letter from HL to Blackwood from the same address (Charlton, Shepperton, Middlesex), whence HL had moved in May 1901. The letter shows that he did not receive revise proofs: 'If there is time kindly have correction on page 9 of enclosed proof transferred to book, it escaped me in book proofs and I find by my M.S. that it was a typewriters error. It is rather important.// I suppose you found it too late to send me revise proofs of book' (quoted in Chaplin, *Henry Lawson*, p. 67). This sounds like page proofs of *Joe Wilson and his Mates*: Blackwood or a reader had evidently been checking final page proofs following receipt of

If it were to be made sense of in Sydney, the 'list of pages, pars, and lines' would need to have referred to the Angus & Robertson edition. So it may be that Lawson and his 'friend' – perhaps Arthur Maquarie – both worked on printer's copy for Blackwood (presumably, printed copies of *While the Billy Boils* and *On the Track and Over the Sliprails*), and Lawson (perhaps alone) on the Blackwood proofs. In either case, it is difficult to see from what source the 'restored' wordings could have come. The changes in the Blackwood collection rarely reinstate deletions from the newspaper texts made in printer's copy of *While the Billy Boils*, and, even in those cases, could have been hit upon independently. For example, 'His Father's Mate' restores from the *Bulletin* the second occurrence of 'three' in '. . . three tall pines—three lonely trees . . .' when *While the Billy Boils* had read '. . . three tall pines. These lonely trees . . .'. However, the *Bulletin* contained the separation of the two sentences and so did *The Country I Come From*. Thus there was less a return to the original reading than a felicitous (but only partial) regathering of it. This points to Lawson's hand at work, but does not establish an actual restoration from retained *Bulletin* copy.

The only other possible source would have been Lawson's original manuscripts, although the difficulty of his preserving them over the years and the fact that they were not used during the 1895–96 preparation of *While the Billy Boils* make this extremely improbable. Lawson often claimed to be 'restoring' wordings. It may have been a semi-automatic defence of an otherwise understandable desire to keep tinkering, and thereby causing extra expense for his publisher. This is the likelihood here.

Collation of the 1896 and Blackwood printings reveals many alterations in wording (what editors call 'substantives'). Although half of the items from *While the Billy Boils* lack any such changes, those that were made are nearly all of a localised kind that could have been made in the margins of a printed copy or without altering the pagination of the

---

HL's marked-up galleys and the incorporation of his changes. An anomaly must have been referred to him for resolution, occasioning his reply.

Blackwood proofs. In addition, the typesetters would have been tempted to regularise the punctuation, spelling, capitalising and word-division ('accidentals') according to their normal practices. However, the stories had already achieved the dignity of print, and the availability of such copy would probably have had the effect of reducing the interpretative leeway with the text of all concerned in its production. Given Lawson's known practice when revising the printer's copy for *While the Billy Boils* it is likely that he made a small percentage, at least, of the several hundred changes to accidentals. Although not this time under the moral pressure of a collaboration with a superintending editor like Jose, Lawson evidently delegated the main job of correction to his 'educated' friend.

The epithet is telling, and it affords us little confidence in attributing variant accidentals to Lawson. In relation to 'The Story of Malachi', for instance, there are almost twenty such changes, mostly tending towards regularisation. There are three changes in wording: two involve a changed position for 'and', leaving only one that perhaps points towards Lawson: Malachi is 'a dreadful fool' in the *Bulletin* and *While the Billy Boils* but becomes the more (or differently) colloquial 'an awful fool' in *The Country I Come From*. But even this is not conclusive. 'Stiffner and Jim (Thirdly Bill)' loses its final 'P.S.' in the Blackwood edition – which could be Lawson at work, except that it deprives the story's title of its explanation.[33] The story is otherwise changed only by a handful of accidentals. On the other hand, 'His Father's Mate', a much longer story, shows about 20 variant accidentals and over 60 variant substantives – but the great bulk of them are changes in the name of the character Tom Hopkins to Bob Sawkins. Nevertheless, a few of the changes suggest Lawson's more localised intervention. Apart from the change mentioned above, there is an alteration from 'Pat Martin lit his pipe, and mounted on the shaft' (1896) to 'Pat Martin felt for his pipe, but remembered himself and mounted on the shaft' (1901). The context is Isley's funeral where the consolation of a pipe, refused, nicely locates, in the unaccustomed setting, the confused emotions of one of the participants.

[33] Cf. 'Steelman's Pupil'; it lost from its ending 'in concluding his celebrated dog-yarn'.

It is necessary to distinguish between the correction of the texts (in large part delegated, and with the normal, additional intervention of the typesetters) and the revision of them, which Lawson evidently took to be his own special province. But it is equally necessary to add that only a few of the sixteen stories and sketches from *While the Billy Boils* show evidence readily attributable to him. 'His Country—After All' and '"An Old Mate of your Father's"' show no substantive variants and the merest handful of accidentals, although 'The Drover's Wife' has more relevant evidence.³⁴ Lawson's creative engagement with the texts of the reprinted items seems, then, to have been variable, and much lighter than his letters imply.³⁵

The volume title could easily have suggested itself from a reading of 'His Country—After All', chosen for the collection, and understandably inflected, for Lawson, by the business of living in England as a colonial Australian and finding a newly sharpened sense of identity against some of the confining aspects of British life. The formation of the Commonwealth of Australia at the start of 1901, a significant Imperial event, may also

---

³⁴ For 'The Drover's Wife', about 20 variant accidentals and 9 substantives are listed in the accompanying edition (Eggert and Webby). It is doubtful that HL was responsible for changing, e.g., the spelling 'enquires' to 'inquires'; but his hand was surely at work in the changed description of the dog Alligator. In 1896, his 'yellow eyes glared unpleasantly also—besides, the dog's chawing-up apparatus greatly resembled that of his namesake'. In 1901, 'his namesake' became 'the reptile he was named after'. In the versions in *Bulletin* and *Short Stories in Prose and Verse* (the latter, for this story, supplied the printer's copy on which Jose and HL worked for *Billy Boils*) there had been a sentence-break after 'unpleasantly'; the running together was initiated by Jose. Although in proofs of *Billy Boils* it was almost certainly HL who abandoned Jose's new wording ('unpleasantly—also he had been named for good reasons') and changed it to the reading given above, HL accepted Jose's pointing and did not overrule it in 1901. '[The Bush Undertaker]', 'Two Dogs and a Fence' and 'Coming Across' are the only others to show substantive variation, and none of it points compellingly to HL.

Some minor changes that represent regularisation might be the responsibility of the friend or the typesetters. E.g., in 'Mitchell Doesn't Believe in the Sack', the purposeful spelling 'git the sack' (in a colloquial speech) becomes 'get the sack'.

³⁵ The accompanying edition (Eggert and Webby) provides the evidence (for what is inevitably, in each case, an interpretative decision as to responsibility) in its foot-of-page listings. The edition's general Note on the Texts, as well as the individual item's Textual note, need to be taken into account when considering the listed evidence. They describe very minor categories of variants that are not systematically listed. Thus, for instance, the count given above for variant accidentals in 'His Father's Mate' ignores the high number of changes to double inverted commas to enclose speeches in *The Country I Come From* (*Billy Boils* used single).

have been a factor; and the sense of *country* in the title is broader than Lawson's frequent use of it to mean locality, as in *up-country*.[36]

Lawson at work in England: The second year

The agreement between the Scottish and Australian firms was announced in every copy of *The Country I Come From*:

> This volume contains a selection of stories from Mr Lawson's 'While the Billy Boils,' 'Over the Sliprails,' and 'On the Track.' It is published by arrangement with Messrs Angus & Robertson, Sydney, and is not for sale in Australia and New Zealand.

It is noteworthy that Blackwood's initial instinct was much the same as Bentley's when republishing Marcus Clarke's novel *His Natural Life* in 1875, despite the fact that it had already been published by the Melbourne George Robertson in 1874 and was still for sale there. Bentley simply brushed that inconvenient fact aside when he took up the novel into his firm's publishing and distribution system. This long established firm, whose name was synonymous with the three-volume novel form (the expensive format intended for the circulating libraries), brought *His Natural Life* out first in this way and thereafter kept it in print in successively cheaper formats until the late 1890s when the firm sold out to Macmillan. The Bentley one-volume format sold well in Australia and by around 1890 the work had established itself as one of a tiny number of classics of Australian literature.[37]

It is hard to believe that George Robertson (of Angus & Robertson) would have accepted a similar relegation. Nevertheless, it is not known which party came up with the idea of a new selection from the Lawson

---

[36] The assertion of country helps explain the rhapsodic 'The Romance of the Swag', written in England (*Australian Star*, 6 August 1902; collected in *Children of the Bush*, 1902): 'The land I love above all others – not because it was kind to me, but because I was born on Australian soil, and because of the foreign father who died at his work in the ranks of Australian pioneers, and because of many things. Australia! my country! her very name is music to me' (*Prose Writings* 499). A computer search revealed no close parallels of the Blackwood title in HL's previous collections.

[37] For an overview of this pseudo-canonising process, see Eggert, 'Australian Classics'. For the publishing history of *His Natural Life*, see the Introduction to the Academy Edition, ed. Lurline Stuart (St Lucia: University of Queensland Press, 2001).

prose volumes of 1896 and 1900 rather than bringing out the two prose and verse volumes from 1896 separately, as initially broached. The result was a cautious decision – which tends to point the finger at the man who was putting up the money: Blackwood.

Another cautious decision was the use of the still-standard (though frequently undercut) retail price for new one-volume fiction of 6s. This was nearly double what Angus & Robertson was charging (3s.6d.) for the combined title *On the Track and Over the Sliprails*, so it was likely to lead to a low sales figure. Still, the rationale was the same as Robertson's in 1896, and if sales were encouraging then repeated, more profitable printings would become feasible. The next record concerning *The Country I Come From* in the Angus & Robertson ledgers is dated 31 December 1900; it shows that sales were indeed disappointing. The Sydney firm, as copyright owner, received royalty of £5.7s.9d. from Blackwood for the stories used from *While the Billy Boils*.[38] Assuming this was roughly half the total receipts (with the other half being in relation to *On the Track and Over the Sliprails*) and that royalties were 6d. a copy, then only 431 copies had been sold in the first half-year, when sales would tend to be at their highest.[39]

This result would not have affected Lawson directly since he no longer had any stake in the stories and therefore nothing to gain financially. But it was an ill omen for sales of the *Joe Wilson* volume that had just appeared in November 1901, once again at the price of 6s. This was the beginning of the Lawson family's second and final winter in England. There had been serious concerns about his wife Bertha's health from October 1900 when she was admitted to Bethnall House, a private asylum at Bethnall Green, London. Lawson's first productive period in England was soon superseded by months of nagging concern over his

---

[38] ML MSS 3269/12/3, fol. 120.
[39] Cf. the sales of Blackwood's edition of Miles Franklin's *My Brilliant Career* (1901), which HL placed and edited for her. It sold 418 copies in the 6s. Home issue and 2,564 in the colonial edition (3s.6d. and 2s.6d.): from a note made by GR in 1931, quoted in *Life* 219. I have rounded down the royalty figure to 6d. to allow for the possibility of the usual calculation of '13 copies counted as 12'. If the initially offered 10 per cent of retail price is used (just over 7d. per copy) then only about 360 copies were sold.

wife's state of body and mind, and there were also the children to think about. Thereafter Lawson worked under a cloud of anxiety. 'I was ill and nearly mad with worry all the time I was writing it [*Joe Wilson and his Mates*]', he later told David Scott Mitchell.[40] He finished the proofs of *The Country I Come From* on the same day that his wife was committed to Bethlem Royal Hospital, her condition having worsened, and where she would stay for four months until 14 August 1901.[41] Truly, ill-luck dogged him. The following English winter would prove too much for Bertha, and her health broke down completely.

A flicker of hope for Lawson amidst the domestic misery must have been the reprinting in December 1901 of 'The Drover's Wife' in *The Bulletin Story Book: A Selection of Stories and Literary Sketches from 'The Bulletin' [1881–1901]*, edited by A. G. Stephens. Published in Sydney by the *Bulletin* Newspaper Company, it was the second volume in a new series, no longer the cheap-format paperback in which the collection containing Lawson's 'His Father's Mate', *A Golden Shanty*, had been issued in 1890. Together with *The Bulletin Reciter* (also 1901), this more handsome series was aimed at promoting Australian literature in the new Commonwealth. 'The Drover's Wife' appeared in heterogeneous company, but it was another canonising sign in the local scene, for this story at least.[42]

The recognition would do little to ameliorate Lawson's situation in London, however.[43] Five of the stories in *Joe Wilson and his Mates* had

[40] Letter, HL to David Scott Mitchell, 11 February 1902 (*Letters* 131).
[41] For the date of Bertha's commitment, see Tasker and Sussex, 'That Wild Run', p. 171. According to the medical records she was suffering from 'melancholia, hallucinations and suicidal tendencies'. When previously admitted to Bethnall House the doctors gave the cause of her insanity as 'lactation and worry' (*ibid.*, pp. 171–2); and HL gave it as 'over-worry and nursing' in his letter to William Blackwood on 15 October 1900 (Blackwood Papers, National Library of Scotland). Their daughter Bertha had been born the previous February; eight months later a hard weaning, assuming it had not already happened, would have been inevitable once the mother was committed. This could well have exacerbated an underlying problem.
[42] 'The Drover's Wife' would be reprinted in [1912 or 1913] in *An Austral Garden: An Anthology of Australian Prose*, ed. Donald McLachlan (Melbourne: George Robertson), pp. 92–103: the source of the text is given as 'From "*The Bulletin Story-Book*" (Bulletin Co.)', p. 103.
[43] There was no immediate payment for the 62 contributors to *The Bulletin Story Book*. The preface stated: 'The risk and expense of this publication are undertaken by the Bulletin

appeared in *Blackwood's Magazine* by October 1901, prior to the volume's appearance.[44] The circulation of the monthly magazine hovered a little over 4,000 copies at the time, plus another 1,000 American sales, so this was a boost for Lawson and ought to have created a demand for his books in those countries.[45] Blackwood had, in addition, secured an agreement with Angus & Robertson that the latter would act as the publisher of the volume in the Australian market. The arrangement put into place what Pinker and Blackwood had envisaged in their earlier letters. Angus & Robertson paid '£14 odd for Set of Electros' [i.e., electrotypes for printing the Blackwood typesetting for the local issues], also paying Blackwood 17.5 per cent of the retail price on the first 2,000 copies and 20 per cent thereafter. Of this, presumably, Blackwood would have to pay Lawson only 3d. or 4d. per copy, a standard amount for colonial sales.[46] Fortunately for Lawson, Blackwood was prepared to give him

Newspaper Company, Limited. Should any profits accrue, a share of forty per cent. will be credited to the writers represented.' George Mackaness records that nearly 4,000 copies were sold (at 4s.6d.), necessitating a second impression in 1902. So HL would have received at least a small payment. *A Golden Shanty* at 1s. had sold 20,000 copies and was out of print by 1901: Mackaness and Walter W. Stone, *The Books of 'The Bulletin': 1880-1952 An Annotated Bibliography* (Sydney: A&R, 1955), p. 48.

[44] 'Brighten's Sister-in-Law' appeared in *Blackwood's Magazine* in November 1900. The second story, 'A Double Buggy at Lahey's Creek', was also completed in August 1900 and published in February 1901. In HL's letter to Pinker of 27 August 1900, he wrote: 'I will be up on Wednesday and will call and have a look through "Double Buggy" yarn. So, if you have it typewritten, do not submit it till I see it . . . Have a third (or, rather the 2nd) Lachey's Creek story on hand, which will complete series for the present' (Pinker Papers, Northwestern University Library, Chicago, quoted in Barnes, 'High Tide', p. 69). The letter shows that while, of the two sections of '"Water Them Geraniums"' both set at Lahey's Creek that appeared in the published volume, '"Past Carin' "' (as 'II') was published in the magazine in May 1901 but 'A Lonely Track' (as 'I') must have been rejected. The published volume also changed the order, moving 'Double Buggy' to the end of Part I. 'The Babies in the Bush' and 'Telling Mrs Baker' appeared in April and October 1901 respectively in the magazine and in Part II in the book. The magazine also published 'The House That Was Never Built' in July 1901; it appeared in *Children of the Bush* (1902): see below and also David Finkelstein, *An Index to Blackwood's Magazine 1901-1980* (Aldershot, England: Scolar Press, 1995).

[45] In David Finkelstein, *The House of Blackwood: Author-Publisher Relations in the Victorian Era* (University Park: Pennsylvania State University Press, 2002): see Appendix 2: 'Blackwood's Magazine Sales, 1856-1915' and, for the average sales for the 1890s decade given below, Table 5 on p. 97.

[46] ML MSS 3269/Lawson, Henry – papers re 1894-1949, vol. 386, fols. 257 (later royalty calculations: see n. 51 below) and 247 (letter, Blackwood to A&R, 27 March 1901). Blackwood issued a colonial edition in 1901 'For circulation in India and British colonies only', and A&R's edition appeared in 1902 (see Mackaness 26–8). Thus simultaneous publication in

an advance on royalties for the *Joe Wilson* volume of £200; and, for the magazine appearances, he had also been paying well (around £20–£25 per story).

The ruinous expense of Bertha's private hospitalisation from October 1900 to May 1901 tempted Lawson to go one step too far with Blackwood. While desperately trying to earn more money from writing stories for *Blackwood's* and a number of other less lucrative magazines with which Pinker was placing his material, Lawson sought – at first through Pinker, successfully – to put pressure on Blackwood for advances. But his finally doing it directly and revealing the full truth of his domestic situation to Blackwood was apparently too intimate, too unbusinesslike, for the otherwise generous Scotsman to tolerate.[47] Thereafter he accepted no further stories from Lawson, and no successor volume to *Joe Wilson*.

Although Lawson was thankful to Pinker for placing his stories and books with Blackwood, he himself had no head for business. As far as placing his books was concerned, there was good immediate income from the advance on the *Joe Wilson* volume. But Lawson had in effect made (or Pinker had made, on his behalf) the same mistake, easier to see in retrospect than at the time, that the Australian women novelists of the 1880s and early 1890s made in publishing with Bentley – that other prestigious but very traditional firm.[48] The business model based

---

Edinburgh and Sydney was aimed at but not achieved (see *Life* 232): this was not a copyright concern as such arrangements were when reached between British and American publishers. It was a practical response to the effect of British reviews on Australian book buyers. The books needed to be available when the reviewing magazines arrived, with no temptation for booksellers to source copies direct from Britain.

Blackwood was averse to Pinker's offering simultaneous magazine publication rights of 'Brighten's Sister-in-Law' to Australian magazines, given that *Blackwood's Magazine* was sold there; the story did not appear. Consistent with this (but, *pace* Roderick, in *Commentaries* 211 and *Life* 224, 226), Pinker did *not* place the *Blackwood's* story 'The Babies in the Bush' in the *Bulletin*. On 8 December 1900, the latter ran only the poem of that title. Nevertheless Pinker was able to sell simultaneous or near-simultaneous magazine rights for some HL stories to English and US magazines. 'Brighten's Sister-in-Law' was published by *Blackwood's Magazine, Littel's Living Age* (Boston) and *Eclectic Magazine* (New York): see the list in Barnes, 'Lawson in London', pp. 34–5 n. 30.

[47] The letter is undated: quoted in Barnes, 'Pinker of Literary Agents', whose interpretation (p. 99) I am following here.

[48] See Eggert, 'Australian Classics'.

on their high-profit, low-printrun three-volume format had collapsed by the mid-1890s. The alternative was dependent on solid continuing sales via world-wide distribution in various Home, Colonial and US editions or arrangements. To achieve this required, on the part of the publisher, both capital and a willingness to take risks. As we saw in Chapter 9, Boldrewood made the right decision in going with Macmillan when that firm approached him for one-volume Home and Colonial rights in 1888, following some moderately good reviews of the three-volume publication with the London firm of Remington. Macmillan was aggressively expanding its Colonial list.

Prestige, however, did not guarantee large sales. The weekly Sydney *Bulletin* sold tens of thousands more copies per issue in the 1890s than the far more prestigious monthly, *Blackwood's Magazine* familiarly known as 'Maga', which averaged only about 5,300 copies per issue across this same decade. When Robert Louis Stevenson's advisor Charles Baxter offered Blackwood the serial rights to his new novel *Weir of Hermiston* for £2,000 he was turned down, explaining to Stevenson: 'You see, an old humdrum house has no machinery for selling these all over the world.'[49] This was despite the fact that the magazine's politics were conservative and Imperialist, and that copies were likely to be found around the Empire. As Joseph Conrad noted in 1911, 'There isn't a single club and messroom and man-of-war in the British Seas and Dominions which hasn't its copy of Maga – not to speak of all the Scots in all parts of the world'.[50]

---

[49] Quoted in Finkelstein, *House of Blackwood*, p. 95. The *Bulletin* was selling 16,600 copies per issue in 1887; its estimated circulation in the 1890s was 80,000; and for the period after 1902 it was 'conservatively . . . 100,000' copies: respectively, Sylvia Lawson, *The Archibald Paradox: A Strange Case of Authorship* (1983; Melbourne: Miegunyah, 2006), pp. 153–4; *The Oxford Companion to Australian Literature*, ed. William H. Wilde, Joy Hooton and Barry Andrews (Melbourne: Oxford University Press, 1985), p. 123; and S. Lawson, *Archibald Paradox*, p. 268. On the alternative business model to Blackwood's, see further Paul Eggert, 'The Bibliographic Life of an Australian Classic: *Robbery Under Arms*', *Script & Print*, 29 (2005), 73–92.

[50] Conrad to his agent, J. B. Pinker, [12 or 19 November 1911]: *The Collected Letters of Joseph Conrad*, 9 vols., *Volume 4 1908–1911*, ed. Frederick R. Karl and Laurence Davies (Cambridge: Cambridge University Press, 1990), p. 506. Despite its modern-day reputation, 'Heart of Darkness' had been serialised in *Blackwood's*, where it was seen probably as another Imperial adventure fiction 'accepted as a critique of Belgian behaviour, having little to do with the British

Australian sales of *Joe Wilson and his Mates* by no means matched those of *While the Billy Boils*: 2,154 in the first year, split evenly between Angus & Robertson's 3s.6d. and 2s.6d. issues. Sales were down to 25 by 1904, but with a distinct revival in 1905 when the volume was split into two series in the firm's Commonwealth Series as *Joe Wilson: Stories* and *Joe Wilson's Mates: Stories* at 1s. each. At this price there were about 10,000 copies sold in 5 years as against only 3,000 in the original format during the first 5 years at the higher prices.[51] In 1902 Blackwood wrote to Angus & Robertson acknowledging their royalty cheque in a rueful tone:

> We are glad to note that the volume has made a good start with you although its reception here has been rather poor. We must recognise however that Mr Lawson's name is now a household word in Australia while here the public have to be educated to appreciation of his work.[52]

As late as 1911, Blackwood, mindful of the £200 advance of royalties that he had still not recouped, rejected an approach from Angus & Robertson to purchase the copyright. For this, the Sydney firm had to wait until about 1920 when its royalties paid to Blackwood, £25 of it in advance, finally exceeded £210.[53]

Lawson had finished his next collection, at first referred to as 'The Heart of Australia', by 11 February 1902. Pinker gave Blackwood first

---

imperial mission upheld and defended so strongly in Maga's pages' (Finkelstein, *Index*, p. xiv).

[51] Thereafter until mid-1919 the two series averaged about 800 sales each per annum. An undated document of royalty calculations details the royalties A&R paid for *Joe Wilson and his Mates* to Blackwood, 1902–09 (ML MSS 3269/Lawson, Henry – papers re 1894–1949, vol. 386, fol. 257: undated, but probably by 17 August 1909: cf. fol. 285). Another such document, dated 29 March 1920 with sales and royalty for 1902–19, is at fol. 315.

[52] Blackwood to A&R, 22 September 1902 (ML MSS 3269/Lawson, Henry – papers re 1894–1949, vol. 386, fol. 263). The cheque was for £54.14s.10d.

[53] GR's intention to acquire the copyright was longstanding: on 11 August 1906 HL had signed over to A&R for £25 whatever remaining rights he possessed in *Joe Wilson and his Mates* and *Children of the Bush* (ML MSS 3269/316/Angus & Robertson Correspondence, vol. 829, p. 23). This included receipt of royalties from Blackwood and Methuen should they ever exceed the £200 advances that each had given him (*ibid.*, p. 25). This still left the necessity of A&R's extracting the main rights from Blackwood and Methuen. The former rejected overtures in 1906, 1909, 1911 and 1912, only apparently relenting in (and certainly no earlier than) 1920. See ML MSS 3269/Lawson, Henry – papers re 1894–1949, vol. 386, fols. 275, 285, 287, 291 (a letter from Blackwood to A&R of 8 March 1911: 'we paid the author a large sum to account of royalties which has not yet been covered'), 293 and 309–13 and 315 (a list of royalties paid to Blackwood for 1902–19).

refusal, and he did refuse it on 15 March 1902.[54] Pinker then offered it to Methuen, whose reader E. V. Lucas (1868–1938) was a neighbour and close friend of Edward Garnett. As we saw in Chapters 8 and 9, Lucas had written on Lawson twice for the *Academy*. Methuen offered Lawson a £200 advance on royalties of 15 per cent and 4d. per copy for colonial-library sales. Pinker considered Methuen an up-to-date firm that knew how to 'push sales' of books, and the advance was a good one.[55] But the Methuen venture would prove no more successful than Blackwood's had, even though a cheap colonial edition was also issued.[56] By the time the work appeared in July 1902 Lawson was back in Australia. He had sent his wife back in advance under the charge of Mary Gilmore and her husband who were in England on their way home from South America in the aftermath of William Lane's failed New Australia experiment. Although at first determined to stay on in England himself, Lawson suddenly changed his mind and departed on 21 May 1902. He sent the proofs back from Naples and Port Said, en route.

Soon, he knew once more, as he had when returning to Sydney from Brisbane in 1892, 'The Shame of Going Back'. But this time the consequences would be irremediable. The following years were ones of continuing health problems for Bertha, their separation, his own

[54] See Pinker's letter to Blackwood, 17 March 1902, acknowledging his of 15 March: Blackwood Papers, National Library of Scotland, quoted in Chaplin, *Henry Lawson*, p. 71.
[55] The quotation is from a letter from Joseph Conrad to Pinker, c. 10 November 1911: Methuen, Conrad states, had only offered an advance of £120 for his collection of short stories *A Set of Six* (1908) and adds: 'I had that amount years before for the *Youth* vol. from B'woods [1900, containing also 'Heart of Darkness'] besides the serial payments for all the stories. As to their ability to push sales I do not see any special evidences of it. One gets the advance and there's the end. I don't question the fact that they sell a lot of books – probably more than any other firm.' The advantage of Blackwood was its being 'a firm owning an old established magazine from whom one would expect some advantages in the way of serial publication' (*Letters of Joseph Conrad*, IV. 502).
[56] The Methuen contract with HL is at ML MSS 3269/Lawson, Henry – papers re 1894–1949, vol. 386, fols. 259–61. Methuen's transfer of rights for £10 to A&R on 10 December 1906 is fol. 260; it was preceded by a letter to A&R (12 September 1906; ML MSS 3269/316/Angus & Robertson Correspondence, vol. 829, p. 33) in which Methuen offered A&R the remaining stock: '100 quires, 12 6/- [i.e. 12 Home-market cloth hardbacks], 42 colonial cloth and 129 colonial paper'. Prior to this, A&R had published a first Australian issue using English sheets, but the first Australian typesetting (containing the stories of *Children of the Bush* but without the verse scattered through that volume) appeared in 1909.

succumbing to depression and his longstanding alcoholism, and periods in hospital and also in prison, caused by Bertha's repeated suing of him for non-payment of maintenance for the children.

His connections with his British publishers fell away. George Robertson stuck by him, and the firm continued as his publisher with two more volumes in 1905 and 1910.[57] According to Thomas Lothian the Melbourne publisher, Lawson more or less trapped him into publishing two other volumes in 1913, neither of which did anything to retrieve his high reputation of the 1890s.[58] The drop in standard is noticeable as early as *Children of the Bush*, and although Lawson was still only 35 when it appeared, his career was mostly downhill from there.[59]

Even with the Joe Wilson stories, Lawson had been frustrated in

---

[57] *When I Was King and Other Verses* and *The Rising of the Court and Other Sketches in Verse and Prose* (Sydney: A&R, 1905, 1910 respectively); the former was also issued in 1905 in two volumes by A&R as *When I Was King* and *The Elder Son*.

[58] The most recent scholarship on the circumstances surrounding the long delayed publication of the two Lothian volumes (*For Australia and Other Poems* and *Triangles of Life and Other Stories*; both, Melbourne: Standard Publishing Co., 1913) is: John Arnold, 'Bringing Lawson to Book: The Lothian Experience', *La Trobe Journal*, 70 (2002), 19–30. Lothian's claim about being entrapped by HL and the bookshop proprietor James Tyrrell (who, together 'spun a story' to Lothian, *Life* 278) was a claim based, as far as Arnold knew, on a conversation between Lothian and Colin Roderick fifty years after the event: this 'is perhaps drawing too long a bow' (p. 29). However, Lothian also reported entrapment as a fact but not involving Tyrrell, in a letter to Harry Chaplin, 12 September 1961, preserved at Sydney University Library (not in Roderick's or Arnold's accounts).

Lothian describes HL as lying drunk at his office door when GR sent him to Melbourne for a break and HL's later telling GR that Lothian had contracted with him for a book when he had not done so. GR advanced HL £50 on the strength of it; in Roderick's account it was backed up by a promissory note in GR's favour signed by Lothian. This led to Lothian's publishing of the two volumes to get his money back as he had felt obliged to reimburse GR: 'I wouldn't have touched either volume if G.R. hadn't advanced the money on a pure lie.' According to Roderick, HL's drunken appearance at Lothian's was on 29 April 1907, the date of his assignment of rights to Lothian of the parcel of writings he had brought with him (*Life* 280–4; *Commentaries* 281–3; and cf. *Letters* 157–8). Lothian's memory was of receiving the papers in Sydney at Tyrrell's (although that was probably a first instalment of materials from HL, prior to those handed over by HL in Melbourne) and the signing happening there.

[59] In 1970, A. A. Phillips described *Joe Wilson and his Mates* as 'the last volume in which Lawson's talent really displayed itself' (*Henry Lawson*, New York, Twayne, p. 50); in 1972 Brian Matthews referred to what he sensed as 'the growing sense of insubstantiality' in the following volumes (*The Receding Wave: Henry Lawson's Prose*, Carlton, Vic., Melbourne University Press, p. 148); and in 1982 Brian Kiernan described the conventions of the stories in *Children of the Bush* as 'those of heart-warming Victorian sentimental melodrama' (*Essential Henry Lawson*, p. 32).

his placement of them with the monthly *Blackwood's Magazine* by its proprietor's need to space them out – the same problem Lawson had experienced with the *Bulletin*. The gathering domestic pressures also militated against the development of his 'power of focussing significance through a single moment or detail' in the short story form, as John Barnes describes it, into what the novel required: the tracing of a process of interaction, personal and intimate, over a period of time in the lives, in this case, of Joe and Mary Wilson.[60]

This would have required the leisure for experimentation, a holiday from the necessity to earn regular money. And it would have required the courage to examine the relationship between men and women, in a period when his own marriage was breaking down. He could already deal evocatively, sardonically, sharply or humorously with the relationships sustaining men under economic distress or family malfunction. He could expertly harmonise the various registers of male comradeship. He would continue to do so, though with increasing sentimentality as he gradually lost his direct openness to it of earlier years and became instead an 'apostle of mateship'.[61]

His best days as a writer of tonally balanced, democratically conditioned and finely perceptive short fiction were over. He died in 1922; but the Lawson interest at Angus & Robertson, and the wider cultural interest in his works and their meanings, did not die with him.

---

[60] See further John Barnes, 'High Tide', *passim* [p. 65]. Colin Roderick had come to the same conclusion via a different route in 1977: 'a colonial Thomas Hardy' might have been able 'to develop the bush into a character that would have given unity to the series . . . Its effect on the people who come into conflict with it is not developed: it is taken for granted, and we are presented with the end result rather than its gradual tragic evolution . . . each instance leaves almost as much to the reader to supply as the author offers him. This, too, is characteristic of the art of the short story' ('Henry Lawson's Joe Wilson', p. 47).

[61] The title of H. P. Heseltine's essay, 'Saint Henry – Our Apostle of Mateship' (*Quadrant*, 17 (1960–61), 5–11), echoes H. M. Green in *An Outline of Australian Literature* (Sydney: Whitcombe & Tombs, 1930), p. 112 ('the apostle and prophet of the gospel of mateship'). Green in turn may have developed it from Fred Broomfield's review of *Billy Boils* in 1896 (see Chapter 11 n. 1) or in later conversation with him. Cf. Broomfield's address to the Fellowship of Australian Writers, 28 November 1930, describing HL as 'ringing . . . the clarion song of universal Mateship': printed as *Henry Lawson and his Critics* (Sydney: A&R, 1930), p. 40.

CHAPTER 11

THE AFTERLIFE OF *WHILE THE BILLY BOILS*

IN 1923, a year after Lawson's death, George Robertson revised his marketing strategy for the 1896 collection. Interest in Lawson had revived. Like every successful publisher, Robertson would have been sniffing the cultural breezes to see which way they were tending. The context for his first decision, and for the firm's later repackaging and expansion of its Lawson offerings in the lead-up to World War II, was the gradual consolidation of a myth of national foundation, with which Lawson would be seen to be intimately connected. As time went by, both sides of politics found they could agree that Lawson, nearly always cast as the 'poet' of Australia, had been its singer and prophet, particularly insofar as national ideals came to be associated with the bush, more insistently and with less variegation than they had been in the 1890s.[1]

On the first day of the year in which Lawson's *The Country I Come From* and *Joe Wilson and his Mates* appeared in Edinburgh (1901) – itself the year following that in which *While the Billy Boils* was divided into two volumes in what Angus & Robertson dubbed its 'Commonwealth Series' – the Commonwealth of Australia was proclaimed. It was the first day of the twentieth century. The movement towards federation of the colonies had been preceded by a series of conventions and premiers' conferences in the 1890s; and the mood for political change had been

---

[1] The originator of the idea of HL as singer and prophet appears to have been Fred J. Broomfield (1860–1941, journalist and subeditor of the *Bulletin*) in his review of *Billy Boils* in the *Australian Workman*, 24 October 1896: 'Of this Australia ['of the miner, the selector, the fossicker, the rouseabout, the swagman'] Henry Lawson is the seer, the prophet, the singer, and the portal-keeper of its temple'.

inched forward by various political and cultural forces, not least of them the aspirations of the *Bulletin*, itself a consciously national newspaper. Week after week from 1880 it had performed a multifarious national conversation, incorporating readers across the Australasian colonies as contributors.

That is not to say that a widespread sense of a single national identity formed overnight in 1901. There was no national capital, nor scarcely a navy; the powerful state premiers had conceded only specified powers to the new federal government; and continuing sentimental attachment to one's former colony was apt to be complemented by a broader Imperial sense of belonging rather than a national identification. What *was* this nation after all? That remained to be seen. In 1913, in the Brisbane *Worker*, we find Grant Hervey opining the lack of an Australian school of literature that might express 'the nation's voice'.[2] Nevertheless, the sharing, by large numbers of men from the various colonies, of a uniform (and uniformed) experience during the Anglo-Boer War and World War I, both in the trenches and the prisoner-of-war camps, would have its slowly accumulating effects.[3]

---

[2] Grant Hervey, 'The Present Status of Australian Literature', Brisbane *Worker*, 25 September 1913, p. 19. With exception of 'the poetic works of Bernard O'Dowd, and the one great novel of this century – Tom Collins's "Such Is Life," a wonderful Australian book that is practically unknown – and the earlier and stronger work of Henry Lawson and a few others', there is 'nothing but a mass of trash'. Ideally, Australian literature 'should help every Australian man and woman . . . to realise his or her responsibility to the nation'. For Hervey, see further Chapter 12 n. 5.

[3] See Amanda Laugesen, *'Boredom is the enemy': The Intellectual and Imaginative Lives of Australian Soldiers in the Great War and Beyond* (Farnham, Surrey: Ashgate, 2012), pp. 17–41, 50–62, 71–7, 87–8, 115–18. The novel experience for nearly all of being overseas with time on their hands, as well as the shock and fatigue of battle, fed a longing for home and thus a heightened sense of belonging to it. The YMCA and the Australian Red Cross established reading huts and libraries for the troops, and books were sent from London to Australian prisoners of war. Laugesen's evidence suggests that their appetite for reading matter was omniverous and fed by pre-War tastes (British and Australian newspapers including the *Bulletin*, mainly British adventure, sporting and sentimental romance novels). C. J. Dennis's *Songs of a Sentimental Bloke*, newly issued in A&R's Pocket Editions for the Trenches in 1916, became a favourite partly because its slang, humour and larrikin disregard for authority, smoothed by romantic sentiment, gave its Australian readers a sense of themselves as marked out from other troops. There were calls from the troops for Australian poetry – useful for recitation, including in concert repertoires – by HL (but not his prose), Adam Lindsay Gordon and Banjo Paterson, and some call for *On Our Selection*, *Robbery Under Arms* and

Death and resurrection

Lawson's death pinpoints the shift in sentiment. He died in poverty on the morning of 2 September 1922, a Saturday. Well known around the streets of inner Sydney as a ruin of a man, a sad alcoholic, he was nevertheless accorded a state funeral – on Monday the 4th. George Robertson and then Phillip Harris, editor of the *Aussie*, approached the State government on the Saturday for a New South Wales state funeral. The requests were turned down; but the chance arrival of the Prime Minister of the Commonwealth of Australia, Billy Hughes, by train from Melbourne on the Sunday morning changed everything. He was visiting Sydney to shore up support for changing his constituency to North Sydney in the next election. Hughes was of the same political party as the New South Wales government – conservative Nationalist. His power base lay in the anti-Labor camp, as well as with former Labor pro-conscriptionists. During the War, he had, Christopher Lee comments, 'used his affinity with the "ordinary" Australian digger to refashion the myths of the radical nationalists into an imperially loyalist account of national development'.[4] A deputation organised by Harris and Mary Gilmore put the case for a state funeral to him. A wily politician, he immediately agreed. He ordered the funeral for the next day at St Andrew's Cathedral in Sydney. The newspapers on the Monday were able to report his tribute: '[Lawson] knew intimately the real Australia, and was its greatest minstrel. He sang of its wide spaces, its dense bush, its droughts, its floods. He loved Australia . . . None was his master. He was the poet of Australia, the minstrel of the people.'[5]

This gathering unto its Establishment breast of the once fire-breathing Republican writer for the *Bulletin* in its radical days, and for the *Worker* of the early–mid 1890s, left the trades unions temporarily shouldered aside. For now, the cause of poetry and the nationalist

His Natural Life.
[4] Lee 50.
[5] 'Henry Lawson. Death Announced. Poet and Prose Writer', *Sydney Morning Herald*, 4 September 1922, p. 8.

politics of the day meant that Lawson's earlier political leanings and the personal disgrace of his post-London years could be air-brushed away. But the upshot was that, over the coming years, his legacy would be able to be appropriated for their own purposes by both the political left and the right.[6]

Lawson's name and identity would be kept constantly before the public for the next nine years by virtue of the efforts of a committee that was soon set up to raise the money for a permanent memorial to be erected near the Art Gallery of New South Wales in the Domain – where Lawson had occasionally slept rough in earlier years. The poet David McKee Wright, a man of Irish and then New Zealand extraction who had arrived in Australia in 1910, published in the *Bulletin* and became editor of its Red Page, wrote the text of the official appeal:

> A nation lives in its art and literature. In Lawson we live, because he spoke for us. Lawson spoke in the authentic voice of this continent; his writings are our word to the world, and our message to the greater Australia of the future. In erecting a memorial worthy of him, we do honour to ourselves, to our country, and to our faith in the destiny of our race.[7]

This high-sounding appeal helped to mobilise the public-school system via the Teachers Federation. Some of Lawson's poems, short stories and sketches began to appear in the *School Magazine*, and school libraries were encouraged to acquire copies of Lawson titles available in print. The schools eventually provided the bulk of the funds necessary for the sculpture by George Lambert, finally erected after many delays in 1931, to great acclaim in the newspapers of the day. Photographs of the monument would appear frequently in the *School Magazine*.[8]

---

[6] This account is indebted to Lee; see Lee 60–2 for the responses in the *Worker* and *Australian Worker*.

[7] Quoted in Lee 74. Wright copy-edited the *Selected Poems of Henry Lawson* for A&R in 1918 and would edit the firm's three-volume edition of the *Poetical Works of Henry Lawson* in 1925. For Wright, see also Chapter 7 n. 10.

[8] See n. 50 below. In a sixteen-page pamphlet produced by the Teachers Federation in 1924 for the anniversary of HL's birth, S. H. Smith, the director of education in New South Wales and a former editor of the *School Magazine*, enjoined schools to build a HL collection (Lee 77–80).

A personal copy of the 1924 Platypus edition (described below) has a bookplate with a

Against this background, the commercial obligation of Lawson's publisher and principal copyright holder was plain: publish, as soon and as much as possible. The firm issued a 'cheap edition' of *While the Billy Boils* in three 'series' in paperback wrappers in 1923 (price unknown, but probably about 1s.). The colour illustrations on the wrappers are by Percy Lindsay. The first volume's is a rollicking scene from '"An Old Mate of your Father's"' inspired by the appearance of the actress Maggie Oliver, who 'stood upon the box seat [of a coach] and tore her sailor hat to pieces, and threw the fragments amongst the crowd' of eager diggers.[9] Once again, the typesetting was that of the 1896 first edition, still with a single pagination throughout, and the paper stock was even bulkier than the 1900 two-series issue. In the haste to publish this cheap edition the division of the stories led to the Contents listing of the last story in the first volume to appear under the list of illustrations rather than at the end of the list of stories. The care that Robertson had lavished on the first impression of 1896 had gone by the wayside. The point now was unabashedly to make money: to this end, the new cover was evidently more important to the firm than the contents. As with the split into two series in 1900, this new subdivision appears to have been a one-off investment (since no copies of any issue later than 1923 have been located): that is, a very large print run, not repeated, and allowed to sell out.

The sales period may have been quite short because a true second edition (that is, a new typesetting) appeared in 1924, in what Robertson, ever keen to stress the formative Australian connection, promoted as the firm's Platypus Series 'in large, clear type on good paper, and strongly bound' in hardback.[10] The new series itself was a creation of 1923, the

portrait of HL 'Presented by the LAWSON MEMORIAL COMMITTEE To "Epping P. S. [Public School, in handwriting]" as a recognition of help in collecting for the fund. 1924'.

[9] The Second Series cover eponymously illustrates 'The Shearing of the Cook's Dog' and the Third has a generic evening scene of two men and a dog around a billy, with cattle lying down and two horses in the background.

[10] Copies from the issues of 1925 onwards carried a series advertisement on the front endpaper. The quotation is taken from an additional refinement: an advertisement on the verso of the dust jacket of a (personal) copy of 1928, First Series: i.e., it is visible only when the dustjacket is removed. Above it is an advertisement for the firm's 6s. Canberra Series, probably so-named to take advantage of the opening of Parliament House (1927). A personal

year after Lawson's death. *Joe Wilson and his Mates* and the other prose volumes were not rushed out in a cheap edition in 1923. Instead, *Joe Wilson* appeared in that year, and thus before *While the Billy Boils*, in the Platypus Series, in two volumes at a standard price for the series of 2s.6d. per volume – as did *On the Track and over the Sliprails*, as well as *Romance of the Swag* and *Send Round the Hat*. Three volumes of Lawson verse (*Popular Verses, Humorous Verses* and *Winnowed Verses*) also appeared in the series in 1924.[11]

The dust jacket of the first of the two volumes of *While the Billy Boils* in the Platypus Series bore the same Percy Lindsay illustration as the first volume of the 1923 three-series issue. The jacket's spine bore a strip from what is almost certainly a fourth Percy Lindsay illustration not otherwise used (cattle on a hillside with a creek in the foreground and trees in the background). Apparently it was not possible to have too much of a good thing. This edition spelled the end of the firm's exploitation of the first typesetting of 1896, at least in hardback format; and in due course, certainly by 1937, the two series of this second edition began to appear in the one volume in keeping with the firm's tradition.

There is no admission in the front or end matter of the Platypus edition that six stories had been excluded: '[Settling on the Land]', 'When the Sun Went Down', 'In a Dry Season', '[An Echo from the Old Bark School]' and '"Dossing Out" and "Camping"' (from the First Series) and 'Jones' Alley' (from the Second). In addition, '"Some Day"' and '"Brummy Usen"' were brought forward from the Second Series to be the last stories of the First. The exclusion of 'Jones' Alley' at first suggests a literary-critical decision-making. (But, if sentimentality was the offence, then why not instead exclude the more egregiously sentimental 'Arvie Aspinall's Alarm Clock' and 'A Visit of Condolence', both of 1892 and

---

copy of 1925 (First Series: from the Circulating Library of the Sisters of Mercy Convent, Surry Hills, Sydney) has the Platypus advertisement as the front endpaper (verso); its (conjugate) recto has the 1923 front-cover (and 1928 dust jacket) illustration in colour, but without the title–author or publisher statements. Evidently, the experimentation with sales strategies continued.
[11] With contents selected and rearranged from the combined-volume *Verses, Popular and Humorous* (1900).

set in the common location, and neither of which received a revision in 1895 – as the material in 'Jones' Alley' did?) But the exclusion of the others from Lawson's mature period (1893–94) does not suggest they were being judged on quality. The explanation is probably commercial. The page design for the Platypus *While the Billy Boils* was not uniform with the 1923 volumes of that series, perhaps because of its delayed issue date; but more generous leading and word spacing meant fewer words to the page. Since price is related to page-extent there must have been a decision that something had to give.[12]

A bibliographical analysis of the printed object shows what did. Excluding front and back matter, the two volumes make up 192 pages and 176 pages respectively. For this edition, there had been a shift to a more economical format, probably in response to the availability of new printing machinery. The line illustrations, although not being counted in the pagination, are printed on the same sheets as the surrounding letterpress; they are not tipped-in as they initially were in 1896. This was a saving. Each sheet, after the first half-sheet for the front matter, now consisted, when folded and trimmed, of sixteen leaves or 32 pages (a 'sixteenmo'), rather than the original eight leaves or 16 pages previously used ('octavo'). Surprisingly, the final leaf in the first volume serves as the endpaper stuck to the inside of the back board; the leaf is conjugate with the first leaf of the final section ('G', 31–32 pages earlier at pp. 157–8). As a result only two leaves bear no text (other than the printer's colophon) in the first volume, with no waste at all in the second. Thus there are, for volumes one and two, exactly twelve and eleven sixteenmo sections, respectively, after the front matter. This was clever bookwork, and it would have reduced the printer's bill; but it meant that the contents of Lawson's 1896 collection were no longer fully represented.

When the Platypus edition was reissued in 1928 it gained a preface by

---

[12] In the Platypus edition, the title of the sketch 'Another of Mitchell's Plans for the Future' was shortened by deleting 'for the Future'; the reason is unknown but the deletion was perpetuated in all A&R printings and subsequent editions sourced from this second typesetting, even after Colin Roderick's edition of HL, *Short Stories and Sketches 1888-1922* (Sydney: A&R, 1972), which restored the original title.

John Le Gay Brereton, Lawson's pal and drinking partner of the 1890s, and now professor of English at Sydney University. The preface was the text of his address on the fifth anniversary of Lawson's death, delivered at Waverley Cemetery in Sydney at Lawson's grave. Brereton distinguished between Lawson's prose writings – which were 'highly prized by good judges of literature' – and his verse: 'He was not a great poet'. But Brereton acknowledged the people's verdict was different, and that '"the poet Lawson" may well stand alone as the typical figure of Australian literature; for his voice is the voice of a great democracy. He speaks for the many; not for the few . . . he saw mateship not merely as the hope, but as the living spirit of his people'. Brereton wound up his oration with his explanation of the qualities of the prose: 'He was never falsely sentimental. You know that from all the best of his prose tales and sketches. Except in his earliest work, he never invested with a deceptive glamour the truth as he clearly saw it.'

Also in 1928 Lawson's editor A. W. Jose, now resident in England, wrote a series of six survey essays, with the series title, 'Australian Literature' for the *Reader* (London). He contended that Paterson and Lawson (as poet) represent:

> the first purely Australian literary movement; and their style owes not a little to Kipling . . . But two qualities mark Lawson out above all his fellows. Not his verse, but his prose – a new thing altogether in Australian literature . . . purely *Bulletin*-begotten . . . [it] ranks him in the eyes of European critics among the masters of the short story; *While the Billy Boils* . . . contains his first and best prose work.

Jose asserts what was fast becoming the orthodox view amongst accredited literary critics: that Lawson was an original and significant artist in prose but not in verse. He also explicitly endorses the Robertson-initiated claim that Lawson's prose was fostered exclusively by the *Bulletin* although (as seen in Chapter 7) Lawson initially published nearly as many stories and sketches in the Sydney labour press.[13]

---

[13] A. W. Jose, 'Australian Literature: IV The *Bulletin* School: Bush Bards', *Reader*, 3.10 (July 1928), 365–9 [pp. 366–7]. The companion essays spanned April–September 1928 in this monthly literary magazine.
The American journalist C. Hartley Grattan, who visited Australia in 1927, ignored HL's

The need for a new typesetting for the Platypus series finally allowed the granting of the request for corrections in future Angus & Robertson printings that Lawson had made soon after the appearance of *The Country I Come From* in 1901. As he reports in a letter to George Robertson in February 1917 (quoted at more length on page 234), he had sent the corrections set out on 'sheets of list of pages, pars, and lines' prepared by 'An educated young Australian friend of mine'. If, he added, the search for the list were 'unsuccessful, we can simply get two good readers to go through *The Country I Come From* and the stories selected for it together'.[14] One or the other must have happened. A spot-check collation of the 1896 and Platypus editions shows that, while the printer's copy was the first edition of *While the Billy Boils*, some new wordings and some deletions from the Blackwood volume were incorporated. But the job was not carried out thoroughly, thus creating an eclectic mixture of readings from the two sources in the new edition, as well as the introduction of new readings caused by the typesetters as they went about their normal duty of making sense of their copy, with its odd spellings and phrasings.[15]

verse while praising the sketches in *Billy Boils* as 'alive to the last degree. Lawson wrote with a delightful ease and clarity, and while he never distorted his pictures or mitigated the hardships of the bushmen, he did introduce a humor that is native Australian': *Bookman*, August 1928; reprinted in Grattan, *Australian Literature* (Seattle: University of Washington Bookstore, 1929), p. 27.

The young Walter Murdoch, then a junior academic at the University of Melbourne, had reached the same conclusion as Jose in 1904 in an essay on several volumes of HL's verse: 'Mr Lawson the poet is not fit to hold a candle to Mr Lawson the story-teller' – whose achievement he had summarised when reviewing HL's latest prose volumes in 1900: 'As a creator of character he is not to be taken seriously . . . [a]nd when he essays to weave a plot, he contrives somehow to bore you. Where he shows real genius . . . is in the presentment of the effect wrought by a man's environment on his prevailing moods . . . these sketches of his contain some of the most poignant things in literature': reprinted in *Walter Murdoch and Alfred Deakin on Books and Men: Letters and Comments 1900–1918*, ed. J. A. La Nauze and Elizabeth Nurser (Carlton, Vic.: Melbourne University Press, 1974), pp. 78, 77.

[14] *Letters* 279.

[15] E.g., HL's renaming of the character Tom the Devil in 'His Father's Mate' as Bob Sawkins for Blackwood was successfully transmitted to the Platypus edition, even though this necessitated multiple changes – as was the deletion of a sentence, which originally read in the *Bulletin*: 'This peculiarity gave a flavour of originality and humour to Tom's utterances, although his nature was far from being witty or humorous.' The versions in *A Golden Shanty* and *Billy Boils* had dispensed with the second half of the sentence. The Blackwood edition deleted the first half as well, as did, following it, the Platypus. A change for Blackwood from the *Billy Boils* reading, 'father's brother got into trouble over a squabble', to '. . . inter trouble over a row'

The new, mixed Platypus texts would be perpetuated over the coming decades as new typesettings were called for, each new typesetting inevitably introducing further changes of its own.[16]

On the boil again, in Britain

In London in 1927, Jonathan Cape used the 1924 second edition of *While the Billy Boils* as copy for its new typesetting, once again in two volumes; as a result it also lacks the excluded six stories. Bibliographically, this is the third edition. The volumes appeared as numbers 38 and 39 in Cape's Traveller's Library series ('A series of books in all branches of literature designed for the pocket') at 3s.6d. But the context for this republication had little or nothing to do with the collection's appearances in Sydney in 1923 and 1924.

Cape's reader since 1921, Edward Garnett, took a special interest in this series. As we saw in Chapter 8, he had long been an admirer of Lawson's prose and, as explained in Chapter 10, had given him assistance of various kinds in England during 1900–02. In his article on Lawson in the *Academy* on 8 March 1902, designed to promote his reputation, Garnett praised the 'apparently artless art' of Lawson's stories and hailed him as 'the representative writer of a definitive environment'. For Garnett, the capacity of the novelist and travel writer to broaden the imaginative confines of British readers by taking them into other parts of the world, while simultaneously satisfying his touchstone of 'veracity', was reason enough to revive Lawson's reputation. In choosing *While the Billy Boils* rather than any of the other prose collections he was probably making much the same commercial decision as Robertson did when choosing *While the Billy Boils* alone for a cheap edition after Lawson's death. It was evidently the best known of the prose volumes.[17]

---

was transmitted to the Platypus except that the phonetic spelling 'inter' went unnoticed or was rejected. And in the story's fourth paragraph the Platypus edition overlooked two minor changes to hyphenation made for Blackwood: see the textual apparatus in Eggert and Webby.
    The changes for the Platypus edition were new: they had not appeared in the two-volume 'Commonwealth series' (copy of 1908 checked), nor in the three-series printing of 1923.
[16] Some examples are discussed in Eggert and Webby, Introduction n. 21.
[17] By c. 1920 A&R owned the copyright to all three obvious contenders: *Billy Boils*, *On the*

In 1933 Garnett went a step further when he included five stories from *While the Billy Boils* in a selection of stories published by Cape since 1921. The volume was called *Capajon: Fifty-four Short Stories Published 1921–1933* (London: Cape, 1933). Those chosen were 'Stiffner and Jim (Thirdly Bill)', 'The Union Buries its Dead', 'The Geological Speiler', 'The Man Who Forgot' and 'Steelman's Pupil' – a slightly surprising preference for Lawson as humourist. Ernest Hemingway was aware of Lawson by 1927 but appears to have read him first in *Capajon*, whereupon he compared the stories favourably to Mark Twain's *Huckleberry Finn*. This was in a letter of 27 September 1933 to Jonathan Cape in which Hemingway ordered the two volumes of *While the Billy Boils* in Cape's Traveller's Library. They were still in his library in Cuba when he died in 1961, and are mentioned in his posthumously published novel *Islands in the Stream*, whose writing dates to the early 1950s.[18] In the novel the writer Roger Davis asks the central character, artist Thomas Hudson, whom Davis is visiting in the Bahamas, for 'those Australian stories you had the last time I was here'. Hudson answers '"Henry Lawson's?"', gets them for Davis, and 'when [Hudson] woke in the night the light was still on in the library'.

Both the Cape edition and Lawson's inclusion in *Capajon* were bright spots, if of limited compass, in an otherwise dismal horizon of failure – at least as regards sales – for Lawson in Britain. When Lawson's daughter Bertha – by 1931 working in the Mitchell Library – urged George Robertson to send copies of her father's works for the display being organised by the Australian Literature Society for an exhibition at Australia House in London, he declined, explaining:

> For twenty-five years I tried hard to interest the Britishers in our books, but they do not care a 'continental' for us or our 'works.' The first exhibi-

---

Track and Over the Sliprails and *Joe Wilson and his Mates*.

[18] Letter to Edward O'Brien, 31 August 1927 (University of Maryland). The novel was originally begun in early 1950 as three linked novella-length pieces, from which *The Old Man and the Sea* was extracted and published separately in 1952. Together with another related tale, the remaining two were first published posthumously in 1970 (London: Collins). The mention is on p. 48. The library's contents are listed in James D. Brasch and Joseph Sigman, *Hemingway's Library: A Composite Record* (New York: Garland, 1981): see items 3760–1.

tion was some sort of a Dominions Exhibition in the early part of this century, and we were duly awarded a gold medal. With the notice awarding it came an account for its cost, so we need hardly say that the medal never came to hand – neither did the set of our publications. The next one was Wembley, the result of which did not affect the British sales in the slightest.

One of our directors, Mr Ritchie, was home a couple of years ago and, at my request, brought out the names of the actual buyers for the great houses like W. H. Smith & Son, Mudie, and so on, and I sent them as samples, without charge, four each of our recent publications. I forget what they were, but I remember that Elliott Napier's 'On the Barrier Reef' and Nettie Palmer's collection of short stories were among them. The letters arrived before the parcels (which went through the Australian Book Co.), and three of the people to whom they were addressed wrote to say that they took no interest in Australian books and did not want to see the samples; three others returned the parcels, unopened; and three declined to take them in.

Please do not think that it is the cost of a set of our publications that I grudge. What I do object to is being concerned in a fiasco. We spent nearly £30,000 on the Australian Encyclopaedia, of vol 1 of which we sent 34 copies to the leading British papers for review. It was enthusiastically received by them, as the enclosed circular will show, but of 50 copies sent to the Australian Book Co. for sale only 5 were sold, and when the second edition came out we had 45 of the old edition returned on our hands. For a year or two we sent all the British review copies of our books through the leading bookseller in the town in which the paper was situated, but it had no effect on sales. You may wonder why we trouble to send books to Britain for review, but the fact is that the English notices are useful to us *here*, not as causing sales in the Old Country. So far as the Encyclopaedia is concerned, up to date we have sold more in Denmark and Sweden than in Great Britain.

If Dr James Booth and his Australian Literature Society would try to encourage the sale of Australian literature *in Australia* they would do their authors a much greater service.[19]

A financial calculation made as at 30 June 1957 shows that, a quarter of a century later, little in relative terms had changed. The document, a

---

[19] Carbon-copy typescript of letter, GR to Bertha Lawson, 4 February 1931 (ML MSS 7587/1/1). In the last sentence of the quotation the words 'in Australia' have been underlined in pencil.

holograph manuscript headed 'TRADE GROUPS', shows that the total of Australian sales for Angus & Robertson titles was 450,513 copies, for New Zealand 32,850, but for the United Kingdom only 12,000.[20]

The collected *Prose Works*: Lawson's divided reputation

In the public arena, it was not a big step from talk about Lawson's representative quality to the assumption that he had no forebears and scarcely any contemporaries worth mentioning, male or female. The committee overseeing the competition for the Lawson sculpture specified in 1926 that what was required was 'a work of art which will suggest Lawson as a typical figure in the beginnings of an Australian literature. They desire that he be represented as an Australian of the Bush, and not of the city.'[21] Both conceptions would have to be addressed and reassessed since both were, in different ways, foundational ones.

In the meantime, Brereton's reporting that 'good judges of literature' believed in the superiority of Lawson's prose writing over his verse did pose the problem for Robertson (who personally preferred Lawson the poet) of whether to memorialise this prose Lawson with an expensive multi-volume collection, in the way that the firm had already done in 1925 with its three-volume *Poetical Works of Henry Lawson*.[22] The very title (*Poetical Works* as opposed to *Verse*) suggests a claim to literary permanence and significance: that the main claim for Lawson lay in the verse.

---

[20] USA sales are recorded as 558 but 'Miscellaneous' (which may include sales via distributors) are 11,400. The value of all 'Actual Sales of A&R books' 'including freights & authors' is given as £511,404 (ML MSS 3269/125/1). Individual items at this 125/1 location and also 125/2 are described because they were unnumbered – and unsorted – when inspected in 2008.

[21] Quoted in Lee 100.

[22] The commercial background for the decision to privilege the verse over the prose is given in a typed list of sales of various HL titles, 1905–22, perhaps made at HL's death in 1922. This document (ML MSS 3269/Lawson, Henry – papers re 1894–1949, vol. 386, fol. 51) shows that, of the ongoing standard hardback and softcover (3s.6d. and 2s.6d.) issues of *Billy Boils*, there were 3,733 sales between 1905 and 1922, an average of 207 copies per year. The figures for *Joe Wilson and his Mates* (1901) are 1,260 and 70. But *In the Days When the World Was Wide* sold 7,668 over the same period for an average of 426, and this in a period when it was partially competing with the relatively expensive edition of HL's *Selected Poems* (1918), edited by David McKee Wright. This title sold 1,434 copies during 1919–22. Nevertheless, this comparison leaves out of account the sales of the cheap two-series *Billy Boils* from 1900, of which 11,000 of each series were printed.

In an earlier letter to Bertha in 1925 Robertson had written:

> If we could find the right editor we should be glad to do an edition of your Father's best prose. Professor Brereton is probably the man for the job, and his Introduction could not fail to be both sympathetic and sane. Next time he happens along I'll speak to him about it.[23]

This intention did not mature into action, but a stop-gap measure – the publication of *A Selection from the Prose Works of Henry Lawson*, edited by George Mackaness – was put into effect in 1928.[24] After Robertson's death the firm published *Prose Works* collections that observed the simple expedient of bringing together the existing published collections rather than selecting from or reordering them. Thus *Prose Works of Henry Lawson* appeared in two volumes in 1935 and 1937, one volume in 1940 and 1948, and then in three in 1964, the last edited by Cecil Mann.[25]

Evidently the absence of the six pieces in the Platypus edition had been noticed for they were replaced in the 1935 *Prose Works*. Because, after the 1937 reprinting, each successor was a new typesetting probably copied from its predecessor, the lost stories and sketches were restored to the tradition. *Prose Works* was arranged in the two-series fashion first used in 1901, with 'The Drover's Wife' always the lead story of the second series.[26] In tandem with the *Prose Works* issuings, however, the second (originally, Platypus) edition of *While the Billy Boils* as a two-series-in-one volume continued to be produced *without* the excluded stories. Copies seen include a 1937 hardback, a 1940 hardback and a 1942 softcover with an illustrated dust jacket.[27]

[23] Letter, GR to Bertha Lawson, 14 October 1925 (ML MSS 7587/1/1).
[24] The Mackaness selection, a new typesetting, was published in Sydney by A&R's Cornstalk imprint and reprinted in 1930. It contained Brereton's Address, retitled 'An Appreciation' and revised. Mackaness would become HL's bibliographer in 1951.
[25] The 1935 typesetting was issued in A&R's Home Entertainment Library. Mann's editorial approach is discussed in Chapter 13.
[26] The copy used in 1935 was probably the Platypus edition since '"Some Day"' and '"Brummy Usen"' still concluded the first series. But, for the lost pieces, some printing of the first edition must have been used.
[27] Adjustments to the stereotyped plates were carried out. Personal copies of 1937 and 1940 containing both First and Second Series have the final four lines of type on the last page (182) of the Platypus First Series shifted back into the previous two openings, creating longer text-blocks, in order to produce a blank page preliminary to the half-title page (p. 183) for

Postwar

Because, in one format or another, *While the Billy Boils* continued to be reprinted in its first- and second-series divisions, postwar literary critics – judging by their references to the work – came to see it as the original format. The early publishing facts had been entirely lost sight of.[28] In 1970 and presumably after an arrangement with Angus & Robertson, Lloyd O'Neil (Hawthorn, Vic.) reprinted under the title *While the Billy Boils* the 1935 *Prose Works* typesetting of both of its series, together in the same volume with the double series *On the Track and Over the Sliprails*. The volume contained 87 stories and sketches in all. Clearly implied in its titling was the belief that *While the Billy Boils* would sell Lawson books but *On the Track and Over the Sliprails* would not.[29] This was another sign of the enduring canonical status of the 1896 collection.

Many print-on-demand artefacts entitled *While the Billy Boils* began to appear for sale on internet sites in the mid-2000s. They were nearly all derived from the inputting of an unnamed source text (in a First and Second Series format) for the internet Project Gutenberg in 2004,[30] usually with unsatisfactory processing applied in order to convert to book norms the plain-text ASCII codes used for inputting (for instance, indented paragraphs rather than blank lines left between paragraphs

the Second Series, whose first story, 'The Drover's Wife', begins on p. 185. A softcover copy of 1942 goes one step further, perhaps a response to wartime paper shortage. Instead of each story commencing on a fresh page as before, the type was rearranged by blocks of lines, so that each story started immediately after the one before it, thus saving 30 pages in the First Series alone. 'The Drover's Wife' now started on p. 155. Line-for-line resetting is another possible explanation of this phenomenon (full optical (machine) collations have not been carried out); but, being expensive, is unlikely.

[28] E.g. Brian Matthews refers to '[The Bush Undertaker]' as 'the most important venture Lawson made upon the madness theme in both series of *While the Billy Boils*': *The Receding Wave: Henry Lawson's Prose* (Carlton, Vic.: Melbourne University Press, 1972), p. 69. The postwar printings include: *(1)* Pacific Books in two volumes or 'series' (Sydney: A&R, 1966, reprinted 1969); *(2)* this same typesetting (the eighth, counting the successive *Prose Works* typesettings) in multiple issues, all from A&R, with an introduction by Chris Wallace-Crabbe dated 1972, but in one volume: Arkon paperback (1973, reprinted 1981, 1983, 1985) and Eden paperback (1988, reprinted 1990), then an Imprint Classics paperback with a new introduction by Wallace-Crabbe in 1991.

[29] See Appendix 3 for a list of postwar printings of *Billy Boils*.

[30] Produced [i.e. transcribed] by Geoffrey Cowling and David Widger, 13 June 2009 (apparently an update: see next note), at www.gutenberg.org/ebooks/7144, accessed 19 December 2011.

as in normal typing, rounded closing inverted commas instead of straight, italics, etc.). When checked in June 2010, *While the Billy Boils* was also available on the iPhone application 'Classic Poems', along with another 16,000 titles simultaneously available for emailing to personal computers. Its text is derived from the same Project Gutenberg inputting as all the rest, except in its first (2004) release rather than its (perhaps?) revised second release of 2009.[31]

The incurious, any-text-will-do practice of the electronic and print-on-demand industries has not gone entirely unchallenged, however, as witnessed by this advertisement for a recent Indian printing which gives a precise provenance for its text and claims to value accurate textual reproduction, even if the climactic selling point is the gold stamping on the cover:

> New. 2009. Reprinted from 1913 edition. PRANAVA BOOKS edition. This is a quality reprint of an old book of historical value. This is an exact/strict reproduction, no changes has been made in respect to the original. A lot of effort has been made to check and improve each page/scan manually for its quality of text and illustrations. This is not a retyped or an ocr'd book. The title of the book, on the cover, is in gold lettering. 398 pages.

Lawson's divided reputation

The republications of *Prose Works*, with counterpart republications of the *Poetical Works*, meant not only that Lawson's works remained readily available in the Platypus and later formats but that they were eminently collectable as large-format hardbacks as well. This was in the period when the Lawson legacy was being continuously disputed by the political left and right.

Three years after Brereton's address at the Waverley Cemetery one of the original reviewers of *While the Billy Boils*, and a former employee of the *Worker* in the early 1890s, Fred J. Broomfield made a significant intervention in the debate in an address to the Fellowship of Australian

---

[31] Accessed 7 June 2010. Originally 'Produced by Geoffrey Cowling', for Project Gutenberg as EBook #7144, released on 1 December 2004; later copied by Freebooks for reuse as part of its Classic Poems application.

Writers at the Forum Club in Sydney on 28 November 1930. The lecture was published the same year by Angus & Robertson as *Henry Lawson and his Critics*. It was partly an answer to the question raised the previous year by the Chief Librarian of New South Wales, W. H. Ifould, when talking to the Henry Lawson Literary Society in Sydney on the topic: 'Has Henry Lawson's Verse any Permanent Value?' His answer: 'Even in the form of his verse, its metre and rhythm, there was a sameness and lack of adaptation to subject.' Thus Lawson's influence 'must mainly be upon the people of his class . . . If Lawson is to live in his writings for future generations it will be because of his short stories and sketches, not because of his poetry.' Like A. G. Stephens before him, Ifould found nothing essentially Australian in Lawson's style but allowed it was there in the 'subject matter'.[32]

Broomfield found this 'arraignment of our poet' to be 'irrelevant and captious'. Although Lawson 'could not spare the time to experiment in new metres, even if he had the taste or the ability to do so', a moral virtue in his writing could be detected: 'he was sincere, honest in speech and meaning, and sympathetic to the innermost heart-core'. This quality informed 'the high merit of his verse no less than of his prose, notwithstanding the incomprehensible bias of the critics' – for 'the same eyes saw, the same hand wrote, the same brain conceived, and the same heart brooded over the trials and troubles and cankering cares and broken lives of those whose fates and fortunes formed the subject of his poems as well as of his prose stories and sketches.' Broomfield's trump card was the claim that 'the Australian of to-day buys his verse in preference to his prose, as book sales conclusively prove, reads and learns it by rote'.[33] But this preference, as we have already seen, was changing.

[32] Published in *Desiderata* (Adelaide), November 1929, reprinted in *Criticism* 247–53 [pp. 253, 250, 251, 249]. On this magazine, cf. Chapter 12 n. 21. In his 1928 Presidential Address to the Sydney University Arts Society, H. M. Green had commented: 'It is curious that a man who could write such crude and clumsy verses – though Lawson's verses are not all like that – should be a master of prose style': 'Australian Literature – A Summary' (offprint 16pp., ADFA Library Special Collections, 'Reprinted from *The Sydney University Arts Journal*, 1928', p. 15.
[33] Broomfield, *Henry Lawson and his Critics* (Sydney: A&R, 1930), pp. 20, 23, 29, 30.

This defence of Lawson's reputation is an early, though in this case undoctrinaire, demonstration of Christopher Lee's contention that, in the interwar period, persistent references to Lawson as poet by figures in the Australian Labor Party tended to tie the Party's agenda to the Australian tradition that Lawson supposedly embodied. The union secretary Lloyd Ross, in his *Fifty Years of Labor* (1940), claimed that 'Henry Lawson became our most popular poet . . . because he was expressing the ideals of the rising Labor movement';[34] and in 1945 the Henry Lawson Labor College was established in Sydney.

The Communist Party of Australia went much further in its ownership claims to the Lawson legacy in the 1950s, in the context of the Cold War. As early as 1938, Katharine Susannah Prichard had published on Lawson in the *Communist Review*. At first the appropriation of Lawson was not unqualified. In a talk Jean Devanny gave in 1942, 'The Worker's Contribution to Australian Literature', she disputed Lawson's right to be seen as 'a true singer of the workers'. Although he possessed 'passionate sympathies with the dispossessed . . . and what he saw he portrayed truthfully', his pessimism about the capacity of workers to do anything to alleviate their condition was only a reflection of his own melancholy that he could not see past.[35]

Understanding literature as a site of class struggle meant recruiting Lawson's *prose* to the banner of socialist realism; but his angry and politically radical early verse such as 'Faces in the Street' and 'Star of

---

[34] Quoted in Lee 121.
[35] Jean Devanny, 'The Worker's Contribution to Australian Literature', an appendix to Devanny's novel of 1935, *Sugar Heaven*, ed. Nicole Moore (Melbourne: Vulgar Press, 2002), p. 258.
   An early-century forerunner was Robert Rives LaMonte's article 'Lawson: Labor's Laureate' published in the American socialist periodical *Comrade*, 2 (October 1902 – September 1903), 199–200, followed in a subsequent issue by reprints, under the heading 'Arvie Aspinall: Two Sketches', of 'Arvie's [Arvie Aspinall's] Alarm Clock' as 'I' and 'A Visit of Condolence' as 'II', pp. 247–9. The article itself is based on biographical information provided by Tom Mills, 'of the staff of the Evening Post, Wellington, New Zealand' (p. 200): 'The object of this little sketch is to introduce to the American comrades a proletarian poet whose lines are known by heart by hundreds of Australian shearers, gold diggers, drovers and swagmen' (p. 199). 'If Lawson had been in the bourgeois sense a "moral man," he could never have written "While the Billy Boils," a series of impressionist prose sketches, which, to my mind, surpass in vividness and realism the best of Gorky's work' (p. 200). 'Lawson is pre-eminently the mouthpiece of proletarian revolt' (p. 200).

Australasia' had an undeniably immediate attraction and more obvious utility to those on the left. Frank Hardy maintained into the 1980s a firm resistance to what he saw as the creeping de-politicisation of Lawson caused by the Academy, especially from the 1960s.[36] The path towards that condition was beaten in the 1950s by a group that Lee calls the liberal nationalists: Vance and Nettie Palmer, A. A. Phillips and Russel Ward. The emergence of this debate about the relative merits of the prose and poetry can be traced, as we saw in Chapters 2 and 8, from the earliest receptions of *Short Stories in Prose and Verse* and then of *While the Billy Boils*. It was continued in Brereton's address in 1927, in H. M. Green's *Outline of Australian Literature* in 1930, and in other places.[37] Because of the continuity of this aesthetic concern it cannot be properly understood as the child of the cultural battle between radical left and the right in the postwar period even though it is true that the aesthetic preference of the Palmers and Phillips was unambiguously for the prose, especially that of *While the Billy Boils* and *Joe Wilson and his Mates*. (This development is the subject of the next chapter.) In clearing the ground, as they saw it, of various illusions, the postwar academics, in their turn, would simply take the already existing preference further and distinguish more finely, according a firmer and more precise valuation of the variable aesthetic successes and failures of Lawson's prose.

Regardless of the merits of proposal and counter-proposal, the fact that the identity of Henry Lawson the writer was being continuously contested, that Lawsons of the left and the right could be appropriated almost at will, kept interest in his published works alive. Readers kept reading him and Angus & Robertson kept publishing, seeking even greater control of the copyrights and continuing to experiment with new forms of marketing.

---

[36] Lee deals with Hardy's literary activism at length (129–43).
[37] The anonymous author of chapter XIII, 'The "Herald" and the Arts', in the commemorative volume *A Century of Journalism: The Sydney Morning Herald and its Record of Australian Life 1831–1931* (Sydney: John Fairfax & Sons, 1931) follows Green's judgement that all HL's work 'is Australian to the core . . . it is by his short stories that he will live' (p. 601). Green is dealt with in Chapter 12.

Sales of the Collecteds

The publication in 1935 of the two-volume *Prose Works* was part of a larger strategy; in essence, it involved a simplification of the firm's Lawson offerings. In 1925 as we have seen, his various volumes of poetry became *The Poetical Works of Henry Lawson* (3 vols.). The extent of its first printing is unknown but there were 820 copies in stock as of October 1937 and 1,690 copies in stock of the *Prose Works*, which was reprinted in that year.[38] *Prose Works* received its third printing, this time in a new typesetting, of nearly 5,000 copies in August 1940 and then, in a one-volume resetting, of nearly 10,000 copies in August 1948. By October 1951 all copies had been sold and Angus & Robertson seems not to have reprinted. *Poetical Works*, now in one volume, also went through several editions from 1939 to 1953. By November 1954 stock-in-hand was nil.[39]

The simplification of the firm's Lawson titles was temporarily complicated by a wartime publishing venture, the Australian Pocket Library, subsidised by the Federal government. The series' titles were selected by the advisory board of the Commonwealth Literary Fund, upon whose deliberations Vance Palmer's influence was central. A number of firms were involved in this scheme to bring a wide range of Australian literary titles back into print at very affordable prices; but in the event they were printed on poor-quality paperstock and with a standard, unattractive cover design.[40] Angus & Robertson published *Winnowed Verses* (1944) and *On the Track and Over the Sliprails* (1945) but neither was especially successful.[41] *While the Billy Boils* did not

---

[38] Handwritten 'Henry Lawson Sales from 1936 to 1954' (ML MSS 3269/125/1). Apparently the two large *Prose Works* volumes sold at 12s.6d. each (advertised at this price on the dust jacket of a 1940 A&R printing of *Billy Boils* (personal copy); the *Poetical Works* volumes sold at 7s.6d.

[39] The printings of *Poetical Works* were: July 1939 (1,013 copies), May 1941 (1,386), November 1944 (5,051), March 1947 (7,440), February 1949 (3,980), November 1950 (3,824), July 1951 (7,544) and April 1953 (7,538): handwritten 'Henry Lawson Sales...' (ML MSS 3269/125/1).

[40] See further, Neil James and Elizabeth Webby, 'Canon around the Hub: Angus and Robertson and the Post-War Literary Canon', *Southerly*, 57.3 (Spring 1997), 51–66; and James, 'A Paperback Canon: The Australian Pocket Library', *Australian Literary Studies*, 19 (2000), 295–305.

[41] As at 1 January 1948, 1,200 unsold copies of the latter were disposed of at remainder prices and 6,877 'used for donations or destroyed'; much the same was true of *Winnowed*

appear in this series, whose commercial failure confirmed Angus & Robertson in the wisdom of their preference for hardback publication.

The firm moved on. The next significant stage is revealed by some comprehensive royalty statements covering the period 1937–54. They were prepared for an approach by Angus & Robertson to the Public Trustee of New South Wales, into whose hands the non-assigned Lawson copyrights had come after his death. Angus & Robertson's proposal was that, in return for £2,500, the copyrights possessed by the Public Trustee should be assigned to the firm, which claimed partial ownership of them in any case and was 'paying in effect 18 years royalty in advance', with all risks, until the expiration of the copyright at the end of 1972.[42] The royalty statements, once extrapolated forwards, showed that £2,500 was one-third of what the royalties would amount to if the Public Trustee owned and was remunerated for all of them at ten per cent of the retail price until 1972. On the figures supplied, the six years 1947–53 had yielded about £2,500.[43] As a result of these negotiations, Angus & Robertson acquired the complete rights and held onto them even after the change in ownership in the 1980s when the firm was taken over by HarperCollins. Although much of the Australian literature list was sold off, HarperCollins was still claiming them in respect of Lawson's unpublished works as late as 2005.[44]

One noteworthy statistic, in view of the longstanding view that Lawson was more popular as a poet than as a prose writer, is that, if for purposes of comparison we ignore the July 1951 and April 1953 printings of *Poetical Works* (as *Prose* was out of print by October 1951 and was not reprinted), then we find that the poetry volume had just over 11,000 sales, only about 1,150 more than the substantially more expensive prose

Verses (carbon-copy typescript, 'HENRY LAWSON/ SALES FROM 1st JANUARY 1948 to 16th SEPTEMBER 1955', ML MSS 3269/125/1).

[42] The firm's partial ownership was pursuant to HL's various assignments of rights over the years. The firm now also claimed 'Exclusive powers to negotiate all other rights (e.g. film, stage, etc.) *subject to* our paying the Public Trustee 50% of all monies so obtained.' The single-page carbon-copy typescript setting out the proposal is headed 'HENRY LAWSON' and in handwriting: 'Mr Iliffe. Please keep this copy' (ML MSS 3269/125/1).

[43] In addition to the two *Works* titles these royalties embraced A&R's *The Children's Lawson*, published in April 1949 in 7,470 copies at 3s.6d. with a further 529 copies in March 1953.

[44] Personal correspondence.

volume (21s. during 1948–51 as against the *Poetical Works* rising from 8s.6d. to 15s.). We can conclude that Lawson the poet and Lawson the short story writer were, at least in the postwar period (1947 or 1948 to 1951), fairly equally balanced in the popular mind. Interest in Lawson had also picked up considerably since the pre-War period. The average per annum royalty at 10 per cent for the years 1936–54 was £211 p.a.; for 1947–53 it was £413 – nearly twice as much.[45]

These figures need nevertheless to be kept in perspective. Angus & Robertson began to publish the novels and prose works of Ion L. Idriess in 1931; he would be a great money-spinner. By 31 December 1961 the total estimated sales of his various titles were over 1.5 million copies.[46] In comparison, the more literary title, Ruth Park's *Harp in the South* (1948) sold not quite 30,000 copies from January 1948 to July 1955, and total sales from her various volumes reached 150,000 by the end of 1961.[47] Most telling, perhaps, are the sales figures for some of the firm's non-literary titles, such as the longstanding success, *The Commonsense Cookery Book* (1916). It had sold 621,000 copies since its first publication; by 1968 this figure had reached 779,000.[48]

After the new arrangements around rights were settled with the Public Trustee, *Prose Works* was reprinted in 1956 in a large print run of unknown size following a period of no availability during 1952–55; 15,000 copies were sold by 1957.[49] The edition was reprinted in 1957 and 1962 (by which time another 5,000 in total had been sold), and again in 1963 (2,000 were sold). It was temporarily superseded by an expensive three-volume collection, *The Short Stories of Henry Lawson*, edited

---

[45] Carbon-copy typesecript 'HENRY LAWSON' (ML MSS 3269/125/1). These figures are in relation to the Collected titles and *The Children's Lawson*; royalties and sales for the Australian Pocket Library edition are unknown, but print runs of 25,000 were originally envisaged.
[46] Typed page headed 'ESTIMATED SALES UP TO 31st. December, 1961' (ML MSS 3269/125/1).
[47] Handwritten sales calculations, top line reads: 'Ivan Southall 149125' (ML MSS 3269/125/2); 'ESTIMATED SALES UP TO 31st. December, 1961' (MSS 3269/125/1).
[48] 'ESTIMATED SALES UP TO 31st. December, 1961', with handwritten additions extending its sales to June 1968 (ML MSS 3269/125/1).
[49] Sales figures in ML MSS 3269/Lawson, Henry – papers re 1894–1949, vol. 386, fol. 173. The list gives 1948–57 as 25,000; as the 1948 print run was 9,862 and 1957 saw another print run, about 15,000 must have been printed and sold beforehand.

by Cecil Mann in 1964; and this was in turn superseded by the more scholarly editions of Lawson's works prepared by Colin Roderick and published from 1967. (These are dealt with in Chapter 13.) But the one-volume *Prose Works* was returned to the marketplace with printings in 1970, 1976, 1979, 1980, 1982 (when its title became *Collected Stories of Henry Lawson*), 1983, 1984, 1986 and possibly later. Lloyd O'Neill released a new typesetting of the same stories in 1979 as *Henry Lawson's Mates* in one volume, and this was reprinted in 1981. Penguin issued the same edition as *Collected Stories of Henry Lawson* in 1987 in the lead-up to the Australian bicentenary, another nationalising moment.

The selections

Aside from appearances of several stories from *While the Billy Boils* in school readers during the period 1924–44, and translations and anthologisings in short-story collections by multiple authors in the interwar period,[50] single-volume selections of Lawson's stories subsequently proved very popular in the postwar period. Angus & Robertson energetically exploited its intellectual property with a number of such selections. (See Appendix 3 for a listing.)

Sales of Colin Roderick's selection *Fifteen Stories* (1959) are estimated to have reached 60,000 by 31 December 1961;[51] he had also selected *Twenty Stories and Seven Poems by Henry Lawson* in 1947. In 1966 Angus & Robertson published Cecil Mann's selection *Henry Lawson's Best Stories* at $3.75 (see Introduction for a description).

The selections proliferated, especially from 1 January 1973 when, fifty years and a day after the end of the year of Lawson's death, the copyright on

---

[50] *The School Magazine* published: 'The Drover's Wife' (1930, 1934, 1938 – a special issue for the 150th anniversary of colonial settlement – and 1942), '[Enter Mitchell]' (in 1939), 'His Country—After All' (1941): details from Lee 242–3, which lists HL's works reprinted in this magazine.

For selective listings of the anthologisings and translations, see: E. Morris Miller and Frederick T. Macartney, *Australian Literature: A Bibliography to 1938 Extended to 1950* (Sydney: A&R, 1956), pp. 280–1; and, for more translations, *The Bibliography of Australian Literature K–O to 2000*, gen. ed. John Arnold and John Hay (St Lucia: University of Queensland Press, 2007), pp. 144–6.

[51] 'ESTIMATED SALES UP TO 31st. December, 1961' (ML MSS 3269/125/1).

the published works lapsed. The field was now open for publishers other than Angus & Robertson. This was a period in which cheaper-format paperback publication for Australian literary titles regained favour after the commercial failure of the paperback Australian Pocketbook Series in the later war years. The new selections usually included stories and sketches from *While the Billy Boils*, which, along with *Joe Wilson and his Mates*, came to represent Lawson's enduring achievement in prose. The lead-up to the Australian Bicentennial celebrations in 1988, and the flourishing of courses in Australian literature around the same time, brought forth a considerable number of Lawson publications, from coffee-table Lawsoniana, to 'heritage' hardbacks, to a rash of cheap paperbacks, to classroom textbooks. New selections have continued to appear – and doubtless will go on doing so for a very long time, in print and other formats.

Although we continue to identify Henry Lawson with the 1890s, printings and reprintings suggest that, in terms of sales and reading experiences, the postwar period, especially from the late 1950s until the end of the 1980s, saw the peak of his popularity. That same book history also suggests that, if he is still to be understood as a quintessential literary figure of the 1890s, it must be a very 'Long 1890s' we are talking about. A book-historical perspective forces this truth out into the open; and it balances, just as it matches, a new awareness (argued at the beginning of Chapter 10) of the heterochronicity of Lawson's actual moment of writing. The implications of both positions for literary study are taken up in the next and final chapters. For now, it is enough to conclude that *While the Billy Boils* has had a very long life indeed.

CHAPTER 12

LAWSON'S REPUTATION IN THE POSTWAR PERIOD

IN 1982 H. P. Heseltine wrote of Lawson criticism: 'Virtually every new account of our most enigmatic author has achieved its own conviction only at the expense of blotting out some of the central features of its predecessors.'[1] In this context, compare the following remarks of Alfred Deakin in one of his numerous notes on his reading, dated 7 November 1896. It was written soon after he had read *While the Billy Boils* and compares Lawson's standing with that of Banjo Paterson:

> An indigenous literature is at last beginning in Australia . . . in all the elements of true power, veracity and grim emotion Lawson is the superior. . . . He speaks for the workman, the tramp, the shearer – the true bushmen – the inner Australian beyond civic or imported influences – the most Australian Australia.[2]

This strikes the very notes that the cultural nationalists would enthusiastically adopt in the 1950s and which a swelling wave of feminist critique, which peaked in the 1980s, aimed at identifying as the dominant masculinist myth of the 1890s – one that needed overturning.

But even in the 1890s much the same dynamic of action and reaction can be seen. In Chapter 8 we saw Turner and Sutherland's near-dismissal in 1898 of Lawson the poet and their studied ignoring of Lawson the short-story writer. Turner articulated the latter rejection in an

---

[1] H. P. Heseltine, 'Between Living and Dying: The Ground of Lawson's Art', in *The Uncertain Self: Essays in Australian Literature and Criticism* (Melbourne: Oxford University Press, 1986), pp. 42–55 [p. 42], originally in *Overland*, no. 88 (July 1982), 19–26.
[2] In *Walter Murdoch and Alfred Deakin on Books and Men: Letters and Comments 1900–1918*, ed. J. A. La Nauze and Elizabeth Nurser (Melbourne: Melbourne University Press, 1974), p. 93.

unpublished lecture that he gave in 1904. The problem was Lawson's catering to the low appetite of the masses for Balzackian seaminess and sordidness.[3] This argument – or, rather, expression of a taste – developed one distinct and continuous strand of the 1890s reaction to Lawson in the successive waves of reviewing of his prose from 1894 onwards. The reaction helps to explain, as we have seen, A. G. Stephens's curiously defensive remarks about the level of achievement of the contents of the *Bulletin Story Book* that he edited in 1901. The reaction also points us towards the conclusion, argued towards the end of Chapter 8, that no uniformly nationalist 'imagined community' sprang into being, fully formed, in the 1890s. The contemporary readership was simply too divided in its tastes and diverted by its abundant sources of magazines and books for this to be the case.[4] And many would-be cultural entrepreneurs and commentators competed for dominance of – or at least struck attitudes in – the literary field, much as they do today.

Coincidentally, 1901 was also the year in which Grant Hervey began to contribute his verse to the *Bulletin*. A blacksmith-turned-versifier, he is remembered principally, when at all, as the writer who was tarred and feathered in 1921 following agitation to set up a separate state around Mildura, a movement that he had offered to lead.[5] Some 324 of his poems

---

[3] Turner deplored the *Bulletin* school as 'sordid', however skilled. HL, along with Arthur Hoey Davis and Miles Franklin, are criticised for stressing the ugliness and seamy side of Australian life as this merely caters to the 'amusement of a class of readers that gloats on the kind of life presented in Rabelais, Balzac or Eugene Sue': Henry Gyles Turner Papers, State Library of Victoria, MS 8062: quoted in Geoffrey Serle, 'Victorian Writers in the Nineties', in *The 1890s: Australian Literature and Literary Culture*, ed. Ken Stewart (St Lucia: University of Queensland Press, 1996), p. 54.

[4] Cf. Jill Julius Matthews's argument, on the basis of a survey of Australian-published turn-of-century magazines, that 'generalist interpretations of the country's past and the possibilities of its people's thought and action have been somewhat distorted ... Across the range of magazines at any one time, there was an extraordinary diversity of opinion and commentary on the many activities of domestic, social, cultural, and political life that makes reliance on two or three "iconic" titles unsafe': 'Hidden Treasures of the Mitchell Library: Sydney Periodicals 1895–1930' (St Lucia, Qld: AustLit, 2010) at www.austlit.edu.au, accessed November 2010.

[5] Later, he called himself Grant Madison Hervey. Both names were pseudonyms of George Henry Cochrane (1880–1933). See further Paul Eggert, 'Colonial King: Grant Madison Hervey, and the *Bulletin* of the 1900s', *The Culture of the Book*, ed. David Garrioch et al. (Melbourne: BSANZ, 1999), pp. 446–67; supplemented by 'Hervey's Contributions to Australian Newspapers and Magazines', *Bibliographical Society of Australia and New Zealand Bulletin*, 24 (2000), 159–60.

appeared in the *Bulletin* during 1901–11. His early attempts at verse were influenced by the Decadence of the 1890s and involved experiments with French verse forms, possibly filtered through Swinburne and Austin Dobson. So 'Legs Talionis: A Stage-manager's Triolets' appeared in the *Bulletin* on 4 January 1902; 'When the Good Old Gods Are Dead' (1 February 1902) is a ballade with 3 stanzas of 8 lines all ending with the same line and with an 'Envoi' addressed to the gods; and 'Concerning a Dead Sweetheart' (same date) is a rondel (15 lines with the opening words used twice as a refrain). They have all the limpness of borrowed form and the blur of feigned emotion. The late-century languor, full of nameless feelings, welling emotion and effeteness, characteristic of his early *Bulletin* contributions, is strangely at odds with the later Hervey, whose thumping rhythms expressed a powerful masculinity that would become a central part of his outlook. His political poem of 1905, 'Wanted, a Strong Man', is typical.[6] The early poems may have been a voice he was trying on: he was still in his early twenties. Nevertheless it all found a home in the turn-of-century *Bulletin*, whose reputation for bohemianism Hervey was continuing. The expense of the illustrations that occasionally accompanied his verse (including some by Norman Lindsay) suggests he was an audience-pleaser, catering to an established taste. Other examples of the variety of the *Bulletin*'s editorial response to existing tastes could be readily adduced.

The cultural environment of the late colonial period in Australia was more variegated than most of its subsequent interpreters were prepared to grant. Previous work by G. A. Wilkes, Leon Cantrell, Ken Stewart and others has already pointed towards such a conclusion.[7] The 1890s literary

[6] 'Wanted, a Strong Man', signed 'G.H.', *Bulletin*, 13 April 1905, p. 24.
[7] For Wilkes, see below. Ken Stewart's introduction to *The 1890s: Australian Literature and Literary Culture* (pp. 1–31), points out that, in HL's account of the bush, there are many 'thugs, con-men, boozers, louts, numbskulls, liars and schoolboyish bushmen' (p. 19); that HL and other *Bulletin* writers were more sensitively attuned to the feminine plight and affected by early feminist politics than has been acknowledged; and that *Bulletin* fiction by no means dominated the publishing output of the period or the available reading matter: 'in many books and periodicals it is hard to find a horse or a gumtree: as in previous decades, love, death, religion and ethical matters are common themes' (p. 8).
Leon Cantrell's introduction to *The 1890s* (in the Portable Australian Authors series: St

ecosystem *can* be cast, as we saw in Chapter 8, as in part a struggle for literary hegemony between Sydney and Melbourne of the time – except that, as I noted, the detractors and acclaimers of *While the Billy Boils* did not line up neatly on either side of the Murray. The Melbourne Deakin's comments, Hervey's hundreds of contributions to the *Bulletin*, as well as the contemporary taste for Imperial-adventure and romance fiction, merely confirm the general observation.

It can be put another way. A century after the 1890s we began regularly distinguishing 'literary' fiction from 'genre' fiction. In view of the overwhelming success of the latter, there was a good deal of anxious discussion about whether Australian 'literary' fiction could survive.[8] Those terms were not used in the 1890s, which was itself a decade of equally rapid change in the fiction market and book trade. A bibliographic study of the formats and printings (including cheap 'yellowback' titles and colonial editions), and where available the sales figures, of Lawson's competitors in the fiction market in the 1890s would surely confirm its congested topography, would further explain why George Robertson designed the physical book *While the Billy Boils* as he did, and prove that Lawson's path was but one of many.

The sudden contemporaneity of Australian literature in the 1890s

Deakin's enthusiastic claim that Australian literature began *now* typified a theme struck in a number of the reviews of *While the Billy*

Lucia: University of Queensland Press, 1977) had already gone part of the way. From his reading for the selection, Cantrell had found that 'the period itself seemed to be unaware of its mythical proportions. Certainly there was a feeling of opportunity and achievement in the air, but it was viewed in essentially modest terms, quite lacking the note of euphoria later writers ascribed to it' (p. xii). He added: 'the variety of Australian nineties' writing has been underestimated' and that 'The truth is that bush life is most frequently depicted in our literature of the 1890s as harsh and destructive of all but the basic urge to survive. Or, if Arcadian, as belonging to a bygone age, now lost. Egalitarian mateship is less common than loneliness and betrayal. Failure is more real than success' (p. xx).

[8] For the evolution of the terms in the booktrade (terms that effectively rewrote the older distinction between 'serious' and 'popular' literature), see Claire Squires, *Marketing Literature: The Making of Contemporary Writing in Britain* (Basingstoke, Hants.: Palgrave Macmillan, 2007), chapters 1–3.

Boils, and it would later be frequently asserted as a fact.⁹ Yet the claim waved away as merely preliminary the prose achievements of Henry Kingsley, Marcus Clarke and Rolf Boldrewood; the fine domestic realism of Ada Cambridge, Catherine Martin and Tasma; and the poetry of Charles Harpur, Henry Kendall and Adam Lindsay Gordon, to name only the obvious candidates. The claim implicitly was that none of this counted because it did not deal with Australian experience or that the authors' styles and attitudes had not been sufficiently moulded by that experience.¹⁰

In retrospect, the wilfulness of the position is striking. While the temptation of critics ever since has been to interpret in ideological terms the 1890s' sense of a break with its past, the simpler explanation has been overlooked or underplayed: that there was a change in literary taste happening, a slightly delayed and differently inflected version of what had already taken hold in Europe, towards new forms of realism. It was a shift that some of the literary elite were welcoming and some were resisting. The subject matter, from this point of view, could be seen as incidental.

And yet it was also not incidental. The nineteenth century was an age of new nationalisms in country after country in Europe, inspired by Romanticism from the beginning of the century and expressed in all art forms. The international Arts and Crafts movement towards the end of the century was aimed at expressing artisanal skills that were in danger of being lost. Folk tales and songs were being deliberately

⁹ E.g. in 1928 by A. W. Jose. Dealing with Australian writing from the earliest colonial period chronologically forwards, he claimed that Paterson and HL represented 'the first purely Australian literary movement' ('Australian Literature: IV The *Bulletin* School: Bush Bards', *Reader*, 3.10 (July 1928), 365–9 [p. 366]); and, in 1932, that the 1890s were 'the birth-years of Australian literature' (*The Romantic Nineties*, Sydney, A&R, p. 21). Deakin wrote: 'There is a greater wealth of insight, of truth of detail and truth of spirit in this volume (While the Billy Boils) than in the whole of the alleged Australian literature which has preceded it' (*Murdoch and Deakin*, ed. La Nauze and Nurser, p. 93). The fact that the Australian Pocket Library (see Chapter 11) chose no title earlier than *Robbery Under Arms* (and then did not proceed with it, as too large for the paperback format) was another confirmation.

¹⁰ It would be repeated by Nettie Palmer in 1924 and Henrietta Drake-Brockman in the late 1960s; by then it had become the accepted wisdom: see Elizabeth Webby, 'Australian Short Fiction from *While the Billy Boils* to *The Everlasting Secret Family*', *Australian Literary Studies*, 10 (1981), 147–64.

collected and published out of much the same impulse. But in Australia, for obvious historical reasons, the situation was delayed and different. An emerging nationalist consciousness is nevertheless readily detectable. Many reviews of *Robbery Under Arms* and other of Boldrewood's novels from the late 1880s congratulated the author (in a way we would not think to do today) on his precise historical recording of a colonial past that was fast retreating from memory. The praise perhaps indexed a contemporary anxiety around the time of the first centenary of European settlement in the Australian colonies. Although in fact expressed in the reviews studied in Chapter 8, this theme, in relation to Lawson, is a mere undertone in them. Francis Adams's book *The Australians: A Social Sketch* had appeared in 1892; it drew together for celebration images and motifs of the Bushman that were already circulating in songs and ballads as part of the colonial oral culture. As John Docker has observed, 'the bush workers c[a]me to have the status of Australia's pre-industrial "folk"'.[11] In this way the path had already been laid for a new talent who would bring the colonial present forward, who would bring it into view for the first time in a nuanced, apparently artless way. Lawson's prose writings thus represent a second wave. They would not, and *could* not after his trip to Bourke, be simply celebratory as he learnt how to make over into the needs of the present, received, romantic-historicising models that would no longer serve.[12] He must have known this in his bones, even if not as a conscious policy, every day that he wrote.

Lawson's painstaking development of an outdoors or bush realism was in this sense almost unavoidable. It chimed, as we saw in Chapter 2, with the demands of the *Worker* and the *Bulletin* for short sketches and stories, and for the interest in life in the bush that the latter had been cultivating since 1886 in 'pars' (pithy, single paragraphs), sketches and ballads contributed by its readers. Although the subject matter in other

---

[11] John Docker, *In a Critical Condition: Reading Australian Literature* (Ringwood, Vic.: Penguin, 1984), p. 35.
[12] E.g., in 'A Christmas in the Far West; or, The Bush Undertaker' (*Antipodean*, 1892), HL on one occasion describes the old hatter as a 'bushman' but, in revising the printer's copy for *Billy Boils* in 1895–96, he changed it to 'shepherd' (see Eggert and Webby). Cf. n. 27 below.

contributions in both weeklies ranged far wider and expressed other, more overtly literary tastes, there was a new taste being formed that would add to and compete with the other elements of the existing mix. Reviewers now recognised it and then hailed Lawson as embodying it. The fact that his publisher was both local and successful fed their enthusiasm. But in order to express their sense of the change in taste – in order to help establish it on a sure footing – many critics felt the need to deny or minimise what had gone before, to 'blot out some of its central features'. That they would encounter resistance from those whose taste had not changed, or not yet changed, was only to be expected.

Later explanations of the significance of the 1890s for the history of Australian culture that overleapt the literary and aesthetic to embrace the more urgently ideological tended to miss the embroiled contest of changing literary taste, and of change resisted. A clarification of kinds was duly achieved, but it tended to conflate the 1890s with the 1950s: at least, that is where the evidence of the later reception of *While the Billy Boils* tends, particularly that of the postwar period. This chapter is therefore focussed less on the left vs right political struggle for ownership of the Lawson legend in the postwar period as on the aesthetic debate around Lawson as prose writer and on its book-historical contexts. It first explores as an essential background the trends of the interwar period.[13]

The interwar period

John Le Gay Brereton's distinction in 1927 between the popular verdict of Lawson as the poet of mateship, the representative of Australian life on the one hand, and the authoritative judgement of literary criticism about Lawson the prose writer on the other, strengthened a note sounded in the first reviews of *While the Billy Boils* in 1896, and, as we have seen,

---

[13] For the political-cultural struggle in relation to HL, see further Lee; John Docker, *Australian Cultural Elites: Intellectual Traditions in Sydney and Melbourne* (Sydney: Angus & Robertson, 1974); and, more generally, Susan McKernan, *A Question of Commitment: Australian Literature in the Twenty Years after the War* (Sydney: Allen & Unwin, 1989). See further, below.

even before 1896. It would continue to ramify in the post-World War II period, especially from the 1960s, when the study of Australian literature began to make its previously marginal presence felt in the curricula of English departments in the universities.¹⁴

H. M. Green in 1930 developed the distinction, though without any explicit mention of Brereton, his colleague at Sydney University, in his fine precursor to his monumental *History of Australian Literature: Pure and Applied*. This earlier book of 1930, *An Outline of Australian Literature*, divides his subject into successive 'periods', of which Lawson's generation is (of course, for a literary historian) not the first, but it is cast as the most distinctive. In the period 1887–1914 'we begin to be modern, and at the same time to be really Australian'. Lawson, as 'the most representative figure in Australian creative literature', is central to that period.

Green describes his *Outline* as only a preliminary to the broader history that he hoped would be ready 'in two or three years'. Nevertheless, the *Outline* is already ambitious, open-eyed and authoritative in tone. Green acknowledges a debt to various printed reference books, mainly introductions to literary collections, and 'especially those by A. G. Stephens'; but otherwise he saw himself as blazing the trail. His touchstone is given in the introductory chapter: 'Australian literature is literature that springs out of Australia, which reflects some aspect of Australian life, though the style alone may be affected and the subject need not be Australian.'¹⁵

The essential context for Lawson, Green argues, was not the various overseas influences that had been cited by reviewers and critics – Bret Harte, Mark Twain, Maupassant and Chekhov (which last he thinks, however, the closest comparison) – but rather the requirements of the *Bulletin* short story:

---

¹⁴ In *The English Men: Professing Literature in Australian Universities*, Leigh Dale records the field's history during the 1920s–1960s: (Toowoomba, Qld.: Association for the Study of Australian Literature, 1997), pp. 147–83.
¹⁵ H. M. Green, *An Outline of Australian Literature* (Sydney: Whitcombe & Tombs, 1930), pp. 70, 109, 5, 14.

> They were inculcated directly in the instructions which were then given on the *Bulletin*'s leader page; by example, in that they were observed in most of the stories published by the *Bulletin*, especially in its Christmas numbers; by the nature of the remarks made to unsuccessful contributors to its Correspondence Column; and also by the emendations made by its editorial staff. In the main they concerned form. At the head of them stood brevity... Finally, the *Bulletin* short story had in it a large element of the primitive. It dealt in high colours and strong contrasts, and, though sometimes beneath a pretence of weariness or boredom, it was bursting with energy. It was the most masculine kind of short story ever written, and one of the most vital. It could never have come from an old or a highly civilised country. Yet it was written, and also constructed, so far as there was room in it for construction, with a considerable amount of skill. It was also original in style.[16]

Green was writing after Ernest Hemingway had begun publishing his very short stories in the mid-1920s, although he would not reach the height of his capacity until the late 1930s and of his fame until the 1950s. That wrinkle aside, Green's deeming of the stories' characteristic vitality as 'masculine' would later open the door for the feminist revisionism of the 1970s and 1980s.

Green's *Outline* appeared in the same year in which George Lambert was completing his sculpture of Lawson the Bushman, for which the schoolchildren of New South Wales had been busily gathering and contributing their pennies for several years. Yet Green, in his praise, trifles with but finally skirts the historical sentimentality about Lawson, which the period almost mandated:

> If the drawing-room and the study were practically outside his experience, he knew the long road and grassless plain, the camp-fire and the up-country shanty as well as the poorer parts of the city, with its slums and by-lanes; and shearer, drover, horse-breaker, spieler and sundowner ... They are at once individual and typical ... Lawson was, by reason of his temperament and the conditions of his life, the apostle and prophet of the gospel of mateship, though in this he may be said to have had also a kind of inheritance from Farrell.[17]

---

[16] *Ibid.*, pp. 106–8.
[17] *Ibid.*, pp. 111–12.

The scholar in Green, witnessed in that last clause, never quite recedes, despite the appropriation of Lawson that so eloquently and idealistically precedes it.

Green was not yet able to make the chronological distinctions in Lawson's achievement that would only become possible in the 1970s when new editorial and biographical scholarship was brought to bear. Content to understand Lawson's prose as an undifferentiated continuum, Green nevertheless nicely defines the narrative point of view we are offered in the stories as being 'neither from the dress circle nor from the "gods,"' but that 'of a member of the company of players'.[18] More technically, he says he is unhappy with Edward Garnett's account of 'Lawson's casualness and lack of form' (see Chapter 8). But Green had nowhere to go in countering it other than to retreat to the other side of the style–subject matter divide:

> Lawson is not only one of the best of all Australian writers; he is the most Australian of all of them . . . If we were set the impossible task of finding some single book to represent Australia, it would have to be one of Lawson's, and for an Australian to read him in another country is to breathe the air of home.[19]

This was because of Lawson's 'far wider humanity' than Henry Kendall's: 'his work was made human and vital by the width and depth and sincerity of his sympathies'.[20] Green's nomination of a moral-imaginative locus of insight would sit uneasily with the facts of Lawson's post-London life, and with the 'limitations' and failings that Green's successors could not avoid naming, especially in the 1960s when the professional literary critics came to deal with him. But the note was a purifying antidote to Henry Gyles Turner's charge of seamy pessimism, and the shocked resistance to new forms of realism and naturalism that had surfaced among many reviewers of *While the Billy Boils*. By the 1930s that had gone by the board; that part of the Long 1890s was over. But the meanings that now began to gather around the earlier decade

[18] *Ibid.*, p. 113.
[19] *Ibid.*, p. 115.
[20] *Ibid.*, p. 110.

and around Lawson's name would redefine the 1890s into an ideological formation that would respond to the needs of a new period.[21]

The postwar period

In his long-delayed two-volume history H. M. Green named what he now called his 'Third Period' (1890–1923) 'Self-Conscious Nationalism'. Though not published until 1961, the history was written by 1954. It brought to a new focus some nationalist notes already present in the 1930 *Outline* but now more strongly evoked by what was going on around him. This Third Period, he now argued, 'began to produce a literature from which the last echoings [of British productions] had almost entirely faded, which had a nature and individuality essentially its own; and the factors that combined in its production were to be found mainly in its own country'. There was a 'self-conscious concentration', Green claimed, 'which took the form, in the literary as in the social and political worlds, of a fervent democratic nationalism: it was based upon a broad social consciousness, a feeling of mutual relationship, that found its most characteristic expression in Lawson's doctrine of mateship'.

The shortage of new British publications in Australia during World War II, together with the nationalism that the war inevitably brought out, had meant that Australian literary and other titles had been in unusual demand. The validation of stoic endurance amongst the Australian fighting men in the crucible of wartime experience equally meant that, after the war, it would be but a short step to the invention of its historical-nationalist underpinning: to Green's claim that 'Lawson

---

[21] For a useful account of the interwar period and the 1940s – including the influence of saga fiction in legitimising colonial and later subject matter and for the influence of P. R. Stephensen's *The Foundations of Culture in Australia: An Essay towards National Self-Respect* (1936) – see Peter Pierce, 'Australia's Australia' in *The Cambridge History of Australian Literature*, ed. Pierce (Melbourne: Cambridge University Press, 2009), pp. 137–55. Cf. David Carter's account of the Adelaide literary magazine *Desiderata*, in which, in the early 1930s, 'there was scarcely any sense that a national [literary] tradition existed' and whose editor stated in 1935: 'Indisputably, but a small percentage of our people is interested in Australian literature only': 'Modernising Anglocentrism: *Desiderata* and Literary Time', in *Republics of Letters: Literary Communities in Australia*, ed. Peter Kirkpatrick and Robert Dixon (Sydney: Sydney University Press, 2012), pp. 85–98 [quoted pp. 96, 97]. See further, nn. 62–3 below.

stands for the equalitarian idealism of the democratic Australia of the day'.[22] The claim was true, except 'the day' was now: the early 1950s.

Vance Palmer

Vance Palmer's influential *The Legend of the Nineties* (1954) shows the conflation of the two 'days' happening. Although the book's title and that of the first chapter indicate he is dealing with a *legend* of the 1890s – a legend about a founding, 'a brief and brilliant first flowering', of Australian literary culture, whose social expression was 'centred in the idea of mateship' – and although he occasionally has to expand his chronological restriction to include the period from Eureka to World War I, and to further restrict the demographic of which he writes to the 'most conscious spirits' rather than the whole country, Palmer nevertheless insists that the legend has 'a close connection with historical reality'.[23] The equivalent of a folk culture, with some jiggling up and down the social scale, was being codified into a legend.

'In what books are we to look for it?', he asks. 'Comparatively few were published during the nineties, and these mainly of a factual kind. The machinery for publishing, in truth, hardly existed, though some publishers were occasionally beginning to issue a volume or two in an experimental way.' Rather, he suggests, the key factor was the 'lively journalism': 'weeklies like the *Bulletin*, the *Boomerang*, the *Worker* gave a suggestion that the national mind was in ferment as never before'. He also emphasises the oral balladry tradition that went before, often exploring the bushranger theme, which gave Lawson and Paterson 'not only a store of incidents and legends to draw upon but an audience used to the imaginative treatment' of the ordinary life around them. Later in the book Palmer states that 'There was an intensity about the spirit of the early nineties that created images and ideas having a continuous force'. He soon answers the question that has been begged: continuous

---

[22] H. M. Green, *A History of Australian Literature: Pure and Applied*, 2 vols (Sydney: A&R, 1961), I. 347, 348, 356–7.
[23] Vance Palmer, *The Legend of the Nineties* (Melbourne: Melbourne University Press, 1954), pp. 9, 10, 10, 9.

until when? It is 'A tradition', he argues, 'that has not been lost'.[24] This locates Palmer's Legend as a consolidation, if not exactly a creation, of the 1940s and 1950s.

Palmer's overlooking the variability in literary production and book publication in the 1890s, as well as Lawson's problematising (rather than simple celebrating) of mateship, suggest that the 1890s was being locked into place as a foundational moment for a nationalism and set of mainly masculine values reflecting the experience of World War II and the currents of Australian culture afterwards. When Palmer writes: 'There was, in truth, nothing to hold people to the country until the dreams of men who had been born in it and conceived a mystical faith in its future with their first impressions gave it a spiritual core', he is speaking generally of white native-born colonists. Lawson was one of them. But the 1899 Lawson of 'Pursuing Literature' and the 1902 Lawson newly returned from England show that the man's Australian spiritual core was sorely tested.[25]

Like a growing number of commentators, Palmer saw that 'the quiet intensity of [Lawson's] prose' was a far superior achievement to that of his verse. In it, 'he founded a tradition of democratic writing that has affected the work of nearly all who have come after him'. The oneness of Lawson's experience with his subject matter was by now a – if not *the* – validating trope of Lawson criticism. Palmer did not fail to draw it into his Legend, generalising it as he went along: 'The [1890s] writer's values were those of the people he brought into his stories, for his experience was likely to have been the same as theirs; Lawson had carried his swag and shared the life of the shearing-shed, Furphy had been a bullock driver; and they were not rendered self-conscious by the necessity of making concessions to an outside audience'. For British writers, 'the style aimed at is a literary one and the point of view is fixed in a secure middle class. In our novels there is not much emphasis on the interior life of the individual; there is more on his activities as a social being, or on his experiences at work.'[26]

[24] Palmer, *Legend of the Nineties*, pp. 10, 13, 68, 167, 172.
[25] Ibid., p. 169. See Chapters 9 and 10.
[26] Ibid., pp. 114, 117, 170.

Whatever its validity, Palmer's distinction drew attention away from the deluge of British writings that Australians were actually reading in the 1890s. If the Legend were as central to that decade as Palmer argues then George Robertson would not have had to strive so hard to get Lawson a hearing as a serious writer. Essentialising statements about the 1890s such as Palmer's misconstrue the period and the author's reception within it. They arise from a belles-lettristic tradition where the stylish gesture at the historical facts was expected and where it was understood that empirical investigation should not get in the way of a shaping that was pleasing and rhetorically effective.

Russel Ward

It is, then, in some ways heartening if also strange to witness a historian, who is otherwise alert to the 'absurdly romanticized and exaggerated', write this:

> It is not necessary to construct from documents a detailed picture of the bushman of the last decades of the nineteenth century for comparison with that of his prototype. The work has been done from the life, and for all time, by Furphy, Lawson and Paterson, and the striking ancestral likeness between their portrait and that sketched in the preceding pages will have been apparent to the reader.... The later bushman [of the 1880s and 1890s] exhibited ... that "manly independence" whose obverse side was a levelling, egalitarian collectivism, and whose sum was comprised in the concept of mateship.[27]

---

[27] Russel Ward, *The Australian Legend* (Melbourne: Oxford University Press, 1958), pp. 1, 167. The historian's methodological jump is less puzzling when it is itself viewed historically. W. K. Hancock's *Australia* (1930) had depicted the social history of the country as conditioned by egalitarianism and a nationalism displacing Anglophile class sympathies. This book provided later literary writers and critics with a historian's warrant, assisted by Manning Clark's 'Tradition in Australian Literature' (*Meanjin*, 8 (1949), 16–22). Clark encapsulates the socio-literary tradition and would later write a biography of HL (see Chapter 13 n. 10).

Ward's 'nomad tribesmen' (p. 10) were a rural proletariat of men working mainly, first, on cattle stations but also as shepherds, and then, increasingly from the 1870s, on the sheep stations rather than as individualist small selectors – which was the determining factor, according to Frederick Jackson Turner (1861–1932), in the American frontier. Trades Unionism in Australia emerged from the shearers in 1886 at much the same time as in the USA and Britain. In time known as the Australian Workers Union it was far more significant than the transport workers and miners unions, and this again was the reverse of the overseas experience.

This quotation comes from Ward's *Australian Legend*. First published in 1958, many times reprinted and still in print fifty years later in 2008, it was based on a PhD done earlier in the 1950s and completed in 1956. Ward's case is about the second half of the nineteenth century, as he traces the actuality of the bushman experience, especially via its multiple recording in folk song and then its conscious promulgation in the *Bulletin* from the mid-1880s. Only with burgeoning literacy and the new railway systems 'did the powerful current come to the surface of events, to dominate formal literature and to provide a native tradition for the new industrial trade union movement'. While these changes helped bring about the demise of the actual bushman ethos by nearly eliminating the distance between the city and the bush, the changes helped make city colonists 'much more conscious of the ethos'. The result was that 'the values and the attitudes of the nomad tribe were embalmed in a national myth, thence to react powerfully, as they still do, upon thought and events'.[28]

The feminist revaluation of Ward's case

Ward's model of a building wave, consolidating into myth in the 1890s, necessarily cast the coming decades as after-effects. Later commentators, especially but not only feminist ones, have accepted the historical case while reversing Ward's valuation of it. They have typically seen a continuity from the 1890s Bushman myth to the celebration at home of the Australian and New Zealand Army Corps (Anzac) disaster at Gallipoli in 1915 – when the really effective Australian Imperial Force (AIF) actions occurred late in the war on the Western Front. The mythologising minimised the role and importance of women in the national ideological formation, a case radically deepened later in the 1980s by the application of the thinking of Julia Kristeva and other poststructuralist thinkers. The land, especially the outback, was now portrayed as having become, by the 1890s, the feminised object of male

---

[28] Ward, *Australian Legend*, pp. 194, 196.

desire and domination. The naturalising of this myth, it was argued, left an ideological and gender legacy with disempowering consequences for women in the post-World War II period. The rediscovery and republication in the 1980s of Australian women novelists and poets from the 1880s and 1890s was, accordingly, welcomed as a counteraction.[29]

A book-historical study of the life of *While the Billy Boils* disputes this series of linked positions, at least in relation to the 1890s. The problem lay in the feminist incorporation into their critique of the increasingly extrapolated nationalist myth. This is not to argue that their battle was not worth the fight. Indeed, the general recognition, now naturalised in political and social debate, that the social, family and legal arrangements of the postwar period needed to be changed if anything like gender fairness and equal opportunity were to be achieved is an enduring legacy of the feminist intellectual movement. But the urgency of the task, I will show, led to some illegitimate intellectual shortcuts that have distorted our view of the 1890s and its aftermath.[30]

Marilyn Lake and Graeme Davison

What would prove to be a very influential essay by Marilyn Lake, 'The Politics of Respectability: Identifying the Masculinist Context', appeared in *Historical Studies* in 1986.[31] It built in part on Graeme Davison's earlier essay of 1978 in which he argued, on strong evidence,

---

[29] The developing feminist case may be traced in: Richard White, *Inventing Australia* (Sydney: Allen & Unwin, 1981); Susan Sheridan, 'Ada Cambridge and the Female Literary Tradition', in *Nellie Melba, Ginger Meggs and Friends: Essays in Australian Cultural History*, ed. Susan Dermody, John Docker and Drusilla Modjeska (Malmsbury, Vic.: Kibble Books, 1982); Sheridan, '"Temper Romantic; Bias Offensively Australian": Australian Women Writers and Literary Nationalism', *Kunapipi* 7.2-7.3 (1985), 49-58; and for Kay Schaffer, *Women and the Bush*, see below.

[30] E.g., the accompanying account of why female authors of the 1880s and 1890s were so soon forgotten after their own period – an account of gender ideology – can at best be only partially true. Elsewhere I have explained the situation as being one of price and availability of books as well as of changing taste – and the first two considerations, at least, are only very distantly an ideological reflection: Eggert, 'Australian Classics and the Price of Books: The Puzzle of the 1890s', *Journal of the Association of Australian Literature* (special issue *The Colonial Present*, ed. Gillian Whitlock), 8 (2008), 130-57.

[31] Marilyn Lake, 'The Politics of Respectability: Identifying the Masculinist Context', *Historical Studies*, 22 (1986), 116-31.

that the bush values were mainly 'the projection onto the outback of values revered by an alienated urban intelligentsia' rather than an autochthonous set of beliefs engendered in the bush, recorded in folk tale as a result, and later taken up by the *Bulletin* writers before spreading across the country as a national myth.[32] In Davison's account, the alienating effects of the 1890s depression on the large group of journalists and writers that the growth of newspapers and magazines had brought together in central Sydney are crucial. The dismal, sometimes apocalyptic view of city life, according to Davison, drew upon a longstanding British tradition of 'rhetorical, quasi-religious verse which descended from the late eighteenth century through Blake and Shelley ... [to] the radical movements of the 1870s and 1880s' and came into Australia via James Thomson and then Francis Adams's *Songs of the Army of the Night* (Sydney, 1888).[33] As far as Lawson – a city dweller, mainly, from the age of 15 – is concerned, a little digging shows that the dates fit, and helps to explain the derivative nature of his early verse. Adams's 'little volume of poems' was 'received' by the *Sydney Morning Herald* on 6 February 1888. Lawson's 'Army of the Rear' was published in the *Bulletin* on 12 May (as 'Song of the Outcasts'), and his rousing 'Faces in the Street' on 28 July. He recalled of the former: 'I can't remember writing it or where I got the idea from'.[34]

Armed with the emerging feminist perspectives of the 1980s, Marilyn Lake pushed the case about the Bushman myth harder, and in a different direction. Starting with the claim that 'The *Bulletin* was the most influential exponent of the separatist model of masculinity which lay at the heart of the eulogies to the Bushman',[35] Lake portrays the nationalist myth about the Bushman as homogeneous and dominant, and she then traces the gradual amelioration of its deleterious effects for women through the Harvester Judgement of 1907 and other legal

---

[32] Graeme Davison, 'Sydney and the Bush: An Urban Context for the Australian Legend', *Historical Studies*, 18 (1978), 191–209 [p. 208].
[33] *Ibid.*, p. 202.
[34] HL, 'A Fragment of Autobiography' (1903–08), in *Autobiographical* 212.
[35] Lake, 'The Politics of Respectability', p. 118.

measures that would provide incentives for men to become honest, sober and industrious supporters of home and hearth rather than to go on thinking of themselves as still somehow part of Ward's 'nomad tribe', wandering from station to station in search of work in the outback.

To what extent this had been a masculine preference for an irresponsible family-free existence as opposed to an economic necessity caused by the depression of the 1890s remains a complicating factor. The easy attraction of versifying the former because of its airy outdoor freedoms, as opposed to the gloominess of the latter, was always going to skew the literary evidence. But in fact Lawson covered both sides of the case, and in his prose the personal and social costs as well as the consolations in mateship – on the track and elsewhere – are registered, whether in a spirit of compassion or of fun.

In characterising the *Bulletin* Lake's strongest evidence, rhetorically-speaking, comes from the least responsible sources: *Bulletin* cartoons and editorial quips, nearly all of 1886–88, and from simple pounding verse more likely to recirculate clichés, sentimentalities and pieties. The potentially subtler workings of fiction of the period, especially but not only Lawson's, go unconsidered. Lake's broad brush inevitably ignores the finer-grained evidence. For example, 'Henry Lawson, unhappily married, returned again and again in his verse to the pleasures of the "careless roaming life" and the nobility of the love between men encountered on the track'.[36] Lake illustrates this with a quotation from 'The Vagabond', published in the *Bulletin* on 31 August 1895 when Lawson was still a bachelor. The poem, which Lake cites from *Winnowed Verses* in a 1944 reprint (and which therefore speaks to its 1940s moment of production as much as to 1895), is actually about the pleasures of going to sea.

Lake also narrows the *Bulletin* letterpress into a single voice ('The Sydney *Bulletin* liked to believe . . .', 'the *Bulletin* portrayed . . .', 'the masculinist press', 'In the *Bulletin*'s view . . .') when Sylvia Lawson had already demonstrated the multi-voiced cacophony – the 'print circus' –

---

36 *Ibid.*, p. 121.

of the weekly.³⁷ Lake's typifying remark that 'the "nationalist" school of writers represented the pastoral workers as cultural heroes' is given an erotic intensification when she claims that 'The lone bushman was these writers' love object'.³⁸ The first claim might be true if either the writers' beliefs could be shown to be identical to one another's and to the *Bulletin*'s, *or* if there were no competition at the time for this gender-ideological push. The late-colonial literary and journalistic marketplace, revealed in cross-section by the early reception of *While the Billy Boils* (explored in Chapters 8 and 11), rules out both alternatives. As for the second claim, in his stories and sketches of the 1890s, it is true that Lawson portrayed, for the men outback, the emotional push and pull of family or girlfriend left behind. But far from being a love object, the 'lone bushman' was usually an eccentric figure of fun or a sad, psychiatric case.

Lawson problematised mateship or placed it in an irretrievable past; he was not its single-minded celebrant. He often reacted against, as he simultaneously explored, an existing set of assumptions about contemporary male behaviours. Tonally subtle and emotionally complex as they often are, his stories and sketches usually resist historical or ideological categorising. Their testimony is more complex.³⁹

Kay Schaffer

Kay Schaffer's *Women and the Bush*, published in 1988 and based on a PhD of 1984, was another, more philosophically radical milestone in the feminist argument about the 1890s and its aftermath.⁴⁰ Starting

---

³⁷ *Ibid.*, pp. 118, 119, 127, 128. Sylvia Lawson, *The Archibald Paradox*, 1983 (see Chapter 2 above, pp. 50–2).
³⁸ Lake, 'The Politics of Respectability', pp. 120, 121.
³⁹ Cf. Christopher Lee, 'Looking for Mr Backbone: The Politics of Gender in the Work of Henry Lawson', in *The 1890s*, ed. Stewart, pp. 95–108. Lee grants Lake her case too readily, to my mind. But he shows that Lake's case does not apply to HL's subtly balanced, quietly despairing explorations of married life on selection farms in the Joe Wilson stories. If anything, 'Lawson's work endorses the logic of the women, the logic of the *Dawn*, the ideology of the family' (p. 108).
⁴⁰ Kay Schaffer, *Women and the Bush: Forces of Desire in the Australian Cultural Tradition* (Cambridge: Cambridge University Press, 1988); 'The Place of Woman in the Australian Tradition: An Analysis of the Discourse', PhD diss., University of Pittsburgh, 1984 (facsimile from University Microfilms International, Ann Arbor, Mich.).

from the presupposition that we are all 'constituted through a linguistic system of meanings', she offers the book as a study of 'the Australian tradition as a discourse' of national identity that marginalises women by 'reading' them, along with the land, as alien, as the 'other' that frustrates male endeavour to conquer or enclose it. Such 'subject/object operations of Western discourse' undergird 'the masculinity of the cultural order', which ought therefore to be found expressed in the 'definitive texts', as she calls them in her PhD dissertation, of the Australian tradition: by Nettie Palmer, W. H. Hancock, Vance Palmer and Russel Ward.

Accordingly, Lawson is a special focus of her study: not 'the man himself' but rather 'the cultural object, handed down to Australians through commentary and cultural practice'.[41] While it must be clear to any reader of the present book that study of the reception of Lawson's writings can be peculiarly revealing as forming part of the 'life' of the works, the temptation to disconnect them from 'the man himself' is no longer necessary – liberating though it must have been for Schaffer and other feminists to frame their arguments solely as discursive critique.

The traditional understandings of 'author' and 'works', confining as they were, needed, I agree, to be burst open: there is more on this topic in Chapter 13. But the move immediately created, for Schaffer, a new other-ing of its own in the explanatory regime she was proposing – discourse on the one hand versus the 'man himself' on the other – even though binary oppositions are consciously identified by her as expressions of the central problem of the Western tradition needing to be exposed and superseded.[42]

Unfortunately, with the new binary went a de-agenting of the individual, a de-privileging of the writing event and the publication event, and a floating temporality for the newly revealed 'discourse'. This condition has, since Schaffer's book appeared, frequently proved to be the case with discursive critique. We employ it because it lends

---

[41] Schaffer, *Women and the Bush*, pp. 10, 15, 111, 112; 'The Place of Woman', pp. 13, 39.
[42] See the list of binary oppositions under the headings 'Typical Australian' and 'Other': Schaffer, *Women and the Bush*, pp. 19–20.

argumentation a generalising sweep and rhetorical power. But insofar as it abandons the field of the empirically verifiable, of which chronology and agency are key vectors, discourse analysis encourages evidential shortcuts and sometimes only gestural argument.

For Schaffer to take this route was to grant as historically accurate whatever claims were made in Lawson's name about 'the man himself', since his status was now reduced to that of 'cultural object', at each and every critic's pleasure. The historical slide in phrases such as 'the bushman-cum-digger'[43] shows Schaffer's basic acceptance of Ward's historical case, even as she reached for a more fundamental ground on which to revaluate its meanings and implications. This retreat into a historical naivety is remarkable now, in hindsight: even though it seemed to many at the time like a fearless breakthrough.

The problem is now, rather, how are the two domains, the discursive and the empirical, to be brought into productive relationship? Chapter 13 addresses this question more directly as one of literary methodology. What may, perhaps, already be claimed is that book-historical and bibliographic methodologies that do not lose touch with agented events and material forms but try to answer the questions that they raise have the capacity to reveal the cultural indexing that long-lived literary works always perform.

What indexing may be drawn from the preceding discussion? First, there are bibliographic-sociological implications. If, as I suggested at the beginning of Chapter 10, there is a heterochronic moment of writing for the individual author so can there be one for a social myth. The 1950s – the period in which Ward came into his own as a historian – saw a concerted effort to collect the ballads of colonial Australia, many of which, as Ward's bibliography shows, provided his primary source material (and that of his friend Vance Palmer too). Ward overlooked the moment of their collection. He had eyes only for their content. There had been an effort of collection and publication of colonial ballads and songs

---

[43] *Ibid.*, p. 115.

in the 1860s (four collections, including the *Queenslanders' New Colonial Camp Fire Song Book* and those by George Chanson and by Alexander Forbes); an increased number in the 1880s probably attributable to the Centenary celebrations in 1888 (six, including *Tibb's Popular Australian Songs and Poems*; the *'Native Companion' Songster* and two of Douglas Sladen's collections published in London). There was a falling-off of publishing interest in the 1890s (just as there had been in the 1870s), until Banjo Paterson notably contributed his reworked *Old Bush Songs* (1905), one of four collections in the 1900s decade. Thereafter there was another lull until the 1950s when at least nineteen were published (e.g. the collections by Hugh Anderson, Vance Palmer and Margaret Sutherland, Douglas Stewart and Nancy Keesing, Bill Wannan, John Manifold, John Meredith, and Marjorie Pizer).[44] This trend continued, decade by decade, peaking in the 1980s, probably again associated with national celebrations, this time the Bicentenary.

The postwar development was paralleled by a similar pattern, beginning slightly earlier, in the collection and publication of bushranging tales and also of a new mythologising of Ned Kelly in print and paint.[45] Regathering the colonial heritage, in its intertwined

[44] These (provisional) figures – which exclude single-author collections of poetry, some of which included verse in ballad form – derive from a search of the NLA catalogue using Library of Congress subject headings relating to ballads, and checked against the AUSTLIT database ('anthologies of poetry': it does not distinguish poetic forms) and bibliographies in published collections of ballads and monographs on ballads. A more thorough search might discover more. Nevertheless, the relativities by decade are striking, as is the fact that the 1890s decade does not stand out: 1860s (4 collections), 1870s (1), 1880s (6), 1890s (2), 1900s (4), 1910s (2), 1920s (2), 1930s (2), 1940s (2), 1950s (19).

[45] My study of the publishing history of *Robbery Under Arms* and of Ned Kelly's Jerilderie Letter (and the various adaptations of his story) shows they followed the same pattern. See Eggert, 'The Bibliographic Life of an Australian Classic: *Robbery Under Arms*', *Script & Print*, 29 (2005), 73–92; this article supplements the account in the Introduction to the Academy Edition of *Robbery Under Arms*, ed. Paul Eggert and Elizabeth Webby (St Lucia: University of Queensland Press, 2005). See also Eggert: 'Peter Carey's *True History of the Kelly Gang*' and 'New Life for the Colonial Classic *Robbery Under Arms*' in *Paper Empires: A History of the Book in Australia*, vol. 3 *1946–2004*, ed. Craig Munro and Robin Sheahan-Bright (St Lucia: University of Queensland Press, 2006), pp. 195–8 and 260–3; 'Textual Criticism and Folklore: The Ned Kelly Story and *Robbery Under Arms*', *Script & Print*, 31 (2007), 69–80; 'The Bushranger's Voice: Peter Carey's *True History of the Kelly Gang* (2000) and Ned Kelly's Jerilderie Letter (1879)', *College Literature*, 34 (2007), 120–39 and at www.austlit.edu.au in *The AustLit Anthology of Criticism*, ed. Leigh Dale and Linda Hale (2010).

but sometimes conflicting strands, into a contemporary national identity took various forms at this time. For instance, on 17 June 1949 an Australian stamp was issued featuring a bust-portrait of Henry Lawson. The design was based on a drypoint by Lionel Lindsay and included a reproduction of Lawson's signature: 109,252,000 copies were printed and circulated throughout the country. There was no special Lawson anniversary needing to be commemorated in this way in 1949. Rather, he was the fourth of five public figures to be thus honoured. The colonial explorer Thomas Mitchell had been accorded the philatelic guerdon in 1946, the wheat researcher William Farrer and colonial botanist Ferdinand von Mueller in 1948. The explorer and first premier of Western Australia throughout the 1890s, Sir John Forrest, would be the last in 1949. The fact that all these designs were issued on stamps at the ordinary letter rate (21/2d.) guaranteed them the widest distribution.

Yet a further indicator that Ward, while attributing his Australian Legend to the 1890s, was a good deal wide of the mark chronologically is provided by economic statistics. If income can be regarded as a proxy indicator of the 'egalitarian collectivism' he claimed was at the heart of the tradition then he definitely mistook the relevant decade. Income disparity between the richest and poorest Australians reduced markedly in the 1940s and 50s from what it had been earlier in the century (and very probably in the 1890s). The income disparity kept reducing, reaching its lowest point in 1980;[46] and, by then (appropriately for a re-dating of the Legend),

---

[46] This is according to the Federal politician and former academic economist, Andrew Leigh in a speech given to the Sydney Institute on 1 May 2012, and partly based on his studies of the historical series of records of Australian and New Zealand annual taxation returns: e.g. Anthony B. Atkinson and Andrew Leigh, 'Top Incomes in New Zealand 1921–2005: Understanding the Effects of Marginal Tax Rates, Migration Threat and the Macroeconomy', *Review of Income and Wealth*, 54 (2007), 149–65.

In the 1910s and 1920s, the richest 1 percent of Australians had 12 percent of national income – 12 times their proportionate share. By the mid-1950s, this was down to 8 percent. By 1980, it was down to 5 percent.

You can see the same pattern if you look further up the distribution, at the richest 0.1 percent – the 1/1000th of Australians with the highest incomes. Back in the 1910s and 1920s, the top 0.1 percent had about 4 percent of household income – 40 times their proportionate share. By the 1950s, this had fallen to 2 percent, and by 1980, it was down to 1 percent. Under the Prime Ministership of Malcolm Fraser, the share of income held by the richest 1/1000th of Australians was only a quarter of what it had been under Billy Hughes.

Lawson's image had been on the Australian ten-dollar note for fourteen years. The disparity has been widening ever since 1980. Appropriately, if a little belatedly for the Legend, Lawson's image was removed in 1993.

These factors and statistics point towards a significant conclusion: that Ward's Australian Legend of the 1890s is more a creation of the twentieth century, and especially of the 1950s. Ward allows that 'A myth, after all, relates to past events, real or imaginary' (194); but he did not see the application to his own writing. Although elements of Ward's Legend were undoubtedly seeded in the more widely literate culture of the 1890s, they did not reach their influential peak until his own decade. And Lawson, especially in his prose, continued to be invoked as its peculiarly important witness.

The feminist historians and commentators needed Ward to be right if his conclusions were to be turned back on him. But in doing so, they strained the evidence unacceptably. One rhetorical closure was effected at the expense of 'blotting out' the other's, while both – understandably for their successive periods – glided over what can only now for the first time be properly appreciated as the book-historical evidence.

So what may we conclude about the nationalists of the 1950s? As I have observed, the slow tide of nationalism that swept through country after country in continental Europe and Scandinavia in the nineteenth century was delayed and differently expressed in settler cultures like Australia's. There were periodic upwellings (the 1890s, and especially strongly in the aftermath of World War II) but also lulls; and then another slow build-up from the 1970s can be discerned in the patterns

---

The collapse of the super-rich is vividly portrayed in William Rubinstein's book *The All-Time Australian 200 Rich List*. Published in 2004, the list covers the all-time richest 200 Australians, from Samuel Terry to Kerry Packer. The cut-off for inclusion in the book is that you had to have wealth of 0.17 percent of GDP, equivalent to $2.7 billion today.

Because Rubinstein's book covers 200 people and about two centuries, you'd expect an entrant every year or so. But the striking thing is that for four decades, from 1940 to 1980, there wasn't a single Australian wealthy enough to make the all-time rich list. For example, Rubinstein points out that in the 1940s and 1950s, there were probably only a handful of people worth more than £1 million, and no-one worth more than £8 million (the cutoff necessary to make the all-time rich list in 1955).

(www.andrewleigh.com/blog/?p=2521, accessed 6 May 2012)

of Australiana and literary-heritage publishing up until the Australian Bicentennial in 1988, before it was overwhelmed, once again, by the international stylistic influences of the postmodern early 1990s. (This is discussed in the next chapter.)

Reactions against the 1890s, especially from feminist critics in the 1980s, must then be read as having partially missed their target for they too ignored the book-historical framework of the myth-busting in which they were so urgently engaged. Much of what has been called the ethos of the 1890s happened later, and Lawson's fate in the marketplace indexes that cultural unfolding.

The professional postwar literary critics

Just as post-World War II critics found language in which to describe the technical innovation of the first-person vernacular narration of *Robbery Under Arms*, so too did they learn to articulate in more-or-less technical terms some of the achievement of Lawson's prose.[47] Nettie Palmer foreshadowed the change. Her private journal of 1925–39 (published as *Fourteen Years* in 1948) anticipates the postwar swing to a privileged aesthetic sphere and absorbs some of the international influences that would result in the New Criticism of the 1940s and after. She deploys a rhetoric of 'shape and significance', of successful prose fiction being 'like a poem', and of completeness: 'A short story must have its own perfection, or it is nothing. The element of completeness, of art, must enter into it so that it lives as a whole in the mind'.[48] The aesthetic

---

[47] The New Zealander Frank Sargeson made the interpretative breakthrough with *Robbery Under Arms* in 1950: see the Introduction to the Academy Edition, ed. Eggert and Webby, pp. lxxix–lxxx.

[48] *Fourteen Years: Extracts from a Private Journal 1925–1939* (Melbourne: Meanjin Press, 1948), pp. 22–3. The entry on HL is given as 9 February 1927, but her actual diary entries were selectively reassembled and revised for publication c. 1947: see Vivian Smith's Editor's Note in *Nettie Palmer: Her Private Journal 'Fourteen Years', Poems, Reviews and Literary Essays* (St Lucia: University of Queensland Press, 1988), pp. 2–5. Cf. F. R. Leavis's series of postwar articles in *Scrutiny* considering various novels and novellas as 'dramatic poems' (e.g. in vol. 17 (1950–51) in relation to D. H. Lawrence's *St. Mawr* and *Women in Love*).

H. M. Green's formulations in his *History* often collapsed the distance between HL's style and subject matter (e.g., see pp. 533, 532), but the newly available idea of works as organic wholes lent a support to HL not present in his earlier *Outline*. Cleanth Brooks and Robert

standards that A. G. Stephens had advocated were being ratcheted-up to a higher notch.

Her identification of Lawson's 'easy, colloquial voice' as the vehicle that 'takes you straight into his own intimate world'[49] was new. Indeed it was almost a technical comment: she saw that it is what makes Lawson stand out from the other short story authors of the 1890s in the *Bulletin*, whose writings she had been reading her way through. 'Who invented the legend', she complains, 'that a band of brilliant short-story writers existed in the 'nineties, and that in examining the files of the *Bulletin* one would stumble upon masterpieces?'[50] Apart from Lawson, she reports, it is not so.

A. A. Phillips and Frederick Macartney

In that same year, 1948, A. A. Phillips noted that previous critics such as Edward Garnett had praised Lawson's apparent artlessness, only then to half-complain of it.[51] But, Phillips observed, Lawson 'had to learn how to be successfully "slight," to find just how little plot he could afford to use without risking the collapse of the structure'. He noted that his 'easy natural glide into the story' helped Lawson give effect to his 'two consciously used devices – effective understatement, and the ironic twist at the danger-points'. Phillips added that Lawson was 'a master of this final reverberation', a method used 'too often and too carefully for it

---

Penn Warren's *Understanding Poetry* (1938, multiple printings of the first few editions; 4th edn 1976) was one source of the new critical vocabulary, which was widely shared.

So Green could now claim, in discussing '[Enter Mitchell]' and 'Mitchell: A Character Sketch', that 'in each there is scarcely a word that is not needed; almost every word is the right one, each is in its place and there is a point in every paragraph; they are almost perfect little organisms from which it would seem impossible to omit a line.' On the other hand, 'The Drover's Wife' 'is less of an organic whole ... there are a few clichés; and ... the pathos, particularly in the final paragraph is a little overweighted' (*ibid.*, pp. 546–7).

[49] N. Palmer, *Fourteen Years*, p. 22; and cf. her commendation of Dick Marston's first-person narration of *Robbery Under Arms* as a 'pleasant expressive idiom' (*ibid.*, p. 28).

[50] *Ibid.*, p. 22.

[51] Arthur Phillips, 'Henry Lawson as Craftsman' *Meanjin*, 7 (1948), 80–90; and see Chapter 8 for Garnett and also for A. G. Stephens's review of *Billy Boils*, which strikes the same note. Phillips also quotes another example: David McKee Wright's claiming, in the Red Page of the *Bulletin*: 'As a writer of prose [HL] can hardly be said to have acquired a style' (p. 81). Phillips further developed his account in chap. 5 of his *Henry Lawson* (New York: Twayne, 1970).

to be accident or intuition': in this, 'Lawson and Chekhov have touched hands'.⁵²

Frederick T. Macartney's bio-critical entry on Lawson in *Australian Literature: A Bibliography* was published in 1956, eight years after Phillips's essay. By then, Macartney felt able both to confirm the existing judgement that 'Lawson in his stories escapes the limitations sometimes imposed on him by verse' *and* point to the 'originality of his technique': 'He writes as one of them ['people of the working class'], creating a familiarity progressing to the total effect.' Macartney refers to Lawson's 'casually natural narrative' and argues that his prose 'cannot be said to owe much to the influence of any particular writer': Kipling 'writes from the middle-class point of view of his time and more as an observer. Lawson creates an impression like that of a bush worker telling a tale prompted by the scenes around him.'⁵³

Nettie Palmer and Macartney were both literary journalists, and Phillips was a headmaster; but the 1950s and 1960s saw a new, firmer professionalising of literary criticism in Australia. An appeal to international standards, and to tighter notions of the aesthetic than traditional belles-lettristic criticism had countenanced, was more or less inevitable, especially in relation to Australian writing as it gradually became established in university courses. Criticism of it needed to survive in a professional discourse that had hitherto found its touchstones abroad. A new outlook and tone of authority, and a willingness to ask difficult and iconoclastic questions, came with the professionalising.⁵⁴

G. A. Wilkes, Stephen Murray-Smith and Brian Kiernan

In 1958 G. A. Wilkes published an essay querying the importance that the Australian 1890s had come to have. The standards he brought to

---

⁵² Phillips, 'Henry Lawson as Craftsman', pp. 82, 85, 87, 86, 87, 88. Some of the alterations that A. W. Jose called for to the endings of stories and sketches on printer's copy of *Billy Boils* show a tone-deafness on his part and a purposefulness on HL's (see Eggert and Webby, textual apparatus).
⁵³ E. Morris Miller and Frederick T. Macartney, *Australian Literature: A Bibliography to 1938 Extended to 1950* (Sydney: A&R, 1956), p. 283.
⁵⁴ Dale's *The English Men* is illuminating and fair on this topic.

bear were self-consciously international and aesthetic. He was intent on distinguishing the literary significance of the decade from the political and the social. In the essay, he allows that the 1890s writers were 'more successful than any before in capturing popular taste', but that 'The true greatness of any literary period, however, is to be estimated by other standards besides these'. He argues that the self-conscious Australianising of literary subject matter in the 1890s is what typically oversimplified its verse and crippled its short fiction: 'this was an age of minor authors', he concludes. Only Lawson and Furphy escape his stricture: Lawson, because he simply takes the Australian environment 'for granted, and get[s] on with the story.' 'Lawson is memorable not for the part of his work – his verse – that reflects the temper of the age, but for the part that transcends it'.[55]

This invoking of the notion that true art necessarily transcends mere 'transcripts of environment' – which were proper to the study of history – became a common one in literary critical evaluations in the 1960s and 1970s, right up until it was undermined as a concept by the poststructuralist movement in the 1980s. It may have been in part born of a felt need to entrench 'English' as a university discipline. It is interesting in any case that the anxiety broadened to the encroachments of sociology upon literary criticism in the 1970s, as we will shortly see. Nevertheless, Wilkes hit the nail on the head when he pointed out that the 1890s ballad and short story of 'marked local colour' was 'but one element in the output of the time'. This needed to be recalled because 'There has been another inflating process at work. As the nineties receded in time, they found a more lively existence – a second life – in anecdote and recollection'.[56] *Henry Lawson by his Mates* (1931) and Jose's *The Romantic Nineties* (1933) are relevant cases in point. The process would become manifest in the essentialising of the role of the *Bulletin* in subsequent nationalist accounts.

[55] G. A. Wilkes, 'The Eighteen Nineties', *Arts*, 1 (1958), 17–26, reprinted in *Australian Literary Criticism*, ed. Grahame Johnston (Melbourne: Oxford University Press, 1962), pp. 30–40 [pp. 33, 34, 37, 40].
[56] *Ibid.*, pp. 40, 33, 34.

Stephen Murray-Smith, founding editor of *Overland* in 1954 and a member of the Communist Party of Australia for thirteen years, wrote a short biographical and critical overview of Lawson in 1962 for the Australian Writers and their Works series. Although affected by debate between *Overland* (est. 1954) and *Quadrant* (est. 1956) over the role of social realism and of working-class subject matter for novels,[57] his study, for which he had read widely, is surprisingly free of partisan comments. He does not count himself as amongst 'Lawson's apostles and supporters' and sturdily accepts the evaluative responsibility of the critic, almost as if the ideological divide did not exist, commenting: 'While Lawson's poetry needs a more adequate appraisal than it has received at the hands of recent critics, it is his stories and sketches that lift Lawson from the rank-and-file of the writers of his period . . . his natural ear was for the rhythms of the prose form rather than of verse'.[58]

Furthermore, Murray-Smith is acute about the failings of the Old Left with regard to Lawson. He confutes the easy equation of socialism and mateship in the 1890s and points out that the fact that the trades union movement created the Labor Party, rather than the other way around, meant there would be no intellectual leadership that might have given the movement a principled or theoretically informed consistency; that instead it would be only pragmatic and empirical. Thus Lawson's disenchantment with the trades union movement, and his loss of radicalism, need, he urges, to be acknowledged but more generously understood.

In accepting his evaluative responsibility as a critic, Murray-Smith could not quite let go of one old piety of the Left. He aimed a barb at

---

[57] David Carter notes that one effect of the studies of the so-called Australian tradition by Vance Palmer, A. A. Phillips and Russel Ward was that 'Realism and democracy, it was assumed, went together ... When *Overland* magazine began in 1954, connected to the Communist Party and the Realist Writers movement, it could name itself heir to a continuous democratic and realist Australian tradition'. The advent of Patrick White's *Tree of Man* in 1955 and *Voss* in 1957, neither of which fitted the tradition, would prove an insurmountable problem for the nationalists but not for the professional critics in the universities: Carter, 'Critics, Writers, Intellectuals: Australian Literature and its Criticism', in *The Cambridge Companion to Australian Literature*, ed. Elizabeth Webby (Cambridge: Cambridge University Press, 2000), pp. 258–93 [p. 271 and cf. pp. 275–6].

[58] Stephen Murray-Smith, *Henry Lawson* (Melbourne: Lansdowne Press, 1962), pp. 7, 37.

the professional literary critics of the day but gave it a nice, historicising twist far more likely in Australia at the time to come from the Marxist critic than the New Critic or Leavisite:

> a reading, say, of *Henry Lawson by his Mates*, the book of recollections published in 1931, shows that, while his stories were regarded with reverence, his verses lingered in people's minds, influenced their thoughts and actions, moved them, inspired them and were made their own.
>
> The critics of today who regard Lawson's verse as beneath contempt betray an aloof particularity that chills the blood. This verse cannot be considered *per se*, neglecting the circumstances of its writing and reception and its effect on the Australia of the day.

Murray-Smith also took aim at another piety that the Lawson legend had been generating over the decades since his death: 'To talk of Lawson as a "tragic" figure is to miss the point that the existential tragedy is a component of all our lives'.[59]

The widely felt Existentialist dilemma of the postwar period – Brian Kiernan writes of it in 1971 as 'the estrangement of the individual from society' – helps explain the attraction and currency of the idea that literary works could transcend their period. In his book *Poetry and Morality* of 1959, the Melbourne critic Vincent Buckley characterised F. R. Leavis's position thus: 'What his criticism has always pointed to . . . is the fact of great literature as transcending a merely individual consciousness, even while it remains firmly rooted in such a consciousness. The universal character of literature is seen to be of a nearly religious kind'.[60]

The consequent sense of mission for literary critics – their identification and elucidation of the transcendent meaning to be found in literary works – helps explain local inflections of Leavisite criticism in Australia. But, as shared use of the term 'transcendent' shows, the Leavisite tag itself merely denoted the more strenuous expression of a view of the role of criticism that was widely felt. As Kiernan put it, aesthetic 'works of the imagination', each considered as 'an autonomous,

---

[59] *Ibid.*, pp. 31–2, 7.
[60] Vincent Buckley, *Poetry and Morality: Studies on the Criticism of Matthew Arnold, T. S. Eliot and F. R. Leavis* (London: Chatto & Windus, 1959), p. 196.

imaginative creation', needed to be treated 'in its own metaphorical and dramatic terms' and 'not as a document in literary or social history'. That meant that the attempt of the cultural nationalists to draw a tradition of Australian writing from the 1890s was doomed since it intermixed the truly literary with irrelevant subject matter: what Kiernan calls mere 'social documentation'.[61] If there was a tradition that could be identified from a study of Australian *literary* works then that was the critic's higher role.[62]

So Kiernan follows Wilkes, asserting that properly literary judgement is essential; and, in his 1974 booklet *Criticism* in the Australian Writers and their Work series, Kiernan argues that H. M. Green had only confused matters and led to a critical stalemate by judging the writers of the 1890s by either 'universalist' or 'localist' standards, 'whichever he feels most appropriate to a particular case'. The result has been that 'For the best part of thirty years, the "Australian tradition" has provided literary critics with the basic framework of ideas and issues. Possibly what is needed if literary criticism is to engage again with the wider culture, and to escape from mechanical exercises in "practical criticism", is a new development in historiography.'[63] He sees this as most likely to

---

[61] Brian Kiernan, 'The Australian Novel and Tradition', in his *Images of Society and Nature: Seven Essays on Australian Novels* (Melbourne: Oxford University Press, 1971), p. 172, 159, viii, 159. Cf. F. R. Leavis's early commentary on the admixture of the literary and the sociological, 'Sociology and Literature', *Scrutiny*, 13 (1945–46), 74–81.

This argument delayed the broader acceptance of Australian literature courses. As a young lecturer in English at La Trobe University in the early 1980s I heard a variant of it – only those Australian works that could stand up to the same high evaluative standards as the British and American ones we taught should be on the syllabus – urged against a proposal to introduce an alternative First Year course that would be in Australian literature alone, justified on the basis of its windfall benefit of talking directly to our students' own experience. As Leigh Dale observes, Vincent Buckley had rejected such 'sociological' justifications (*English Men*, p. 161).

[62] There was a history to this ambitious claim. Vance Palmer had tilted in this general direction in 1935 when he commented, in the context of a newspaper debate about the future of Australian literature: 'there are columns of gossip about books and authors in all our papers, but little sense of values. Criticism in Australia has lagged badly behind creative work' (quoted in Dale, *English Men*, p. 152). In Adelaide, *Desiderata* (see n. 21 above) saw itself as accepting this responsibility in the 1930s.

[63] Brian Kiernan, *Criticism* (Melbourne: Oxford University Press, 1974), pp. 37, 46. In 1963 Leonie Kramer had argued similarly: 'criticism cannot fulfil its proper function if it rests on a narrow basis of nationalistic fervour or provincial self-consciousness': 'Literary Criticism in Australia', *Overland*, no. 26 (April 1963), 25–7 [p. 27]. Cf. also John Docker's account of

come from historians on the New Left such as Humphrey McQueen.

But this prognosis sits ill with the final sentence in the booklet where he says that he agrees with other critics that 'we are moving towards a higher state of cultural development and that literature will both express this and help us to attain it.'[64] Literary criticism must therefore articulate the necessary tradition for creative writers. Unfortunately, this belief cast critics as a priestly class who would nurture and license the writers. This was never going to happen. It was pure illusion, although a logical development of the special cultural significance of the literary critic's role, as Kiernan and others saw it. No wonder that Michael Wilding and his group were busily shaking off the nationalist tradition in their creative writing at more or less the same time and looking for inspiration and examples elsewhere – though whether they were shaking off Lawson, or the short-story tradition that had subsequently been attached to his name, is another matter entirely.[65] Nevertheless, Kiernan's sense of the

---

the social mission of literature and criticism encouraged by *Meanjin* in the 1940s and 50s: *Australian Cultural Elites*, chap. 6. Clem Christesen was the founding editor of *Meanjin*, 1940–74. By 1943, as David Carter observes, it was seen as a serious reviewing journal, distant 'from "mere" journalism'. It helped bring about 'a new confidence in talk about an Australian tradition' especially in the late 1940s: 'Critics, Writers, Intellectuals', p. 270.

[64] Kiernan, *Criticism*, p. 47.

[65] Certainly the identification of HL with the tradition they were reacting against was deliberate. Cf. *(1)* Murray-Smith in 1962: 'Today, perhaps, we often feel the need to revolt against what many have come to feel is the dead hand of the nineties holding us back from uninhibited cultural expression; and it is true, as I have said, that the success of Lawson has encouraged to this day a host of worthless imitators' (*Henry Lawson*, p. 32). Cf. *(2)* Michael Wilding in 1978: 'So there is the nationalist cult of the short story, with Henry Lawson as the particular native genius and the fount and source. The Australian story began with Lawson, the myth read: so anthology after anthology was produced beginning with Lawson ... A narrow, reduced tradition of the short story took its increasingly barren way on; it became established, enshrined, protected and the literary magazines gave it a home': Afterword to *The Tabloid Story Pocket Book*, ed. Wilding (Sydney: Wild and Woolley, 1978), pp. 303–4. Cf. *(3)* Frank Moorhouse in 2007: 'as with all young writers, my group also saw itself as essentially severed from the older Australian writers and certainly from the "bush school"': 'On Being a Writer in Australia', *Australian Author*, 39.1 (April 2007), 7.

However, in a review of Douglas Stewart's collection *Short Stories of Australia: The Lawson Tradition* (1967), which contained stories up until 1940, John Barnes challenged Stewart's claim for the existence of a Lawson 'school' of short story writers: 'Lawson and the Short Story in Australia', *Westerly*, no. 2 (July 1968), 83–7. In 1981 Elizabeth Webby remarkably extended the challenge, arguing that the realists of the first half of the twentieth century were like HL only in subject matter or locale but not in style or approach. She concludes that 'the so-called Lawson tradition' was 'distinctly mythical' and that Hal Porter and Frank

looming stalemate of critical method was real enough; he would himself in due course see a way through the dilemma. Once again, it would be in relation to Lawson. (This is dealt with in Chapter 13.)

Brian Matthews

A more coherent approach, and in a less strenuous vein, was adopted in Brian Matthews's *The Receding Wave*. The first book-length study of Lawson's prose by a professional literary critic, it was published by Melbourne University Press in 1972, in between Kiernan's two accounts; but it is, in some of its operating assumptions, consonant with Kiernan's.

Matthews's first chapter, 'Beginnings', sets the scene for his account of Lawson's development into a major writer. He examines first 'The Union Buries its Dead' and then 'The Drover's Wife'. The chapter has a firm narrative thrust about Lawson's growing powers and humanistic insight, one that is picked up nicely in the next two chapters about the later Joe Wilson stories. Matthews evaluates 'The Union Buries its Dead' with some shrewd commentary about the rag-tag burial of the drowned man whose name is unknown:

> the ruthlessness of the portrayal is too eager: the grim logic, the over-conscious detachment, the complete inversion of the accepted are all so trenchantly done that they evoke often the opposite effects. It is nihilistic and ruthless, but unsure; Lawson too eagerly rejects the sympathetic possibilities of the incident and the result is that his most vigorous assaults on sentimentality become in themselves sentimental by implication.

Lawson's intention is 'to disturb, to menace us by the horror of veracity'. Comparing the burial scene to one in Albert Camus's Existentialist novel *The Outsider*, Matthews concludes that 'Lawson lacked the literary tradition, sophisticated society and, indeed, the rich scholastic resources which helped Camus to achieve [his] lucid control and civilised irony, and which supplied the cutting edge of restraint.'[66]

Moorhouse are more like HL in their self-conscious awareness of audience than the earlier writers who were supposed to be part of his 'school' ('Australian Short Fiction', p. 147).
[66] Brian Matthews, *The Receding Wave* (Melbourne: Melbourne University Press, 1972), pp. 8, 11, 12.

In 'The Drover's Wife', which Matthews then goes on to discuss, 'the same ruthless pessimism is evident' but finally the story 'implies that human attributes may well be the ennobling and enduring consolation in a ruthless and spiritually debilitating environment . . . [L]ife remains hard, cruel, potentially tragic, but human worth rescues it from being a bad joke'. Matthews accordingly judges it 'the more accomplished story in many ways'; it represents 'an important stage in Lawson's attempts to communicate the powerful impressions of the land and its people'.[67]

Apparently at a late stage in the writing of this book some new bibliographical information came to Matthews's attention. It may have been Colin Roderick's 'Commentary' in his 1970 edition of *The Bush Undertaker and Other Stories*, based on inspection of the printer's copy for *While the Billy Boils* in the Mitchell Library (A1867–8). What Matthews now had to face was that his case about the superiority of 'The Drover's Wife' did not square with the chronology of composition: that the supposedly inferior 'The Union Buries its Dead' 'it appears, was the later story of the two' – as in fact it is.[68] Matthews acknowledges the anomaly but, since he had no way of fusing it with his humanist evaluation, he simply passes over it, leaving this part of his narrative of Lawson's development of his narrative art (a rise and fall, when we are still at this point on the rise) curiously unsupported by chronological particulars. So he also misses the development in Lawson's narrative experiments of 1892 and especially 1893, and shows, in this book, little interest in the results of Lawson's trip to Bourke in late 1892.

Matthews's chapter 2, called 'The Drover's Wife Writ Large' and reprinted from *Meanjin* where a version of it had appeared in 1968, deals with the Joe Wilson stories, focussing on '"Water Them Geraniums"'. Once again the commentary is adeptly sensitised to the prose and moves in widening circles. He describes the story's 'personal, looser, less cryptic and less consciously tight-lipped style' and refers to the 'master strokes which so frequently lie beneath the deceptive surfaces of Lawson's best

[67] Ibid., pp. 12, 15, 16, 15.
[68] Ibid., p. 14.

work; so completely integrated into the mood and spirit of the writing that the effect is wrought almost on the subconscious'. Matthews goes on: 'Because they so constantly and consciously walk this knife-edge of madness Joe and Mary and Mrs Spicer have about them implicitly a pathetically intense desire to remain linked with some broader ill-defined stream of life', something the drover's wife herself cannot achieve. He concludes: 'they are fighting to remain in the human race'. With this eloquent declaration, Matthews is able to extract Lawson from the clutches of the old debate about his local or his universal representativeness and to insist that, with these stories, 'Lawson's art has assumed a breadth and power in relation to which the bush milieu of his stories no longer stands as a limiting factor.' Matthews praises this later 'Lawson's delicate understanding of man's desperate need to know himself involved in humanity (perhaps this is the real Lawson mateship) and his fear and horror when, for whatever reason, he begins to lose himself and his human landmarks in the labyrinths of alienation and endless physical stress'.[69]

The Existentialist dilemma, and the consequent obligation of the literary critic to find a countervailing source of lived value in literature, hang heavy over statements like this, which reach towards complete generality and in which the individual literary work becomes subsumed. This was taking Lawson out of the 'Australian Tradition' by bringing him into relation with broader contemporary concerns, while also demonstrating his right to a place in that international discourse.

No wonder the postwar period saw a disconnect between literary criticism and literary scholarship: the latter – referring to the full range of editorial, bibliographic, biographic and literary-history scholarship – was apt to seem only an irritating interruption to a more urgent moral and humanistic pursuit. Yet for his chronology of the Joe Wilson stories Matthews depends on Bertha Lawson's dating them as from their stay at the Native School in Mangamaunu in New Zealand (1897) where Lawson worked as a teacher. Thereafter, in Matthews's larger case about Lawson, a severe decline in quality sets in; it is dealt with in his later

[69] *Ibid.*, pp. 18, 19, 23, 24, 27.

CHAPTER 12 . LAWSON'S REPUTATION IN THE POSTWAR PERIOD

chapters. That case left Matthews with the obligation to explain how the more ambitious and resolved nature of these stories of marriage and family life, of 'the elusive intricacies of human relationships' on a selection, came about.[70]

He speculates that:

> Mangamaunu . . . forced upon Lawson what was for him a unique combination of circumstances: he was living in an isolation and a relative solitude which together encouraged, indeed virtually enjoined, introspection; his day-to-day relationship with his wife was a central, constant and somewhat obsessive element in his consciousness and not, as before, shared with a variety of distractions, no longer chronically interrupted by quixotic absences or frenetic sprees; and he was in an environment different and distanced from Australia, yet in some ways reminiscent of it. These, I think, were the indispensable conditions for the writing of *Joe Wilson*, the conditions which most informed and most shaped his masterpiece when he finally came to write it.[71]

In a footnote added late in production Matthews adds a reference to an article by Colin Roderick – which Matthews says he has not read because it is 'not in print at the time of writing' – demonstrating that the Joe Wilson stories were actually written in London some years later;[72] and there is an added and uneasy parenthesis on page 119 '(even though its [their] actual writing probably belongs to a later date)'.

Obviously there was a mismatch, but the times in which Matthews wrote were not propitious for resolving it. Biographical and bibliographical scholarship, and even literary history, were not in a fertile relationship with literary criticism. So, although Matthews's argument yearns for biographical support, it is methodologically cut off from a commitment to follow through, since the real action was taken to be elsewhere. (Much the same problem held for the New Critics, as we will see in Chapter 13.) The humanism was taken to be *in* the art. This was the province of the critic; it gave warrant to sensitised accounts of the writing. Yet critical accounts were, one sees in retrospect, accounts of

---

[70] *Ibid.*, p. 120.
[71] *Ibid.*, p. 120.
[72] *Ibid.*, p. 184.

the reading experience in the present, sensitive to the broader cultural needs of that present. As the critics reached for more general, moral-humanistic conclusions, they tended to conflate what had been published with their reading of it, or, put another way, to conflate the identified meanings in the reading present with the intention or achievement of the artist. Of course, the conflation lent the criticism, at its best, a seductive power. Under this critical gaze, the artist's life became merely secondary. Studying it was the province of the scholar not the critic. But without the scholarship the argued case of the critic was always going to be vulnerable. Lawson happens to provide a particularly clear case of it.

Matthews's account in his chapter 10 ('The Rise and Fall of Mitchell') of the evolution of this character's 'wry, sad, complex personality' provides another example that will help clarify the present argument. 'As Mitchell evolves', Matthews argues, he can be seen to be 'moving slowly in the direction of other complex characters: Mrs Spicer, Joe Wilson, Mary and Brighten's sister-in-law' – as opposed to the Steelman character who never changes. In the Mitchell stories, on the other hand, 'objects and aspects of the surroundings engender a momentary or cumulative tension without themselves achieving any symbolic status'.[73]

Matthews observes that 'Mitchell arrives quietly' in the first of the Mitchell stories in *While the Billy Boils*, '[Enter Mitchell]'. The critic next considers 'Another of Mitchell's Plans for the Future' (item no. 19 in the 1896 collection), then moves on to 'On the Edge of the Plain' (no. 16) and thence into the 'quiet symbolism' and deepened meaning of 'Shooting the Moon' (no. 25) and '"Some Day"' (no. 35). Thus it comes to seem that the sequence within the collection is roughly indicative of the relevant stage of the evolution in Lawson's writing.

In fact, as we saw in Chapter 4, '[Enter Mitchell]' was not a Mitchell story originally at all. It only became so in revision for the 1896 collection; indeed, the inscription changing the sketch's title of December 1894

---

[73] *Ibid.*, pp. 100, 102, 104.

from 'That Swag' may be Jose's.[74] So the argument about evolution becomes problematic: *when* is it to be considered as having happened? If it is late 1895–96 as the volume was being prepared for typesetting (as it must be if '[Enter Mitchell]' is to be considered as the first) then the other stories no longer fit the evolutionary arc. The next sketch mentioned, 'Another of Mitchell's Plans for the Future' dates from July 1893; 'On the Edge of the Plain' is May 1893; and 'Shooting the Moon' and '"Some Day"' are September 1894 and July 1893 respectively.

I do not adduce these facts in a spirit of one-upmanship. Far from it, as I admire the confident argumentation, as well as the sensitivity of the close readings that typify *The Receding Wave*. It is indeed, I think, one of the outstanding examples of postwar Australian literary criticism in book form. Yet its contribution to today's debate is not its offering us a reading of Lawson for all time, but rather its revelation of what it felt like to be reading Lawson in Matthews's professional position in the late 1960s and early 1970s in Australia. That it conflated the two kinds of report (for all time and everywhere as against for now and here) is the upshot of a methodology of literary criticism that enjoyed widespread support at the time and, as I have suggested, was an understandable response to the (by the early 1970s, ebbing) tide of Existentialism.[75] The facts that I have adduced also point, more generally, to the incompatibility of the two main forms of postwar endeavour in the literary field, despite the fundamental commitment to the importance of the aesthetic object that they shared. The literary-critical mode of reasoning was constantly tempted into narratives of meaning-making and cultural generalisation that the bibliographical, biographical and other contextual scholarship simply did not and could not support; and neither had any way of bridging the gap. There was a great lost opportunity involved in the post-

---

[74] See Chapter 4 n. 21.
[75] Cf. Dale: 'An examination of titles of Masters theses in the *Union List of Higher Degree Theses* suggests that … Leavisism was at its strongest in Australia in the early seventies' (*English Men*, p. 140). Economists say that the moment of peak in a market can be identified by the irrational behaviour of buyers desperate to enter it while they still can; the crash ensues. And so it was in this case too.

World War II division of the literary kingdom – in what proved to be the lead-up to the post-structuralist rush. Just as the literary nationalist frame for criticism was brow-beaten, in the universities at least, by imported and then naturalised New Critical and Leavisite approaches, so would it be the turn of the latter in the 1980s to receive much the same treatment, with the rise of literary Theory. My concern is that we not repeat the mistake again, now that the latter period, at least in its higher theoretical reaches, is over.

Just as Lawson and *While the Billy Boils* have been present at each stage of this process, so too should they be when new methodological experiments in literary studies are being canvassed – as they are in the next chapter.

CHAPTER 13

AUSTRALIAN LITERARY CRITICISM AND SCHOLARLY EDITING FROM THE 1980s

WHILE THE BILLY BOILS AS CROSS-SECTION

That *While the Billy Boils* should have acted as a gauge of successive formations of Australian culture until the 1970s, at times as a lightning rod of disputation, is a confirmation of the importance of Lawson's collection. This is what enduring literary classics with long reception histories – themselves sustained by repeated, varied and adapted production-events – are capable of revealing. Mention has already been made of the flourishing of heritage and Australiana publishing that swept up *While the Billy Boils* with it during the lead-up to the Australian bicentenary celebrations of 1988. The listing in Appendix 3 of postwar Lawson prose selections, as well as reprintings of *While the Billy Boils*, helps document that moment. It proved, however, to be an artificial stimulus, a peak in an ongoing cultural graph, for publishing interest in Lawson fell away in the mid-1990s.

The years 1990–91 saw three printings, 1992 one more, one each in 1994 (a new typesetting) and 1995, and then a gap until 2000 when normal commercial Lawson prose publication resumed, with printings in 2000, 2001, 2002, 2006 and 2009.[1] Sydney University Press from 2004 also published printed transformations of the digital texts (eight volumes of Lawson) that it had prepared and mounted from Project Gutenberg sources in 1997; and Dodo Press in Gloucester, UK followed suit in 2007–08. One notable fact however is that, during the Lawson

---

[1] *Robbery Under Arms* had a similar fate: two printings in 1990, another in 1994 and then nothing until 2001.

prose-drought of the later 1990s, translations, adaptations for children and musical settings of his prose works continued to appear (the last, in some number), showing the continuity of his popular, if not 'literary', appeal during that late postmodern period, with its conscious internationalising of taste.

The professional academic sphere saw the continued entrenchment of the ideological–discursive approach to Lawson and to the 1890s, initiated by the feminist interpretations of the late 1970s and 1980s – though more in the guise of established fact than as new discovery. But as that drum was beating, a counter-rhythm is also audible in Australia, one that would spread from the biographical and bibliographical into the literary historical and literary critical arenas. It goes on today, and it is the subject of this final chapter. Towards the end, I sketch a future direction for literary study – empirical, potentially productive, but not exclusive – as foreshadowed in Chapter 1.

The writing now becomes, inevitably, more speculative and broad-ranging, and the impersonal tone of the earlier chapters gradually changes register. I have asked myself whether I am far enough away from events in which I have taken part to see them clearly, and I have to admit that I am probably not: so the buyer must beware. On the other hand, the advantage of this tack of articulating what I take to have been a counter-rhythm, and then, towards the end of the chapter, generalising its implications, may allow others to take over into their own thinking and critical practice what I am proposing, in some adapted form most likely – or to contest it – just as they see fit. In all of this, *While the Billy Boils* has proved to be a wonderfully convenient illustration: in fact it is only by engaging in the close-reading book-historical practice of the kind I have been presenting that the general case for an expanded literary criticism, for me, came into being.

H. P. Heseltine

H. P. (Harry) Heseltine's two essays on Lawson – twenty-two years apart – afford a convenient index to the shift in thinking about the study of

Lawson. As the first Australian literary academic to have received a PhD in English in the United States, Heseltine may be said to have been the first properly accredited New Critic in Australia. The PhD was awarded in 1956 at Louisiana State University at Baton Rouge, where Brooks and Warren had taught and where, as Heseltine records in his memoir *In Due Season*, the 'legacy of their New Criticism remained'.[2] Once back in Australia Heseltine turned his mind to the literature of the country, and his first article on Lawson appeared in 1960.[3] By then, as we have seen, Lawson's reputation had become a battleground between the nationalists in Australia who looked back to the 1890s for the initiating moment of the Australian character and who especially admired his stories and sketches, and members of the Communist Party and the Left in general who put more emphasis on Lawson's early radical ballads. Both camps saw Lawson as the apostle of mateship.[4]

The professional literary critics, as we saw in the last chapter, had a broader humanist agenda that reflected the Existentialist anxieties of the period. There was an appetite to believe that mankind was still living in a post-World War I, T. S. Eliot-style wasteland; that therefore literary expressions of this anxiety (whether written before or after World War I) were of considerable value; and that the highest role of the critic was to evaluate.[5] Those literary works that afforded answers to the dilemma or

[2] Heseltine, *In Due Season: Australian Literary Studies, a Personal Memoir* (North Melbourne, Vic.: Australian Scholarly Publishing, 2009), p. 50. Cleanth Brooks (1906–94), author of *The Well-Wrought Urn* (1947) was professor of English at LSU 1932–47. Robert Penn Warren (1905–89) joined the same department shortly after Brooks. They were co-founders of the *Southern Review* in 1935 and co-wrote the influential textbooks *Understanding Poetry* (1938) and *Understanding Fiction* (1943).
[3] Heseltine, 'Saint Henry – Our Apostle of Mateship', *Quadrant*, 5 (1960–61), 5–11.
[4] For the origin of this term, see Chapter 10 n. 61.
[5] Cf. the 'teenage Leavisite' John Docker: 'The Leavisite analysis of a text . . . was always dissolving into a version of cultural history . . . very much influenced by an apocalyptic mood about the decline of civilisation, shared by Pound and Eliot and Yeats as well as by Leavis': *In a Critical Condition: Reading Australian Literature* (Ringwood, Vic.: Penguin, 1984), p. 11. The attendant anxiety (even if we think of it now as a passing cultural phase) suggests a more charitable interpretation than that they were 'colonising' a professional turf to the exclusion of untrained critics and historians (p. 86): they had also been using literature to try to understand more widely felt concerns.
   Docker might have added Joseph Conrad to his apocalyptics list. Popularly known prior to World War II as a writer of fine tales of the sea, Conrad thereafter became known primarily

that allowed it to be understood anew would be deemed to be serious or significant. So, in 1967, Stephen Murray-Smith could praise that

> compassion and universality of vision that you find in those rare people who have been touched, one might say, by the finger of God. In nearly two hundred years we have been lucky to find one such man among the twenty million or so who live or have lived on our shores. We shall be lucky to find another, but at least we have Lawson. And if Australians were divested of all other sources of spiritual judgment and values, we could do far worse than draw on him.[6]

In this professional context, high valuation of Lawson as a simple celebrator of mateship was out of the question. Certainly this was the case for Heseltine, newly attuned as he was to Lionel Trilling's psychologically angled approach to literature. For Heseltine, the celebratory reflex ignored the fact that Lawson's stories rarely venerate mateship in an unproblematic way or, when they do, are weakened by it; that, when positively seen and functioning well, mateship is portrayed as being in an unreachable past; and that for the rest of the time it is 'simply the rough, sometimes brutal community behaviour of vigorous and desperate men' or 'a last ditch stand against madness' in the face of an anti-human landscape often leading to insanity.[7]

Although this essay was a particularly fresh one, Heseltine had, in 1960, little chronological attunement to the periods across which, and the contexts in which, the works he was discussing had been written and published. Lawson had died in 1922. Heseltine declares that his source is Lawson's collected *Prose Works* (1948), a large-format single volume (described in Chapter 11). He quotes across this substantial tome at chronological random. The unspoken assumption seems to

---

in educational settings as the author of the previously little-known novella of 1899, 'Heart of Darkness', and of a few novels of profound psychological tension (*Nostromo, The Secret Agent, Under Western Eyes*). The dates of the postwar New American Library edition of *Heart of Darkness*, introduced by Albert J. Guerard and now with a separate identity rather than buried in the collective title *Youth and Two Other Stories*, and of the Norton classroom edition are indicative: 1950 and 1963 respectively.

[6] S. Murray-Smith, 'Introduction' (dated '1967') to *Henry Lawson's Best Stories*, ed. Cecil Mann (Penrith, NSW: Discovery Press, 1968), p. [x]. On Murray-Smith, see Chapter 12 pp. 300–01.

[7] Heseltine, 'Saint Henry', pp. 10, 9.

have been that, since works are aesthetic entities, they are or should be, if worthy of the critic's attention, timeless in their aesthetic quality. In this, Heseltine was A. G. Stephens's and Nettie Palmer's inheritor, except that, now, New Criticism lent an even firmer literary objecthood to the works being discussed.

A limitation of this approach can be seen in Heseltine's discussion of '"Rats"'.[8] In this sketch, three shearers see another man in the distance fighting violently with what appears to be a woman. They rush up, only to find that he is an old man and that the other figure is in fact his swag. They conclude he has gone mad – ratty – in the dust and poverty and isolation of the outback. They make fun of him by encouraging him to go a few more rounds with his swag, and they pretend to bet on the outcome. They enjoy the energetic display of his madness but, at length feeling sorry for him, give him meat and money and then leave, looking back only to see him start the fight again. That is the end of the story as it first appeared in the *Bulletin* on 3 June 1893.

Lawson revised it for its appearance in *Short Stories in Prose and Verse* in 1894 where it gained a concluding paragraph that now gave it an unambiguously comic conclusion:

> And late that evening a little withered old man with no corks round his hat and with a humourous twinkle instead of a wild glare in his eyes, called at a wayside shanty, had several drinks, and entertained the chaps with a yarn about the way in which he had 'had' three 'blanky fellers' for some tucker and 'half a caser' by pretending to be 'barmy.'[9]

But in 1895–96 in preparing printer's copy for *While the Billy Boils*, Lawson crossed out this new paragraph, and A. W. Jose, his editor, confirmed the deletion. The result is that the comic twist was rejected in favour of the more disturbing ending of the original version.

In 1960 Heseltine did not know about these alternative endings and did not realise that the 1894 ending challenged his interpretation. By 1982, when he came back to write on Lawson again, Manning Clark's

---

[8] *Ibid.*, p. 9.
[9] HL, *Short Stories in Prose and Verse* (Sydney: L. Lawson, 1894), p. 5.

biography had appeared in 1978, providing much new information about Lawson's life and arguing a case about his psychological dividedness. So too, in 1970, had the first instalment of Colin Roderick's textual scholarship (of a selection of Lawson's stories and sketches, including '"Rats"') and also his 1972 complete edition – although, as explained below, its editorial completeness remained basically compromised until its *Commentaries* supplement appeared in 1985. Thus Heseltine, in 1982, was able to range more confidently across Lawson's life and writing career. He was in effect, giving himself the liberty not just 'to submit his [Lawson's] work', as he says, to the 'procedures' of literary criticism (which he had tried to do in 1960) but to embrace literary scholarship (biographical, bibliographical), despite both of those pursuits being still in an only moderately developed phase for Lawson.[10]

However, in the first half of the 1982 article, it is as if nothing had changed. This first half stays in touch with the concerns of 1950s and 1960s criticism. The 1982 essay at first adopts a traditionally New Critical methodology, identifying a pattern of references to, and situations of, death and resurrection – 'Lawson's central theme'.[11] The method of finding a pattern of motifs and then erecting them into an assumed generative principle, which is only later identified with the author's thought (in the sense here of Lawson's being 'profoundly representative'), substitutes an ostensible subject matter for the operative tension in Lawson's stories.[12] The darker ones do not, I believe, so much reveal a bitter new insight into the conditions of human existence as *take* the bitterness of the insight, swallow its unavoidability, register the cost. They are about moving on, minimally, in this knowledge.

[10] H. P. Heseltine, 'Between Living and Dying: The Ground of Lawson's Art', in *The Uncertain Self: Essays in Australian Literature and Criticism* (Melbourne: Oxford University Press, 1986), pp. 42–55 [p. 42], originally in *Overland*, no. 88 (July 1982), 19–26. Roderick's 'first instalment' was in *The Bush Undertaker and Other Stories*, ed. with Preface and Commentary by Colin Roderick (Sydney: A&R, 1970). Manning Clark's biography was *In Search of Henry Lawson* (South Melbourne, Vic.: Macmillan, 1978).
[11] Heseltine, 'Between Living and Dying', p. 49. The stories are said to demonstrate 'that it is man's lot to be held somewhere between living and dying' (p. 45), with '[The Bush Undertaker]' discovering 'the possibility of redemptive change' (p. 47).
[12] *Ibid.*, p. 42.

The second half of Heseltine's essay is, however, decisively new. He admits himself to be perplexed. Absorbing the meaning of the scholarly editor's identification of alternative endings for "'Rats'" – endings that, depending on which is preferred, alter the whole import of the story – Heseltine states that this situation

> must provoke questions about Lawson's intentions in writing the story, about the validity of a commentary so completely based on a doubtful text . . . Whatever Lawson's conscious 'intentions', his imagination was demonstrably capable of entertaining at least two possible interpretations of the same events . . . the question of primary interest concerns the nature of that discrepancy and the reasons for its appearance.[13]

This is a revealing moment in Australian literary-critical history. What we have is an honest registration of a problem with a methodology that had hitherto served professional critics well. The thing that was thought to be stable, to be the object of the literary critic's attention – and therefore, in its stability, justifying the ordinary procedures of that methodology – had turned out to be unstable after all. In other words, a newly introduced source of relevant information was calling for a renovation in the practice.

The problem was that this was the very moment when the poststructuralist theory movement swept across the Australian literary terrain, making the question of adjustment and renovation, or of change of focus, irrelevant. The opportunity was there in the early 1980s; more scholarship was coming; but the timing was unlucky. The study of literary works as privileged objects of attention was challenged by the at-first more exciting and liberating study of the discourses that texts instantiated. This pushed authorship and intention to one side; it vaporised what, in the Introduction, I nominated as the two organising principles of literary-historical scholarship – chronology and agency. Chronology was seen as operating horizontally within a period or a Foucauldian episteme, and agency was transferred from author-as-creator to the discursive system.

---

[13] *Ibid.*, pp. 51–2.

Bizarrely for a New Critic, though less so for one whose interest in literature and psychiatry was by now longstanding, Heseltine argued that Lawson's 'divided and ambivalent self', which the 1978 biography had demonstrated, was nowhere more evident than in the 'textual history of these final paragraphs' of '"Rats"'. This argument pushed Heseltine to qualify the very conclusions that his ordinary methods had only just identified in the first half of the same essay:

> The great stories of his flowering time are precisely those in which he refuses to let ambivalence, uncertainty, distress be resolved by the comforts of doctrine, any absolutes of belief or action. His primal sense, that is to say, of human existence held between living and dying stubbornly opposes the seductive symbols of death and rebirth to which it is so regularly submitted.[14]

Here was an attempt – whatever its merits – to interfold the new scholarship with interpretation. And Heseltine was able now, in 1982 as he could not in 1960, to identify the writings of 1892–95 as 'the highwater mark' of Lawson's career, with a glance also at the Joe Wilson stories, whose chronology of composition, as we saw in Chapter 12, was still cloaked in some mystery.[15]

More generally, here was a New Critic potentially remaking his notion of what a work of literature *is*, a notion that had been naturalised by the protocols of the material book (especially of a tome like *Prose Works*) and further entrenched by the working assumptions of New Criticism. Without an expansion of the object of critical attention, there could be no recourse to traditional literary-critical procedures of the kind that Heseltine and his forebears and contemporaries saw as natural. The 'work' was always going to need redefining: just as Heseltine was on the edge of saying in 1982, but did not quite say.

In his personal career this was the moment when Heseltine moved to the Royal Military College Duntroon, charged with creating a larger department of English for the tri-service Australian Defence Force

---

[14] Heseltine, 'Between Living and Dying', p. 52.
[15] The mystery was clarified in large part by Colin Roderick's answer to Clark's biography, called *The Real Henry Lawson* (Adelaide: Rigby, 1982).

Academy, whose campus was then under construction.[16] What he found at Duntroon was a small group of colleagues intently at work on the first *Oxford Companion to Australian Literature*.[17] Australian literary history was being engaged for the first time in narrative form with an encyclopaedic scope and organisation. When published in 1985 the book was hailed by some as a portent of a new era for the study of this literature, and a recognition that it had come of age. Not all were happy since the *Companion* could be seen, from a then-progressive point of view, as going against the incoming tide of literary theory. Moreover, it paid a great deal of sympathetic attention to the 1890s, and could be seen (though not fairly, I think) as a crowning achievement of the nationalist case. The attention paid to the forgotten, including to a great many women authors, which an encyclopaedic approach necessarily brings out, was a welcome counteraction.

Taking advantage of the momentum thus created, Heseltine moved to create a literary database of Australian literature (AUSTLIT)[18] and then (logically, after his experience with Lawson) to establish a series of scholarly editions of works of Australian fiction that the *Companion* had identified as undeservedly neglected: the Colonial Texts Series (from 1988).[19] This is where I myself come into the account. The development

---

[16] RMC Duntroon housed the Faculty of Military Studies of the University of New South Wales from 1968. English had been taught there, although not as a university discipline, since 1911 when the first professor, V. J. R. Miles was appointed, followed by L. H. Allen (with a Leipzig PhD on Shelley and himself a poet) in 1918. From 1986 ADFA housed a much upgraded University College of the same university. At both institutions, English was one of several undergraduate programs in the Bachelor of Arts.

[17] William W. Wilde, Joy Hooton and Barry Andrews, *The Oxford Companion to Australian Literature* (Melbourne: Oxford University Press, 1985).

[18] AUSTLIT was launched as an online database at ADFA in 1988. It was re-engineered using new ('FRBR') protocols and relaunched, now as the property of a consortium of universities, in 2001 (www.austlit.edu.au). It was headquartered at first at ADFA and later at the University of Queensland. Current indexing of a range of literary periodicals and newspapers since the early–mid 1980s, together with some substantial retrospective indexing projects in the 1990s and 2000s, meant that, by May 2012, it contained more than 750,000 work records and 135,000 agent (author, publisher) records.

[19] Planning began in 1985; six of the eight titles in the Colonial Texts Series (1988–2004) are by women authors. Heseltine also moved to instal Australian literature as one of the two priority areas for the ADFA Library, with the result that its rare books and manuscripts collections grew into a significant resource, available to the research sector.

helped create the groundwork that in due course enabled the Australian Academy of the Humanities to establish the Academy Editions of Australian Literature.[20]

These were, however, only elements of a larger national story. What I have been describing was by no means the highroad of professional endeavour in Australian literary studies, neither at the time, nor afterwards. Poststructuralist theory, which was quickly taken over into tertiary-level curricula in the 1980s, taught a generation of Honours and PhD students to condescend to such endeavours as merely philological and as hailing from a long-discredited, positivistic past.[21] This was a fate for which, ironically, New Criticism had long prepared the way by deeming bio-bibliographical study to be merely preliminary to the engagement of the critic face-to-face with 'the work itself'.[22]

Brian Kiernan and the *Essential Henry Lawson*

Heseltine was not the only one rethinking his position in the early 1980s. Brian Kiernan's work, far more focussed on Lawson than Heseltine's had been, is another intriguing example.

Compared to his work of only a few years before, Kiernan's Introduction to his Portable Australian Authors *Henry Lawson* selection (1976) is a halfway house to something new. Required to select from the full range of Lawson's writing – verse, stories, sketches, journalism and letters – he began to understand his own role as commentator and critic differently:

> Between the best of the sketches, short stories, and verses and the inferior, and between his 'imaginative' work generally and his 'non-imaginative' writing, there are many links. In his journalism, his autobiographical writings, and his letters can also be found the dominant themes of his fiction and verse. These reveal a continuity of concerns, illuminate his

---

[20] Its editorial board began work in 1992; ten titles appeared during 1996–2007.
[21] Cf. D. C. Greetham, 'The Resistance to Philology', in *Margins of the Text*, ed. Greetham (Ann Arbor: University of Michigan Press, 1997), pp. 9–24.
[22] The *locus classicus* of this position is: René Wellek and Austin Warren, 'The Mode of Existence of a Literary Work of Art': first published in 1942 in *Southern Review* and in Wellek and Warren, *Theory of Literature* (1948) as 'The Analysis of the Literary Work of Art'; then with the revised title (London: Cape, 1966), pp. 142–57.

personality and his artistry, and show his critical involvement with the changing society he lived in.[23]

The advantage of Kiernan's new, bio-bibliographical awareness about Lawson became obvious in his far more considered essay, 'From Mudgee Hills to London Town', which served as an Introduction to his selection, *The Essential Henry Lawson* in 1982.[24] It is a strong piece of work that showed a new maturity about the achievable role of the literary critic now obliged also to bridge across to literary scholarship. (Although we now see literary criticism as a form of literary scholarship the two were routinely and polemically differentiated, 'scholarship' referring to the broad range of editorial, bibliographic, biographical and literary-historical considerations argued to be relevant to the particular work.)

In 1976 Kiernan had followed Brian Matthews in plotting a decline in Lawson's writing from immediately after the Joe Wilson stories; but in 1982 he would go a different way. Matthews had put it down to the 'fragility' of Lawson's talent, which Lawson himself did not understand. However, a letter to George Robertson of January 1897 suggests that he did, at least sometimes:

> You mustn't take notice of the drivel to the effect that I should write a long novel – anything in fact save what I *have* written. That was originally one man's idea. If I had published a novel, they would have said it was jerky and disconnected and I should try my hand at short stories and sketches. My line is writing short stories and sketches in prose and verse. I'm not a novelist. You will find a man to write you an Australian novel soon enough. If you were a builder, would you set the painters to do the carpentering?[25]

Nevertheless the evidence cited in Chapter 2 shows that Lawson was often pushed by the pressure of the marketplace to try to write longer short stories (rather than what came more naturally to him: sketches or sketch-stories) and the pressure was now being brought to bear to write

---

[23] Brian Kiernan, *Henry Lawson* (St Lucia: University of Queensland Press, 1976), p. ix.
[24] Brian Kiernan, 'From Mudgee Hills to London Town: A Critical Biography of Henry Lawson', in *The Essential Henry Lawson*, ed. Kiernan (South Yarra, Vic.: Currey O'Neil, [1982]), pp. 1–40.
[25] *Letters* 66–7.

novels. Probably at least in part because, as John Barnes has suggested in relation to the Joe Wilson stories, this would have meant meeting the emotional challenge of sustained introspection at a time when his marriage was crumbling, Lawson could not manage it when in London.

Kiernan cites interesting new biographical evidence in his 1982 essay, suggesting not 'a steady rise and then fall, but constant fluctuations' as Lawson repeatedly fell back on the attractions of melodrama and sentimentality.[26] Robertson announced 'The Hero of Redclay: A Novel' in the firm's advertising section dated January 1896, bound-in with copies of Lawson's *In the Days When the World Was Wide*, as ready '*Shortly*'. Lawson frequently referred to a projected novel while in New Zealand in 1897 and at the end of 1897 spent some weeks fruitlessly rewriting 'Hero of Redclay' materials as a melodrama for the stage for Bland Holt. And again in England in 1900–02 he talked about completing a novel. But he never did. All this points to a continuing misunderstanding on Lawson's part of his organisational capacities and persistence.

The now-assumed relevance of this sort of evidence to literary criticism, together with Kiernan's subtitling his 1982 essay 'A Critical Biography of Henry Lawson', shows that he had emerged from the New Critical-cum-Leavisite mindset that had been holding so many of his generation captive.

He was also the editor of the texts he had selected for both the 1976 and the 1982 volumes. Since a scholarly editor has to establish the reading text in every detail, the editorial approach enacts the editor's sense of what the text of a work is. Yet this concept was becoming less stable, and to make editorial decisions in light of it can be a vertiginous business. So it is not surprising that, in view of the prestige of Colin Roderick's editions of Lawson, Kiernan basically followed his lead in simply preferring the text of the last authorised version.[27] However, this brought a chafing restriction with it, as he soon realised: so Kiernan

---

[26] Kiernan, 'From Mudgee Hills', p. 35.
[27] 'Usual editorial preference is for the last version the author approved, even if tacitly' (*ibid.*, pp. 41–2).

breaks his own rule of thumb for 'His Father's Mate' by sourcing it from the *Bulletin* 'for historical reasons' because it was 'later heavily revised and abridged'. With '"Rats"', although Kiernan (after Roderick) duly takes his text from *While the Billy Boils*, he includes in square brackets the final paragraph Lawson added in *Short Stories in Prose and Verse* since it shows him turning the sketch into a more complex story, thus 'finishing on a note of comic reassurance'.[28] Editorially, of course, this was having it both ways. If his breakout from a New Critical paradigm in his criticism was not matched by a parallel advance in his thinking about the editing, it could not reasonably – in 1982, just before the revival of the new editorial theory of the 1980s – have been otherwise.

With his textual criticism Kiernan went as far, in the circumstances, as he could have gone. He comments, for instance, that 'a pattern of development, in technique if not always in quality, is discernible in, or behind the fifty-two pieces that make up the prose collection' but that the pattern is 'elusive . . . because the arrangement is not chronological'. Kiernan had Roderick's 1972 *Short Stories and Sketches* edition to work from. It gives dates of composition by year only, often by a two or three-year span and sometimes in square brackets – presumably (but this goes unexplained) to show the dating was speculative. In fact, the great majority of the composition dates are speculative, and those in square brackets only more so that the rest. In general, the dates that are known for sure are not composition dates but publication dates, and these Roderick did not provide in full until the *Commentaries* volume in 1985. So, unless Kiernan were to have done the archival work himself, he did not have a chronology of newspaper publication dates to go by. Thus, the argument about the 'pattern of development', while not untrue, remained only a claim in the absence of the archival work necessary to recover the chronologies.

[28] *Ibid.*, pp. 41, 101. Again, Kiernan felt the need to publish a non-authorised version of the sketch-essay 'Succeeding in London' and to place it out of chronological order (see p. 304). He takes 'A Visit of Condolence' and 'A Day on a Selection' 'from the second printing of WBB (1896)' because it 'incorporates corrections to the first printing' (p. 41). He presumably means the Second Thousand (again, following Roderick: see n. 56 below); but the first three Thousands were printed as a single impression, so their text is the same. The first change occurred in the third impression (Seventh–Ninth Thousands): see Chapter 7 n. 25.

Similarly, in a confusion that is both biographical and bibliographical Kiernan suggests that, in *On the Track and Over the Sliprails* (1900), Lawson 'was deliberately extending the sketch stories that had made him famous . . . to the length preferred by English publishers of books and magazines', and that this was a process 'discernible among the later stories in *While the Billy Boils*'.[29] This latter claim does not stand up to scrutiny: of the fourteen stories or sketches eight pages or longer in *Billy Boils* only four of them date to 1895–96.[30]

Again, Kiernan argues that '*While the Billy Boils* shows Lawson developing different techniques, working simultaneously in a number of genres'.[31] This is true in the sense that the collection (understood in a timeless, aesthetic sense) represents such efforts; but it is false if 'simultaneously' means 1896, since the statement then conflates original composition or publishing dates with the date of the collection. Discussions of the place of individual stories in the Joe Wilson sequence – and Kiernan is by no means alone in this – also fall foul of a similar problem. Such critics usually mean the published sequence; but, insofar as the aesthetic acclaim is a description of Lawson's writing, they ignore the fact that the stories were not written in the published order. So, although Kiernan is aware of the reverse order of writing of the two stories that make up '"Water Them Geraniums"', he describes the results of their placement in the published *Joe Wilson* sequence by an appeal to the themes struck throughout.[32] As long as this traditional proceeding seems to appeal to something objective (the thing or aesthetic object in which the themes are struck) the chronological ordering is assumed not to bear on the question.

This is an odd proceeding in a critical biography: it marks a failure to pursue the newly emerging method as far as it might have been. It

---

[29] *Ibid.*, p. 26.
[30] They are: 'Going Blind', 'Some Reflections on a Voyage across Cook's Straits (N.Z.)' ['Across the Straits'], 'Jones' Alley' and 'The Geological Speiler'. The others of 1895–96 are shorter: 'For Auld Lang Syne', 6 pages; 'An Unfinished Love Story', 7; 'Two Dogs and a Fence', 3; 'Steelman's Pupil', 7; 'Our Pipes', 5; 'Steelman', 4; and 'The Old Bark School: An Echo', 2.
[31] Kiernan, 'From Mudgee Hills', p. 21.
[32] See *ibid.*, pp. 28–9.

betrays a rhetorical habit, a literary-critical shorthand, that does not bear scrutiny. In such cases, we need clarity on the question of whether we are praising the author or the publisher (*whose* sequence is it?). The book-historical method I have been pursuing puts stress on the relationship of author and publisher, and opens it up for inspection. It points to the larger question: Are we interested in the writing or in the publication? Or both, if they are separable moments in the life of the work? For most authors we have either too little information or time to make the distinction. But with literary classics, especially if they are supplemented by archival holdings, we are now often able to undertake the deeper and more chronologically extended study.

Fortunately, Kiernan's errors were of the kind that could be remedied. All that was needed was a fuller commitment to the necessary literary scholarship: biographical, textual and bibliographical. At least Kiernan was beginning to see how to shake off the intimidating effect of trusting volume-publication dates alone and restricting oneself to study of the recognised literary genres. Now everything Lawson wrote was grist to the critical mill: foreground and background came simultaneously into view. There was, as it were, an *authorial* intertextuality to be described and understood.

Colin Roderick's editions

Enter Colin Roderick: except, of course, he already *had* entered, before this shift in literary critical awareness; and, indeed, to a certain extent, his work may be said to have caused the shift. Responsible critics could not ignore the new information he was bringing to the table, even if their training and backgrounds made it difficult to digest. But where were Roderick's editions coming from?

What is not immediately clear is the relationship of his prose editions to one another. The three volumes of the poetry (1967–69) present no such problems, nor do the *Letters* volume (1970) and his selection of criticism of Lawson (1972). But what the prose volumes contain is at first unclear. The last sentence of the two-page Introduction to

Autobiographical and Other Writings (1972) notes: 'As with Volume One, *Short Stories and Sketches* [1972], the contents of this volume [Two] are dealt with in detail in the *Commentary* forming Volume Three of the series.'[33] This last volume is mentioned on the verso of the half-title page as being '*In the Press*', but the prospect of financial loss led to its delay until 1985. The early instalment of Roderick's work provided in 'Commentary' to his 1970 selection for Angus & Robertson, *The Bush Undertaker and Other Stories*, shows that he was well under way by that time. But he was by no means finished. A 'revised and corrected' edition of this selection appeared in 1974, followed by many reprints from 1975 until at least 1988. Most readers who have come upon Roderick's editorial scholarship have encountered it here rather than in the *Short Stories and Sketches* volume of 1972 (xxiv + 935 pages) or in its revision, entitled *Henry Lawson the Master Story-teller: Prose Writings* (xx + 961 pages). It appeared in 1984, immediately before *Commentaries* in 1985. Although this is not declared in its blurb or introduction, comparison of the Contents pages shows that *Prose Writings* incorporated a number of the essays that had appeared in the 1972 *Autobiographical* volume. These replaced some of the fiction-memoir material originally in *Short Stories and Sketches*. Evidently, the publisher wished to supersede the two 1972 volumes with a single one; and the individual entries in *Commentaries* are cross-referenced by page and section to it. As a result, some of the pieces that appeared only in *Short Stories and Sketches* received no commentary, and this is also the case for most of the material in the *Autobiographical* volume. Fortunately, all of the stories and sketches in *While the Billy Boils* were unaffected by this compromised outcome.

Although Roderick's task was a vast and mainly editorial one its links to the prevailing tenor of the times that I have been uncovering in the literary criticism may also be detected in the editing. To make this argument I need first to outline how Roderick approached his task. In his earlier selection *Fifteen Stories* (1959) Roderick divided his selection into the sections: Background (Out Back), Humour, Pathos and Sympathy.

---

[33] *Autobiographical* xiv.

The introduction describes Lawson as 'a true poet... A great deal of his poetic feeling, and the best of his art, went into his short stories. They are charged with poetry and are as much poems as any that are arranged in stanzas and measured verses'.[34] By thus defining Lawson's short stories this move might seem at first to represent an ingenious attempt to heal the rift between the cultural-political Left and Right, which had preferred one form over the other. But it is not that at all.

Poetry and drama are the oldest literary forms and self-evidently worthy of study; but the novel had only been widely recognised as such in the early twentieth century. Henry James's *The Art of the Novel*, edited by the New Critic and poet R. P. Blackmur in 1934, brought together James's prefaces to the revised New York Edition (1907–09) of his novels. The Blackmur volume became a seminal document. Although the volume also contained James's prefaces to his collections of novellas and short stories, special pleading for the short story continued to be needed before the form would be generally considered worthy of academic study. In 1959, Roderick evidently believed the case still needed to be made; and it would not be until 1976 that Brian Kiernan could go one step further and distinguish the Lawson sketch from the short story in the confidence that the sketch would also now be treated as a work of art.[35] But it is the appeal to the status of poetry as a justifier that is most revealing in Roderick's argument and that aligns him with the postwar climate of opinion about literary works, and therefore of the role of the critic. The attitude continued to be reflected in the introductions to Roderick's scholarly editions and it would necessarily affect the editorial stance he enunciated for them and adopted in them. (In the 1959 selection he made no statement about the source or treatment of his texts at all.)

Roderick edited the verse first, choosing, in each case, the last

---

[34] HL, *Fifteen Stories*, ed. Colin Roderick (Sydney: A&R, 1959), p. ix.
[35] The sketch shows no narrative development but is left 'to reverberate in the reader's mind' (Kiernan, 'From Mudgee Hills', p. 16), whereas the short story, such as 'Going Blind', is 'a *story* in the fullness of its dramatic development and its manipulation of the narrator's point of view, so that he becomes an observed, not merely an observing, character who extends the implications of the story' (p. 22).

authorised version as his text but providing an apparatus of variants that allows the reader to reconstruct earlier versions. Although reconstructing a textual descent in reverse, up the textual tree, is harder than down it, as would have been the case had he chosen early versions as reading texts, the information to do so is nevertheless presented on the reading page. His explanatory notes are extensive and helpful, usually revealing suggestive biographical and textual links. His edition of the *Letters* came next; and once again the notes are extraordinarily helpful for the later reader and scholar. There are, inevitably, many subsequently discovered letters not in the volume (e.g. the Lawson correspondence with Garnett, Pinker and Blackwood, drawn upon in earlier chapters); and, to my mind unfortunately, Roderick decided to regularise in a thoroughgoing way Lawson's 'capricious spelling', his abbreviations and 'careless punctuation', giving the letters a formality and an air of careful consideration that are misleading.[36] The motive may have been partly the usual copy-editing imperative of eliminating inconsistencies; but it also may have been, in part, a protective instinct. Roderick's Lawson-as-artist needed to seem more conventionally literary than he was.

Roderick came to edit the prose last, when he was already committed to preferring final authorised versions. The editorial policy is probably an unknowing continuation of a policy first adopted by the New Biblio-

---

[36] *Letters* 31. In a sample check, letter 20 in *Letters* (HL to A&R, 3 September 1896), collated against the original (ML MSS 314/45, pp. 69–75), reveals the following alterations. HL's wording 'Having been working at my trade – I go to graft again this afternoon' is defensibly emended to 'Have been working . . .'; the sentence, 'It is a decent camp, well built and much fresher cleaner and healthier than the city', gains commas ('fresher, cleaner, and'); 'the east' (meaning the Eastern colonies) and 'The tothersiders' (their inhabitants) becomes 'the East' and 'The Tothersiders'; 'Floor of gal' iron cases' becomes 'Floor of galvanized iron cases'; ampersands are expanded; perfectly clear monetary amounts (e.g. 2/6, 15/) are formalised (2s. 6d., 15s.); and 'They made us buy – or at least the married men had to – buy night-soil pans' is restored to syntactic tranquillity by bringing the second 'buy' back before the dash. To standardise in these ways (nearly 50 occasions) the usages of a man who was working by day as a painter and writing his letter in the tent in which he and Bertha were living is a questionable advantage. One error suggests that the proofs were not checked against the original in ML or against a photocopy of it: HL stops his underline before 'perfect' in the emphasised sentence '*Must have English edition of "Billy Boils" perfect*' (*Letters* 61–3). HL's characteristic spelling 'speilers' is regularised to 'spielers': just as the title of 'The Geological Speiler' would be in *Billy Boils* and by Roderick in *Prose Writings*.

graphers in the early part of the twentieth century (e.g. in R. B. McKerrow's edition of Thomas Nashe of 1904–10) and one that continued to affect editorial thinking into the late 1930s, as in McKerrow's *Prolegomena to the Oxford Shakespeare* (1939), where he nearly, but not quite, breaks out of the early-century mould.[37] The spectre that haunted them was the history of Shakespeare editing, which had often been wilful and subjective.

Roderick's policy follows theirs by not presuming to intervene in a text known (or deemed) to have been finally authorised by the author. In practice for Roderick 'authorised' means Lawson needed to have been involved, or suspected of having been involved, in the preparation of the particular collection of verse or prose for the press. This criterion typically involves the rejection of the texts of manuscripts, in that relatively small proportion of cases where they exist. It also involved rejecting versions that had appeared in newspapers and magazines – or in prior book collections that were later (according to Roderick's criterion) superseded. Where gross editorial intervention in some of Lawson's late works occurred Roderick finds justification to break his own rule of thumb and restore an earlier text.

This editorial policy means that, in the great bulk of cases (and all of those in *While the Billy Boils*) Roderick denies himself the right to edit eclectically even where he knows or suspects that the text, although authorised by Lawson, had been altered by others.[38] There was in fact a new editorial methodology that afforded a reasoned justification for eclecticism and that was widely used, especially in the USA, from the 1960s. It largely superseded Pollard and McKerrow's amongst Anglo-American scholarly editors. This newer method was developed in the

[37] For a discussion, see Richard Bucci, 'Tanselle's "Editing without a Copy-Text": Genesis, Issues, Prospects', *Studies in Bibliography*, 56 (2003), 1–44.

[38] E.g., for 'His Father's Mate', where Roderick becomes a victim of his own editorial policy. He strongly criticises A. W. Jose's condensation of the story for *Billy Boils* – which supplies his reading text – because it 'catastrophically shifted the point of approach of the work and altered the line of communication with its basic theme' (*Commentaries* 6). Roderick expresses a very strong preference for the original version, rather than the one authorised by HL, to the extent of providing the original in full in an Appendix to *Commentaries*. That volume's entries are sprinkled with expressions of regret about HL's acceptance of editorial changes (e.g., in 'Bogg of Geebung' and 'A Visit of Condolence', pp. 10, 18).

1950s, initially in Britain, and is still fairly widely practised. It has the advantage of recognising that textual descent involves an inevitable drift away from the texture of the author's original. Over and apart from the obvious opportunity for copy-editors to make alterations in a text being prepared for publication, successive copyings of a document (by amanuenses, and then by typesetters of first and successive editions) meant that inattention or the pressures of standardisation would affect the author's usages. These include spellings (which can be meaning-laden, especially for Lawson's non-standard usages), the rhythm enacted by the author's punctuation as he heard the sentences unfold in his head, the marking of certain words for capitalisation or for other special attention (as Lawson often did, by placing them within inverted commas), and the division of a story into sections, used by 1890s newspapers, that would typically be dispensed with in book form.

Thus the new approach, argued by W. W. Greg for seventeenth-century works and then by Fredson Bowers for later American works, was to choose the earliest extant version, on the grounds that it was the one most likely to preserve these features. Then the editor could introduce into that copy-text only those wordings in later versions known to be, or deemed on critical grounds to be, the author's.[39] This would produce the text of final authorial intention, while stripping out the textual alterations of others. Roderick gives no indication of having been affected by this postwar tradition. It is possible that he was not even aware of it: it was more widespread in the USA than in Britain, whose traditions were more influential on Australian English departments in those days. And there was relatively little scholarly editing of literary works happening in Australia where access to the primary documents, typically held in overseas locations, was difficult and expensive. Furthermore, Roderick's career had been in publishing and the book trade until 1966 when, in his mid-fifties, he took up the new Chair in Australian Literature at James Cook University.

---

[39] This was a constrained right. The editor was to be guided wherever possible by bibliographical considerations: that is, by reconstruction of the likely production process.

Roderick's editorial approach was a reflection of the postwar commitment to the aesthetic object as organic and self-contained. He chose what he took to be the nearest and surest way of securing it. The Greg–Bowers approach was more flexibly responsive to the empirical factors of textual dissemination and thus demanded more of the editor. But it was essentially in pursuit of the same goal: the author's finally intended text.[40] This was important in the postwar literary-critical climate I have been describing. Both methods took into account those complicating biographical factors that literary critics widely deemed to be irrelevant to consideration of the texts of literary works. Those factors could be taken into account temporarily, in a preliminary way by the critic, but were primarily the business of the scholarly editor. Once the reading text of the work had been established by the editor, it would *present* the work. It would be a single text that could stand alone, nakedly itself. Its textual lineaments – those ambiguous and complicating historical markers of its textual descent through time, through multiple copyings, editings and typesettings – could now be safely removed from the interpretative scene. Scholarly editions would record them as a matter of course, but usually at the end of the volume where the textual apparatus would function as a list of rejected readings, rather than of alternative ones.

Thus Roderick's editorial approach to the texts can be said to have been unusually old-fashioned. Yet he also, I noted above, created the ground for a germination of new thinking that I have noted in both Heseltine's and Kiernan's work on Lawson. How can this be?

Scholarly editors cannot restrict themselves to the writings of an idealised artist figure. The editor must examine those textual markers I mentioned: must follow the author-as-professional or would-be professional writer through the dusty byways, and not only the highways, of a writing career. Biographical enmeshment of the writing is inescapable, as is, consequently, the enmeshment of the author's contemporaneous

---

[40] Other comments about Roderick's various editions, particularly *Prose Writings* and *Commentaries*, appear in earlier chapters, where relevant to the discussion; and some technical-editorial comments will be found in the Introduction to Eggert and Webby.

writings (in whatever genre, and whether public or private) with one another. There is, as I have termed it, an authorial intertextuality to consider.

This awareness (which his notes show Roderick to have been thoroughly immersed in, even if he phrased it differently), together with his interest in the psychological dimensions of Lawson's creativity, meant that he needed to reconcile the biographical dimension with his sense of what a *work* is. His textual policy was a principal route towards a reconciliation. He effected it by closing the dimension down, by hemming the work in. As shown in Chapter 4, this committed him to accept the Jose–Lawson texts of late 1895–96, with all their loss of edge, of linguistic marking and of social-tonal location that copy-editing brought with it. The experimental Lawson of 1892–94 is systematically excluded from Roderick's reading texts, despite the developmental chrono-logic that he professes is indispensable to any proper understanding of Lawson's unfolding works. This latter commitment needs explaining. It was Roderick's second editorial means of effecting a reconciliation between the textual and the biographical.

It involved the sequencing of the stories and sketches, which in turn raised the overarching questions, for Roderick, of what an author is and of how 'a complex developing creative mind' may be understood, especially if he is a 'genius' such as Lawson – 'a mind possessed, a mind beyond the inhibiting control of normality'.[41] In his introduction to *Commentaries* Roderick states:

> The purpose of this book is to trace the nature and the course of development of that creative mind. It is accordingly a study in the psychology of literary creation . . . The stages of his development as an artist can be discerned only by a study of his writings in association with these comments and through debate on them.
>
> Lawson was a divided man: the social personality went one way, the creative artist the other. They coexisted independently yet criss-crossed unceasingly . . . The process is observable, but only by taking the relevant

[41] *Commentaries* x–xi.

series of stories and setting them out in the chronological order of composition and in relation to Lawson's verse and his letters.[42]

Without the proper sequencing of the stories and sketches, and without Roderick's running commentaries on them, there could, in other words, be only misunderstanding. The two together – sequencing and commentaries – would create the sense of a developing artistic maturity and unity that we could henceforth identify as 'Lawson'. 'In that sense', Roderick concludes, 'these commentaries reveal the growth and development of what was essentially a poetic mind.'[43] The Wordsworthian ring of the phrasing is unmistakeable.

The editorial principle of arrangement of contents that he would employ in 1972 in *Short Stories and Sketches* and again (with some alterations) in 1984 in *Prose Writings* is first stated in his preface to *The Bush Undertaker and Other Stories* in 1970. There, Roderick accepts without demur A. G. Stephens's criticism in his 1896 review of *While the Billy Boils* concerning the need for its contents to have been 'classified and put in sections', organised by character (Mitchell, Steelman) or theme ('a bush sequence, a city sequence, and so on').[44] Roderick's justification is essentially an aesthetic one:

> It is obviously not possible to include in a selection all the stories comprising any particular sequence. What is desirable is that Lawson's development of the sequence be illustrated in stories of high literary quality, and that the unity of the sequence be demonstrated and preserved. It is on these principles that the present selection has been made.

The editorial desire to achieve 'unity' is the collective counterpart to the textual policy he adopted for the individual works. The fact that 'unity' was to be observed as a principle when many of the components of the supposed unity were not – and, in a selection, could not – be present is striking.

Roderick goes on:

---

[42] *Commentaries* ix–x.
[43] *Commentaries* xi.
[44] *Bulletin*, 29 August 1896. See Chapter 8 pp. 173–4.

> This selection is the first to carry into effect the belief – in which I share – that Lawson did aim at harmonious sequences of stories, however separated in time the composition of the individual stories may have been. ... This is not to say that these sequences, or the stories comprising them, are autobiographical. Far from it. Lawson has warned us against reading them as such. ... Such unity as this selection aims at, then, rests in the presentation of sequences of stories that reveal an artist's development towards self-realization through the activity of created characters in the world of his mind.[45]

In Chapter 2, I argued that dependence on Stephens's critique of *While the Billy Boils* is dangerous. It ignores the feedback loop between the actual circumstances of Lawson's writing and sale of his stories and sketches. Writing and sale must typically have gone one by one, a situation that Lawson first, and then only temporarily, overcame in 1900–01 when writing the Joe Wilson sequence for (as he vainly hoped) the one publisher, *Blackwood's Magazine*. It probably also overstates the number of pieces that the *Bulletin* was holding back and so could not be selected for *While the Billy Boils* and later volumes.

In a postwar literary-critical climate that valued aesthetic unity and integrity highly the editorial yearning for unity was a natural one. There were two unities to be had: one of *work* and one of *world*. The annoying particularities of a life lived and of inconsistent writings written needed to be reconciled with these overarching requirements. This may help explain some of Roderick's irritability with the feckless and irresponsible, and cripplingly self-divided, Lawson that he portrays in his biography – which Roderick finally came to write at the close of a very long career. He turned eighty in the year in which it appeared, 1991.

Roderick's sequences

Roderick's sequences were, first and foremost, a reaction against the ordering of stories by original published volume, which the 1935 and successive editions of *Prose Works of Henry Lawson* had observed: *While*

---

[45] *The Bush Undertaker and Other Stories*, ed. Colin Roderick (1970; revised edn 1974: reprint Sydney: A&R, 1975), pp. 6–7.

the Billy Boils First Series appeared first, followed by the Second Series, then *On the Track*, then *Over the Sliprails*, and so on. In 1964, Cecil Mann's new three-volume edition perpetuated this ordering but added some of Lawson's uncollected writings (which had been 'harvested from newspaper sources and other sources in the Mitchell Library' by the bibliographer George Mackaness), together with some essays about Lawson, in his third volume.[46]

Roderick was scathing about this edition in private correspondence to George Ferguson at Angus & Robertson, especially about Mann's failure to detect the gross copy-editorial intervention in Lawson's Elder Man's Lane series (1912–15), and for including stories that had no part in the series and excluding others that did.[47] Roderick might have added that Mann's editorial policy for the texts was not even declared in the first volume but had to wait for the second, as if it were an oversight barely worth mentioning. The edition would receive a devastating bibliographic review at the hands of Dennis Douglas in 1966.[48] Nevertheless, Mann declared a belief that Roderick would make his own. The collected stories and sketches, he claimed, 'are held together . . . by voice, as a composite work, a single book, rather than only a collection of assorted writings scattered over a lifetime. In sum they are the book of that life – a book that provides a key to our legendary Lawson.'[49]

The internal sequencing of both the 1935 *Prose Works* and Mann's 1966 edition was misleading in that it gave only the roughest guide to a story's date of composition if the interpreter was trying to outline

---

[46] *The Stories of Henry Lawson*, ed. Cecil Mann, 3 vols. (Sydney: A&R, 1964), III. xi.
[47] Letter, Roderick to George Ferguson, 20 September 1970 (NLA MS 1578, Special Set 38a, Guardbook 8), and cf. *Commentaries* 373–4.
[48] Dennis Douglas, 'The Text of Lawson's Prose', *Australian Literary Studies*, 2 (1966), 254–65. Mann's policy involved: *(1)* acceptance of the texts of the published book forms of all of HL's stories and sketches; and *(2)* a jocular wave of the hand at categories of emendation enacted silently: 'such as corrections of old misprints' and 'the hitherto swarming plague of now unnecessary quotation marks and such similarly surviving oddities as "dingo (wild dog)" and its bracketed kind' (*Stories of Henry Lawson*, II. vii). Mann also confidently misinformed his 'general readers' that *Billy Boils* 'in its two parts' was 'originally published as separate books' (I. ix, x).
[49] *Stories of Henry Lawson*, ed. Mann, I. xiii.

Lawson's development of that 'composite work'. Many stories and sketches had been published in newspapers years before the date of the volume in which they were first collected; and some, appearing in the next collection, had been written before the preceding one – and so on. In his preface to his 1966 selection *Henry Lawson's Best Stories* Mann wrote: 'A thought for variety, to ensure sustained and continuous reading interest and enjoyment, has chiefly influenced the sequence arrangement of contents; departing from chronology, for instance, as of no real value in any such compiled and patterned book as this, if ever of value at all in any Henry Lawson context.'[50] This was the belles-lettristic background – by 1966, a defensive and rather amateurish one – against which Roderick had to mark out his own editorial departures. As he later explained in *Commentaries* (1985), the process of gradually creating character types such as Steelman and Mitchell 'is observable, but only by taking the relevant stories and setting them out in their chronological order of composition and in relation to Lawson's verse and his letters'.[51] This made eminent sense. However, Roderick compromised the chronological principle by subsuming it within an ordering based on thematic or character sequences.

While Roderick gave A. G. Stephens's review of *While the Billy Boils* and Lawson's angry letter to Robertson in response as the source of his authority for this decision, it was in the service of an overriding aesthetic desideratum. Roderick had hit upon an ordering and unifying principle that he hoped would demonstrate his literary-critical case about Lawson's developing artistry. He came to believe that the contents would be more effective if arranged in sequences, even though there is no evidence that they were sequential as written. Although Lawson later claimed Stephens's idea about sequences in *While the Billy Boils* was originally his own, Lawson himself, as far as we know, never specified their contents. So there can be no question of recovering them. And again, as far as we know, Lawson made no recommendation about the

---

[50] *Henry Lawson's Best Stories*, ed. Cecil Mann (Sydney: A&R, 1966), p. vi.
[51] *Commentaries* x.

works available for the volume but not selected. The net result was that Roderick was obliged to construct the sequences rather than discover them.

In Roderick's papers in the National Library of Australia, there are two lists, one in lead pencil, the other a later typed version but dated in pencil 1969. They are described as the 'Classified list of Lawson's stories arrived at by Colin Roderick for Vol. 1 of *Collected Prose*. With original holograph draft'.[52] In the holograph draft only some of the titles of the groupings subsequently used for the 1972 edition are present: 1. Seminal Stories; 2. Early City Stories; 3. Early Bush Stories (a) Inner Bush (b) Out Back. In the typescript they are all present. In a letter to George Ferguson of Angus & Robertson on 30 August 1970 Roderick described his plan for the *Prose Writings* edition as being dictated by the sequences, which are intended to lend strength and power.[53] The letter also adds that the contents will be comprised of four parts according to chronology.

In the event, there would be two: Part I, 1888–1902 and Part II, 1902–22. And the early groupings given above evolved into a much fuller series. Part I consisted of:

1. Beginnings, 1888–91
2. The City – I, 1892–3
3. Up the Country – I, 1892–4
4. Out Back – 1, 1892–4
5. Stiffner, 1893–5
6. Mitchell – I, 1893–4
7. Bush and City, 1893–5
8. New Zealand – I, 1893–6
9. Steelman, 1894–7
10. City Characters, 1894–7
11. Boyhood and Youth, 1894–6
12. Mitchell – II, 1894–9

And so on. Part I has eighteen sequences in total, two of which (New

---

[52] The lists are at NLA MS 1578/286; the quotation is from the detailed description of 'Special Set 39'.
[53] NLA MS 1578, Special Set 38a, Guardbook 8.

Zealand II, 1897; and London, 1901–2) consist of only one piece each; and Part II has another eight sequences.

The list shows how the ordering worked at cross-purposes to the principle of chronology that Roderick was also citing and that his poetry volumes had in fact observed. It is a principle that has not dated. But in the list above it is only secondary, serving more as a rhetorical underpinning for the dominant ordering by theme, character and place. The datings are year by year, with the years frequently overlapping. Thus the list shows how much like a publisher's editor rather than a scholarly editor Roderick was treating the stories' ordering; and how fully interpretative it was. (Alternative groupings are easily conceivable; and, as we have seen, Roderick had to alter them for *Prose Writings* in 1984.) In sum, there was a great deal of direction of the reader going on. The fact that Roderick was editing in the 1970s rather than the 1890s, and with an outlook on literature that had crystallised in its mature form in the postwar period, meant that his attempt to demonstrate an improved Lawson actually created one of his devising, which had never seen the light of day, neither in Lawson's time nor in the fifty years afterwards. Although working in the name of authorial intention in establishing the texts, the intentions Roderick was actually serving with the sequences were those of an ideal publisher's editor of his own invention – one whom Lawson might have had but didn't.

The 1972 edition itself gave, at the end of each story or sketch, the date of composition, usually by year, the name of the collection in which the piece first appeared, and a symbol to indicate if Lawson had ever revised it.[54] It was not until the appearance of *Commentaries* in 1985

[54] In his two-volume edition *Henry Lawson Complete Works*, Leonard Cronin advanced Roderick's mixture of year-by-year presentation and thematic organisation by intersequencing HL's verse and newspaper writing with his sketches and short stories: 'The works are arranged chronologically and thematically (according to their year of composition), showing Lawson's progression of ideas, themes, and the external and internal influences on his work' (vol. 1, *A Camp-Fire Yarn: Henry Lawson Complete Works 1885–1900*: Sydney: Lansdowne, 1984, p. xi; vol. 2 (1984) is *A Fantasy of Man . . . 1901–1922*). But providing no evidence for the annual datings (some are wrong, others are speculative – just as many of Roderick's were), and simultaneously accepting the late authorised texts rather than those of the year in question, left the edition open to the same objections as Roderick's. The edition, however, does not

that the bibliographic data about first periodical publication were given. The information was often accompanied by a summary of some of the textual changes evident between these first publications, the changes marked on printer's copy for *While the Billy Boils* (A1867–8), changes inferred as having been made on its proofs, and the later changes for those stories collected again in *The Country I Come From* in 1901.

By 1972, Roderick had explored the bibliographic complexities of at least a selection of the stories, as his commentaries to his *Bush Undertaker* volume of 1970 shows. Evidently, *Commentaries* was in active preparation by then. Although he states in a letter in 1976 that he had written a great many of the entries he then turned to other things, only completing the volume in March 1982.[55] But of course by then, given the existence of the 1972 edition, the die had already been cast. While I see no indication that Roderick would have changed his mind from the editorial course he adopted in 1972, there are a few glaring errors in the introduction to that earlier volume that show that it would have benefited from some delay.[56] Immersion in the manuscript and bibliographic evidence was necessary but it appears not to have been fully done. Admittedly, there was a *great* deal of evidence to master, and Roderick took on a job, with self-confidence, that no-one else had dared undertake. Realistically, it was one for a team.

It was inevitable, then, that Roderick would make mistakes of fact or inference, some of them more than trivial; but the later *Commentaries* present itself as a scholarly one.

[55] Letters, Colin Roderick to Stuart Marshall, 6 July 1976 (NLA MS 1578, Guardbook 17); Roderick to Marion[?] and Olaf [Ruhen?], 14 March 1982 (Guardbook 18).

[56] Roderick refers to the two stories in Bertha's holograph manuscript added to bulk out *Billy Boils* as 'The Geological Spieler' and 'Taking Stiffner Down' – when the second one was actually 'For Auld Lang Syne'. (The Stiffner story is extant in manuscript in ML A1862 but was not published in HL's lifetime.) He adds that his source is 'the text of the second thousand' of *Billy Boils* because HL pointed out to GR 'a few accidental errors and these were corrected for the second impression' (*Short Stories and Sketches*, ed. Roderick, p. xvi). But the printing of the sheets for the first 3,000 copies was done as a single job. Had Roderick collated copies of the First and Second Thousands or studied A&R's Publishing Ledger, which has an entry for the printing, he would not have made the error. The Ledger would also have suggested to him that the probable composition date of 'For Auld Lang Syne' was shortly before the date of payment for it, recorded as 25 April 1896 – not 1895 as he states in both the 1972 and 1984 editions, and without enclosing the year in square brackets.

volume will remain of permanent value as a report on the thinking of a scholar hard at work trying to bring the over-abundant evidence under some sort of control. Because it is broken up into entries, story by story, the production histories of the individual volumes tend to be broken up as well. The complexities of *While the Billy Boils* for instance, which my earlier chapters have demonstrated, were not fully faced because the evidence was never brought together as a single unit with its indications and counter-indications resolved into a coherent narrative.

This makes *Commentaries* a hard volume to use unless one knows the basic situation in advance. The evidence is not laid out well and the claims based on documents and inferences from documents are sometimes advanced as factual when they are only interpretative. Composition dates are only one example. Roderick's claims typically suffer from a lack of citation: whatever entry one is reading, one suspects that the hard evidence must be elsewhere. But sometimes, as I have shown, it is not there at all.

Roderick: Conclusion

Because Roderick's textual policy mandates the choice of the last authorised version this means that, as one tries to follow Lawson's development, one is not only baffled by the invented sequences, which interrupt the chronology, but also one lacks the texts of earlier versions that are needed if one is to observe the development of which Roderick speaks. He only provides a selection of their variant readings. His drawing attention to them discursively rather than in apparatus forces the reader to consult his reading text, find the place he is referring to, and perform the notional replacement. Since the reporting is not systematic, one cannot tell what else may have changed that relates to the disclosed alteration – and thus one is typically at the mercy of Roderick's interpretations, which can be dogmatic.

Like all editions, Roderick's 1972 and 1984 editions of the prose, when considered together with *Commentaries* of 1985, may be seen as the enactment of a textual argument. Understandably for his period,

Roderick believed that the case about Lawson's artistry needed proving, that *it* was the central problem. But no-one has believed so since. The long succession of Lawson selections since 1972 suggests that the judgement is beyond doubt. The real question for a scholarly edition is: How is the study of Lawson best served? The accompanying edition to this book proposes a different answer to Roderick's but only in relation to the 52 stories and sketches brought together as *While the Billy Boils*. In presenting the sketches and stories in chronological order and in their original newspaper texts, it raises the question: What kind of literary criticism might such an edition enable and how might it understand itself?

A new literary criticism of Lawson?

As part of a discussion of the literary-critical directions available in Australia in the early 1980s Harry Heseltine rapidly surveyed those arising from what were then the still-new promptings of poststructuralist theorists, concluding that 'too ardent a study of context – structural, cultural, historical – may blot out the original object of regard'.[57] Avoiding this outcome is a challenge for any new proposal that would merit the adjective 'literary'. Yet there can (and should) be no thought of return to a New Critical past, even if some of its regard for the literary work may still be cherished and, indeed, as I shall propose, defended in a theoretical manner. The question becomes: How is it possible to validate reasoned and sensitive interpretation in the present while acknowledging the fact that it inevitably participates in the discourses of its own moment? And that, of course, the work being discussed did likewise but at an earlier time?

Since the first chapter, I have been pressing on the conceptual boundaries of the work. Much of the evidence has been historical and bibliographical, about the versions, productions and readings of Lawson's *While the Billy Boils* stories and sketches over the decades since

---

[57] Heseltine, *In Due Season*, p. 200.

the 1890s. One's own criticism in the present (in response, it is likely, to a printed object or electronic artefact from the very recent past) is necessarily a further instalment in that history. Its advantage is that it is a report from the here and now, with the distinctive context of one's particular here and now. In due course, it takes its place in the long line of responses that, together over time and in response to materialised texts being read, *realise* and constitute the work. I gave a brief account of this in the Introduction in going back to the arguments of aesthetic philosopher Roman Ingarden, and I return to it below.[58] My proposal emerges from what I take to be this textual and material condition. As foreshadowed in the Introduction, what I am proposing is that we revive the notion of the *work* but expand it conceptually, leaving the New Critical inflection of the term behind. We should, I am arguing, no longer remain content with *text* standing in for the work in an apologetic way, nor automatically grant the term *discourse* the explanatory capacities we have been used to accord it.

For the professional literary critic, what goes with this expanded definition of the work is a more thoroughly informed style of literary criticism and history (and ultimately of editing) than we are used to. It is one that newspaper and magazine reviewers, given the restrictions and imperative deadlines of the genre, can scarcely be expected to provide. There is no reason why our literary conversation cannot take place on multiple levels or at multiple stages – indeed, there is every reason why, in a healthy literary culture, it should. That said, I cannot provide here a detailed response to all 52 sketches and stories in *While the Billy Boils*, for that would be another book in itself, although the new edition implicitly issues the invitation to others. But I can give a sense of what I believe ideally needs to be taken into account in the practice of literary criticism that I am prefiguring.

I have already shown in Chapter 2 a tissue of commonality between

---

[58] The argument is advanced theoretically in Eggert, *Securing the Past: Conservation in Art, Architecture and Literature* (Cambridge: Cambridge University Press, 2009), chap. 10; and with some extension in 'Brought to Book: Bibliography, Book History and the Study of Literature', *The Library*, 7th series, 13.1 (2012), 3–32.

Lawson's writings and the editorial agendas being pursued and audiences addressed in the newspapers in which he appeared. In dealing with this, I would not allow myself the tempting shortcut of making such loosely historicising claims as, for instance, nationalist discourse or the discourse of the Bushman-cum-digger spoke through them. Under this explanatory regime, the writing becomes the passive instance of the discourse, its particularities tend to lose their relevance, and the reader's active aesthetic engagement with the work tends to get left out in the cold, unsupported by theory and methodology.

I would still want to test such claims for whatever truth-value they might contain, but I would do it in relation to the histories of the story or sketch under discussion. Material meanings would be relevant here, and the allowable length of contributions would become a significant matter. Again, some pieces by Lawson are given illustrations in the *Bulletin*. These graphic works tend, visually and stylistically, to talk to the others in the same issue and over time. Since every illustration presupposes a response on the part of the illustrator, whether thoughtful or superficial, to the verbal text – and thus becomes, in the critic's sense, a 'reading' of it – the graphic interpretation in effect draws the Lawson piece into the multi-voiced cultural conversation that was enacted week by week in the newspaper-magazine. The paid-for illustration is thus a calibrator of contemporary tastes, to which the illustrator (with one eye necessarily on the audience) needed to attach the story, rather as a blurb for a book does today. The task of understanding the filaments of this intertwined conversation in which Lawson was being located will become more practicable once the *Bulletin* is made available as a digitised newspaper on a discovery service.[59]

Insofar as the weeklies' material meanings could be elicited I would relate them to the texts of Lawson's works. I would look very closely at the effects on these meanings of the series of alterations subsequently made by Jose, Lawson and the typesetters. And I would look, as best I

---

[59] The *Bulletin* is not yet available on the NLA's TROVE database (trove.nla.gov.au), though I have been informed (25 July 2012) that it will be digitised once funding becomes available.

could, at the effect, for the particular work, of Robertson's sequencing. That would help reveal the collaborative meanings of the work, meanings that were lost, for some readers, after the Platypus edition removed some stories and shuffled others and that were eliminated for most readers in the postwar period, especially from the 1970s, once their primary access to *While the Billy Boils* came via edited selections of Lawson's stories or works as a whole. The two positions in the sequence of 'The Drover's Wife' would be, as we have seen, a special object of attention, as would the relationship (another collaboration) of Mahony's illustrations in the 1896 collection with the stories or sketches they were illustrating. The medium of the illustrations (photographic process engraving in the early printings, replaced by cruder line-illustrations as the pricing of the collection went down when divided into two series in 1900) would bear on this since it changed the nature of – yokelised, one might say – Lawson's outback figures into caricatures of themselves, as the long process of retrospective creation of the 1890s began.[60] Such questions about the material meanings of the printings and collections down the decades, and about related contemporaneous publications of works by other authors, could be productively asked at every stage.

For the story or sketch being interpreted, I would ponder the meaning of changes made in proofs (described in Chapter 6) and think about them in relation to their likely agents of inscription. Perhaps most productive would be to read the stories and sketches in their chronological order of first publication and to try to elucidate the stages in Lawson's evolution as a prose writer from 1888 until 1896, and with a glance forward to the changes made in 1901 for *The Country I Come From*.

Apparently minor things (that are not, in fact, minor), such as getting the date right, will feed into such criticism by suggesting the appropriate comparators. 'Jones' Alley', for instance, is dated as written in 1892 in both Roderick's *Short Stories and Sketches 1888–1922* of 1972 and his *Prose Writings* of 1984. His *Commentaries* specifies its serialisation in the *Worker* as 1, 8 and 15 June 1892, and this determines its position in

---

[60] For the redrawn illustrations see Appendix 2.

Roderick's sequencing.[61] Although the story seems to have been written at the same general time as 'A Visit of Condolence' (*Bulletin*, 23 April 1892) and 'Arvie Aspinall's Alarm Clock' (*Bulletin*, 11 June 1892), it was not in fact published until 1895 on the same June dates. Roderick's misdating is understandable because of the common subject matter. But the superiority of 'Jones' Alley' strongly suggests that Lawson retained original papers and revised the story before its serial publication in June 1895. Its narration is more firmly third-person omniscient; there is no appeal to sentimentality; and its resonant ending has been often quoted in the criticism. As neither 'Arvie Aspinall's Alarm Clock' nor 'A Visit of Condolence' has anything like this note or the tonal control of the rest of the story, it is likely that 'Jones' Alley' was either the last of them to be written (and benefits from coming last) or, more likely, that it benefits from the linguistic control that Lawson developed as he wrote the later tales of 1893–95.

Once 'Jones' Alley' is recognised as being partially of 1895 the image, at the end of the story, of the Irish policeman walking very slowly away 'like an automatum' falls into place.[62] It aligns with the stoicism of the outback figures of the 1893 stories who are variously enduring failures of love or fortune or who are unable to return to the domestic conditions that would allow a regathering of ordinary social life. They too have put their emotional lives on a sort of permanent hold – the only way they can deal with disappointment. The story or sketch typically catches them in the act of remembering the initiating circumstances. In 'Jones' Alley' the Irish policeman has deliberately turned a blind eye to Mrs Aspinall who, aided by Billy Anderson and his 'push', is absconding with her few sticks of furniture that could lawfully be seized by her landlord as recompense for her unpaid rent.

From time to time, in the kind of criticism I am sketching, I would measure the distance between my own responses and those of earlier

---

[61] *Commentaries* 18.
[62] For the unusual spelling ('automatum'), which locates the writing within the newspaper advertising culture of the period, see Commentary for the story in Eggert and Webby.

readers as recorded in the reviewing periodicals and newspapers, to try to see what I was not seeing. To seek to understand the difference thus revealed by contextualising the earlier judgments would enrich our understanding not only of the earlier criticism, but of Lawson's work itself. Exploring what else Lawson's contemporaries were reading and thus the place of his writings in that reading – to what extent his writings were exogenous and to what extent endogenous – was not a priority for those elaborating the 1950s legend of the 1890s, or for those who subsequently critiqued it. Turning that around will become easier as bibliographic identification of the borrowing records of circulating libraries gradually becomes part of our ongoing conversation, as the retrospective coverage of the existing AustLit database becomes more complete, with our knowledge of publishing networks as a result maturing, and if the gathering of readers' experiences into database form begins to generate usable (and disputable) patterns. It would also be to answer the question, by means of an enriched empirical base, of the extent to which the colonial scene of reading was truly cosmopolitan (or transnational) as well.

Book history and a future for literary criticism

Anglophone book history has, over the last fifteen years or so, signalled its liberation from old-fashioned memoirs of the firm, in favour of a form of study sensitised to newer so-called 'material' conceptions of production and reception. Interest in a wider range of players and motivations in the book scene has been licensed. In this bold advance, some book historians have flexed the muscles of their new freedom by deliberately refusing to grant any methodological precedence to classic literary works on the grounds that they are aesthetically superior to the other titles on the lists of the publisher being studied. A book-democracy has been declared.

The new attunement to the circumstances and effects of book production means that we will be less likely to believe the traditional House accounts of their own role as handmaidens of literature. De-privileging the literary – knocking it off its belles-lettristic pedestal in the pre-professional book-historical period – has been part of the area's coming of age. The assumption is shared by many book historians, particularly if they have backgrounds in English literature.[63] The move does not get the argument very far theoretically, though. It leaves, exactly where it was, the problem of whether we are talking about books or about works; and, indeed, many book historians shuttle between the two terms as if there were no difference between them. Those literary scholars who tend to think of the concept of the *work* as embarrassingly old-fashioned are especially liable to slip and slide over the distinction.

The historians, drawing upon another tradition, have developed their own methods, having tended to rely on the inspection of official archives and the analysis of trends within one or more publishing houses across a historical period. Decisive price *vs* format analysis, as developed by William St Clair and Simon Eliot for the late eighteenth- and nineteenth-century book trades, has been another leading shoot of book-historical study. Histories of readership, such as those of Jonathan Rose and Martyn Lyons, represent another notable initiative.[64] However,

---

[63] E.g., David Finkelstein, *The House of Blackwood: Author–Publisher Relations in the Victorian Era* (University Park: Pennsylvania State University Press, 2002). He argues that 'the process of producing print for public consumption . . . can no longer be viewed simply as a linear path from producer (author) to disseminator . . . to consumer'. Referring to various shifts in allied fields towards a cultural materialism that is more sensitive to historical contexts, he describes the 'social and cultural factors [that] feed into the process of production, dissemination, and reception of individual works' and argues for acknowledging the 'democratized spaces' of the print shop where the literary value of what is produced is immaterial (pp. 15, 16, 19).

[64] See, e.g., St Clair, *The Reading Nation in the Romantic Period* (Cambridge: Cambridge University Press, 2004); Eliot, *Some Patterns and Trends in British Publishing 1800–1919* (London: Bibliographical Society, 1994); Rose, *The Intellectual Life of the British Working Classes* (New Haven: Yale University Press, 2001); Lyons and Lucy Taksa, *Australian Readers Remember: An Oral History of Reading 1890–1930* (Melbourne: Oxford University Press, 1992); and Lyons, *A History of Reading and Writing in the Western World* (Basingstoke, Hants.: Palgrave Macmillan, 2010).

I leave out of this brutally abbreviated sketch of recent trends in book history the sociological slant of the French *annales* school of book historians from and after the 1970s, precursors of the current boom in Anglo-American forms of book history; the materialist interest of anthropologists in meaning-bearing cultural objects; and recent calls for unrolling book history into the continuities of pre-alphabetic marking systems, orality and various kinds of media literacy.

the situation I am describing leaves would-be literary practitioners grasping for an alternative theory of, or empirical approach towards, book history.

The 'material' fetish

This problem was raised for me in reading Laurel Brake's *Print in Transition 1850-1910* (2001), which, among other things, takes Finkelstein's case one crucial step further. Her emphasis is on the importance of serialisation in all forms (fiction, periodicals, encyclopaedias and other reference books issued in parts) during 1850-1910. A dethroning of the book goes with it:

> In a framework of material culture, I want to treat the wrappers and advertisers that, with the letterpress and illustration, make up part-issues and periodicals, as part of what we designate the 'text' to be studied. In this perspective the discourses of higher journalism such as history, literature and science are situated far closer to other commodities in the marketplace than in the reductive and apparently normative high cultural volume forms in which they principally reach us.[65]

By way of example, Brake notes the odd juxtaposition of an advertisement for the Scottish Widows' Fund on the back wrapper (recto) opposite the last page of Book VIII of *Daniel Deronda* (1876), where Gwendolen is discovered 'crushed on the floor. Such grief seemed natural in a poor lady whose husband had been drowned in her presence'. Brake comments: 'This chance parallel between the letterpress and the advertisements underlines the consanguinity of the discourses of commerce and culture, the heteroglossia of these hybrid texts which serially produce regular, pervasive dialogue.'[66]

She shows that the apparatus of publishing was continuous across periodical and book formats. Each took advantage of the other through pricing differentials that justified serialisation of novels and even of long short stories and poems. Reviews of books that were published

---

[65] Laurel Brake, *Print in Transition 1850-1910* (Basingstoke, Hants.: Palgrave Macmillan, 2001), p. 27.
[66] *Ibid.*, p. 45.

in periodicals were then excerpted for publication in advertisement sections bound-in at the end of the very same titles; book publishers conducted their own successful House magazines; and so on. The evidence is plentiful.

Brake's general conclusion, announced near the start of her book, is that 'in the nineteenth century the spheres of the book and the serial inhabited one and the same galaxy'.[67] Literary study, she argues, ought to attend to this salient fact, from which libraries' binding practices – discarding wrappers, advertisements and other matter considered ephemeral – have tended to shield us. Although she does not put it this way, one may say that, in the period Brake covers (which conveniently includes the 1890s), the work's materialised base typically brought it into some dubious company – which is where its earliest readers encountered it. In this argument, the thing that is wrong with the concept of the literary is that it is associated (for us) almost exclusively with the book. Recovering the contemporary reading experience requires we go beyond its respectable confines.

The emphasis in the present study on understanding Lawson's writing career as an evolving, active response to the practicalities of periodical publication, subsequently affected by his negotiations with a new set of players as the collections were produced in book form, sits well with Brake's argument, as does acknowledging the broader tastes of 1890s readers than those envisaged in the legend of that Australian decade. Similarly consistent is the decision in the accompanying edition to privilege Lawson's newspaper and magazine texts, and to record the changes made for the book forms of the stories and sketches at foot of page.

Brake refers to her kind of enquiry as horizontal book history. It collapses the boundaries between book and periodical, and can embrace periodicals (as whole titles) as 'texts' worthy of study in themselves, enjoying a semi-collective authorship and participating in 'discourses of a nineteenth-century cultural formation'. This approach, she argues, dissolves 'the hypotheses of vertical studies of single titles,

[67] *Ibid.*, p. 26.

editors and writers'.[68] Earlier in her book she aligns such study with the methodologies of New Criticism whereas study of the discourses of the periodicals she sees as closer to poststructuralism. It is at this point that the parallel between my approach and Brake's ceases.

The forging of a new material-culture emphasis has been a hallmark of the recent phase of book history, and Brake's work takes it an important step further. However, the disadvantages of rejecting vertical studies are obvious. The baffling generality of claims about the shared discursive formation of books and periodicals, their 'consanguinity of discourses', their sharing 'the same galaxy', and the claim that whole periodicals can be treated as single texts to be studied, suggests to me that the banner of the 'material' that the book-history movement unfurled as its own twenty years or more ago has become something of a fetish in need now of bibliographic counterbalancing. Otherwise the claims reduce to the status of truisms, rhetorically impressive to be sure, but perilously close to empty. The example of the part-issue of *Daniel Deronda* can only be seen as significant in an unspecific and unintended way, and then only for some contemporaneous readers (who made – what? – of it) rather than for the makers. The fact is worth knowing about in case it is indicative of something more important; but – standing as an unexplained, apparently inexplicable, event – *how* significant is it? Put theoretically, how can the production and reception of the extraordinary juxtaposition of the two texts be grounded?

Bibliographical reasoning often allows us to reconstruct production events: in principle, this applies as much to the production of advertising wrappers as to canonical works such as *Daniel Deronda*. An analysis of the gathering of copy for both forms, identification of the agents of the separate texts, and of the printing environments in which the two productions took place, and then their final conjunction at the binder's would offer an explanation that was specific and that uncovered something of the varying intentions of the different textual agents. Assuming sufficient bibliographical information could be elicited

[68] *Ibid.*, p. 82.

from the copies themselves or from archival holdings, an empirical explanation would emerge. A series of such analyses over time of the production events of *Daniel Deronda* in book form might well reveal, by cutting across, the cultural rhythms and tensions of successive historical moments. Such a project would also potentially offer an explanation of the ongoing importance for successive sets of readers (and publishers and printers and booksellers) of a remarkable novel. The writer of the advertisement for the Scottish Widows' Fund, on the other hand, almost certainly does not deserve this kind of attention, especially not if it impoverishes study of *Daniel Deronda*. But I am talking about George Eliot's novel as a work, not as a book.

Thus I see no reason to believe that commitment to the horizontal kind of study need involve undermining the vertical. To assume that it must, only exposes the erroneous assumption that postwar understandings of what works and authorship are can never change and that the role of the literary critic cannot broaden either. There is no need, I believe, for the literary scholar-turned-book historian to remain in reaction to New Criticism, no need to reject the triad of author–work–oeuvre – although there is definitely a need to understand them afresh, as I have been trying to show with Lawson. Similarly, I see no need to downplay the cultural importance that the book form maintained for authors, reviewers and readers. But there is definitely (I agree with Brake) a need to shine more light on the crucial role played by periodicals in the careers of authors, the kinds of writing this material form encouraged, and the consequently catholic experience of their periodical readerships.

Conclusion

I am arguing that we can do this by modeling our understanding of works on their material forms, their chronologies of production and in terms of the agents who originally produced them, in their successive versions. I include as agents all those readers who *realise* works every time they are read. Mute objects in material form, texts live only by our grace as we read them. It gives us joy to extend their lives as they enter into ours, extending, expanding, confronting our imaginative life in the present. The aesthetic dimension emerges from the encounter: it *becomes* the encounter for the reader. The acknowledgement of the act of reading as part of the life of the work potentially allows a realignment of any and every work's historical and aesthetic legibility.

Typesetting is, before it is anything else, a form of reading; and so is copy-editing. Both are agented acts of interpretation or construing, and both usually result in changed wordings, whether great or small. Publication is an act of reproduction carried out in the name of the work, done usually for commercial motives in relation to real or supposed market opportunities. Reviewing is another act of reading that leaves a report of the encounter, and marginalia in books in personal and public libraries all over the world bear cryptic memoranda of such encounters. All these acts are done in the present, one that soon falls into the past. All bring the work back into full being temporarily; when completed, they resign its status to a material one only, awaiting the next realisation. Our later discussion of the work is really a discussion of what we remember of the reading experience; when we reach a point of disagreement we check by returning to the material object, which once again yields up its text to us.

From this point of view the work emerges, not as a transhistorical essence, not as aesthetic object ideally shaped for New Critical study, but as a series of historical processes. For a literary classic, this includes a set of material products, all of which claim to present or represent the work. To accept this starting point is to be able to model the relationship between the material object and the readings carried out in the name of the work; and it is to redefine the fundamental unit of literary study.

All of these processes are historically marked. All are agented. All can be studied. The material object, inherently inert, rises onto the level of meaning only in the act of reading, whether that reading is allographic (of the text) or autographic (of the material *object*: in this case, the newspaper, magazine or book).[69] If reading involves human

---

[69] This is Nelson Goodman's distinction in *Languages of Art: An Approach to a Theory of*

participation, then text (meaning) acts in a dialectic with document: the two dimensions require one another to establish their identity as such. The dialectic is not a transcendent one – as the humanist postwar literary-critical style conceived of it. Rather it is a process.

From this point of view scholarly editions of the work do not supersede all previous editions and printings. Rather they propel the life of the work further into the future, in an altered form, by intervening in it critically and appealing to criteria and information previously overlooked. So scholarly editors, like all editors, are agents in the ongoing life of the work, not its embalmers. Editions are one form of argument about the work. They are subject to the same textual and documentary condition of all printings carried out in the name of the work. It has been the business of the present book to study that condition for a set of works that gained the collective title *While the Billy Boils* in 1896. The accompanying edition is intended as an intervention in the reading and study of them.

My hope is that we will be able to find conceptual room for the aesthetic so that book history can revive and refresh literary study and not just act as another escape route for lecturers in English or other literatures. My contention is that this can be done if we look again at what the Oxford bibliographer Kathryn Sutherland referred to in 1996 as 'the manifestly relegated concept of the work'.[70] Her description of the fate of the term is understandable. It had by then been widely superseded by *text* and *discourse*. To use the term *work* was to admit to the illusions of New Criticism or Leavisism, or to the even more old-fashioned, pre-professional belletrism.

The folly of this supersession is now clear to me. The ongoing currency of any work must, I believe, be conceptually included in it; and the work's capacity to go on doing work in readers' imaginative lives offers a way of marrying the material and the aesthetic. The arena of reception is

---

Symbols (Indianapolis: Bobbs-Merrill, 1968).
[70] Kathryn Sutherland, 'Looking and Knowing: Textual Encounters of a Postponed Kind', in *Beyond the Book: Theory, Culture and the Politics of Cyberspace*, ed. Warren Chernaik, Marilyn Deegan and Andrew Gibson (Oxford: Office for Humanities Communication, 1996), pp. 11–22 [p. 16].

where the argument about a work's (current) meanings resides. The *work* is a convenient concept that offers boundary lines around the constantly shifting relationship between a printed, digital or other document and the meaning raised from it by the reader. But the concept of the work validates the notion of reader response both to the materiality of the book and (far more importantly in most, but not all, cases) to its lexical text or texts.

In practical terms, what this work-grounded approach to literary study offers is a way of bringing the history of works in their material and textual forms together with the receptions of those forms. When one can do that one has a better chance of understanding what one is commenting on than when one limits oneself to a purely aesthetic or discursive approach. Logically, the reception in the present both renews the work – since it extends its life either in the reading or in the commentary, or both. Its special privilege is that it is the only moment of reception capable of bringing to bear the concerns and sensitivities of the present onto the reading of the work that derives (as all works do) from the past.

A book-historically inflected, bibliographically sharpened literary criticism, focussed on the work, gains depth and precision from the 'thick description' of the text-production events, spread out over time, that it requires. Because the exploration of a work's production–consumption spectrum necessarily engages study of the reading experience over time, the approach imperatively raises larger, more general questions about cultural and discursive shifts, and shifts in taste: shifts that the work itself indexes. This is a literary methodology that knows where it starts: with the aesthetic experience of reading the text of a work in the present. It is an experience that, once attended to as an intellectual problem in itself, begins to open up for every work some or all of the kinds of questions that the present study has been pursuing for *While the Billy Boils* – as well, undoubtedly, as many others that it has not.

APPENDIX 1

A PRODUCTION HISTORY OF EDWARD DYSON'S *RHYMES FROM THE MINES*

In 1896 Edward Dyson's *Rhymes from the Mines* was shadowing *While the Billy Boils* through the press. As Dyson lived in Melbourne, correspondence between him and Angus & Robertson was necessary. This surviving evidence, together with the production documents for *Rhymes from the Mines* that survive in part, help to confirm the analysis of the production of Lawson's prose collection, mainly reconstructed from bibliographical evidence, offered in Chapter 5.

Dyson proposed a volume of verse to Angus & Robertson probably in early November 1895. (*The Man from Snowy River* had appeared on 17 October 1895.) He submitted his manuscript in three instalments, probably a mixture of holograph manuscript and newspaper clippings.[1]

Arthur Jose's initial comments for Angus & Robertson were prepared by early May 1896 at latest. It is not obvious what form they took but they were evidently passed on to Dyson. He revised as 'needed' but disagreed with Jose's suggestion that the poem 'Battered Bob' be excluded.[2] On 15 May 1896, Robertson predicted that the book would become available by the 'end of June'.[3]

ML A1907 is the printer's copy. A mixture of clippings and holograph manuscript, it has Jose's and Dyson's alterations on it; some of Dyson's are clearly in response to Jose's. It also contains a Contents page in Dyson's handwriting (with a later pencilled pagination-calculation of

---

[1] Letter, Dyson to GR, 17 February [1896] (ML MSS 314/28, pp. 747–51).
[2] Letter, Dyson to GR, 4 May [1896] (ML MSS 314/28, pp. 759–61).
[3] Letter to W. R. C. Burt of the Melbourne *Age* (ML MSS 3269/71/4, fols. 200–1).

121 pages) and another list of poems (in Jose's handwriting) 'Additional' (50 pages). Jose has marked a few 'too poor to put in'. These markings, and his alterations to the texts of the clippings and holographs, may have made up Jose's initial comments.

Proofs were prepared. Jose's later (extant) comments are keyed by comment number to a document that is not A1907: presumably to the first (galley) proofs. One of his comments pre-supposes text that Dyson has added to a clipping of 'The Old Whim Horse' in A1907 and that would have appeared in the proofs.[4]

On 21 May 1896 Dyson sent a letter to Angus & Robertson with a new version of a poem to which Jose had objected. Dyson requested 'revises' on 24 May but they had not arrived by 1 July.[5] He still did not know whether Robertson intended to include four poems, of which he, Dyson, thought little. Robertson was evidently deciding which should be included and their sequence. This selection process dragged on.

In his letter to Robertson of 'July 1 [1896]' Dyson stated: 'I have been waiting upon further proofs of Rhymes from the Mines for close on three weeks with the greatest impatience. Is there any hitch? It would be a pity to defer the publication for long, as the decided mining boom now on would certainly help sales'.[6] And, on 24 November 1896: 'to receive a request for copy at this stage was the last thing I bargained for'. The request was to rewrite 'The Song of the Stampers'. Dyson asked Robertson simply to delete it and urged a reduction in the retail price from 5s.

Jose was correcting one copy of the proofs as they appeared in batches and this was being sent to Dyson with his own set for correction: 'when I have made small alterations in his corrections, I have struck them out in his proofs and entered them in mine.'[7] The holograph Preface in A1907 is marked in pencil: 'Mr Jose for report 23/7/96 Referred to E.D. 24/7/96'; but the Preface would have been submitted last, together with

---

[4] ML MSS 314/28, pp. 803–9.
[5] ML MSS 314/28, pp. 663, 665, 695.
[6] ML MSS 314/28, p. 695.
[7] ML MSS 314/28, p. 706.

the introductory verse. So this date may refer to these last pages alone and their proofs. Publication finally occurred in December 1896 in time for the Christmas market.

APPENDIX 2

THE CURIOUS HISTORY OF THE FRANK MAHONY ILLUSTRATIONS IN *WHILE THE BILLY BOILS*

Traditional but slow copper-plate engraving had given way in the nineteenth century to lithography and end-grain wood engraving for book illustration: lithography was flexible and fast; end-grain blocks were extremely durable. By late in the century, photogravure and process engraving had become fairly well adapted for the reproduction of paintings – or, as for *While the Billy Boils*, Frank Mahony's inkwash and line drawings, five of the former and three of the latter, and a line vignette for the title-page. (All but one of the originals are preserved at the Mitchell Library and are reproduced here.[1])

For the latter processes a photographic image of the original was exposed to a sensitised copper plate, etching it through successive 'bites' and stoppings-out to match the tones of the photograph. Process engraving required the careful removal, under a magnifying glass, of the plate's ragged edges or the opening up of its dark areas with a graver where the bite had been imperfect. The finished plate was mounted on a block 'type high', thus enabling the printing of illustrations and text in the same pass through the press. Photogravure involved intaglio printing and therefore had to be done separately; illustrations needed to be neatly glued onto the gutter edge of the adjoining printed section.

---

[1] At ML PX *D195 as part of A&R's artwork (353 original drawings) purchased (separately from MSS 314) in 1959. The exception is the illustration for 'A Day on a Selection'. Also present, of relevance to HL, are: *(1)* the title-page vignette for *In the Days*; and *(2)* three illustrations for *On the Track and Over the Sliprails*, dated 1900, one of which was used (inside the front boards) – for the special issue of 50 copies with 'Thin Lips and False Teeth'. The back inside-boards illustration for the double volume is not present.

APPENDIX 2 . THE FRANK MAHONY ILLUSTRATIONS   359

The first impression of 3,000 copies of *While the Billy Boils* was letterpress-printed by Websdale, Shoosmith in Sydney using stereotypes. The fact that the illustrations were tipped-in shows that they were printed separately; this was confirmed by the review of *While the Billy Boils* on 29 August 1896 in the *Sydney Mail*, which reported that they were 'admirably reproduced by the Electric Photoengraving Company'.

However, behind the scenes, some experimentation to achieve the desired standard had been necessary. A letter dated 6 June 1896 from George Robertson to James MacLehose & Sons, the Glasgow book retailer and publisher to whom Robertson had been apprenticed as a boy, shows he had had to resort to that firm to secure a satisfactory result: 'We are afraid our Local Printers made a mess of the Lawson & Paterson Photogravure blocks – but we hope Annam[?] has been able to put them right again By this time we hope that the 3000 each we asked you to print are well in hand if not on the way.'[2]

It is clear that some copies of the illustrations were printed in Sydney (for Robertson later had a special issue of twelve copies prepared); but they were rejected, along with an extra, line illustration of two swagmen sitting talking, drawn by Walter Syer. It was used in the special issue only, on the inside front cover: see Illustration 12.[3] Robertson then sent

---

[2]   ML MSS 3269/71/3, fol. 67. The Ledger record of this printing (24,000 plates – i.e. 3,000 copies of 8 plates – for £6.7s.) is dated 1 August 1896, whereas the entry for the printing and binding of the volumes themselves (done by Websdale, Shoosmith of Sydney) is dated 23 September 1896 (ML MSS 3269/11/1, fol. 46). The charge for 9 blocks (£10.2.3) was charged on 10[?] July: the title-page vignette must have been printed in Sydney, presumably via a steel or an end-grain wood engraving. An entry for 12 September 1898 lists the return to A&R (after the printing of a new impression of *Billy Boils*) of a 'Line block': ML MSS 3269/12/2, fol. 44.

[3]   The special issue is distinguished from the normal trade issue by containing an early state of the illustrations, which lack their captions, and the Syer illustration dated '8/96'. (The Syer original is in ML PX *D195; for Syer, see Chapter 3 n. 28.) GR must have had the copies specially bound. He gave at least two of them to his book collector–customers, David Scott Mitchell and the barrister Adrian Knox (1863–1932). In their copies (ML A823/ L425.1/1A1 and 1A2) there is a handwritten note by GR opposite the Syer illustration:

   D S Mitchell Esq/ With the publishers' compliments/——/ This is one of twelve copies/ with plates unlettered and W Syer's vignette on endpaper. The plates, we regret to add, are not so well printed as in the ordinary edition!/ A&R

Evidently the Syer illustration was a rejected experiment, intended to improve the look of the volume. GR perhaps decided that the vignette went one step too far towards popularisation and away from the dignity of the London-quality printed book he was seeking. The copies

the Mahony blocks to Glasgow for further processing, but photogravure cannot have been the method used. This is shown by the second impression of *While the Billy Boils* – also of 3,000 copies, but with a change of printer to McCarron, Stewart of Sydney. This printer incorporated the plates for the illustrations with the type matter rather than subsequently tipping-in. This fact, together with the fact that there is no observable difference between the illustrations in the two impressions, shows that the method used in Glasgow was process engraving, not photogravure, and that the re-processed blocks were sent back to Sydney for reuse.[4] As both processes involved photography, Robertson's imprecise terminology in the letter is understandable.

Later impressions continued with the same method. Not being tipped-in, the illustrations with their blank versos became, for printing purposes, part of the page count that made up each sheet. Thus adjustments to the gatherings were necessary. This was true for McCarron, Stewart, who changed from the original octavo (16-page) gatherings to sixteenmos (32-pages) printed on a larger machine, and for Websdale, Shoosmith who resumed responsibility with the third impression and went back to the octavo format.[5]

In the second impression, the illustration for 'On the Edge of a Plain' (opposite p. 98) was replaced with a redrawn version, signed by Mahony and dated 'Sept 96': see Illustrations 4 and 5. The reason for the replacement is unknown; some mishap may have necessitated the

---

have the advertisement section at the back dated August 1896; no reviews of *Billy Boils* are quoted.

[4] The other possibility – that GR sent the original illustrations to Glasgow for a completely new processing – is ruled out by his next extant letter to MacLehose of 11 July 1896. Speaking of his intention to have *Billy Boils* printed in England for Home market distribution (see Chapter 7 pp. 154–8), he added: 'we will send an advance copy with the originals of the illustrations and a set of matrices [to allow stereotype printing of the type matter]': ML MSS 3269/71/3, fol. 79. The despatch is recorded at ML MSS 3269/11/1, fol. 79 (entries for the 'English Ed.' of *Billy Boils*).

[5] McCarron, Stewart left the printed signatures of the gatherings: A, B, C, etc.) as they were, despite adopting the sixteenmo format for printing, gathering and sewing. GR had originally approached Websdale, Shoosmith for quotations for the second printing, either with 'the plates in each case to be printed along with the letterpress' or 'printed separately and tipped in': ML MSS 3269/71/4, fol. 337, dated 10 September 1896. See further, Chapter 7 pp. 153–4.

renewal. The captions were also re-typeset for the second impression.[6]

The style of the replacement illustration shows a notable deviation from the original. It is not simply a copying and seems to be differently inspired. It had, by September 1896, been many months since Mahony had been working closely with Lawson's texts. In the *Bulletin* version of 'On the Edge of a Plain' – which, as explained in Chapter 5, Mahony must have read – the mate's attitude, whether standing or sitting, is not stated: so Mahony was at liberty to have him standing up. But, in revising the text in printer's copy, Lawson newly specified the mate as being in a sitting position, along with Mitchell. So Mahony's sketch *had* matched the text but now did not. The fact that he kept the mate standing in the revised version of the sketch shows he did not read the version in *While the Billy Boils*, or, if he did, chose to ignore it.

Thus, whatever the influence that led to the changed stylisation, it was not Lawson. The standing figure (Mitchell's mate) is awkward in the first version but the faces and clothing are more fully realised. In the second version Mitchell's mate loses his weather-beaten look and becomes almost elegant. Mahony was effectively dispensing with the down-at-heel realism of the first version, appropriate to Lawson's text. Both men are in the shade in the first version; the second is much more open in composition. The trees and background are now more functional, with a hint of Art Nouveau in their patterning against the sky. The style of the illustration, especially the use of vertical strokes for the background trees, is somewhat similar to that of George Lambert and Fred Leist (and is distantly related to the more full-blown Art Nouveau of David Souter) in *Bulletin* cartoons of the period.[7] Another possible (English)

---

[6] Tiny shifts in the position of the type in the captions are revealed by optical (machine) collation. Further, the second impression's caption to the illustration for 'The Drover's Wife' uses numeral 1 instead of capital I in the first of its two examples in 'Mother, I won't never go drovin'; blast me if I do!'. The first, third and fourth impressions – printed by Websdale, Shoosmith, unlike the second – correctly use 'I'; and identical settings of the other captions (except that of 'Macquarie's Mate', whose caption was reset with another, very minor textual change) suggest that they too were originally stereotyped and reused when Websdale, Shoosmith resumed responsibility.

[7] For some examples, see Patricia Rolfe, *The Journalistic Javelin: An Illustrated History of the Bulletin* (Gladesville, NSW: Wildcat, 1979): for Souter, pp. 130–1; George Lambert, p.

source is the *Idler* where economic line and languid poses were to be seen during 1895–96.

The illustration for 'The Drover's Wife' is one of the five tonal illustrations in *While the Billy Boils*. The result in a (personal) copy of the Twelfth Thousand from the fourth impression is particularly good, slightly better than the best of the results noted in copies inspected of the First Thousand. Paradoxically if one regards the question from an editorial point of view, the original intention (of Mahony and Robertson) was better materialised at this later stage than in the first printing: the process was inherently liable to variation, depending on the care that was or was not taken during the printing. If one gives the paradox one further twist, it could be argued that the reproductions that appear in the present volume represent a further refinement and are therefore closer to the intention, even though the technical process used is one that could not have been anticipated in 1896. The illustrations are reproduced here from high-quality digital photographs of Mahony's large-format originals in the Mitchell Library, but with foxing marks, now present in the originals, reduced in prominence.

After that fourth impression the five tonal reproductions were abandoned for newly cut line-illustrations, much cruder than the other three originally drawn in 1896. The redrawings (signed by Mahony: three undated and two '1899') for the cheap editions are also present in the Mitchell Library: they are crudely done, but they are not the same size as printed copies so they were not simply traced. Perhaps the original blocks had worn and were judged to need replacing.

The illustration for 'The Drover's Wife' is one of the casualties (compare Illustrations 6 and 7). But it had a worse fate in store. The adjustment to the gatherings entailed by taking the illustrations into the page count from the second impression onwards, described above, had at first no visible effect for the reader. But, with the division of the title into two 'Series' in 1900, what became a blank leaf at the end of the First

119; Leist, p. 47. I thank Dennis Bryans for these suggestions and for identifying process engraving as the technique used.

Series paperbacks had, in the two-Series-in-one-volume hardbacks, to be excised, thus leaving a stub, between pages 168 and 169. This was a trivial matter except that, as a result, the Second Series now had a number of pages inconvenient for folding (174 in total, including the illustrations and final colophon on the verso of the final page of text, p. 333) whereas 172 pages can be folded easily by introducing a 12-page section (or a 4 and an 8) amongst the otherwise octavo gatherings.[8] The two inconvenient pages became the illustration for 'The Drover's Wife' and its blank verso: this leaf now had to be tipped-in, and indeed it was at first, as a (personal) copy of 1902, the Thirteenth Thousand, shows.

For the 1913 and subsequent issues the printing was transferred to W. C. Penfold & Co. Whether deliberately (to save on costs) or as the result of some mix-up, Penfold's printings omitted the inconvenient illustration altogether: and this became, for readers of the best known story in the collection, a significant visible effect until it was restored in 1923 for the three-series paperback volumes printed by Marchant & Co. for Angus & Robertson.[9] True to form, a different omission occurred in this printing: the drawing of Steelman, opposite page 113.

---

[8] The Thirteenth Thousand (1902) has, between octavo signatures T and W, an unsigned folio (2 leaves, [U]) followed by a quarto (4 leaves, signed V): personal copy.

[9] Personal copy of 1915 (Penfold); NLA copy of 1923 (Marchant).

APPENDIX 3

POSTWAR PRINTINGS OF *WHILE THE BILLY BOILS* AND PROSE SELECTIONS

This is a list of *(1)* post-World War II publications of *While the Billy Boils*; *(2)* postwar Lawson prose collections, and selections of Lawson containing stories or sketches from *While the Billy Boils*; and *(3)* postwar anthologies by multiple authors including items from *While the Billy Boils*. Pre-1946 printings are dealt with in the relevant chapters above: the printings in Lawson's lifetime in Chapters 2, 7 and 10 and the subsequent ones in Chapter 11. Entries are given here in the chronological order of their first printing.

The list has been derived from inspection of personal and library copies, reprint statements on copyright pages, the catalogues of the State Library of New South Wales and the National Library of Australia, and secondhand bookseller listings in abebooks.com (accessed in June 2010). Where ABEBOOKS provided the sole source of information on the existence of a particular printing its date is followed by an asterisk (*) to indicate it is unconfirmed.

The list's reliability is limited by that of its sources. It does not include translations or limited-edition fine-print publications. Nor is it intended to substitute for what is still badly needed: a complete descriptive bibliography of Lawson's works that would supersede the once-standard but now out-of-date, incomplete and bibliographically imprecise *Annotated Bibliography of Henry Lawson* (1951) by George Mackaness. The listing in *A Bibliography of Australian Literature K–O to 2000*, gen. ed. John Arnold and John Hay, will be found to be of further assistance – but it is not a descriptive bibliography (St Lucia: University of Queensland Press, 2007; pp. 143–9).

Despite the incompleteness of the present listing, especially in section *(3)*, the number of the collections, selections and anthologies, and especially of their reprintings, remains striking, at least until the early 1990s: see Chapter 13, pages 270–1 and 311–12 for a discussion. The abiding popularity of 'The Drover's Wife', 'The Union Buries its Dead' and '[The Bush Undertaker]' is also notable: see Chapter 10 n. 29.

1. Post-World War II publications of *While the Billy Boils*

While the Billy Boils First Series (Sydney: Angus & Robertson, 1966). REPRINTED 1969.

While the Billy Boils Second Series (Sydney: Angus & Robertson, 1967).

While the Billy Boils: 87 Stories from the Prose Works of Henry Lawson (Sydney: Angus & Robertson, 1970). Contains the 1935 *Prose Works* typesetting (see Chapter 11 pp. 261–2) of the First and Second Series and also the double series *On the Track and Over the Sliprails*. REPRINTED (London: Hale, 1972); in paperback (Sydney: Rigby, 1975), (Windsor, Vic.: Budget Books, 1979), (Windsor, Vic.: Currey O'Neil, 1980, 1981, 1982), (South Yarra, Vic.: Claremont, 1990), (Sydney: Rigby Seal Books, 1995).

While the Billy Boils: First and Second Series (Sydney: Angus & Robertson, 1973; Arkon Paperbacks imprint), Introduction by Chris Wallace-Crabbe. REPRINTED (Arkon) 1977, 1981, 1983, 1985; (Eden) 1988, 1990; (Imprint Classics) 1991 with new introduction by Chris Wallace-Crabbe.

While the Billy Boils (Sydney: Sydney University Press, 2004). Print-on-demand artefact based on an e-publication taken from a copy of the 1896 first edition (Sydney: University of Sydney Library, Scholarly Electronic Text and Image Service, 1997).

While the Billy Boils (Gloucester, UK: Dodo, 2007). Print-on-demand artefact probably based on the Project Gutenberg EBook #7144, released on 1 December 2004.

While the Billy Boils: The Original Newspaper Versions, ed. Paul Eggert with explanatory notes by Elizabeth Webby (Sydney: Sydney University Press, 2012). Scholarly edition.

2. Post-World War II Lawson prose collections, and selections containing items from *While the Billy Boils*

Twenty Stories and Seven Poems, with Observations by his Friends and Critics, ed. Colin Roderick (Sydney: Angus & Robertson, 1947).

Prose Works of Henry Lawson (Sydney: Angus & Robertson, 1948). REPRINTED 1956, 1957, 1962, 1970, 1976, 1979, 1980; then 1982 as *Collected Short Stories of Henry Lawson*.

The Children's Lawson, selected by Colin Roderick (Sydney: Angus & Robertson, 1949).

The Selected Works of Henry Lawson, ed. Lyle Blair ([East Lansing]: Michigan State University Press, 1957).

Fifteen Stories, Introduction by Colin Roderick (Sydney: Angus & Robertson, 1959). REPRINTED 1962, 1966, 1968,* 1969, then in Angus & Robertson Classics 1975, REPRINTED 1978, 1982, 1985, then in 1988 under Angus & Robertson's Eden Paperbacks imprint as *Bill, the Ventriloquial Rooster and Other Yarns*.

The Stories of Henry Lawson, ed. Cecil Mann. 3 vols. (Sydney: Angus & Robertson, 1964). See Chapter 13 p. 335.

Best Stories, Preface by CM [Cecil Mann] (Sydney: Angus & Robertson, 1966). REPRINTED 1968, then under Angus & Robertson's Pacific Books imprint, 1970 (twice),* then in Angus & Robertson's Classics, 1973, REPRINTED 1975, 1979 and 1980, then in The Australian Classics (Penrith, NSW: Discovery Press), Introduction by Stephen Murray-Smith, then REPRINTED by Angus & Robertson in Australian Literary Heritage Series 1981, then under Angus & Robertson's Arkon imprint 1983, 1984, 1986, by then in Australia's Great Books edition (Kensington: Australia's Times House, 1984), then (North Ryde, NSW: HarperCollins, 1986), then retitled as *The Drover's Wife and Other Classic Stories* (North Ryde, NSW: HarperCollins, 1988), REPRINTED 1991.

Humorous Stories, selected by Cecil Mann *(1)* (Sydney: Angus & Robertson, 1967). REPRINTED 1968, 1971 (Angus & Robertson's Pacific Books imprint), 1975, 1977, 1980. *(2)* Same typesetting but with stories rearranged and illustrations by S. T. Gill added: (North Ryde: Angus & Robertson, 1987), REPRINTED 1989. The format of the following reprints may be either *(1)* or *(2)*: (North Ryde, NSW: HarperCollins, 1986),* REPRINTED 1987, then 1988 as *The

Loaded Dog and Other Humorous Stories, 1988, 1990, (NSW: Cornstalk, 1991),* (North Ryde, NSW: HarperCollins, 1992, 2000).

Stories for Senior Students, ed. Colin Roderick (Sydney: Angus & Robertson, 1962).

The Bush Undertaker and Other Stories, ed. with Preface and Commentary by Colin Roderick (Sydney: Angus & Robertson, 1970), revised edition 1974, REPRINTED 1975 (twice), 1977, 1979, then under Arkon Paperbacks imprint 1982, 1983, 1986, 1987 (twice), then under Eden imprint 1988, 1989,* then under Collins/Angus & Robertson imprint 1990; then a new typesetting in 1994 (Imprint Classics series), REPRINTED 2002. See Chapter 13 p. 326.

Selected Stories, Introduction by Brian Matthews (Adelaide: Rigby, 1971). REPRINTED 1974, 1975, 1981 (lacks Introduction), 1984.* The 1971 issue would presumably have been licensed by Angus & Robertson, but there is no note of this in the front matter.

Short Stories and Sketches 1888–1922, ed. Colin Roderick (Sydney: Angus & Robertson, 1972). Scholarly edition. As *Henry Lawson the Master Storyteller: Prose Writings*, ed. Colin Roderick (Sydney: Angus & Robertson, 1984). Expanded edition. See Chapter 13 pp. 325–41.

The Best of Henry Lawson for Young Australians, illustrated by Arthur McNeil (Sydney: Paul Hamlyn, 1973).

The Drover's Wife and Other Stories, Introduction by Alan Brissenden (Hornsby, NSW: Hodder & Stoughton, 1974).

The World of Henry Lawson, ed. Walter Stone (Dee Why, NSW: Hamlyn, 1974).

Favourite Stories, selected by Walter Stone (West Melbourne, Vic.: Nelson, 1976). REPRINTED 1976, 1977.

Henry Lawson, ed. Brian Kiernan, in Portable Australian Authors series (St Lucia: University of Queensland Press, 1976). REPRINTED in 1980, 1982, 1985, 1987, 1988, 1991 (as Henry Lawson, *Stories, Poems, Sketches and Autobiography*).

Tales from Henry Lawson, adapted by Margaret McPherson (West Melbourne, Vic.: Nelson, 1977).

Henry Lawson's Mates: The Complete Stories of Henry Lawson (Hawthorn, Vic.: Lloyd O'Neil, 1979). New typesetting of *Prose Works*. As *Collected Stories of Henry Lawson* (Ringwood, Vic.: Penguin, 1987).

Stories of Henry Lawson, illustrated by Louis Silvestro (Sydney: Angus & Robertson, 1980),* REPRINTED 1981, 1986.*

The Essential Henry Lawson, ed. Brian Kiernan (South Yarra, Vic.: Currey O'Neil, [1982]). See Chapter 13 pp. 320–5.

A Camp-Fire Yarn: Henry Lawson Complete Works (2 vols.), ed. Leonard Cronin, introduced by Brian Kiernan, vol. 1 *1885–1900*, (Sydney: Lansdowne, 1984). See Chapter 13 n. 54.

An Illustrated Treasury, illustrated by Dee Huxley, selected by Glenys Smith (Sydney: Lansdowne, 1985). REPRINTED Chatswood, NSW: New Holland Publishers, 2011.

The Penguin Henry Lawson: Short Stories, ed. John Barnes (Ringwood, Vic.: Penguin, 1986). REPRINTED 2009 with preface by John Tranter; and as part of an omnibus volume *The Penguin Book of Ballads and Short Stories* (Camberwell, Vic.: Penguin, 2003).

Recollections: A Selection of Autobiographical Works, ed. Leonard Cronin (Frenchs Forest, NSW: Reed, 1987).

Henry Lawson Favourites, illustrated (Hawthorn, Vic.: Currey O'Neil, 1984), revised edition 1986, then under Viking O'Neil imprint (Ringwood, Vic.: Penguin, 1987). Also in large-print format (Melbourne: Australian Large Print, 1987).

The Picador Henry Lawson, ed. Geoffrey Dutton (Chippendale, NSW: Pan Macmillan, 1991).

Selected Works ([Melbourne]: Modern Publishing Group, 1992).

Selected Stories (Pymble, NSW: HarperCollins, 2001). Claims to use Roderick's *Master Storyteller* (1984) texts; a new typesetting re-organising the contents back into original volume divisions.

Henry Lawson, ed. Geoffrey Blainey (Melbourne: Text Publishing, 2002).

Henry Lawson's Greatest Stories, introduction by Barry Oakley (Rowville, Vic.: Five Mile Press, 2006).

Short Stories in Prose and Verse (Gloucester UK: Dodo Press, 2008), a print-on-demand artefact.

Henry Lawson in New Zealand, ed. Charles Ferrall (Wellington, NZ: Steel Roberts, 2011). Foreword by Vincent O'Sullivan.

3. Post-World War II anthologies by multiple authors including items from *While the Billy Boils*

Australian Round-Up, ed. Colin Roderick (Sydney: Angus & Robertson, 1953). 'His Country—After All'.

A Century of Australian Short Stories, ed. Cecil Hadgraft and Richard Wilson (London: Heinemann, 1963). 'The Drover's Wife', 'The Union Buries its Dead'.

Favourite Australian Stories, ed. Colin Thiele (Adelaide: Rigby, 1963). 'The Drover's Wife'.

Southern Harvest: An Anthology of Australian Short Stories, ed. R. F. Brissenden (Melbourne: Macmillan, 1964). '[Enter Mitchell]'.

Short Stories of Australia: The Lawson Tradition, ed. Douglas Stewart (Sydney: A&R, 1967). 'The Drover's Wife', '[The Bush Undertaker]'.

Best Australian Short Stories, ed. Douglas Stewart and Beatrice Davis (Hawthorn, Vic.: Lloyd O'Neil, 1971). 'The Drover's Wife', '[The Bush Undertaker]'.

An Australian Selection: Short Stories by Lawson, Palmer, Porter, White and Cowan, ed. John Barnes (Sydney: Angus & Robertson, 1974). 'The Drover's Wife', '[The Bush Undertaker]'.

Classic Australian Short Stories, ed. Judah Waten and Stephen Murray-Smith (Melbourne: Wren, 1974). 'The Union Buries its Dead'; 'Shooting the Moon'.

Jack London and Henry Lawson, ed. Esmor Jones (London: Harrap, 1976). '"Board and Residence"', 'Hungerford', 'The Union Buries its Dead', 'The Drover's Wife'.

The 1890s, ed. Leon Cantrell (St Lucia: University of Queensland Press, 1977). '"Dossing Out" and "Camping"', 'The Union Buries its Dead', 'The Drover's Wife', '"In a Wet Season"'.

Australian Short Stories, ed. Kerryn Goldsworthy (Melbourne: Dent, 1983). 'The Union Buries its Dead'.

The Australian Short Story: An Anthology from the 1890s to the 1980s, ed. Laurie Hergenhan (St Lucia: University of Queensland Press, 1986). 'The Union Buries its Dead'.

The Oxford Book of New Zealand Short Stories, ed. Vincent O'Sullivan (Auckland, NZ: Oxford University Press, 1992, 1994). 'Stiffner and Jim (Thirdly, Bill)'.

Great Australian Short Stories (Noble Park, Vic.: Five Mile Press, 2002). Miniature book. 'That There Dog o' Mine', 'Going Blind', 'Mitchell: A Character Sketch'.

The Macquarie PEN Anthology of Australian Literature, ed. Nicholas Jose (Crows Nest, NSW: Allen & Unwin, 2009. 'The Drover's Wife', 'The Union Buries its Dead', 'In a Dry Season'.

The Penguin Book of Australian Bush Writing, ed. John Ross (Camberwell, Vic.: Penguin Viking, 2011): '"In a Wet Season"'.

APPENDIX 4

ANGUS & ROBERTSON'S RECORD-KEEPING

THIS account of materials located in the Angus & Robertson collections at the Mitchell Library, State Library of New South Wales, supplements the account of the firm's record-keeping given in Chapter 3. Jennifer Alison made good use of the firm's correspondence in her history of Angus & Robertson to 1900, and she itemises the series of letterbooks in the firm's archive.[1] However she made relatively little use of the evidence in the ledgers. They are peculiarly relevant here, given the focus of attention on a single title.

George Robertson seems to have been a meticulous financial record-keeper. The most relevant documents in the firm's archive at the Mitchell Library are two publishing ledgers. Both have one or more openings devoted to each successive title being published. Entries in them mostly have a cross-reference to journals. The actual transactions (orders and payments) would presumably have been done daily, and recorded in a Purchases Journal or Cash Book, and possibly other Day Books, themselves the later source of the information recorded in the ledgers.[2]

The ledger books were not primarily tracking cash flow but were, rather, a means of subsequently determining whether a particular title had generated profit or loss. Debits for a title were recorded on the left-hand page of the opening. They are referred to there as '*To*' costs (i.e. debits attributed *to* the book being produced). On the right-hand

---

[1] In ML MSS 3269/71–75: see Alison 13–14.
[2] The two ledgers are ML MSS 3269/11 and 12. There is a Purchases Journal at ML MSS 3269/13/1. Only one Cash Book is extant, that for 1899–1909, at ML MSS 3269/13/3.

page, credits were recorded. They are referred to as '*By*' values (i.e. value accrued, even if not yet realised, *by* means of copies so far printed and bound). Thus the first opening for *While the Billy Boils* records, on its left-hand page, costs for the period up until 23 September 1896, amounting to £459.4s.9d.

It was a requirement of this form of bookkeeping that the right-hand and left-hand page-totals could be made to balance at any time so that an assessment of how the title was faring could be achieved. Similarly, if another opening was required to continue the recording (typically for reprints) a balance would be struck for the first opening and the overall debit or credit carried forward to the beginning of the new one. To achieve the balance before payment for copies had been received a nominal amount representing the wholesale value of bound copies was entered on the right-hand side: in this case, 'By 3000 Copies. (W. S. & Co.)' at 3s. per copy, totalling £450. Thus a 'Debit Balance' for this opening was recorded as £9.4s.9d.[3]

In this ledger, *While the Billy Boils* is at first treated as a single title on folio 46 (i.e., stamp-numbered opening '46'). Its first entry is dated 30 November 1895 and does not have an amount brought forward at the top of its left-hand page – as would be expected if it had a predecessor. This is therefore the first extant ledger record dealing with the Lawson prose collection. In this ledger, folios for other titles follow until, at folios 78 and 79, the recording for *While the Billy Boils* resumes but splits into the 5s. cloth-bound edition and the English edition. At folios 120 and 121 the recording further splits into paper-bound and cloth-bound. Then a reversal occurs in the next ledger book: its folios 81–2 regather, for the title as a whole from January 1898, all orders and copies received.[4] (The

---

[3] ML MSS 3269/11/1, fol. 46. In some cases to achieve a balance, the cost of printing so-far unbound volumes was entered on the right-hand side to offset a corresponding charge on the left. This cost represented the value to the firm even if saleable copies were not yet available. When bound, they would normally be warehoused by the printer until required (see Chapter 7 n. 15). If they were then credited on the right-hand side a second time (at the wholesale rate for bound volumes) then the original printing cost was transferred back to the left-hand side to enable an accurate final balance to be achieved.

[4] ML MSS 3269/11/2. It is continued (from July 1899) in a ledger named '3': ML MSS

successive publishing formats are dealt with in Chapters 7 and 11.)

Until 30 June 1897 (the end of a financial year) the credit side of the ledgers recorded copies received or printed, credited at a wholesale rate, as mentioned above. From 1 July 1898 the calculation was done off actual sales of stock. It was calculated as stock brought forward from a previous opening, less complimentaries; this number, minus the stock still on hand, provided sales information for the financial year.

There is also a payments record book, which was being kept for a separate purpose; in the case of *While the Billy Boils* entries start at August 1897.[5] With the printed column headings 'Paper', 'Cloth', 'Stereos and Blocks', 'Portraits', 'Printing. Typewriting', 'Advertising. Postages', 'Complimentary Copies', 'Royalties' and 'Sundries', this record book duplicates, but often with later dates, orders recorded in the ledger just mentioned above on its folios 81–2.[6]

Doubtless the still relatively young publishing firm was experimenting with record-keeping as it went along. The ledgers provided a managerial overview, title by title. The information in them was always open to error, duplicated entry or omission on the part of the bookkeepers. However, the habit of end-of-folio and, later, end-of-financial-year reconciliation of debits and credits acted as a check. There is also evidence of a later hand (perhaps an auditor's) on some of the folios.

Typesetting was not separately charged, so it must have been part of the original printing charge. But author's corrections and the cost of preparing stereos and their matrices appear separately.[7] The Private Ledger starts on 1 July 1897.[8] It seems to have been the partners' way of keeping financial oversight of the whole operation rather than title-by-title. The subdivisions include Royalties Account, Copyright Account and Sales Account.

3269/12/3, fols. 119–20.
[5] ML MSS 3269/11/3, fol. 28. This is not a recording of debits and credits for a title, but of payments made for that title by category.
[6] ML MSS 3269/11/2.
[7] ML MSS 3269/12/2.
[8] ML MSS 3269/12/1.

In addition, a Publishing Progress Register kept track, for each title, of materials despatched (proofs, paper, cloth etc.) and of proofs and bound copies received. The firm's Publishing Review and Complimentary Copies Register lists copies sent out for review or as complimentary copies sent to booksellers and school inspectors. This was done in an effort to secure firm orders rather than operate on a more hazardous sale-or-return basis.[9]

Finally, a Manuscripts Register for the period 1 October 1896 – 21 April 1937 lists between 6,000 and 7,000 manuscripts that were considered for publication.[10] There are no formal readers' reports in this register, but they are occasionally to be found in correspondence volumes.

As the firm grew, the archival effort to keep track of all copyrights and licences must have grown in proportion. Collections of verse and short stories, each with multiple copyrights, would have presented a particular problem. By 1920 Angus & Robertson had established a card catalogue of all works whose copyright it possessed.[11] This catalogue grew over the years. It was supplemented by various 'Scrap Books' to which cuttings of the copyrighted works were added.

---

[9] ML MSS 3269/23/2.
[10] ML MSS 3269/23/1.
[11] As for the year, HL's sister Gertrude O'Connor (Susannah Gertrude m. Job Falconer; they lived at his property Cobberah near Dubbo) inscribed the date 2 August 1920 on Card 419 for the poem 'Faces in the Street' in ML MSS 314/247. She went through the cards adding biographical information, some of it inaccurate.

INDEX

1890s. *See also* Sydney–Melbourne rivalry
  booktrade in, 77–9
  economic depression in, 40, 287
  income disparity in, 294
  heterogeneous identity of, 193, 273, 274–5, 284
  reading tastes in, 79n, 193–6, 204, 223, 277–8, 349
  seen as originary, 275–6, 279, 284
  as a construction of the 1950s, 224, 275n, 283–4, 295, 344, 346
  Graeme Davison on, 287–8
  Russel Ward on, 285–6, 295

Academy, 162n
Adams, Francis, 277, 288
Age (Melbourne), 82, 137, 355n
Alison, Jennifer, 77n, 162n, 211n, 212, 218n, 371
Anderson, Benedict, 21, 273
Andrews, B.G., 116n
Angus, David Mackenzie, 77, 78, 201, 219
Angus & Robertson. *See also* Robertson, George
  early publishing, 79–80
  uses Macmillan as model, 80–2, 129, 176–7, 215–16
  cross-subsidises literary publication, 82
  sends books to troops, 181, 249
  record-keeping of, 371–4
  storage of printed sheets, 144n, 372n
  publishing arrangement with Blackwood, 241
  overseas distributors of, 154n, 159n
  buys up HL copyrights, 86n, 149, 209–11, 244, 258n, 266, 268
  profits earned from HL books, 211–19
  distribution inferior to Macmillan's, 217–19
Antipodean, 56, 65, 66, 67n, 147, 277n
Archibald, J.F. (editor, *Bulletin*), 42n, 50, 51, 52–3, 71n, 73, 74, 82, 92, 193n
  nominated consultant on *WBB* selection, 73, 112
  sends HL outback, 29, 42, 199
  dissuades Paterson from reviewing HL, 165
  defers publication of manuscripts, 51, 60, 112
  admires Zola, 55
Argosy, 229
Argus (Melbourne), 165, 175, 182, 196
Arnold, John, 246n, 364
AustLit, 8n, 79n, 190n, 233n, 273n, 293n, 319, 346
Australasian, 196
Australian Medical Gazette, 166
Australian Pocket Library, 267, 269n
Australian Socialist League, 65

Balzac, Honoré de, 273
Barnes, John, 191n, 207, 220–1, 225, 228n, 229n, 230n, 232n, 241n, 242n, 247
  documents HL's London problems, 226
  challenges idea of a 'Lawson school', 303n
Barton, G.B., 50n, 205n
Bathurst Free Press, 172
Becke, Louis, 186
  HL's fiction more 'trustworthy' than, 179
  plagiarised by Boldrewood, 193n
  and Walter Jeffrey, *The Mutineers*, 137, 138n, 162n

Bentley, Richard (publisher), 137n, 238, 242
Blackmur, R.P., 96, 327
Blackwood (publisher), 157–8, 161, 202, 228–39, 241
Blackwood's Magazine, 202, 241, 243
Boake, Barcroft, 215
Bode, Katherine, 27n, 190n
Boldrewood, Rolf, 168, 195, 205n, 276
   American editions of, 8n
   anglophile orientation of, 26
   literary earnings of, 215–17, 224
   HL's fiction more 'trustworthy' than, 179
   seen as historically accurate, 277
   prefers HL's verse to prose, 182n
   plagiarised Louis Becke, 193n
   promoted by Macmillan, 81, 243
   use of vernacular, 94, 96–7
   Robbery Under Arms, 34, 50n, 94, 96–7, 129, 171–2
Bookfellow, 206
booktrade
   in 1890s Australia, 77–9: booksellers, 78, 163n; shortage of type, 144
   imperial, 19–20, 130n, 155, 157, 180, 224–5, 230–2, 242n, 258–60
   collapse of three-decker novel, 133, 242–3
Boomerang, 39, 42n, 147,182, 283
   HL on staff of, 38, 41, 45n, 48, 50, 65, 208
Boote, Henry E. (editor, *Worker* (Brisbane)), 69n, 75–6
Boothby, Guy, 8n, 223
Bourdieu, Pierre, 13, 21n
Brady, E.J., 187, 206
Brake, Laurel, 348–51
Brereton, John Le Gay, 70–2, 113, 184n, 261, 263
   nominated consultant on *In the Days*, 73, 112
   collects HL clippings, 114
   on HL's reading, 34n
   working on HL's proofs, 83n, reviews HL, 68n
   reviews Paterson, 74
   puffs HL, 74, 112
   judges HL's prose superior to verse, 255, 260, 266, 278–9
Bright, Charles, 105
Brooks, Cleanth, and Robert Penn Warren, 296n, 313

Brooks, Emma (HL's aunt), 42, 313
Broomfield, Fred, 164n, 171, 174, 247n, 248n, 263–4
Bryans, Dennis, 362n
Buckley, Vincent, 301, 302n
Bulletin, (Sydney). *See also* Archibald, J.F., Stephens, A.G.
   nationalist agenda of, 25, 38, 82, 248–9
   interest in fictional technique, 90
   initially thought disreputable, 190–1
   cultivates brevity, 39n, 51
   circulation figures, 243
   book series, 38, 50n, 240
   political proximity to the *Worker*, 46–7
   out-pays *Worker*, 63, 204–5, 211
   HL's pride at appearing in, 37–8
   HL's contributions to, 42, 50–7
   promotes HL's A&R sales, 74, 115, 147, 165n
   credited with launching HL, 148, 187, 255
   Walter Murdoch on, 182
   H.M. Green on, 279–80
   nurturing role recognised, 179, 186, 187
   ethos romanticised in 1950s, 224
   condemned for separatist masculinity, 288
   plans for digitising, 343

Cambridge, Ada, 8n, 191n, 223, 276, 287n
Cantrell, Leon, 215n, 274, 275n
Cape, Jonathan (publisher), 257–8
Cargill, Henry C., 74n
Carter, David, 8n, 10n, 21n, 282n, 300n, 303n
Casanova, Pascale, 17, 21
Champion, 137, 169, 176, 200n
Champion, Henry Hyde (bookseller and editor), 137, 165
Christesen, Clem, 303n
Clark, Manning, 285n
Clarke, Marcus, 8n, 35n, 168, 187, 188, 190, 191, 192, 206, 276
Clipper (Hobart), 64n
Cole, E.W. (bookseller and publisher), 78, 160
Conrad, Joseph, 192, 227n, 230, 243, 245n, 313n
Cosmos, 105
Crane, Stephen, 230
Creed, Mrs, *see* Mack, Louise

Cronin, Leonard, 338n
Cunninghame, F., & Co. (printer), 159n

Daily Worker, 49, 62
Dale, Leigh, 279n, 302n
Daley, Victor, 73, 215
  At Dawn and Dusk, 162n, 218n
Damrosch, David, 17
Davis, Arthur Hoey. *See* Steele Rudd
Davis, William Walter ('Baldy', station owner), 43
Davison, Graeme, 37n, 215n, 287–8
Dawn, 36, 38, 65, 290n
Day, J. Medway (editor, *Worker*), 69
de Serville, Paul, 192–3
Deakin, Alfred, 25n, 192, 272, 275, 276n
Demaine, William Halliwell, 65
Dennis, C.J., 249n
Devanny, Jean, 265
Dickens, Charles, 34, 69, 223
  influences HL, 54–5
Dimock, Wai-Chee, 17, 22–3
Dixon, Robert, 21n, 22
Dixson, Sir William, 86n, 102
Docker, John, 277, 278n, 302n, 313n
Douglas, Dennis, 335
Dymocks (bookseller and publisher), 7, 163n, 195
Dyson, Edward, 83, 134, 187, 205, 215
  use of dialect spelling, 91, 96
  literary earnings, 215n
  Bull-Ant, 190
  Rhymes from the Mines, 91, 96, 97, 128, 138, 151, 153, 137, 355–7

education
  HL's, 33–4, 67
  of workers, 39
  in NSW, 77, 251
  in British Empire, 18, 172, 313n
Eliot, George, *Daniel Deronda*, 348, 350–1
Eliot, Simon, 347
Eliot, T.S., 222, 313
Emerson, Ralph Waldo, 24, 223
English, James F., 10n
Eureka Stockade, 37, 45, 171, 283
Evans, George Essex, 56

Farrell, John, 76n, 92n, 170, 171, 175, 215, 280

Ferguson, David G., 165, 168, 172
Ferguson, George (A&R), 335, 337
Finkelstein, David, 16n, 241n, 243n, 347n
Foucault, Michel, 11–12, 317
folk songs and ballads, 286, 292–3
Furphy, Joseph, 222, 223, 224, 249n, 284, 285, 299

Gallop, Jane, 10n
Garnett, Edward, 52, 196–8, 220, 227–9, 245, 257–8, 281, 297
  criticism contrasted with A.G. Stephens's, 198
  on class-based criticism, 197
Gaunt, Mary, 135n
General Laborers' Union of Australasia, 43, 45
George, Henry, 46n
Giles, Paul, 24
Gilmore, Mary, 41n, 71n, 245, 250
globalisation, 19–20, 312
Golden Shanty, A, 38, 110–11, 122, 240, 241n, 256n
Goodchild, Keighley, 151
Goodman, Nelson, 353n
Gordon, Adam Lindsay, 68n, 179, 187, 188, 195, 206, 249n, 276
Gordon, James W. (friend of HL), 43n, 44, 114n
Gouws, John, 223n
Grace, A.E., 46
Graham, R.B. Cunninghame, 228, 229n
Grahame, Jim. *See* Gordon, James W.
Grattan, C. Hartley, 255n
Green, H.M., 214–15, 247n, 264n, 266, 279–83, 296n, 297n, 302
Gundagai Times, 56n

Hancock, W.K., 285n, 291
Hardy, Frank, 266
Hardy, Thomas, 187, 197, 247n
Harpur, Charles, 276
Harris, Phillip (editor, *Aussie*), 250
Harte, Bret, 34, 54, 97, 168, 170, 223, 279
Head, Walter W. (editor, *Worker*), 41, 48, 151n
Hemingway, Ernest, 258, 280
Henley, W.E., 94
Henry, O. (W. S. Porter), 53
Hermes, 68, 74

Hervey, Grant, 249, 273–5
Heseltine, H.P., 184n, 247n, 272, 312–20, 331
   practising New Criticism, 313, 315–18
   faces critical aporia, 317–18
   warns against over-discursivity, 341
heterochronicity
   of books, 222–4
   of social myth, 271
Hickey, Bernard, 229n
Hinderaker, Eric, 18
Hirsch, E.D., 6
Holt, Bland, 322
Howe, Stephen, 19n
Hudson, W.H., 196n
Hughes, Billy, 294n
   orders HL's state funeral, 250
Hummer, 41

Idler (London), 165, 362
Ifould, W.H., 264
Ingarden, Roman, 6, 342

James, Henry, 230, 327
James, Neil, 267n
Jarvis, Doug, 90
Jefferson, George, 227, 228n, 229
Jeffrey, Walter, *see* Becke, Louis
Jonathan Cape *See* Cape, Jonathan (publisher)
Jose, Arthur, 85, 128, 232n, 276n
   biography, 88
   copy-editing HL, 88–97, 101–3, 104, 105, 106, 107, 117–19, 121–5, 137–8, 140, 141–3, 157, 236, 298, 315, 343
   copy-editing Edward Dyson, 355–6
   provides title for *WBB*, 149–51
   uses Macmillan's Kipling as model, 82, 93–7
   edits to placate English critics, 90, 92, 95–6, 332
   reviews *WBB*, 178
   as critic of verse, 96n, 97
   on Sydney and Melbourne aesthetics, 81
   sees Lawson and Paterson as originary, 255, 276n
   credits *Bulletin* with launching HL, 255
   admires *Bulletin*'s nationalism, 82
   values Lawson's prose over verse, 255, 256n
   likes Kipling's work, 80

   unimpressed by Paterson, 134
   caricature of E.E. Morris, 191n
   Pagliaro on, 90
   Roderick on, 90
Juta, J.C. (South African publisher), 154n, 162, 180, 181n

Kiernan, Brian, 38, 246n, 301–4, 320–5
   distinguishes sketch from story, 327
   sees literature as autonomous, 302
   partial adoption of book history methods, 324–5, 331
Kingsley, Henry, 8n, 168, 222, 276
Kipling, Rudyard, 98, 131, 165, 191n, 195, 223
   model for A&R publishing HL, 80–2, 93–7
   use of dialect spellings in dialogue, 81, 93–4
   verse recited by HL, 97
   HL compared to, 170, 178, 255, 298
Kirkpatrick, Peter, 21n
Kirkpatrick, Rod, 65n
Knox, Adrian (book-collector), 359n
Kramer, Leonie, 302n
Kratzmann, Gregory, 215n
Kristeva, Julia, 286

Labour press, 39–41, 48. *See also Boomerang, Daily Worker, Hummer, Patriot, Worker, Worker* (Brisbane)
Lake, Marilyn, 288–90
Lambert, George, 251, 280, 361
LaMonte, Robert Rives, 265n
Lane, William, 40–1, 71n, 245
Larsen, Niels (HL's father), 33–4, 35, 36
Laugesen, Amanda, 249n
Lawrence, D.H., 230, 296n
Lawson, Bertha, (née Bredt, HL's wife), 124, 126, 136n, 199–201, 203–4, 225–6, 239–40, 242, 245–6, 306, 328n
   works as amanuensis for HL, 85, 105n, 119n, 124–6, 127n, 137, 140, 339n
Lawson, Bertha (HL's daughter), 204, 240n, 258, 259n, 261

Lawson, Henry
LIFE AND CAREER
   early life, 33–7
   education, 33–4, 67
   reading, 34–5, 97, 168

Lawson, Henry *(cont.)*
  deafness, 35, 37, 44, 168
  writing habits, 48–9, 169
  contributions to the *Worker*, 45–9, 187
  contributions to the *Bulletin*, 42, 50–7
  travels to: Melbourne (1887), 37;
    Bourke (1892–3), 42–4; New Zealand
    (1893–4), 48–9; New Zealand (1896),
    136; Perth (1896), 199; New Zealand
    (1897), 201; London (1900–02), 204,
    225–45
  socialistic sympathies of, 39–40
  on mateship, 47–8, 314
  becomes disaffected with trades unions,
    62–3, 300
  language, 95, 97–103
  use of dialect spelling, 91–2, 98–9
  agreements and contracts, 38, 148–9,
    255, 276n
  economics of writing, 204–14, 216–17,
    219–20, 230–1
  copyright expiration, 270–1
  pessimism in, 167, 179, 187, 192
  sentimentality in, 175, 197, 304
  realism in, 96, 167–9, 171, 179, 192,
    277–8, 285, 298
  debate on worth of verse vs prose,
    181–2, 255, 256n, 264, 266, 278, 284,
    298, 301, 313, 327
  story sequences by, 57–62, 173–4, 177,
    308–9, 333–4
  projected novel, 321–2
  praised as social historian, 171–2
  seen as originary, 38, 255, 276n
  compared to: Chekhov, 279, 297; Gorky,
    265n; Harte, 170; Kipling, 170, 178,
    255, 298; Paterson, 272; Twain, 258
  mythologised as bushman, 248
  co-opted to nationalist myth, 171, 248,
    250–1, 313
  appropriated by the Left, 251, 265–6, 313
  absorbed by the Establishment, 250–1
  memorialised, 251, 260, 280, 294, 295
  popularity peaks in 1950s and 1960s, 271
  WORKS: VOLUMES
  Short Stories in Prose and Verse (1894),
    64–70, 97, 119n, 167, 202, 233
  In the Days When the World Was Wide
    (1896), 49n, 70, 73–6, 84n, 92, 112,
    116, 137–9, 147, 155, 157, 162n, 164,
    181, 189, 201, 205, 208n, 209, 212,
    213n, 217, 260n
  While the Billy Boils (1896). *See separate main entry*
  On the Track and Over the Sliprails
    (1900), 84, 86n, 114, 119n, 133, 149,
    200n, 208n, 218, 226–7, 231, 239,
    258n, 262, 267, 324
  Verses, Popular and Humorous (1900),
    200n, 214, 218, 226n 253n
  The Country I Come From (1901), 5,
    186–7, 196n, 218, 226, 233n, 234, 235,
    236, 237n, 238–40, 256, 339, 344
  Joe Wilson and his Mates (1901), 133,
    226–7, 240–2, 244, 246n, 260n, 266,
    271
  Children of the Bush (1902), 43, 119n,
    200, 226n, 227n, 238n, 241n, 244n,
    245n, 246
  later Collected editions, 267–70
  WORKS: INDIVIDUAL POEMS
  'The Cambaroora Star', 41n
  'Faces in the Street', 38, 209, 265, 288,
    374n
  'For'ard', 49n, 61, 174
  'The God-Forgotten Election', 74n
  'Golden Gully', 38n
  'Here's Luck', 61n
  'The Paroo "River"', 61n
  '"Sez You"', 61n
  'The Shame of Going Back', 42, 245
  'A Song of the Republic', 37, 38
  'The Star of Australasia', 112, 174n
  'The Waving of the Red', 45
  'The Wreck of the *Derry Castle*', 114
  WORKS: INDIVIDUAL SKETCHES, STORIES
  AND ESSAYS
  'Across the Straits'. *See* 'Some
    Reflections on a Voyage across Cook's
    Straits (N.Z.)'
  'Another of Mitchell's Plans for the
    Future', 101, 103, 143, 254n, 308–9
  'An Article on Man', 47
  'Arvie Aspinall's Alarm Clock', 54, 175,
    253, 265n, 345
  'Baldy Thompson. A Sketch of a
    Squatter', 43, 62, 111n, 123
  '"Board and Residence"', 60, 100, 233

Lawson, Henry *(cont.)*
- 'Bogg of Geebung', 38, 53, 111n, 123, 132, 329
- 'Brighten's Sister-in-Law', 192n, 227, 241n, 242n, 308
- '"Brummy Usen"', 57, 118, 253, 261
- 'The Bush Undertaker'. *See* 'A Christmas in the Far West; or, The Bush Undertaker'
- 'A Camp-fire Yarn', 57, 101, 143
- 'The Cant and Dirt of Labor Literature', 62
- 'Chicken Pies', 85, 111, 118
- 'The City and the Bush', 62–3
- 'Coming Across.–A Study in the Steerage', 64n, 100, 140
- 'A Christmas in the Far West; or, The Bush Undertaker', 56, 65, 66, 119n, 175, 178, 232, 237n, 262n, 277, 316n, 365
- 'The Darling River', 46n, 132n
- 'A Day on a Selection. A Sketch from Observation', 120, 122, 157n, 323, 358
- '"Dossing Out" and "Camping"', 60, 100, 108, 120, 142, 253
- 'A Double Buggy at Lahey's Creek', 192, 227, 241n
- 'Drifted Back', 62
- 'The Drover's Wife', 2, 3, 55, 65, 84n, 89n, 104, 107, 108, 110, 111n, 118, 119n, 120, 122, 131, 132, 134, 139, 140, 141, 142, 145, 159, 160, 172, 175, 184, 232, 237, 240, 261, 262n, 270n, 297n, 304, 305, 344, 362, 363, 365
- 'Enter Mitchell'. *See* 'That Swag'
- 'For Auld Lang Syne', 41, 85, 105, 111n, 124–5, 126, 132, 137, 142n, 174n, 210n, 324, 339n
- 'A Fragment of Autobiography', 34–5, 37, 288
- 'The Geological Speiler', 57n, 85n, 105n, 111n, 124–5, 126–7, 132, 137, 140, 149n, 258, 324, 328, 339
- 'Going Blind', 60, 63, 98, 174–5, 324n, 327
- 'His Colonial Oath', 58
- 'His Country—After All', 64, 232n, 233, 237, 270n, 369
- 'His Father's Mate', 38, 54, 107, 110–11, 122, 128, 145, 175, 232n, 233, 235, 236, 237n, 248, 256n, 323, 329
- 'He'd Come Back', 63
- 'Hungerford', 60, 89, 122n
- 'In a Dry Season', 53, 253, 370
- '"In a Wet Season." Along the Line', 44n, 60, 100, 114, 118, 123
- 'An Incident at Stiffner's', 61
- 'It Was Awful', 85n, 111, 118
- 'Jimmy Grimshaw's Wooing', 227
- 'Jones' Alley', 54n, 63, 65n, 119n, 137, 142n, 157n, 166n, 174n, 253–4, 324n, 344–5
- 'A Leader of the Future', 45
- 'Letters to Jack Cornstalk', 227n, 229
- 'Louth, on the Darling', 45
- 'Macquarie's Mate', 57n, 61–2, 65, 67n, 70, 89n, 116, 232, 233n, 361
- 'The Man Who Forgot', 58, 232n, 233, 258
- 'Mitchell: A Character Sketch', 57, 102, 123, 297n
- 'Mitchell Doesn't Believe in the Sack', 57, 108, 109, 122, 145, 232n, 233, 237n
- 'The Old Bark School: An Echo', 63, 84, 253, 324n
- '"An Old Mate of your Father's"', 45, 47, 57, 114, 135, 179, 232n, 233, 237, 252
- 'On the Edge of a Plain', 57, 103, 116–17, 142, 308, 309, 360–1
- 'On the Tucker Track', 200n
- 'Our Pipes', 63, 101, 102, 104, 118, 125–6, 324n
- '"Pursuing Literature" in Australia', 41n, 50n, 75n, 169, 183, 203, 204–5, 208n, 284
- '"Rats"', 57, 65, 89, 143, 232, 233n, 315, 316, 317, 318, 323
- 'Remailed', 62, 99, 100, 108, 110, 142n, 174
- 'Settling on the Land'. *See* '"Tom's Selection." (A Sketch of Settling on the Land)'
- 'She Wouldn't Speak', 61n, 63, 107, 110, 111, 123, 125, 128, 132
- 'The Shearing of the Cook's Dog', 45, 57, 252
- 'Shooting the Moon', 62, 101, 110, 122, 142n, 145, 308–9
- '"Some Day." A Swagman's Love Story', 45, 57, 101, 143, 253, 261n, 308–9
- 'Some Popular Australian Mistakes', 47
- 'Some Reflections on a Voyage across

Lawson, Henry *(cont.)*
  Cook's Straits (N.Z.)', 63, 100, 114, 140, 324n
  'Steelman', 63, 142n
  'Steelman's Pupil', 64, 105, 110, 122, 124, 126, 232n, 233, 236n, 258, 324n
  'Stiffner and Jim (Thirdly Bill)', 61, 62, 232n, 233, 236, 258
  'The Story of Malachi', 38, 53, 104, 125–6, 232n, 233, 236
  '"Stragglers": A Sketch Out Back', 57, 143
  '"Succeeding": A Sequel to "Pursuing Literature"', 204n, 228
  'Taking Stiffner Down', 63n, 85n, 339n
  'That Swag', 63, 101, 122n, 270n, 297, 308–9
  'That There Dog o' Mine. An Australian Sketch', 103
  'Three or Four Archibalds and the Writer', 53
  '"Tom's Selection." (A Sketch of Settling on the Land)', 58, 89, 120, 122n, 138
  'Two Dogs and a Fence', 64, 94, 126, 232n, 233, 237n, 324n
  'An Unfinished Love Story', 64, 104, 111n, 118, 123, 124, 125, 136, 139, 157n, 175, 324n
  'The Union Buries its Dead. A Bushman's Funeral. A Sketch from Life', 65, 142, 232, 258, 304, 305, 365
  'A Visit of Condolence: A Study from Life of a Sydney "Larrikin"', 54, 104, 116, 118, 123, 141, 175, 196n, 253, 265n, 323n, 329n, 345
  '"Water Them Geraniums"', 227, 241n, 305, 324
  'When the Sun Went Down', 58, 84n, 175n, 253
Lawson, Louisa (HL's mother), 33, 36–7, 67n, 73, 165n
  establishes *The Dawn*, 36, 38
  publishes HL's *Short Stories in Prose and Verse*, 65
Lawson, Sylvia, 50–2, 243n, 289–90
Le Gallienne, Richard, 165
Leavis, F.R., 296n, 301, 302n, 309n, 310, 313n, 322, 353
Lee, Christopher, 250, 251n, 266, 270n, 278n

Leigh, S.T. (Sydney printer), 133
Leist, Fred (illustrator), 361
libraries, circulating, 21, 34, 77, 78, 82, 194, 195, 223, 238, 346
Lindsay, Lionel, 294
Lindsay, Norman, 160, 274
Lindsay, Percy, 252, 253
Lockley, J.G., 83n, 194
Longfellow, Henry, 223
Lothian, Thomas (bookseller and publisher), 180n, 217, 229n, 246
Louisson, Jack (NZ friend of HL), 49n, 64, 68n
Lucas, E.V., 179, 207n, 245
Lukin, Gresley, 65n
Lyons, Martyn, 347

Macartney, Frederick T., 298
Maccallum, Hugh (A&R), 89, 90, 91n, 116, 119n, 134, 138, 201, 219–20, 232n
McCarron, Stewart & Co. (Sydney printer), 153, 360
Macintyre, Stuart, 25n
Mack, Louise, 119n
Mackaness, George, 78n, 147n, 159, 161, 241, 261, 335, 364
McKernan, Susan, 278n
McKerrow, R.B., 329
MacLehose, James, & Sons (Glasgow publisher), 76, 130, 151–2, 154n, 155–6, 158, 359, 360n
Macmillan (publisher)
  Kipling editions a model for A&R, 82, 129
  successfully publishes Boldrewood, 81, 129, 215–17, 243
  publishes Paterson, 218n
  buys Richard Bentley & Son, 238
Mahony, Frank (illustrator), 55, 56, 74, 115–17, 134–5, 141, 145, 152, 159, 164, 172, 344, 358–63
Mann, Cecil, 1–2, 3, 261, 270
  belles-lettristic editing principles, 335–6
  edition of HL savaged, 335
Maquarie, Arthur Frank (friend of HL in London), 229, 235
Marchant & Co. (Sydney printer), 159n, 160n, 363
Martin, Arthur Patchett, 180n, 188
Martin, Catherine, 223, 276

Matthews, Brian, 58n, 177n, 246n, 304–9, 321
　contemporising, humanistic criticism, 305–6
　developmental theses undercut, 309
Melbourne. *See* Sydney–Melbourne rivalry
Melbourne Review, 180n, 196
Melville, Adam Graham (Melbourne bookseller), 193–4
Methuen (publisher), 155–7, 217, 220, 226, 228, 244n, 245
Milford, Humphrey (publisher), 159
Mills, Tom (NZ friend of HL), 48–9, 136, 139, 265n
Minns, G.E. (illustrator), 56n
Mitchell, David Scott, 204n, 220n, 228, 240, 359n
Moretti, Franco, 26
Morrah, Herbert (editor, *Argosy*), 229
Morris, E.E., 191
Mount Alexander Mail, 172
Mullen (Melbourne bookseller and publisher), 7, 163n
Murdoch, Walter, 182, 230, 256n
Murray-Smith, Stephen, 182, 300–1, 303n, 314

nationalism as literary paradigm, 16–18, 20, 21, 24–5, 50–1, 82, 187–8, 190, 248–9, 276–7, 282–96, 302–3, 310, 343
New Australia colony, 40, 245
New Bibliography, 328–9
New Criticism, 6, 14, 96, 175, 296, 307, 310, 320, 341, 342, 350, 351, 353
　Heseltine practising, 313, 315–18
New Zealand Mail, 49, 50n, 61, 147, 204
New Zealand Times, 49, 61n, 147

O'Dowd, Bernard, 249n
Ogborn, Miles, 19
Ogilvie, Will, 52, 128–9, 187
O'Hagan, M.D., 56n
Osborne, Roger, 8n
Oxford University Press, 159, 160n

Pagliaro, Teresa, 90, 94n, 96, 102, 149n
Pahiatua Herald, 61, 62n
Pall Mall Gazette, 61n
Palmer, Nettie, 259, 266, 276n, 291, 296–7, 298, 315

Palmer, Vance, 51, 266, 267, 283–5, 291, 292, 300n, 302n
Park, Ruth, 269
Parker, Arthur (friend of HL), 65n, 114n
Paterson, A. B. ('Banjo'), 52, 56n, 62n, 70, 151, 194, 195, 211, 219, 249n, 272, 283, 359
　verse mock duel with HL, 47
　dissuaded from reviewing HL, 165
　assists HL with business affairs, 203
　seen as too pessimistic, 179
　seen as authentically Australian, 187, 255, 276n, 285
　on George Robertson, 77, 79n
　The Man from Snowy River, 71–2, 74–5, 80, 84n, 107n, 128, 134, 135, 139, 155, 218n, 355
　Rio Grande's Last Race, 90
　Three Elephant Power, 138n
Patriot (Maryborough, Q.), 64, 65n, 147
Penfold, W. C. & Co. (printer), 60n, 363
Pentland, Young J., 78, 144, 147n, 153, 157, 162, 219
Perel, Irvine ('Jack', editor, *Patriot*), 64–5
Phillips, A.A., 246n, 266, 296–8, 300n
Pierce, Peter, 282n
Pinker, J.B. (literary agent), 229–32, 241–2, 243n, 244–5, 328
press cutting agencies, 114–15, 156, 162
Prichard, Katharine Susannah, 265
Propsting and Cockhead (Hobart bookseller), 152

Quiller-Couch, Arthur, 94

Reader (London), 255
reading
　as aesthetic experience, 9–10, 354
　and community, 21, 176
　as accretive process, 14, 352
　as index of cultural change, 10, 354
　as dialectic, 352–3
　by authors, 14
　in publishing processes, 352
　time-conditioned, 309
　danger of essentialising individual, 307–8
　transnational perspectives on, 21–3
　'distant', 26–9
　histories of, 16

effects of infrastructure on, 29–30
HL's, 34–5, 97
preferences in 1890s Australia, 79n, 193–6, 204, 223, 277–8, 349
at war, 181, 249n
Review of Reviews for Australasia, 149, 165, 168, 172, 191
Robertson, George (A&R)
  biography, 76–7
  as publisher, 20, 76–7, 79–82
  raises local production standards, 20, 80, 129–30, 148, 152
  uses Macmillan's Kipling as model, 80–2, 129, 176–7
  superintends production of *WBB*, 120, 122, 123, 127–41, 144–52
  splits *WBB* into two series, 131–3, 159–60, 213
  marketing initiatives, 20, 137, 153, 160, 162–6, 180
  publishing local writers an idealistic 'hobby', 82
  scrupulous about HL payments, 210–12, 246
  relations with HL strained, 199–202
  despairs of selling books to Britain, 258–9
Robertson, George (Melbourne), 7, 56n, 78, 79n, 163n, 190n, 191, 238
Roderick, Colin, 325–41
  on HL's language, 99
  psychiatric focus in *Letters* and in *Life*, 225
  Selected editions of HL, 270
  contents of editions of HL's *Prose*, 325–6
  critical of Jose's regularising copy-editing, 90
  regularises spellings in editing HL's letters, 328
  accords stories poetic status, 326–7
  'final intention' editing of prose, 328–31
  bio-bibliographic scholarship conflicts with aesthetic approach, 332–3, 338
  favours sequences in HL stories, 333–8, 344–5
  problems in using his *Commentaries*, 339–40, 344–5
  Life under-documented, 208
  scholarship encourages changed approach by other critics, 305, 331

Rolfe, Patricia, 361n
Rose, Jonathan, 347n
Ryan, John Tighe (editor, *Catholic Press*), 56, 79n

Said, Edward, *Orientalism*, 17n
St Clair, William, 27–9, 347
Sargeson, Frank, 97n, 296n
Schaffer, Kay, 287n, 290–2
School Magazine, 251, 270n
Serle, Geoffrey, 190, 211n, 273n
Shakespeare, William, 191n, 193, 223, 329
Shenstone, Fred (A&R), 102n, 227, 232n
Sheridan, Susan, 287n
Simpkin, Marshall, Hamilton, Kent & Co. (publisher), 154–5, 156n, 158, 162, 178, 180, 217–18
Sladen, Douglas, 151n, 180n, 188, 293
Smith, Beaumont, 210
Souter, David (cartoonist), 361
Spence, Percy (illustrator), 56n
Squires, Claire, 275n
Steele Rudd, 50n, 113n, 249n
Stephens, A.G., 50, 112–13, 215n, 315
  on HL's finances 206
  assessment of HL: natural spontaneity, 68, 169; strength comes from feeling, 75; should write more complex narratives, 59, 122, 173–4; quintessentially bush Australian, 198; sometimes flawed by sentimentality, 175; local rather than universal, 184–5
Stephensen, P.R., 282n
Stevens, Bertram, 34n, 97n, 184n
Stevenson, R.L., 94n, 197, 243
Stewart, Douglas, 303n
Stewart, Ken, 189n, 193, 274
Stone, Walter, 74n, 78n
Sussex, Lucy, 225, 240n
Sutherland, Alexander, 196. See also Turner, Henry Gyles, and Alexander Sutherland
Sutherland, Kathryn, 16, 353
Sydney *Bulletin*. See *Bulletin* (Sydney)
Sydney Mail, 34, 50, 183, 191, 359
  on Australian readership, 79n, 193–4, 204
Sydney–Melbourne rivalry, 81–2, 182, 184, 189–90, 192, 193–4, 274–5
Syer, Walter S., 102n, 116n, 359

phantom contents list for *WBB*, 82–5, 111, 115–16, 123

Tasker, Meg, 225, 240n
Tasma, 8n, 223, 276
theory. *See also* New Criticism, nationalism as literary paradigm
  distant reading, 26–7
  discursive critique, 291–2, 312
  feminist critique, 279, 286–92
  transnationalism, 17, 21–24, 26
  postcolonialism, 12, 17, 18
  poststructuralism, 7, 17, 317, 320, 341, 350
  'material fetish', 348–51
  the work: 'life of', 6, 341–2, 351–2; distinct from 'book', 347; accretive, 352; as dialectic process, 15, 352–3; draws stability from the material document, 14–15
  a book-history inflected literary criticism proposed, 341–57
trades unionism, 39–41, 285n, 300
  HL as unionist, 43, 45
  HL disenchanted with, 62–3, 300
Town and Country Journal, 38, 167, 191
Trilling, Lionel, 314
Trollope, Anthony, 223
Truth (Gympie), 75n
Truth (Sydney), 38, 50n, 57, 58, 147
Turner, Henry Gyles, 196, 272–3
Turner, Henry Gyles, and Alexander Sutherland, *The Development of Australian Literature*, 166, 188–9, 192, 196, 204n, 272
  reviewed, 191–2
Turner & Henderson (Sydney bookseller and publisher), 79n, 163
Twain, Mark, 34, 97, 168, 173, 223, 258, 279
Tyrrell, James, 71n, 79, 217, 246n

unions. *See* trades unionism
University extension lectures, 88, 172, 195
Unwin, T. Fisher (publisher), 220, 227–9

Walch, Garnet, 150
Wallace-Crabbe, Chris, 58n, 262n
Ward, Humphrey, 94n
Ward, Russel, 266, 285–6, 295
Warren, Robert Penn. *See* Brooks, Cleanth,
  and Robert Penn Warren
Warung, Price, 79n 167, 172
Watt, A.P. (literary agent), 155, 156n, 157, 158n, 217n
Webby, Elizabeth, 50n, 94n, 196n, 216n, 217n, 267n, 276n, 293n, 296n, 303n
Websdale, Shoosmith (Sydney printer), 80, 106n, 130, 135, 153, 156n, 158, 159, 160, 359, 360, 361n
Wellek, René, and Austin Warren, 6, 320
While the Billy Boils
  agreement for, 112, 149
  contents list of, 109–10, 120–1. *See also* Syer, Walter S.
  order of stories in, 107–10, 118–24, 131, 145–6, 160, 176–7
  title of, 149–51, 176
  Kipling books used as model, 80–2, 93–7, 129, 176–7
  physical get-up of, 128–30, 148, 152, 163, 164, 166
  sequence of production events, 112–26, 139–41
  Jose's copy-editing of, 88–97, 101–3, 104, 105, 106, 107, 117–19, 121–5, 137–8, 140, 141–3, 157, 236, 298, 315, 343
  illustrations for, 55, 109–10, 115–17, 131, 145, 152, 160, 344, 358–63
  typesetters of, 105–6
  galley proofs for, 119–20, 137
  costing for, 130–2, 140, 152–3, 157
  marketing of, 162–6, 180
  attempts at UK publication of, 155–8
  profit earned, 212–14
  profit compared to that of *Robbery Under Arms*, 214–18
  proofing of, 141–4
  early sales of, 153–61
  reviews of, 162–87
  second edition (A&R, 1924), 252–4
  stories omitted from second edition, 253
  third edition (Cape, 1927), 257
  division into series perpetuated, 262
  title '*WBB*' becomes iconic, 257–8, 262
  electronic editions of, 262–3
White, Patrick, 215n, 300n
White, Richard, 287n
Wigg, E.S. & Co. (Adelaide bookseller and publisher), 78n, 150, 163n
Wilde, W.H., 41n

Wilding, Michael, 303
Wilkes, G.A., 274, 298–9, 302
William Blackwood and Son. *See* Blackwood
Wilson, Kathleen, 18
Winks, Robin, 18
Wood, Billy (friend of HL), 43n
Woods, Susan Nugent, 150–1
Woods, W.A. (A&R), 136
Wordsworth, William, 76, 333
Worker
  genesis of, 41
  demands conciseness, 39, 277
  pay rates of, 50n, 63, 204
  as bookseller, 49, 69, 165
  circulation levels of, 46
  championed mateship, 47–8
  HL appointed provincial editor of, 62
  HL falls out with, 49, 62
  readership helps shape HL's language, 99–100
  role in nurturing HL overlooked, 148, 187
Worker (Brisbane), 40–1
  reviews HL, 75
Wright, David McKee, 151n, 251, 260n, 297n

Zinkhan, Elaine, 154n, 156n, 158n, 217n
Zola, Emile, 55n

www.ingramcontent.com/pod-product-compliance
Lightning Source LLC
Chambersburg PA
CBHW050848160426
43194CB00011B/2077